Tasmania

THE BRADT TRAVEL GUIDE

THE BRADT STORY

The first Bradt travel guide was written by Hilary and George Bradt in 1974 on a river barge floating down a tributary of the Amazon in Bolivia. From their base in Boston, Massachusetts, they went on to write and publish four other backpacking guides to the Americas and one to Africa.

In the 1980s Hilary continued to develop the Bradt list in England, and also established herself as a travel writer and tour leader. The company's publishing emphasis evolved towards broader-based guides to new destinations – usually the first to be published on those countries – complemented by hiking, rail and wildlife guides.

Since winning *The Sunday Times* Small Publisher of the Year Award in 1997, we have continued to fill the demand for detailed, well-written guides to unusual destinations, while maintaining the company's original ethos of low-impact travel.

Travel guides are by their nature continuously evolving. If you experience anything which you would like to share with us, or if you have any amendments to make to this guide, please write; all your letters are read and passed on to the author. Most importantly, do remember to travel with an open mind and to respect the customs of your hosts – it will add immeasurably to your enjoyment.

Happy travelling!

Hilary Bradt

Hilary Bradt

19 High Street, Chalfont St Peter, Bucks SL9 9QE, England
Tel: 01753 893444 Fax: 01753 892333
Email: info@bradt-travelguides.com
Web: www.bradt-travelguides.com

Tasmania

THE BRADT TRAVEL GUIDE

Matthew Brace

Bradt Publications, UK
The Globe Pequot Press Inc, USA

First published in 2002 by Bradt Travel Guides Ltd
19 High Street, Chalfont St Peter, Bucks SL9 9QE, England
web: www.bradt-travelguides.com
Published in the USA by The Globe Pequot Press Inc, 246 Goose Lane,
PO Box 480, Guilford, Connecticut 06475-0480

ISBN 1 84162 056 4

British Library Cataloguing in Publication Data
A catalogue record for this book is available from the British Library

Library of Congress Cataloging-in-Publication Data applied for

Photographs
Front cover Blue Lake, near Gladstone in northeast Tasmania (Matthew Brace)
Text Matthew Brace (MB), Robert Jones (RJ), Steve Lo (SL), Tom Keating (TK), Tourism
Tasmania (TT), Geoff Murray (GM)
Illustrations Carole Vincer
Maps Steve Munns

Typeset from the author's disc by Wakewing
Printed and bound in Italy by Legoprint SpA, Trento

Author

Matthew Brace is a foreign correspondent, travel writer and photographer based in Sydney. He was born in Britain and began travelling in earnest in 1988 in Central America and has spent a large part of his time since overseas, mainly in tropical countries. He is a fully trained, professional journalist and is the freelance Australasia correspondent for the *Observer* and *Geographical Magazine*. He contributes occasionally to many other titles.

Contents

Acknowledgements

Above everyone I must thank Michele McGinity at Tourism Tasmania who has been a tireless source of information, ideas and mirth. Without her help and the wide resources of her organisation, on which I have leaned heavily, this book could not have been written. Their website, brochures and network of contacts were all invaluable.

I would also like to thank Patricia Sabine and her staff at the Tasmanian Museum and Art Gallery for providing detailed information which has filled the natural history sections of this book.

The Government Parks and Wildlife department was extremely generous in allowing me to base a number of the walks in this book on ones it has developed over the years, particularly a series of excellent Great Short Walks that it promotes to visitors.

Rob Pennicott and Tonia Cochrane made Bruny come alive; Geoff King in Marrawah gave me a Tasmanian devil experience I will never forget; Graham Wells in Stanley taught me a priceless penguin lesson; and Ron Hedditch in Latrobe introduced me to the Tasmanian platypus.

Much thanks goes to Craig Williams in Scottsdale for his valuable help and bush survival tips, and to Simon Houghton and his animals for their unconditional generosity and warmth, and for his wonderful sense of humour.

I am indebted also to Andrea Wood in Strahan for her kindness and patience with me, and to Wayne and Gill Homan in Bicheno for their generosity and superb oysters.

Finally, I'd like to express my gratitude towards Dal and Kath Hyland of Hobart who housed and fed me through a bitterly cold June week, and my girlfriend Erin for being patient with a grumpy hermit while he wrote this book.

FEEDBACK REQUEST

You, the readers, can make an incalculable difference to further editions of this guide by writing to me about your trip. If, upon your return home, you can find time to send a postcard or longer note with any updates or corrections to the information I have provided, it would be greatly appreciated. Happy travels.

19 High Street, Chalfont St Peter, Bucks SL9 9QE, England
Tel: 01753 893444 Fax: 01753 892333
Email: info@bradt-travelguides.com
Web: www.bradt-travelguides.com

Introduction

I had to wonder, setting out to write this book, whether I was doing Tasmania a disservice. Was I sending people there who would scuff up the walking tracks, disturb the nests of the rare 40-spotted pardalote, and leave tonnes of rubbish in the national parks for Tasmanian devils to cut their paws on or to get washed out to sea and end up choking an albatross to death?

And then I remembered I was writing for Bradt Travel Guides, whose focus has always been on minimal impact and sound environmental practice, and that put my mind at rest. Nevertheless you will still find copious notes on best practice in the next few hundred pages which I implore you to follow for I have deep feelings for this place and would hate to see it harmed.

Journalists are not meant to show too much sentimentality in their work. 'Stiff upper lip, just get the story,' our news editors tell us but there are times when we are moved and find it hard to describe what we see coldly and without a personal accent. Writing about Tasmania was doubly hard for me as not only is this island ravishingly beautiful but it is in such a wonderfully clean and healthy state that you pray to all the gods you know that it will stay that way. In 14 years of travel to more than 40 countries I cannot remember a place as pristine. You almost do not want to breathe in case a rogue germ escapes. I was constantly gathering up the sweet wrappers in my car every time I stopped to get out in case a gust of wind caught one and blew it out to stain the landscape.

Subsequently, on my return to Sydney, I sat for several days at my computer not knowing quite how to describe this place to you in a way you would believe.

Also, as a journalist, I suppose I am always looking for the catch, trying to sift through the 'PR speak', and find the facts. Tasmania cannot all be beautiful can it? Surely there are some really bad areas as well? Well, no, actually; with one or two very minor exceptions it is quite astoundingly picturesque. And the people, there must be a few rogues – after all, they are descended from convicts? I am sure one or two are hiding somewhere but I have always found Tasmanians to be among the most pleasant, giving and genuinely friendly people in Australia, and in turn I rate the Australians as one of the most welcoming and warm populations on the planet.

Visitors can bask in the added luxury of knowing that Tasmania is a modern state in a modern nation with all mod cons and buses that leave on time, clean toilets that work, and exotic food served in fine restaurants. Regular travellers to the developing world might miss the unpredictability of African train timetables or the platforms full of faces staring at you open-mouthed as if you have landed from Mars that afternoon. Much as I love roughing it through the tropics, the ease of being in an ordered and safe place was welcome and comforting. Wilderness with washbasins, and *wasabi* ... and wine.

Tasmania restored a good amount of my faith in the world, and continues to do so as I pop down from Sydney as often as possible. Walking the Overland Track, I remember standing on Cradle Cirque with my Queensland hiking pal Graham and we looked in silence and in rapture for countless miles into the far distance.

We could see nothing man-made: no roads, towns, logging operations, power lines, factory smoke, not even an aircraft vapour trail. There were no artificial sounds or smells; it was all completely natural.

Note on prices and contact numbers

Unfortunately prices go up and places change hands. I have done my best with this book to include up-to-date information but what is current now might not be in the month that you are reading these pages. For this reason the prices quoted here should be treated as rough guides rather than as pin-point accurate. All prices are quoted in Australian dollars.

For accommodation, I found the star-rating system in Tasmania to be misleading. I visited several four-star places that were bad and inhospitable; on the other hand, I visited a pub and some units with no stars and virtually no services in the rooms which became some of my favourite places to stay for their location, friendly staff and value for money.

For this reason I have included as many website and email contacts as possible so that you can double check details and the look of places to stay. I would encourage you to refer to Tourism Tasmania's excellent website: www.discovertasmania.com. I have also tried to include any tourism awards that places have won as this too gives a good indication of quality.

In terms of contacts, all were correct at the time of going to press, including new email and website addresses and postal addresses in certain regions that have altered their street names, but it is possible some numbers may change in time. If you are unlucky you might call a Tasmanian coastal caravan park and instead get a Chinese laundry in Melbourne – but it is unlikely.

And finally, as there is some debate over the use (or not) of apostrophes in Tasmanian place names, I have decided to follow the path more travelled and exclude them from all proper names, even when this looks grammatically incorrect.

Part One

General Information

Sugar glider

Background Information

FACTS AND FIGURES
Location
The heart-shaped island of Tasmania lies between 143° and 149° east and 40° and 44° south, equivalent in the northern hemisphere in terms of latitude to the temperate regions of the northern Mediterranean, and in the United States to the Great Lakes, northern Midwest and west to Oregon. It is the smallest and most southerly state in Australia, whose vast mainland lies across the 240km-wide Bass Strait. South of Tasmania there is nothing but the remote, windswept Macquarie Island and miles of tempestuous Southern Ocean until one reaches landfall on the wastes of Antarctica. Tasmania is roughly a one-hour flight south from Melbourne, one and a half hours from Adelaide and two from Sydney.

Size
The island is 304km west to east at its widest point (between Mawson Bay and St Helens Point) and 281km north to south (between Cape Grim and the South East Cape). Tasmania covers 68,314km², similar in size to the Republic of Ireland, the American state of West Virginia, and to the Japanese island of Hokkaido.

Population and religion
At the last census in 2001 Tasmania's total population was 470,000, showing a drop of 3,300 since 1995. Tasmania is the only state or territory to have witnessed an overall population decline during the past three years (1997–2000). Most Tasmanians are descended from the British who were the first settlers and made up the lion's share of the convicts. Increasingly, however, residents can trace their roots back to a host of nationalities who found their way here. Around one-third are Anglicans, 22% Catholic and 8% belong to the Uniting Church in Australia, an amalgam of Protestant churches (Congregational, Methodist and Presbyterian) similar to the United Reform Church in England and the United Church of Christ in America.

Languages
English is the national language of Australia. There are so few Aboriginal descendants left on Tasmania that indigenous languages have died out.

Government
Since January 1 1901, Australia has been a federation of six states and two territories, and its government has been based upon a written constitution. Although the country is autonomous, the Queen of England is still the head of state and is represented by the Governor General of Australia, Peter Hollingworth.

Tasmania, like all other Australian states, has a three-tier system of government. The national or federal government, based in the nation's capital Canberra, follows Britain's Westminster system but with American-style federal arrangements. It is

3

mainly responsible for the national economy, immigration, defence, foreign policy and communications. There is a lower House of Representatives with 148 members, to which Tasmania sends five members, and an upper Senate to which each state sends 12 senators (territories send two each).

The current Australian Prime Minister is John Howard, whose conservative Liberal Party rules in a coalition with the National Party. Howard was appointed for a third term on November 10 2001. However, Tasmania is a Labor state federally and in state politics with all five federal constituencies remaining Labor at the last national election. At the time of writing a state election was due in 2002.

In Tasmania the state government is based in Hobart and is in charge of health, housing, transport, education and law and order. The state parliament also has two houses: the lower House of Assembly with 25 members, and the upper Legislative Council which is traditionally non-partisan.

The final tier is local government, which operates in 29 divisions and has authority derived from state parliament Acts.

Capital
Hobart is a lively, friendly city in the south of the island situated on a natural harbour at the mouth of the River Derwent. Mount Wellington (1,270m) rises to the west and the city is protected from the ravages of Storm Bay by a spit of land called South Arm. It is a centre for Antarctic research, a growing tourism destination and has a thriving arts scene.

Major towns
There are blissfully few large towns, leaving more room for wilderness and natural beauty. Launceston is Tasmania's second city and the third oldest in Australia, older than both Melbourne and Adelaide. It is considered the capital of the north and is situated on the Tamar River. The river and town are named after their English predecessors in Cornwall. Devonport and Burnie on the north coast are more industrial. The car ferries from the mainland dock at Devonport while Burnie's deep water port is used for cargo. The west coast capital is Strahan which is more of a seaside village than a town. Inland is the former mining town of Queenstown.

Economy
Traditionally, agriculture and mining have been Tasmania's mainstays but tourism is becoming increasingly important. Farming occupies almost 2 million hectares, just less than one-third the total land area. Beef cattle makes up a quarter of the agriculture market with sheep farming accounting for 14%. Tasmania is Australia's fruit and vegetable bowl with apples, beans, berries, bulbs, carrots and grain crops all abundant, as well as specialist crops such as opium poppies, lavender, saffron and cut flowers.

The overall export value of metals and minerals in 1995–96 was A$701.8m (US$350m, UK£255.2m) and the industry employed 4,669 people.

Tasmania receives more than 530,000 visitors each year of which about one-fifth are from overseas. Forestry and fishing are also important industries.

Roughly 45,000 (9.4%) work in the public sector, 32,200 (6.8%) in retail, 25,000 (5.3%) in manufacturing and 18,700 (3.9%) in tourism.

Currency
The unit of currency is the Australian dollar. The rate of exchange in late 2001 was around US$1 = A$2; UK£1 = A$2.75.

HISTORY

Places of remoteness and great beauty do not necessarily boast a peaceful past and Tasmania is no exception. With your face pressed into a breeze of the freshest air on earth and your feet planted at the edge of the cleanest of streams, it is hard to imagine this as a place of horror but there are numerous ghosts abroad on this island, victims of decades of pain and suffering that chiefly occurred after the arrival of the Europeans.

We can date Tasmania's human history with some certainty to at least 23,000 years ago. As with all reflections over time the facts are only as solid as the experts can make them and on occasion educated assumptions are required based on the evidence before us. The swift decimation of Tasmania's earliest human inhabitants, the Aborigines, has left us with some crucial chapters missing in the history of this island. They took to their graves the stories of their culture and their long existence here and we have had to piece history together from archaeological finds. What we can say for sure is that Tasmania and Tasmanians have lived full lives. This island has lurched from peace and harmony to terror and desecration – often within a historical heartbeat.

Pre-European history

Tasmania's oldest inhabitants were Aboriginal people who crossed by foot from what is now mainland Australia when Bass Strait was not a sea channel but a land bridge. At that time, during the last Ice Age roughly 10,000 years ago, the world's sea levels were considerably lower and Australia's land mass was about one-fifth larger than it is today. Aboriginal people are believed to have originated either further north in what is now the Indonesian archipelago or further east in Melanesia. Papua New Guinea was linked to northern Australia by a northern land bridge.

Those who made it to Tasmania did so while searching for lush grasslands and more water and game, or were driven here by rival warring tribes. They were later cut off from their cousins, or enemies, as the waters rose, the land bridge was flooded and Tasmania became an island roughly 12,000 years ago. As a result of centuries of isolation they developed physical and cultural differences from those on mainland Australia. They were darker skinned and had frizzy hair while the mainland tribes were lighter and had generally straight hair. It is unlikely their numbers ever exceeded 4,000 but it was almost certainly a steady if not growing population, and, for a while, before people appeared in the southern reaches of South America, they would have been the world's most southerly group. Culturally there are interesting idiosyncrasies too. Unlike mainland tribes, Tasmania's Aborigines cremated their dead. The boomerang never made it to Tasmania primarily because it was not needed for hunting as it was on the great plains of the outback.

Archaeologists have pieced together Aborigines' diets and lifestyles mainly from bones and charcoal unearthed at many sites. Most early ones are to be found in the north and west of the main island and on the smaller northern islands indicating that this is where the land was most conducive to hunting and gathering. They used boats made from rolled up eucalyptus bark to launch food expeditions around neighbouring islands as well as catching seals in the summer months.

If you happen to experience one of Tasmania's rough weather days (and the likelihood is you will, even in summer) look out to sea and try to imagine the dangers of steering a crudely made bark boat through the boisterous, churning seas around this island's coastline with little more than a pole or even with someone swimming alongside and pointing the boat in the right direction.

Tasmania's Aborigines ate practically anything from kangaroo, which were hard to catch, to echidna, an Australian monotreme that closely resembles a porcupine and has such poor eyesight that its breed was fair game. (Monotremes are egg-laying mammals. They make up a rare order of mammals – *Monotremata* – of which just two types exist: the platypus and the short-beaked echidna. They possess only one opening for both digestive and genital organs.) The only exceptions came as a result of their religious beliefs, similar to those of mainland tribes, which prevented them from eating their animal *totem* or the creature from which they believed they were descended.

Women from coastal communities would dive for crayfish and abalone (two of Tasmania's most popular and lucrative marine products to this day). We know the extent of their seafood diets by the presence of piles of shell and bone known as *middens* that appear all around the coastline. However, carbon dating has revealed that within these middens lies a mystery. There are no remains of scaled fish for the past 4,000 years whereas before that such food was a staple. As yet the jury is out on why, although one suggestion is that with a rise in sea levels seafood became more plentiful and easier to catch than scaled fish and so replaced them in tribes' diets.

On the main island tribes hunted kangaroos in the Florentine Valley west of Mount Field National Park on land that is now on the eastern boundary of the Franklin-Gordon Wild Rivers National Park. In caves they left behind the charred remains of great feasts and even the odd flake tool. One such cave, although further west, is Kutikina on the Franklin River near the Elliot Range of mountains, and halfway between the river's junction with the Jane River and where it becomes the Gordon River. The people living here during the last Ice Age would definitely have won the accolade of the world's most southerly inhabitants. They hunted wallaby across the harsh tundra and made tools called scrapers that were still being used here in the 1800s.

Despite the chilly and often icy winters there is little evidence of Aborigines wearing more than a kangaroo pelt to keep warm and to carry babies. Instead it seems they coated themselves in what must have been a particularly pungent paste made from charcoal, animal fat and ochre. Ochre, a rusty-brown, iron-based pigment, was extracted from earth and rock dug from mines around the island, notably at Mount Gog, Mount Housetop and Mount Vandyke in the northwest. At Mount Gog archaeologists discovered a network of trenches, holes and tunnels; the best preserved trench is 35 metres long and 1.5 metres deep. The miners used a chisel principle, banging in wedged sticks with rocks and levering them to prize out blocks of sediment. They would dry the material on flat stones and extract the powdered ochre remains, which were used for cave and body decoration. As you tour the island look out for the remains of other ochre mines at Welcome River, Queenstown and Point Hibbs along the west coast; Louisa Bay, Melaleuca Lagoon and Randalls Bay Rocks on the south coast; Ouse in the Derwent valley; Russel Plains and Swan Island in the north; and Sandford and Maria Island on the east coast.

Around 15,000 years ago, the climate gradually became warmer and wetter and rainforest replaced tundra and cool temperate scrubland. The wallabies moved into the last patches of open country and the dwellers of Kutikina bade a final farewell to their ancestral cave home and moved with them. They would have carried their possessions, including several tools made of sinew, seaweed, stone and wood, in home-made baskets.

Tasmania had nine tribes which were themselves split into smaller sub-groups called bands and hearths. Hearths were basically family units of from two to 11 people, nearly always related. They would cook and camp together. A hearth would be part of a bigger band of maybe 50 people, each led by a hunter-warrior man, and with rights to hunt and gather on a certain area of land. Bands had similar cultural traits and spoke the same languages but disputes arose from time to time when land boundaries became confused and areas overlapped; on these occasions harmony depended on how well each got on with its neighbours.

As well as middens and charcoal remains in caves, the Aborigines left us other clues which are much harder to piece together. Stencil paintings and rock carvings have been found in Tasmania although not in the same numbers as on the mainland. Some art is believed to pay homage to important symbols of the Tasmanians' religious beliefs. There are unexplained rock carvings at Mount Cameron West and at High Rocky Point on the west coast. The ones at Mount Cameron West have been carbon dated to 1,650 years ago and bear some similarity to ones found in the central Australian deserts but remain as yet unexplained. There are hand stencils adorning cave walls and rock faces in the Derwent Valley which were done with a mixture of ochre, blood and animal fat.

When not engaged in their own brand of interior decorating, the Aborigines were partial to song and dance. They told stories of courage, love and loss through elaborate songs with three-part harmonies, melodies reminiscent of Melanesian society which they may have passed down through the generations. If so, these songs have survived for a fantastic 60,000 years. Originally, dances aped the movements of kangaroos and emus but later, after the arrival of the Europeans, they mimicked instead dogs, horses and guns.

Aborigines are known to have made necklaces of shells and animal and plant fibres for both men and women to wear, and to have had some knowledge of astronomy.

The Aboriginal belief system is fiendishly complicated. Most non-Aboriginal people do not attempt to understand it. I have spent two years trying to fathom its complexities and have resigned myself to listening and accepting it. According to this system, all things were created during a period called the 'Dreaming' or 'Dreamtime', with the land being made first, followed later by animals and the rest of nature. Subsequently, all people have direct links with the land which they consider to be 'alive' and full of spirits. They also have close ties to their non-human 'totem' or ancestor being, be it a tiger snake, kangaroo or kookaburra.

Stories of the Dreaming are colourful and full of morals and adventure and make great reading for adults and children. Every Aboriginal group has a different take on the story with different characters but keeping the similar creation theme. According to today's descendants, the **Tasmanian Aboriginal story** goes as follows:

> Parlevar was the first Aboriginal, created by the spirit Moihernee who gathered some earth, carried it skyward and designed a man with a kangaroo tail and legs without knee joints. Parlevar could not lie down and had to sleep standing up.

> Dromerdeener, the great star spirit, saw this and decided to help Parlevar. He cut off his tail, cured the wound by rubbing grease on it, and made knee joints for him. When Parlevar sat down for the first time he said, 'Nyrerae' – it is good. Parlevar stayed in the sky for a very long time. Eventually he came to the land by walking down Laway teeney – the sky road or Milky Way. Later Moihernee and Dromerdeener quarrelled and Moihernee was forced to leave the sky and came to live on the land near Louisa Bay in southwest Tasmania. There he fought with many evil spirits

who lived in the ground at Toogee Low – the land near Port Davey.
Moihernee's wife followed him and went to live in the sea. Their many
children came down from the sky in raindrops. When Moihernee died he
went to Krib-biggerer near Cox Bight. There he was turned into a large
rock that stands majestically on a point near the sea.

What to most of us appear as rocks and valleys and grassy plains are in fact areas of
sacred importance to the Aborigines. Walking up Uluru (formerly Ayers Rock) in
the Northern Territory (which is still allowed) has been likened to the sacrilege of
tourists daily defacing the dome of St Peter's in Rome. Disrupting an Aboriginal
historical site in Tasmania can cause similar offence.

Aboriginal historical sites

Full-blood Aborigines may be no more in Tasmania but they left several important
sites behind them as a legacy. Many sites are sacred and advice should be sought from
Tourism Tasmania and the Aboriginal Information Centres in Hobart and
Devonport before visiting them. Some might be off limits to non-Aboriginal people.

Some sites were occupied several times through the ages. Cave Bay on Hunter
Island was a hunting camp which has been dated to roughly 22,000 years ago. It
was abandoned during the Ice Age about 10,000 years ago but, when the sea
reached its present level about 6,000 years ago, the Aborigines returned having
abandoned hunting for a new skill – fishing. Hunter Island camp was abandoned
once more 4,000 years ago and reoccupied 1,500 years later, roughly around 500BC.
However, as recently as the 1800s, Aboriginal people were still known to go to the
island in the summer months to hunt wallabies and mutton-birds and gather
shellfish washed up in rock pools along the shoreline.

Cape Barren Island in the Furneaux Group is also a breeding ground for
muttonbirds. For the final 20 years of the 19th century there was an Aboriginal
reserve and school on the island.

By the turn of the century the Cape Barren Aborigines were exporting seal skins
and seal and sea elephant oil, and mutton-birding was thriving. However, the
government stepped in and ordered them to begin farming which was never going
to prove fruitful in such barren soil. Crime and alcoholism ravaged the
communities, fuelled by European settlers who paid Aborigines in alcohol (to
which they have a low tolerance). One well-intentioned European, George
Augustus Robinson, was appointed by Governor George Arthur to take charge of
a mission to Bruny Island, south of Hobart. A group of 25 Aborigines, including
Truganini (see box, page 10), agreed to join him in the venture. It was an
experiment in assimilation between white and black. Robinson was a bricklayer
and taught the group how to make and lay bricks. The Aborigines were fed and
clothed but the project failed and within 12 months almost half of the group had
died from bronchitis or pneumonia.

Robinson was not disheartened however and, having predicted the widespread
decimation of the population on the main island, he persevered with a plan to
establish a settlement. In 1834 he landed on Flinders Island with a group of 135
Aborigines, once again including Truganini, where they were to be 'civilised and
Christianised'. A small gaggle of thatched huts was erected and the settlement
named Wybalenna which means black men's house. But this effort also failed. The
group had been taken from different tribes as Robinson had toured the main
island, and they did not always get on. The physical barrier of the stretch of water
between them and the rest of their kin made them homesick; they could not adapt
to the changes in diet; and they were angered at visits by sealing fleets of white

sailors trying to barter for – or steal – Aboriginal women. The group soon began to wither and die as a result of their isolation, and the project collapsed. In October 1847 the remaining 47 were shipped to Oyster Cove near Hobart but they lived in crude houses and soon they too fell victim to disease. By 1867 there were just three survivors: William Lanney, Mary Ann and Truganini.

The eastern shore of the Derwent estuary near Hobart is an important site as this is where the first inhabitants are thought to have lived. The Moomairremener people gathered every autumn near Risdon Cove after spending the summer months in the lush north of the island. For thousands of years the band wintered here living off abundant shellfish and seaweed. With the return of the sun in spring they made their way back inland to begin a summer of hunting. At Gellibrand Point there are middens, stone artefacts and an old Aboriginal campsite.

Nearby at Bedlam Walls are caves used by Aborigines for thousands of years and at Shag Bay is a stone quarry where each autumn and winter they made tools for the approaching kangaroo-hunting season. The Moomairremener celebrated life with feasting, singing, dancing and that most noted of Aboriginal traditions, storytelling. Shag Bay is also a site of mourning for Aboriginal people, for here in 1804 almost 100 of their band were killed by white soldiers. That year, as usual in autumn, the people arrived for the start of the hunting season but found a group of white farmers had set up camp on their traditional lands. They were fishing for oysters and hunting emus and swans, and were reported to be intoxicated. Two members of the Moomairremener approached to remonstrate with the farmers who shot them dead before they could flee to warn their people. The hunt began as normal but, when the hunters came into view of the new camp, soldiers among the white settlers opened fire with muskets and a cannon.

To save face, the military involved in the slaughter sent a despatch to Lieutenant-Governor David Collins, Tasmania's first governor. It described a heroic event in which the small group of white settlers and soldiers had defended itself bravely against a vicious and unprovoked attack by savage natives. However, one white farmer who had witnessed the barbarism, Edward White, later issued a damning report detailing the savagery with which the soldiers had attacked the Aborigines who were doing little more than partaking in a traditional hunt. No-one was ever charged or chastised for the violence.

Rocky Cape is a fantastic Aboriginal site and a must-see for anyone touring the western reaches of the north coast. It is now a national park so normal rules apply (see *Chapter 3*). The caves they used are still there and in places the midden deposits are in the order of six metres deep, the result of at least 8,000 years of continuous use. In fact Rocky Cape's ancient midden sites provide the most complete record yet found of Aboriginal coastal life in Australia. This was the land of the Tommeginer people, who were one of the eight bands of the northwest coast tribes. They moved nomadically, following the seasons around the tribal territory between Table Cape, near Wynyard, and Macquarie Harbour, on the west coast near Strahan. The middens here have revealed they had a varied diet including seals, fish, birds and small mammals, spiced up with bracken ferns, the tubers of lilies and washed down with pith from the grass tree. But September's spring weather brought swans and ducks to the coastal lagoons and egg collecting was almost a daily event. During the summer months from October to March the Tommeginer ate mutton-birds and hunted the then abundant elephant seals off the coast. They were sophisticated, making and using a wide variety of tools to catch and cook food, as well as creating cloaks from possum skin, and inventing a precursor to the rubber-tapping device which allowed the sweet sap from the cider gum to seep out and be collected.

TRUGANINI

Truganini was one of Australia's most famous Aborigines, as much for the events she lived through as her own loyalties. She was also known as Lalla Rookh and Ludgudge. She was born in 1803 of the Nuenonne tribe, whose country had been Bruny Island and the Channel area of the mainland. This was the same year Van Diemen's Land was first settled by white Europeans. Her mother and husband were both murdered by white men and her sister abducted by rampaging sealers.

Truganini went with George Robinson on his expeditions around the island as he tried to encourage Aboriginal people to join projects designed to assimilate them with a degree of decency into European culture. She was his vital conduit, introducing him to various tribes and gaining him audiences with their leaders, and then translating between the two parties. She lived in, and survived, the Flinders Island settlement and was later moved to Oyster Cove. She could have stayed in the straits and lived on Badger Island but she chose to return to her country and stay with her companions from Wybalenna, the settlement begun by Robinson on Flinders Island. After she watched them die around her, she too became weak and ended her days living with a woman in Hobart called Mrs Dandridge.

She was thought to be the last full-blood Tasmanian Aborigine and when she breathed her last in 1876 an entire culture died with her. Her people, who had been here for 50,000 years, had been wiped out in less than 100. To add insult to injury her spirit was not allowed to rest even after death. Her skeleton became a morbid exhibit in the Hobart Museum.

She would have to wait another 100 years until her bones were cremated and her ashes scattered in the D'Entrecasteaux Channel between the mainland and her beloved Bruny Island. Today a small plaque in the penguin breeding grounds on the Neck between North and South Bruny commemorates her and looks out over the water.

Recently historians have discovered that some outlived her on the Bass Strait islands and elsewhere. Their descendants are today's Tasmanian Aborigines.

Other important Aboriginal sites include Steep Island (now a game reserve), West Point, and Mount Cameron West on the northwest coast north of Marrawah. Also four islands just off Flinders Island: Babel Island, Mount Chappell Island, Badger Island and Great Dog Island. All are now nature reserves. In the southwest, Kutikina Cave and Ballawinne Cave are noted sites, and, in the southeast, Wargata Mina.

European arrival

The first European to see Tasmania was the Dutch explorer Abel Janszoon Tasman, who spied the west coast in 1642. He is said to have immediately named two peaks near the coast after his two ships, Mount Heemskirk and Mount Zeehan. Tasman had no idea this was an island but tactfully named it Van Diemen's Land after his patron, the Governor-General of the Dutch East Indies Company, Anthony Van Diemen. With equal diplomatic aplomb, he named the tiny island off the east coast after Van Diemen's wife and to this day beautiful Maria Island bears her name. Maatsuyker Island off the south coast and Schouten, just south of the Freycinet Peninsula, also owe their names to him.

As European nations were in full empire-building mode, any new lands were seen as potential possessions, the site of colonies and the sources, perhaps, of great riches. There is some speculation over who went ashore. It could have been Tasman himself or a few of his crew. They probably rowed in on a small ship at Blackman Bay on the Forestier Peninsula, near the current town of Dunalley where a monument to him stands today. The Dutch flag was raised but the men soon realised they were not the first humans to walk these shores. They saw notches cut in trees and smoke coming from up the hillsides. Some even claimed to hear human voices, yet no contact was made with the Aborigines. The Dutch sailors also found large paw prints in the earth, almost certainly those of the now extinct Tasmanian tiger or thylacine. A lack of evidence of minerals and a windswept coastline put them off further investigation, and they left with not the most positive of impressions of the country and headed for New Zealand. Although some early European visitors had genuine thought for the indigenous population, there was little chance the two groups would have seen eye to eye, so vastly different were their cultures and desires.

The first meeting between Tasmanian Aborigines and Europeans was in 1772 when a French navigator, Captain Nicholas Marion du Fresne, spent five or six days ashore at Frederick Henry Bay on the Forestier Peninsula, east of where Hobart now stands. The French had sailed from the west via Mauritius, as Tasman had, and were on a scientific mission. They went ashore in search of fresh water and took gifts to present to the Aborigines. Initially the meeting was harmonious despite the Aborigines rejecting the gifts, which confused the French. But when a few Aborigines threw stones at du Fresne's boats, the *Mascarin* and the *Marquis de Castries*, the French retaliated with gunfire, killing at least one and injuring several more.

Over the next 20 years several noted explorers visited the east coast. Captain Tobias Furneaux was accompanying James Cook on his second voyage to the Southern Ocean in 1773 when the mission's two boats, the *Adventure* and the *Resolution*, became separated in heavy seas on February 8. In the maelstrom, Furneaux grabbed his copies of Tasman's charts and made for Van Diemen's Land. Next day he landed at a spot on Bruny Island south of Hobart that became a favourite sheltering place for several of his fellow explorers. He named the wide sweep of calm water Adventure Bay after his ship. Once repairs were completed he headed north, exploring previously uncharted parts of the north coast at the eastern end of Bass Strait. Had he had favourable winds he might have carried on west and discovered that Van Diemen's Land was in fact girt by sea, but the elements blew him east to New Zealand where he rejoined Cook.

Cook did not land on Tasman soil until his third southern expedition in 1777, when the *Resolution* and *Discovery* sailed into Adventure Bay in January looking initially for food and water but with a mission to weigh up the trading potential of this great southern land. As far as he was concerned, Van Diemen's Land was an extension of the vast land mass of New Holland to the north, whose east coast Cook had charted on his first voyage here in 1770. Again gifts were offered and again they were refused, but there was much fascination on both sides in the other's weapons. The Aborigines were terrified by a display of musketry by one of the British sailors, who shot apart a piece of wood. This time there was no violence. Cook rested in Adventure Bay on at least three occasions, as did the ill-fated Lieutenant William Bligh while en route from Britain to Tahiti in the *Bounty* in 1788 to collect breadfruit trees to take to the sugar plantations in the West Indies for cheap slave food. Bligh found a tree inscribed with 'AD1773' by a sailor from Furneaux's unplanned landing. His crew planted apple trees, vines, orange and lemon seeds, cherry stones, plums, peaches and apricots, pumpkins, corn and other vegetables. They also had amiable meetings with Aborigines. Penguin Island in the bay was Bligh's last landfall before the mutiny that unseated him in the South Pacific.

But Bligh would see Adventure Bay again four years later when he returned with the *Providence* and the *Assistant*. He spent two weeks with the Aboriginal people of Bruny Island but found that, despite his previous crew's diligent horticulture, only one apple tree remained standing.

Further up the east coast, another English navigator, Captain John Henry Cox, on the brig *Mercury*, landed at Shoal Bay on the western side of Maria Island in July 1789. He met Aborigines and reported them as peaceful, 'very merry, laughing and mimicking our actions'. He described their boats made from dug-out tree trunks, their bark huts and scores of middens along the shore.

The French Rear-Admiral, Bruni D'Entrecasteaux, and Captain Huon de Kermadec, in charge respectively of the *Recherche* and the *Esperance*, were dispatched to these southern waters to search for a missing expedition led by the explorer Comte de la Perouse that was four years late in returning. They were passing the waters south of Van Diemen's Land and looking for the by now quite famous Adventure Bay, but they misread their charts and ended up 25 miles southwest in a bay they named Recherche. D'Entrecasteaux made use of this error by charting and taking depth soundings – very accurately as it turns out – in the channel between the main island and Bruny Island. No prizes for guessing that this is now known as the D'Entrecasteaux Channel! He also explored the Huon River and the Port Esperance areas, and further north around the coasts of Bruny Island and up to Ralph's Bay and the River Derwent. Again there were friendly meetings with Aboriginal tribes, this time with frequent and welcome gift swapping. Some sailors even shared meals of seafood, gathered by the women who dived for long periods of time in the chilly waters. One allowed himself to be daubed in a charcoal paste while an Aborigine tried to work out the squeaky technicalities of his violin. D'Entrecasteaux was clearly taken by these harmonious meetings and wrote in his log: "Oh, that civilised people who pride themselves on the extent of their knowledge could learn from this school of nature."

But all these great explorers missed one crucial geographical point. It was George Bass and Matthew Flinders, on a mission from the Governor of New South Wales, John Hunter, in October 1798, who proved Van Diemen's Land was an island. The charting of Bass Strait cut the time of the voyage from Europe to the colony at Port Jackson in New South Wales (later to become Sydney) by some days, and meant any livestock taken on board at the Cape of Good Hope would have a better chance of surviving the trip. The large numbers of seals spotted frequently in Bass Strait drew European sealing boats by the score. They began reaping their blubber harvest in 1798 and soon also started trading with the Aboriginal tribes of the north coast. Seal and kangaroo skins, and Aboriginal women, were exchanged for flour, tobacco, tea and dogs. Sealers and whalers were among the most despicable of sorts and almost universally mistrusted. Some gangs simply raided the tribes for women and killed any men who tried to protect them. Through the loss of women and many deaths, the once 500-strong North East tribe numbered only 72 men and six women by 1830.

Bass and Flinders also brought back positive reports on the soil and vegetation of the island which was an important factor in the eventual decision of the British to establish settlements here in 1803 and 1804. Already this island had been earmarked as a good spot to house a tough penal colony for convicts who re-offended once in Port Jackson. After some tense moments with the French, who were also contemplating colonising the island, the British finally claimed it for

King George III. The first settlement was established at Risdon, on the eastern bank of the Derwent River, with 49 people (including 21 male and three female convicts) in early September 1803. Each free settler was given a 14-year lease on five acres of land, two ewes, six bushels of wheat, tools, nails, clothing, garden seeds and, for one year only, stores and two convict labourers to work the land.

In actual fact Risdon was not ideal. The settlement moved across the Derwent and Hobart was born. First contacts between the settlers of Hobart Town and the Aboriginal people were often friendly but this did not last long. The Aboriginal people may have thought the settlers could be accommodated if they were willing to trade and share some of their foods and ways of life. The colonists had other ideas, expecting the Aborigines simply to move over and become second-class citizens. They felt the indigenous people had little, if any, right to the land because they did not really occupy it effectively. In other words, they were not farmers and so were somehow inferior. Settlers, escaped and freed convicts, and bushrangers (outlaws) took over Aboriginal land, abducted children for forced labour, raped and tortured women, and murdered whole groups. This was compounded by a military operation in 1830 called the Black Line which rounded up the Aboriginal people in newly settled districts.

Penal colony

The first shipment of convicts arrived at Sullivans Cove, near Hobart, in 1804. The English had thought Port Jackson (Sydney) was remote and rough enough for prisoners but nothing could compare to the wilds of Van Diemen's Land. Even the name conjures up thoughts of forbidden lands and final outposts. As a result of this early move south, Tasmania has the longest European history of any state after New South Wales.

Of the 160,000 men, women and children sent to Australia as convicts between 1787 and 1868, almost half ended up in Van Diemen's Land. They were invariably second offenders or habitual criminals, along with several political prisoners including Chartists, Luddites and the union activist George Loveless, founder and leader of the Tolpuddle Martyrs. Loveless' crime was establishing Britain's first agricultural union for which exile was deemed an appropriate punishment. He was later pardoned.

Several detention sites were set up. The first was built in 1822 on Sarah Island amid the turbulent waters of Macquarie Harbour on the west coast. It became notorious for the appalling conditions and the treatment of its inmates. Here the worst convicts slaved to construct ships out of Huon pine, cut from forests along the Gordon and Franklin rivers on the mainland and rafted across the harbour to the island. Had the authorities sat and thought about using ship building as a form of labour for convicts on an island they might have realised the risk they were running.

Sure enough, a boat was used by a group of 112 convicts to mount an escape. 62 of them perished in the icy waters, nine were killed and the remaining 41 recaptured. Each caught escapee was lashed to within an inch of his life.

Maria Island was a penal settlement from 1821 but 11 years later the prisoners were moved as it was decided it was not cost efficient. The Cascades Female Factory was a women's prison in Hobart established in 1827 on the site of an old brewery. It was in a marshy part of town totally unsuitable for habitation by the women and, especially, their children. The local paper dubbed the place the 'Shadow of Death Valley'.

The most famous penal site was Port Arthur on the Tasman Peninsula where the British built an early Alcatraz from where no-one could escape. There is only one way in and out of the Tasman Peninsula by land and that is along the narrow strip of land called Eaglehawk Neck which was heavily guarded by soldiers and a line of vicious dogs. Any attempt to escape by sea would bring certain death from hypothermia in the icy waters or by falling prey to sharks. In Port Arthur convicts were incarcerated in wooden, and later stone, cells but it is unlikely they saw much of their humble abodes as they were worked hard. There were several separate prisons which all serviced the main township where thriving industries included timber milling, shipbuilding, coal mining, brick and nail production, and furniture and shoe making. Transportation to Australia ceased in 1853 and the penal colony closed in 1877, its walls having heard the desperate laments of 12,000 prisoners.

Tasmanians tend to agree that roughly half of them are descended from convict stock with the other half related to free settlers. Some are proud of their roguish ancestors but others still feel it a slur to be of convict lineage. The convicts have left Tasmania with a rich architectural heritage – bridges, roads, cottages and courthouses were all erected by men in chains. They came from all walks of life. Most had little education and had been forced into crime to survive in a rapidly industrialising Britain. Many of their crimes were petty, such as stealing a sheep, clothing or the odd vegetable.

But there were also educated men with skills that meant they could escape the cycle of poverty and crime in a new place and become clerks, draughtsmen or even doctors, all essential for building the new colony.

For about the first ten years of settlement there were more convicts than free settlers, so the convicts had to fill positions of responsibility such as medical assistants or 'trusties' in the gaols, on top of their day jobs digging coal mines or making boats. Many female prisoners were given to settlers as house servants. In the 1830s the authorities designed a probation system which farmed out newly freed convicts to paid work in the colony. If he remained out of trouble he would be offered paid work as a settler's servant. However, this backfired somewhat when it was discovered the colony did not have enough money to honour its payments, so the settlers refused to honour theirs as well. As a consequence it was back in the clink for the convicts until a better and cheaper plan could be thought up.

Those who did escape and remained at large were branded 'bushrangers' for their survival skills. They were Tasmania's highwaymen, robbing wealthy travellers of their jewels and clothes on remote trackways at night. Two of the most famous were Martin Cash and the chivalrous crook, Matthew Brady. In the mid-1850s, support for convict transportation in Britain was waning and the government was forced to admit the experiment of sending convicts to Van Diemen's Land had made the prison and probation problem worse rather than better. At that time the island was given the new name of Tasmania.

Was one of your forebears an early settler or convict in Tasmania? Many people come here to find information for their family trees. Genealogical research takes time and will be easier if you prepare before you arrive. The Genealogical Society of Tasmania encourages people to research from their homes first but then to get in contact with them when coming to the island. They can be found at 19 Cambridge Road, Bellerive, Hobart, Tasmania 7018; tel: 6243 6200. Also the Archives Office of Tasmania is at 77 Murray Street, Hobart, Tasmania 7000; tel: 6233 7488 or 6233 7490.

Economic strides

The Van Diemen's Land Company was chartered in England in 1825 with a grant of 141,640 hectares in the northwest to invest money in livestock breeding and sheep for wool. The first block of land was 8,094 hectares at Circular Head, Stanley, demarcated in 1826. Much of the early white exploration of Tasmania was done by company surveyors. The company lost heavily in the late 1840s and, despite finding gold on company land, it was dwindling in importance by the 1850s.

Tasmania then supported a number of industries. Barkmilling enjoyed a spell of importance in the 19th century on the east coast, where black wattles were used to extract tannic acid for the leather industry. Sealing and whaling were mainstays through many of the fledgling years of European settlement. Whales were caught in estuaries as well as on the open ocean, meaning whalers got rich quick selling skins and blubber. We can get an idea of the size of the whale populations from records taken by crew on the barque *Cheviot* in 1843, who caught 17 in six weeks in a coastal bay and in 1844 sailed into Hobart with 40 large casks (known as 'tuns') of sperm whale black oil. The *Camilla* in 1844 delivered 28 tuns to the Hobart dockside. The following year, Captain Irvine of the *Martha* and *Elizabeth* reported seeing 300 whales during his passage from Sydney to Hobart.

So voracious were these industries that in a century they almost wiped out entire populations of whales and elephant and fur seals. The Australian Whaling Commission was established to regulate catches in 1948. Under the International Whaling Agreement, Australia was allowed a quota of whales which for 1951 was 650 humpbacks per season.

Exploratory sperm whaling began in 1955 and eight years later the International Whaling Commission banned humpback whaling. As the IWC imposed more restrictions the industry died here and the last Australian whaling station closed in 1978.

Mineral and metal exploration unearthed several valuable seams which contributed greatly to Tasmania's coffers through the 19th and 20th centuries.

Gold and tin were struck in the 1870s. Silver, lead, zinc and copper were later found on the west coast. More recently, magnesite was discovered in the northwest of the island. If the deposit is rich and plentiful enough it could result in Tasmania becoming a key exporter of this metal which is refined into magnesium.

Such was the lust for easy money and power that with each strike came prospectors and environmental degradation. The devastation can still be seen, especially at Queenstown in the west. As the last miles of the main A10 cross-island road from Hobart twist and turn down the western flanks of the West Coast Range of mountains, the forests suddenly end and a stark moonscape of stained rock and mud prevails.

The centres of Hobart and Launceston grew steadily throughout the 19th century. In fact Australia's second largest city, Melbourne, was founded by an expedition that set out from Launceston in 1835. Roads and railways were laid across the island's challenging terrain, often taking years to complete as they inched through tortuous mountain passes. Slowly they usurped sea travel, which used to be the only way of getting between the east and west coasts.

Australia became a federated nation on January 1 1901, of which Tasmania was its smallest state, but Tasmanians still fought wars alongside British and other Commonwealth troops and were inextricably linked to the Crown. Unless Australia declares itself a republic, Tasmanians will continue to share the same queen as their fellow Aussies and the Commonwealth.

Today's Tasmania
Mining, fishing and forestry have continued to be important industries but lately tourism has become a major income earner for the state with 272,000 leisure

visitors in 2000/2001. Tasmania is a leading centre for nature tourism with so much of the state protected in parks and reserves, and such diverse flora and fauna. It is also a magnet for those who enjoy outdoor and 'adrenaline' activities. Try the mammoth 10-day hike along the South Coast Track or mountaineering along the testing Port Davey Track; hop on a raft for a rollercoaster white-water ride down the Franklin River; try a sea kayak expedition on the surging waters around Schouten Island. The boldest visitors who have a few months to spare – and a lot of books to read (or write) – can apply to do a stint in the lighthouse on Maatsuyker Island.

There's an awful lot of science going on here too. Tasmania is a leading Australian science base with probably the world's biggest and most diverse collection of Antarctic research agencies based here. A number of pioneering wildlife projects are also underway in the state including cutting-edge research into protecting and breeding seahorses, and tracking Great White sharks by satellite to learn more about their habits.

The island is also blessed with a disproportionately wide array of arts and entertainment. There are theatres and concert venues in the main towns, galleries and museums throughout the state, and a wealth of historic buildings to explore. Every two years in March and April, national and international bands, dance troops, poets, musicians, artists and many other acts descend on Tasmania for the 10 Days on the Island festival.

Historic buildings have survived from each stage of Tasmania's past, making the state an excellent destination for architecture and heritage seekers. Many have been continuously used while others have been lovingly saved and restored. Most towns have fine examples of buildings which can be traced from the early period of timber houses and shops through the Georgian, Regency, Federation, Victorian Revival and Italianate schools to the art deco styles of the 1930s. The National Trust owns many properties and records information about many more. Almost all are open to the public.

It could be due to the pioneer spirit nurtured in this wild place or to an intense love for their home island but many Tasmanians consider themselves loyal to the state first, with Australia most definitely in second place. Any thoughts of allegiance to England, from where most of Tasmania's early white settlers originated, is fading with each generation.

Aboriginal rights

Advances have been made in Aboriginal rights since they were given the vote in 1967, although some argue the pace of reform is glacially slow. Those living on the outer islands were given federal government funding in 1972 and work was undertaken building and cleaning the islands. An Aboriginal Information Centre was established in Hobart. Five years later a National Employment Strategy for Aborigines was established to boost the training and placing of indigenous people. Housing allocation schemes were set up in Hobart, Launceston and Burnie, and an Aboriginal Housing Policy Committee launched in Hobart. In 1979 the Tasmanian Aboriginal Education Consultative Committee was formed to advise the state government on needs.

The Tasmanian Aboriginal Centre is responsible for repatriating artefacts from museums and private collections around the world. It is known as 'cultural retrieval' and includes the finding, gathering, recording and practising of old traditions such as language, story-telling and crafts. In 1988 the remaining collection of Tasmanian Aboriginal bones held in museums were handed over to Aboriginal trustees, and six years later an Aboriginal heritage strategy was drafted giving Aboriginal descendants control of site records and the power to grant or deny permits. Today, the Tasmanian Aboriginal Land Council is in charge of preserving culture and heritage and significant Aboriginal sites, and it looks after land management issues.

On October 18 1995, Premier Ray Groom announced that 12 significant sites were to be handed back to Aboriginal ownership: Steep Island and Mount Cameron West in the northwest; Babel Island, Mount Chappell Island, Badger Island, Great Dog Island and Cape Barren Island in the northeast; Kutikina Cave and Ballawinne Cave in the southwest; and Wargata Mina, Risdon Cove and Oyster Cove in the southeast – a total area of 3,800 hectares. This was the result of an 18-year fight for an Aboriginal Land Claim and marked the first time since the Europeans arrived and claimed Tasmania for a distant monarchy that any land had been given back to the original inhabitants. A ceremony took place at Risdon Cove where the land title documents were handed over on December 10 1995.

A Tasmanian Aboriginal lawyer and activist, Michael Mansell, described the return of the land to Aboriginal ownership as a sea change from a position of terrible shame to one of empowerment. 'They and their grandparents and great grandparents fought for years for land rights without results,' he said. Two years later, on August 13 1997, a statement of apology for the so-called Stolen Generation was unanimously supported by the Tasmanian Parliament. The Stolen Generation was a particularly gloomy chapter of Australian history in which missionaries coaxed, and in some cases forcibly removed, children of mixed Aboriginal and white blood from their poor families to bring them up in white environments. No matter how many times apologists say the missionaries had only good intentions, the fact remains that hundreds, possibly thousands, of children were taken from their homes. Many have spent years trying to trace their real parents, often with no success. Most of us can only begin to imagine the traumatic effects of this separation. Aborigines across Australia have been campaigning for an apology from the federal government which they say will acknowledge the wrongs of previous administrations and move the debate forward, perhaps towards an Aboriginal bill of rights.

As yet there has been no apology; in fact there was a firm refusal from the conservative government in power (run by John Howard) as this book went to press.

You are unlikely to encounter the race debate in Tasmania as the Aboriginal descendants here are so few in number, but it is worth noting that all is not well in Australia when it comes to race relations. No matter how many tourist brochures you see containing photos of smiling Aboriginal people clutching gaily painted boomerangs and didgeridoos, the fact remains that the majority of them lead a Third World existence, and – most disturbingly – the majority of white Australians seem fairly happy to keep it that way. Aborigines have been oppressed from the day the first Europeans arrived and nowhere more obviously than in Tasmania, where the full-blood race has vanished.

Archaeological finds are helping to fill in the missing chapters in the ancient history of the island state. In the 1980s, rock paintings were discovered in the southwest believed to be 20,000 years old, graves of 100 Aborigines at Wybalenna on Flinders Island, and hand stencils dating back 10,000 years to the last Ice Age in a cave in the Cracroft Valley in the south. There are almost certainly more to emerge.

In October 2001, members of the Aboriginal community were increasing pressure on the Tasmanian government to return land at Eddystone Point in the northeast. Already land at Oyster Cove, south of Hobart, has been successfully reclaimed and there is a similar campaign over Rocky Cape, in the northwest.

World news

Tasmania has been put on the world map in recent years by two key events. The battle to save the Franklin River from a massive damming project in 1983 grabbed international headlines. The famous Tasmanian Green activist and politician, Dr Bob Brown (now a senator in the federal parliament), and the well-known British conservationist, Professor David Bellamy, were both jailed for their parts in the blockades. The protest was a success and the region is now a beautiful and precious World Heritage Area. Another major event happened at the Port Arthur Historical Site on April 28 1996, when lone gunman Martin Bryant shot dead 35 tourists and staff, and injured many more. The incident prompted the newly elected Australian Prime Minister, John Howard, to hurry through tough new gun laws across the country.

Blue gum

Practical Information

WHEN TO VISIT

Tasmania is really a summer destination (November to March), when the weather and the waters are warmer, the meadows are full of wild flowers, and more animals are out and about. Temperatures do not start to pick up until early October, and the seas are cool to swim in for at least another month after that. Summer days are longer too, as Tasmania operates a daylight saving policy from early October to late March. Summer evenings are light until 21.30.

As the western half of the state gets more than four times the amount of rain that the eastern side gets, it follows that Christmas Day could be hot, dry and sunny in Bicheno but miserably wet and cool over in Strahan. Maximum temperatures in Hobart will be up in the high 20s and low 30s centigrade during summer, and rainfall is low.

The three mid-summer months of December, January and February are the busiest, when the island comes alive with festivals, concerts, food fairs, exhibitions and sporting events. They also constitute the main tourist season, so if you are planning to visit during these months it pays to book accommodation, tours and hire cars some months in advance. The Christmas and New Year period is hectic, especially in Hobart, which plays host to thousands of yacht fanatics celebrating the end of the annual classic Sydney to Hobart yacht race. Competitors set out from Sydney Harbour on Boxing Day, with the first boats cruising up to Derwent about four days later. Summer is good for bushwalking but is also a busy time on the tracks. The most popular route, the Overland Track, can feel like a city marathon. Try to avoid walking during school holidays at this time.

Spring and autumn are perfect for bushwalking and are best for sightings of migrating whales and pods of dolphins and for spotting flocks of leaving and arriving birds. Spring tends to be especially windy in the Roaring Forties (the term used to describe Tasmania's latitudinal position, between 40° south and 44° south). It is ideal for flower lovers. Peak flowering times for most species are September to February.

The fruit groves burst into blossom in August and September. Lowland wild flowers show off their colours from September to December, with upland varieties coming later, from December to February. The stunning fields of lavender blush purple in December and January. There are flower shows throughout the summer.

Late summer and early autumn brings Tasmania's biggest arts festival, 10 Days on the Island, which is held in late March and early April every two years.

In late autumn and early winter the beech forests of the southwest turn their leaves, painting the hillsides a rich rust-red and gold. In the Huon Valley the apple carts strain under the weight of the year's crop. The orchards are carpeted with 'windfalls', and on still, misty mornings the scent in the air is intoxicating.

Winter days (June to August) on the east coast can be beautiful and many Tasmanians head there for weekends. The air is keen and cool and the sky clear, and long walks along lonely beaches are bracing and cleansing. Bushwalking in higher altitudes is much tougher and in some cases impossible unless you are an experienced and well-equipped mountaineer used to operating on snow and ice. Hobart's cosy pubs come into their own during the winter with log fires, good Guinness and often a local musician strumming in the corner.

Surfing is good all year due to regular swells but requires a warm wetsuit with hood from June to October. The brown trout fishing season runs from August to April, the rainbow trout season starts in October and ends in May, and the sea run trout season is from August to December.

HIGHLIGHTS

It is hard to get a better introduction and feel for this island than at the Tasmanian Museum in Hobart where colourful displays give information on flora, fauna, history and development. Be sure to visit the mega-fauna room.

More than half of all visitors go walking in Tasmania according to official figures. Some of the most spectacular tracks can be found along the cliffs of the Tasman Peninsula. The Tasman National Park was only opened in 1999 and hugs the east and south coasts of the peninsula from Eaglehawk Neck to Curio Bay. All the walks are excellent, with dramatic views in almost every direction. There are impressive geographical features such as sea caves, a blowhole, a sea arch and a tessellated pavement. Walkers can take a leisurely two-hour stroll on their own or with a local guide, or get kitted out for a week-long hike which includes practically the whole park coastline. Also relatively new (opened in June 2001) is the Tahune Forest AirWalk near Geeveston in the Huon Valley, a thrilling aerial walkway through the eucalyptus canopy.

If messing about in boats is your thing then head for the Collingwood River, where it crosses the A10 east–west highway in the World Heritage Area. This is the put-in point for rafting trips down the Franklin river system. The trips take either one or two weeks depending on how far you want to go. From the put-in point to Sir John Falls on the Gordon River is about 80km. They are led by experienced river guides and are a superb way to experience this magical wilderness. Rafters spend days drifting through pristine Huon pine forests and running the rapids, and nights camping on the river bank among the tea-tree bushes.

One way of getting out of the bush is by seaplane which offers another awesome experience.

Tasmania's fairy penguins are a must-see. On summer nights there are hundreds at the southern end of Godfreys Beach, at Stanley on the north coast, waddling between their miniature caves and yapping like puppies. All penguin watching at night must be done with torches covered by red cellophane and flash photography is not recommended.

The Tasmanian devil is like no other animal. At once fascinating and terrifying, it needs to be seen to be believed and a good place to do that is at Marrawah in the far northwest with local landowner and guide, Geoff King (Joe to his friends). Geoff takes small groups to a shack by the water's edge on a deserted and usually wildly windy beach that devils regularly visit. You sit and wait and listen for the first crunch of bones as they begin devouring a wallaby carcass.

Picking a Tasmanian beach is near impossible as so many are bright white and crystal clean, but a personal favourite is Abbotsbury in the Mount William National Park. Apparently few people get to this park which is surprising because it involves a fairly straightforward dirt-track drive and is easily reached on a day trip from Scottsdale and St Marys. The beach is a magnificent stretch of perfect, powdery sand and the dunes are criss-crossed with quoll and devil tracks – it's human prints that are hard to find. Sea eagles hop along in the surf lazily looking for dead fish.

Abbotsbury's northern extent is marked by a cluster of granite rocks painted bright orange by lichen. Above them, completing this idyllic scene, is the graceful Eddystone lighthouse.

Queenstown in the west gets a bad press most of the time. Indelibly stained by a century of mining, it comes as a bit of a shock to those who have driven through the verdant beauty of the central mountains and are heading down the western flanks hoping for more before they reach the coast. But it occupies an essential chapter of Tasmania's history and should be seen, especially by those who have not visited, and are not planning to visit, any mining towns on the mainland. Australia may have survived for many years 'on the sheep's back', as was said of the wool trade, but mining has been a real mainstay, and rough-and-tumble mining towns are part of the Australian psyche. Queenstown lost much of its raucous edge as the mines closed and the miners took their picks and moved on, but there is still a thin seam of pioneer lawlessness here. Despite the through-flow of tourists it still has a Wild West flavour.

The best all-round access to Tasmania's wild beauty is probably at Russell Falls in Mount Field National Park which is considered something of an island treasure. The easy track can be negotiated by some wheelchairs and families can take strollers along it too.

For arguably the best view in Tasmania, take the delightful ferry ride across to Bruny Island and head south to the Cape Bruny lighthouse. Looking out from here there is no land until Antarctica save for the three rock stacks Pedra Blanca, Sidmouth Rock and Eddystone Rock. Only Pedra Blanca is visible without binoculars, and that only on a clear day. In the bay at the bottom of the cliffs below the lighthouse, abalone divers can sometimes be seen risking their lives for a lucrative prize.

SUGGESTED ITINERARIES

All our itineraries are based on driving a hired vehicle but segments of some are possible by public transport, depending on bus and minibus schedules.

Day trips
From Hobart

Self-drive loop tour of the **fruit groves of the Huon Valley** in autumn, heading south via Fern Tree to around Huonville, with lunch at Cygnet, and returning through Snug and Kingston. Pick up some apples from the roadside stalls as you go. If you wish to travel by bus, Hobart Coaches run from the capital to Kettering through Kingston and Snug. Tassie Link run their minibus to Huonville via Kingston.

Length 130–140km. *Time* 6 hours with stops.

Self-drive loop tour to **Richmond via Sorell**, heading east across the Tasman Bridge and a quick drive up **Mount Rumney** for the view, then across Pitt Water to Sorell and north to Richmond for lunch and a historical tour. Back via Risdon Vale and Bowen Bridge. Tassie Link go to Sorell, where passengers must change to catch a connection to Richmond, then return the same way.

Length 70–80km. *Time* 4–5 hours with stops.

Cyclists could comfortably cruise down through **Bellerive** and **Lauderdale** to the tip of the South Arm peninsula at **Opossum Bay**. Take lunch and a flask of tea to have at **Cape Contrariety**, overlooking Betsey Island.

Length 35–45km. *Time* 6–8 hours with stops.

Fit walkers can stride out from their hotel and scale **Mount Wellington** in a day, but an easier way is to catch either a No 48 or 49 bus from Franklin Square in the city centre to Fern Tree, then try one of the walks that start from there. Buses run to the top from December until mid-February.

Length and time From Hobart to the summit and back is 16–20km and would take 8 hours with stops. The bus to Fern Tree takes about 20 minutes and the return or loop walks from Fern Tree to the summit are between 10km and 14km, which could take from 3–6 hours with stops.

Tour with the Wilderness Society (130 Davey Street, Hobart, TAS 7000; tel: 6224 1550; fax: 6223 5112; email: tasmania@wilderness.org.au; web: www.wilderness.org.au/tasmania) to the **Styx Valley** to visit the giant eucalyptus trees.

Length 120–150km. Time 6–8 hours with stops.

From Launceston
North to **George Town** and **Low Head**, east to **Pipers Brook** vineyard for lunch and wine tasting, and back to Launceston via Lilydale.

Length 150–160km. *Time* 6–8 hours with stops.

North to **Beaconsfield** and **Narawntapu National Park**, take a bush walk and have a sandwich lunch, and then return via **Seahorse World** at Beauty Point.

Length 150–160km. *Time* 6–8 hours with stops.

From Wynyard
Along the coast to **Stanley** to climb the **Nut** and see penguins, and return via **Rocky Cape National Park**.

Length 200km. *Time* 8 hours with stops.

South to **Hellyer Gorge** to take a bush walk through tree fern gullies, and back the same way.

Length 90–110km. *Time* 6–8 hours with stops.

Two days on the island
Hobart to Tasman Peninsula
Day one Hobart to Tessellated Pavement and Eaglehawk Neck; take a short bush walk to the Tasman Blowhole or Tasman Arch. Overnight in Taranna (at Convict Station B&B).

Day two Visit Nubeena and White Beach, then spend the afternoon at Port Arthur historical site before returning to Hobart (maybe by boat plane).

Hobart to Cockle Creek
Day one To Cockle Creek by car or bus via Tahune Forest AirWalk. Take a short afternoon walk along the South Coast Track, and stay overnight at a youth hostel.

Day two Back to Hobart via the Hartz Mountains National Park and Huon Valley.

Hobart to Mount Field National Park
Day one To the park, afternoon walk and overnight stay at Tyenna Valley Lodge.

Day two Morning walk to Russell Falls and return to Hobart.

Launceston to Mount William National Park
Day one To the park via Derby for the craft centres, and spend the night at St Helens.

Day two Return via the cheddar cheese factory in Pyengana.

One week on the island
East coast–Midlands
Day one Hobart to Orford to catch ferry to Maria Island. Afternoon bush walk and camp the night.

Day two Morning bush walk and ferry to Orford, north to Freycinet Peninsula via Spiky Bridge, and overnight in Freycinet.

Day three Walking trails in Freycinet and north to do evening penguin tour and overnight in Bicheno.

Day four To St Marys via Douglas Apsley National Park for short walks. Overnight in St Marys.

Day five Return to Hobart via Fingal, Campbell Town and Oatlands, with stop in Oatlands for historical building tour. On to Richmond and stay the night.

Day six Morning historical tour of Richmond, and back to Hobart for late lunch on the harbour.

Mountains
Day one Hobart to Gordon Dam and return to Mount Field National Park to stay overnight.

Day two Walks in the park and tour of Styx Valley.

Day three To Derwent Bridge via Tarraleah. Overnight at Derwent Bridge.

Day four Walk from Lake St Clair information centre along the southern end of Overland Track to the first hut and return to Derwent Bridge to spend the night.

Day five Back to Hobart with lunch at Bradys Lake.

North
Day one Launceston morning tour, and to Lemonthyme Lodge for the night via the caves.

Day two Either to Cradle Mountain for a day walk along the northern end of the Overland Track and a return to Lemonthyme Lodge, or straight on to Murchison Highway and north via Hellyer Gorge to Wynyard.

Day three Either Lemonthyme Lodge to Wynyard, the Rocky Cape National Park and on to Stanley to see the penguins and spend the night, or Wynyard to Boat Harbour, Sisters Beach and Rocky Cape National Park, and Stanley for the night.

Day four Morning tour of Stanley, then to Marrawah to view the Tasmanian devils. Return to Stanley for the night.

Day five Return to Launceston via Bass Highway passing through Penguin, Ulverstone and Latrobe.

Two weeks on the island
West
Day one Hobart familiarisation (getting to know the Tasmanian capital) and overnight in Hobart.

Day two Bruny Island for penguins and the night.

Day three Full day and night in Bruny.

Day four To Mount Field National Park and stay overnight.

Day five Day trip to Gordon Dam, and overnight in Mount Field.

Day six To Derwent Bridge for walks and the night.

Day seven To Queenstown for mine tour and overnight.

Day eight To Strahan and tour of Sarah Island followed by accommodation in Strahan.

Day nine North to the mining museum at Zeehan, on through Rosebery and Hellyer Gorge, and overnight in Wynyard.

Day ten Rocky Cape National Park, tour of Stanley, evening devil watching at Marrawah, and overnight in Stanley or Marrawah.

Day eleven Bass Highway to Burnie and south to Cradle Mountain to spend the night.

Day twelve Short walk along northern end of the Overland Track, then drive to Mole Creek to see caves and stay overnight in Deloraine.

Day thirteen South along Lake Highway to Hobart.

Day fourteen Hobart to shop.

East

Day one Hobart familiarisation, and overnight in Hobart.

Day two Bruny Island for penguins and the night.

Day three Full day and night in Bruny.

Day four To Tasman Peninsula for walks and overnight stay in Taranna.

Day five Port Arthur and more walks or sea kayak tour around Tasman Island.

Day six Travel to Orford and take the ferry to Maria Island to camp overnight.

Day seven Maria Island walks, ferry to Orford and drive to Freycinet Peninsula for the night.

Day eight Full day and night on Freycinet.

Day nine Morning walks on Freycinet, afternoon drive to Bicheno for evening penguins and overnight stay.

Day ten To Mount William National Park via St Helens, and overnight in Ansons Bay (camping only).

Day eleven To Bridport and Pipers Brook for wine-tasting, and overnight in George Town.

Day twelve Morning tour of George Town, and afternoon and evening in Launceston.

Day thirteen To Hobart via Oatlands for heritage building tour, overnight stay in Hobart.

Day fourteen Hobart to shop.

For the Overland Track, you need a day to get to either starting point from Hobart, at least five days to walk it (seven allows a comfortable pace), and a day for the return to Hobart. For the South Coast Track, you can double this and include at least one short plane flight into or out of Melaleuca.

If you are thinking of staying longer than a month then consider some trips to the outer islands such as King Island for a few days of camping and cheese-tasting, or Flinders Island to trace Aboriginal history, or even a voyage south to Macquarie Island to spot albatross and penguin colonies. There are also several volunteer projects you can join, mending footpaths or helping wildlife.

TOUR OPERATORS
Australia

Goway Travel 350 Kent St, 8th Floor, Sydney 2000; tel: 800 227 268 or 02 9262 4755; fax: 02 9290 1905; email: res@goway.com.au; web: www.goway.com/tasmania/index.html.

World Expeditions 3rd Floor, 441 Kent St, Sydney, NSW 2000; tel: 02 9264 3366; fax: 02 9261 1974; email: enquiries@worldexpeditions.com.au.

Canada

Goway Travel 3284 Yonge St, Suite 300, Toronto, Ontario M4N 3M7; tel: 800 387 8850 or 416 322 1034; fax: 416 322 1109; email: res@goway.com; web: www.goway.com.

France

Australie Autrement 14 rue Servandoni, 75006 Paris; tel: 01 44 07 04 98; fax: 01 56 24 91 13; email: info@australieautrement.com; web: www.australieautrement.com.

Australie.net Tel: 0825 888 353; email: info@australia.net; web: www.australie.net.

Germany

Australia Plus Reisen Partnachstr 6, 81373 Munchen; tel: 089 72 6694 0; fax: 089 72 6694-44; email: australiaplus@t-online.de; web: www.australiaplus.de.

Best of Australia Ostwall 30, 47608 Geldern, Germany; tel: 028 31 13 32 09; fax: 028 31 13 32 12; email: head.office@bosp.de; web: www.bosp.de.

Boomerang Reisen Christophstr 36, 70180 Stuttgart; tel: 0711 6079600; fax: 0711 6079603; email: stuttgart@boomerang-reisen.de; or Waldstr 1, 04105 Leipzig; tel: 0341 984520; fax: 0341 2113363; emailleipzig@boomerang-reisen.de; web: www.australien.com.

Karawane Reisen Schorndorfer Str 149, 71638 Ludwigsburg; tel: 071 41 28 480; web: www.karawane.de.

Kiwi Tours Franziskanerstr 15, 81669 Munchen; tel: 089 7466250; fax: 089 746625 99; email: info@kiwitours.com; web: www.kiwitours.com.

Netherlands

Barron & De Keijzer Heemraadsingel 107, Rotterdam; tel: 010 4780000; email: rotterdam@barron.nl; or Noordermarkt 16, Amsterdam; tel: 020 6258600; email: amsterdam@barron.nl; web: www.barrontravel.com.

Special Traffic/Kuoni Entrada 211–214, 1096 EE Amsterdam; tel: 020 3989292; fax: 020 3989202; email: info@specialtraffic.nl; web: www.specialtraffic.nl.

New Zealand

Air New Zealand Destinations Tel: 0800 737000 for reservations or 0800 737767 for travel centres; web: www.airnzdestinations.co.nz.

Travel.co.nz 52 Emily Place, Auckland; tel: 09 359 3860; fax: 09 308 9727; web: www.travel.co.nz.

Travel Online Level 4, The Domain, 103 Carlton Gore Road, Newmarket, Auckland; tel: 09 358 5617; email: info@travelonline.co.nz; web: www.travelonline.co.nz.

South Africa

Goway Travel 71 Loop St, 5th Floor, Cape Town 8001; tel: 021 424 0070; fax: 021 424 2130; web: www.goway.com.

Thompsons Tours 1st Floor, Dunkeld West Shopping Centre, cnr Bompas Road and Jan Smuts Av, Dunkeld West, Johannesburg; tel: 11 77 07 677; fax: 11 32 52 840; or 5th Floor, Atlantic Centre, cnr Oswald Pirow Dr and Louis Gradner St, Foreshore, Cape Town; tel: 21 40 89 500; fax: 21 40 89 596; or FNB House, 4th Floor, 151 Musgrave Rd, Durban; tel: 31 25 03 100; fax: 31 20 13 203; web: www.thompsons.co.za.

UK

Australian Affair Hillgate House, 12 Hillgate St, London W8 7SP; tel: 020 7616 9191; email: contact@australian-affair.com; web: www.australian-affair.com.

Austravel 50–51 Conduit St, London W1R 9FB; tel: 0870 166 2070; email: westend@austravel.com; or 17 Blomfield St, London EC2M 7AJ; tel: 0870 055 0213; email: city@austravel.com; web: www.austravel.com. Branches also now in Birmingham, Bournemouth, Bristol, Edinburgh, Leeds and Manchester.

Bridge the World 45–47 Chalk Farm Rd, Camden Town, London NW1 8AJ or 4 Regent Place, Regent St, London W1R 5F; tel: 0870 444 7474; fax: 020 7734 6455; email: sales@bridgetheworld.com; web: www.bridgetheworld.com.

Classic Connection Concorde House, Canal St, Chester CH1 4EJ; tel: 01244 355504; email: cc@itc-uk.com; web: www.itc-uk.com.
Kuoni Travel 84 Bishopsgate, London EC2N 4AU; tel: 020 7374 6601 or head office Australasia sales 01306 741111; email: australia.sales@kuoni.co.uk; web: www.kuoni.co.uk. Closed Saturday.
Tailor Made Travel 18 Port St, Evesham, Worcs WR11 6AN; tel: 01386 712005; email: sales@tailor-made.co.uk; web: www.tailor-made.co.uk.
Travelbag 3–5 High St, Alton, Hants GU34 1TL; tel: 0870 730 3201; web: www.travelbag.co.uk.
Travel Mood 246 Edgware Rd, London W2 1DS; tel: 020 7258 0280; fax: 020 7402 4107; email: sales@travelmood.com; web: www.travelmood.com.

USA

ATS Tours 2381 Rosecrans Av, Suite 325, El Segundo, CA 90245; tel: 1800 423 2800 or 310 643 0044; fax: 310 643 0032; email: info@atstours.com; web: www.ATStours.com.
Austravel 51 East 42nd St, Suite 616, New York, NY 100017; tel: 1800 633 3404 or 212 972 6880; fax: 212 983 8376; or 5959 Airport Boulevard, Suite 106, Los Angeles, CA 90045; tel: 1800 633 3404 or 310 338 0574; fax: 310 338 9643; web: www.aus-vacations.com/tas.html.
Brendan Tours 15137 Califa Street, Van Nuys, CA 91411-3021; tel: 818 785 9696; fax: 818 902 9876; email: info@brendantours.com; web: www.brendantours.com.
Goway Travel 5865 South Kyrene Rd, Suite 2, Tempe, AZ 85283; tel: 1800 387 8850; fax: 800 665 4432; email: res@goway.com; web: www.goway.com.
Newmans Vacations 6033 West Century Bd, Suite 970, Los Angeles, CA 90045; tel: 1800 421 3326 or 888 592 6224; fax: 310 215 9705; email: newmans@newmansvacations.com; web: www.newmansvacations.com.
Qantas Vacations 300 Continental Bd, Suite 610, El Segundo, CA 90245; tel: 1800 348 8139 or 1300 322 6359; fax: 310 535 1057; email: booknow@qantasvacations.com; web: www.qantasvacations.com.
Swain Australia Tours, 6 West Lancaster Ave, Ardmore, PA 19003; tel: 1800 227 9246 or 1800 642 6224; fax: 1610 896 9592; web: www.swaintours.com or www.DownunderDirect.com.
United Vacations (no postal address); tel: 1888 854 3899; web: www.unitedvacationssp.com.

Tasmanian Travel Centres on mainland Australia

If you are already in Australia when planning a Tasmania jaunt check out the following Tasmanian Travel Centres:

New South Wales 60 Carrington St, Sydney 2000; tel: 02 9202 2004.
Victoria 259 Collins St, Melbourne 3000; tel: 03 9206 7901.

SPECIALIST TOUR OPERATORS

Tasmania is a dream destination for those who love the outdoors. It is an island full of adventure, soft or hard. Below is a run-down of the possibilities and some reputable companies who can organise them. Some specialise in one thing while others run several different activities. It is not a definitive list.

Bushwalking

With more than 1,000 miles of trails winding across the island, bushwalking must rank as the most popular outdoor activity in Tasmania. Walks such as the Overland Track and the South Coast Track are legendary. The authorities have done well, however, not to limit the accessibility of these walks merely to the physically able and fit. There are walks lasting less than one hour, with wide, even paths along the flat and through gentle mixed forest or coastal heathland. Many are suitable for young children and the elderly, and some can accommodate wheelchairs. I am indebted to Tasmania's Parks and Wildlife Service for producing a brilliant booklet called *30 Great Short Walks*, and for giving us permission to use their suggestions in this guide. Look out all over Tasmania for the Great Short Walks sign which is made up of a 'W' and a boot print. Copies of the colour brochure can be obtained from Tourism Tasmania or any visitor travel and information centre on the island.

Those in search of a challenge have also come to the right place. Some of Tasmania's walks will test even the toughest of outdoor folk. Frenchmans Cap tests even hardy and experienced walkers, the Overland Track is no picnic even in fine weather, and the South Coast Track is long.

A quick word about huts. They are wooden, and have no electricity or running water or mattresses. Some have bunks, in others you will have to use the floor. There are tables and benches and they have coal heaters, but supplying coal to huts is expensive and the heaters generate a lot of ash waste which degrades the environment around the huts. So do not light the heaters if the thermometers in the huts read 10°C or more. Putting on extra clothing is a non-polluting way of getting warm. Psychologists and social anthropologists would have a field day examining hut etiquette. Everything is on a 'first come, first served' basis, but there are always some who take advantage. Walking the Overland Track, I was overtaken every evening by four rather obnoxious policemen friends from Victoria who sped up over the last two hours of the walking day to make sure they got their spaces in the huts before everyone else. They then spread out their gear and made others feel like they were intruding. By all accounts, though, this is rare and most people are friendly, chatty and willing to share. One night, over a game of cards with a woman from Queensland, I swapped some of my rather foul and squashed dried apricot biscuits for some of her anti-inflammatory tablets which fixed my painful knee.

Where relevant in the later chapters of this guide I will feature details of **short walks** (under four or five hours), **day walks** (up to eight hours), and **long-distance walks** (two days and longer). Most bushwalkers stride out under their own steam, or in small groups of friends or others they have met on their travels. There are opportunities, however, to join guided tours. Try the following companies:

Craclair Tours Tel/fax: 6242 7833; email: craclair@southcom.com.au; web: www.southcom.com.au/~craclair. Short, easy walks of one or two days in length combined with yacht cruises and historical tours of both the Cradle Mountain region and the western mining areas. Also an 8–10 day tour to walk the length of the Overland Track.
Freycinet Experience Tel: 1800 506 003 or 6223 7565; fax: 6224 1315; email: walk@freycinet.com.au. 4-day guided walk along the east coast for people of moderate fitness. Some steep sections but not difficult scrambles. First two nights under canvas with fresh fish, oyster and wine suppers; last night at the eco-award-winning Friendly Beaches Lodge. Accommodation on twin-share basis.
Tasman Bush Tours Tel: 6423 4965; mobile: 0418 373113; fax: 6423 6259; email: tasmanbush@tasadventures.com. 6-day Overland Track tour with guides and loan of walking and camping equipment; 5-day tour to the summit of Frenchmans Cap via the North Col; and a 3-day expedition into the Walls of Jerusalem. Camping.
Tasmanian Expeditions 110 George St, Launceston, TAS 7250; tel: 6334 3477 or 6334 0427; fax: 6334 3463; email: info@tas-ex.com; web: www.tas-ex.com. 3-day Cradle Walk with just day-packs, exploring lakes, waterfalls, and rainforests of Cradle Valley, including a climb up Cradle Mountain. Nights in cabins. 13-day bushwalking, cycling and rafting tour.

Hikes and camping in Cradle Mountain-Lake St Clair, and the Walls of Jerusalem. Cycling along the east coast and rafting on the Picton River south of Hobart.

Sea kayaking

This is easier than river kayaking in some respects. The kayaks are wide and pretty hard to capsize, they have larger holes to sit in, which means if they do turn over they are easier to scramble out of, and you are unlikely to encounter rapids at sea. Despite the effort required to paddle, this is one of the most relaxing ways to see Tasmania. You can opt for easy half-day tours drifting through Hobart's docks and up the Derwent River or go for the really tough stuff, circumnavigating Tasman Island under towering cliffs.

Try the following companies:

Freycinet Adventures Tel: 6257 0500; mobile: 0419 321 896; fax: 6257 0447; email: coastalkayak@vision.net.au; web: www.tasadventures.com. 1-, 3- and 5-day tours around Freycinet coast and Schouten Island. Observing Aboriginal middens and walks to Wineglass Bay. Nights at wilderness camp.

Roaring 40s Tel: 6267 5000; fax: 6267 5004; email: rfok@ozemail.com.au. 2-hour paddles from Hobart around the docks and up the Derwent River; 1-day and 5-day tours through the sheltered coves and waterways of Bruny Island and the D'Entrecasteaux Channel.

Rafting

There can be few places so exhilarating to experience the joys and adrenaline of whitewater rafting as down the Franklin and Gordon River system. Most trips are through grade two to four rapids with only the occasional grade five (severe) rapid when the rivers are in flood. Most trips can be undertaken with no experience, but one or two are unsuitable for novices. There are day trips and ones that can last two weeks.

Try the following companies:

Aardvark Adventures Grove Rd, Glenorchy, Hobart, TAS 7010; tel/fax: 6249 4098; mobile: 0408 127714; email: aardvark@tasadventures.com. Run rafting trips on the Mersey River.

Peregrine 258 Lonsdale St, Melbourne, VIC 3000; tel: 9662 2800; mobile: 018 056 896; fax: 9663 8618; email: franklin@peregrine.net.au. Run Franklin River trips departing from Hobart.

Rafting Tasmania Tel: 6239 1080; fax: 6239 1090; email: raftingtas@tasadventures.com. 5-day Franklin River rafting trip begins with travel by bus and 4WD and a climb to the start of the river. Visit an Aboriginal cave at Kutikina, join the Gordon and paddle to Sir John Falls. Camping. Also tours on Derwent.

Cycling and mountain biking

In keeping with Tasmania's pristine environment, using nothing but pedal power is a good way to travel. There are some spectacular rides along the coasts, some tougher ones inland and through the mountains, and one or two arduous, off-road scrambles. You can bring your own bike, or hire one from the tour company or from a private hire firm. Always make sure your bike is spotless before pedalling out into the wilds in order to prevent the spread of the root rot fungus *Phytophthora cinnamomi*.

Try the following companies:

Cycling Adventures Tasmania Fax: 6244 3251; email: rowanburns@hotmail.com. 1-hour, half-day and all-day tours from Hobart, both for those wanting to take it easy and for the fitter cyclist.

Tasmanian Expeditions Tel: 6334 3477; fax: 6334 3463; email: tazzie@tassie.net.au. 2-day tours cycling and canoeing from Launceston through the South Esk River valley. 4-day tours from Launceston to Freycinet. 6-day Heritage Cycle tours stopping each night at National Trust accommodation.

Sailing

It is in the blood of most Australians to sail. More than 75% of the population live on the coast after all, and their ancestors nearly all got here on a boat of some description. The seas around the island can be rough and unpredictable, which means Tasmania is not the ideal place to learn to sail. You might be better off doing that on Sydney Harbour or on the Great Barrier Reef. However, if you just want to get out there on the water under sail, then try the following company:

West Coast Yacht Charters Tel: 6471 7422; mobile: 0419 300994; fax: 6471 8033; email: wcyc@tasadventures.com. 2-hour crayfish dinner cruise on Macquarie Harbour ('bring your own' and licensed), and 2-day Gordon River and Macquarie Harbour cruise, including Sarah Island.

Diving (and snorkelling)

Diving in Tasmania is for the hardy. Even in the warmest months this is cool water. It is also spectacular as you will rarely dive with better visibility. You can frequently see many metres in all directions. As these are temperate waters, you will not find the corals of the Great Barrier Reef or other tropical areas. Instead there are giant kelp forests, vast granite boulders creating exciting swim-throughs, 10–30m drop-offs and cliff walls, southern rock lobsters and leafy sea-dragons, and numerous shipwrecks. The best diving is along the east coast and around a few of the northern islands. Try the following company:

Dive Tasmania Mobile: 0417 013518; email: dive@tasadventures.com. Organise dives at Eaglehawk Neck on the Tasman Peninsula, including Cathedral Cave (a honeycomb of passages and massive entrances) and 30m-high kelp forests; two dives at Bicheno, including Granite Boulders Drive (swim-throughs and drop-offs) and Giant Kelp Forests; and three on King Island with plenty of wrecks and night dives.

Scenic flights

A wonderful way to see this magical island and to get into remote areas without so much as packing a rucksack. Try the following companies:

Freycinet Air 109 Friendly Beaches Rd, Friendly Beaches; tel: 6375 1694. Flights over the Freycinet Peninsula.
Par Avion Tel: 6248 5390; fax: 6248 51177; email: paravion@tassie.net.au; web: www.paravion.com. 2-hour flights twice daily from Hobart over the southwest wilderness, with stops for lunch and the option of camping overnight. The cost is $132–264. The company also operates one-way flights to or from Hobart for bushwalkers doing tracks in the southwest ($138), and can arrange food drops for walkers out there for the long haul. It also runs a flight up the east coast, with a stop at Maria Island.
Schutt Aviation Tel: 9580 3033; fax: 9580 8955: email: info@schuttaviation.com; web: www.schuttaviation.com. Also have a flying school.
Tasair Regional Airlines Tel: 1800 062900; web: www.tasair.com.au. Run flights over Freycinet Peninsula, the southwest wilderness and Tasman Peninsula. Adults pay $77–176.
Tasmanian Seaplanes Tel: 6227 8808; fax: 6227 9721; email: scenic@tas-seaplane.com; web: www.tas-seaplane.com. Short flights over the southwest wilderness, the southeast and the Tasman Peninsula, including stops at Port Arthur.

Wilderness Air Tel: 6471 7280; fax: 6471 7303; email: wildernessair@tasadventures.com. Seaplane flights from Strahan to the headwaters of Gordon, or over Frenchmans Cap.

Rock climbing, abseiling and rappelling

Australia has high standards of safety when it comes to adrenaline sports and, with all its natural beauty and interesting rock formations, Tasmania is a good spot to learn to climb and abseil. Organisers will use pretty much any vertical surface they can find, so there is a wide choice of venues. There are also opportunities for more experienced climbers. When contacting operators, let them know exactly how much experience you have had. Rappelling is abseiling, but face-first and running down the cliff. Try the following companies:

Aardvark Adventures Grove Rd, Glenorchy, Hobart, TAS 7010; tel/fax: 6249 4098; mobile 0408 127714; email: aardvark@tasadventures.com. Offer a 140-metre abseil down the mighty Gordon River Dam, the highest commercial abseil in the world. Suitable also for beginners.
Freycinet Adventures Tel: 6257 0500; mobile: 0419 321 896; fax: 6257 0447; email: coastalkayak@vision.net.au. Half-day and full-day climbs and abseils around the beautiful cliffs of the Freycinet Peninsula. All standards catered for.
Summit Sports 444 Huon Rd, South Hobart, TAS 7004; mobile: 0418 362210 fax: 6223 1741; email: summit@southcom.com.au; web: www.summitsports.southcom.com.au. Run climbing and abseiling trips on the Freycinet and Tasman Peninsulas, and on Mount Wellington outside Hobart which is handy if you only have a short stay in the city.
Tasmanian Expeditions Tel: 6334 3477; fax: 6334 3463; email: tazzie@tassie.net.au. Half-day and full-day climbing and abseiling in Launceston's Cataract Gorge. All standards catered for.

Caving

Caving requires skill, concentration and, for the more serious expeditions, a good deal of underground experience. Statistically it is one of the more dangerous sports. Aesthetically it is one of the most exhilarating. A good contact is Debbie Hunter, who runs Wild Cave Tours in the north, is conservation officer for the Mole Creek Caving Club, and the first point of contact for the state's cave rescue operations. Her tours have a strong emphasis on environmental issues and she limits the groups to a maximum of eight but prefers just two or three in each party. To contact Debbie Hunter, tel: 6367 8142; email: debhunter@tassie.net.au or debbie@wildcavetours.com; web: www.wildcavetours.com. Also try the Australian Speliological Federation (web: www.caves.org.au) who produce the *Australian Caver* newsletter.

In Hobart, try Jeff Butt at the Southern Tasmanian Caverneers Club, the oldest caving club in Australia (tel: 6223 8620; web: www.tased.edu.au/tasonline/caving).

Surfing

Grab your board and head for the waves, but don't forget your wetsuit – this is cool-water surfing. Waves rolling into Tasmania are big, anywhere in the 3–6 metre category, especially when the big ocean swells are running in. Marrawah, on the northwest coast, has some of the best surf breaks as the waves hitting here have come clean across the Southern Ocean from South America, missing the Cape of Good Hope. They are not suitable for beginners. Likewise some of the beaches around the south of the Tasman Peninsula: the local surfers won't let on where it is, but there is a beach down here which has recorded gigantic waves and is apparently to be used in a global search for a 100ft mini-tsunami monster. They call it 'Fluffies'. Beginners can catch some lovely waves on the beaches along the north coast, the east coast north of Bicheno, and on the South Arm Peninsula near Hobart. Local surf shops know the swells and the best breaks to head for day-to-day. They hire boards and wetsuits too. Also check out *Surfing World* magazine (web: www.surfingworld.com.au). It is worth noting that although Tasmania's waters are well stocked with fish, White Pointer sharks (Great Whites) are present here, so avoid surfing where you see people spearfishing or diving for abalone.

Surfing Tasmania are an outfit worth contacting (mobile: 0417 589089; email: chris@tassiesurf.com; web: www.tassiesurf.com). They organise surf packages for a day or a few days, using Zodiac dinghies to get around quickly to catch the best of the swells.

Skiing

For skiing, head for Ben Lomond and Mount Field National Parks. Ben Lomond (tel: 6390 6279) is the more established centre, having been the first base of the Northern Tasmanian Alpine Club in the 1930s. Despite its designation as a national park in 1946, skiing was encouraged. The season runs from July to September, and skiing costs extra to the park fees. Mount Field (tel: 6288 1149) caters mainly for cross-country skiing and apparently you cannot hire skis here any more.

Jet-boating

This is pure adrenaline on the water. A speed boat will whisk you at a great pace across the waters of the Huon or the Derwent rivers.

Try **Huon River Jet Boats** (tel: 6264 1838; fax: 6264 1031; email: huonjet@tassie.net.au) or **Devil Jet** (tel: 6261 3460) for 30-minute rides.

Sky-diving

If you have never done it before, then Tasmania is ideal for a first jump. They run tandem jumps here where you are strapped to an instructor who can give you second-by-second guidance in steering and technique as you descend from 10,000ft.

Try **Tassie Tandem Skydivers** (tel: 6390 6250; mobile: 0418 293 698; email: tassky@hotmail.com). They offer brief pre-jump training and then take you to 10,000ft where you jump attached to an instructor.

Horse riding

A gentle way to see the countryside. There are rides available in most centres, mainly for half-day or day tours. Some are closing due to high liability insurance costs so check first. Try the following companies:

Ferndale Horse and Deer Trails Tel: 6375 1311 or 6375 1871; mobile: 0407 509 918. This company is based in Bicheno; beginners and experienced riders are welcomed for trail rides into the Douglas Apsley National Park (safety hats provided).
Tullah Horse-back Tours Tel: 6473 4289; email: pielark94@hotmail.com. Beginners and experienced riders welcome for trail rides ranging from one hour to one day (lunch and safety hats supplied). Also organise wagon tours.

Rides are also available at **King Island Holiday Village** (tel: 6461 1177; fax: 6461 1387; email: kiholiday@tasadventures.com) and **Silver Ridge Retreat** near Mount Roland (tel: 6491 1727; fax: 6491 1925; email: silverridge@southcom.com.au).

Fishing

There are scores of places to go fishing in Tasmania, whether you are an expert or looking for a first lesson. Trout is the big freshwater catch. The brown trout fishing season runs from August to April, rainbow trout from October to May, and sea run trout from August to December. Ocean fishing is possible too, by chartering a boat. Try the following companies:

Auprey Tours Tel/fax: 6330 2612; email: ausprey.tours@tassie.net.au. Trips in the central highlands and northern rivers.

Lakeside St Clair Wilderness Holidays Tel: 6289 1137; mobile: 0417 591 289; fax: 6289 1250; email: lakestclair@trump.net.au. Trips and accommodation in the Lake St Clair region.

London Lakes Fly Fishers Lodge Tel: 6289 1159; fax: 6289 1122; email: garrett@londonlakes.com.au; web: www.londonlakes.com.au. This is a specialist fly-fishing estate and a famous destination for anglers. Owner Jason Garrett is a former captain of the Australian fly-fishing team. Lessons available.

Pepper Bush Peaks Adventures Tel/fax: 6352 2263; email: pepper@microtech.com.au. Half-day and full-day trips on rivers, lakes or ocean. Craig Williams is an excellent bush chef and will pan-fry a brown trout for lunch.

Tasmanian Fly-Fishing School Tel/fax: 6362 3441; email: tasflyfish@vision.net.au. One-day beginner schools and one-day trout guiding trips.

RED TAPE
Visas/ETAs

If you are planning a holiday visit or a short business trip to Australia you will need to apply for either a visa or an ETA (Electronic Travel Authority). Anyone who is not an Australian citizen needs an ETA, which will let you spend up to three months in Australia. With the exception of New Zealand citizens travelling on New Zealand passports, all foreign nationals must obtain a visa/ETA before travelling to Australia. An ETA is equivalent to a visa but there is no stamp or label in your passport and there is no need for you to visit an Australian diplomatic office to submit an application. Applications for ETAs can be submitted through travel agents or airlines. Approved applications are electronically recorded on Australian Government systems.

When you arrive at an airport to check-in on a flight to Australia the airline check-in staff can electronically confirm that you have authority to board the flight. The Australian Government has now made it possible to arrange an ETA via the internet by submitting applications directly through the website (www.eta.immi.gov.au) and following the prompts. When an application for an ETA is submitted through this site, all you need to do is enter the details from your passport and your credit card information. The application is processed immediately. The Australian Government's Department of Immigration claims to be able to approve an ETA in most cases within 30 seconds. You can also check your ETA status if you applied through this site by clicking on the Check Your ETA button. A Visitor ETA is for those travelling as tourists or to visit friends and who wish to stay for up to three months on each visit within a 12-month period. A Short Validity Business ETA is for those travelling on business and intending to make just one visit to Australia. It entitles the holder to one visit to be made within 12 months and permits a stay of three months from the date of arrival. A Long Validity Business ETA is for those travelling frequently to Australia for business purposes over a long period of time. It is valid for the life of your passport, for multiple visits each of up to three months only. This type of ETA is not yet available through the website. Apply through travel agents or airlines.

All applications processed through the website are subject to a service charge of A\$20. Payment is by credit card only (American Express, Diners Club, JCB, Mastercard and Visa). There will be an entry on your credit card statement against Visa services of A\$20 for each ETA application processed by this site.

Airlines may refuse to allow travellers to board their aircraft without valid visas/ETAs and passports, so get your visa before you buy your flight. Tourists are not allowed to work during their stay in Australia.

ETA-eligible passport holders
ETAs are available to holders of the following passports approved for ETA: Andorra, Austria, Belgium, Brunei, Canada, Denmark, Finland, France, Germany, Greece, Hong Kong, Iceland, Ireland, Italy, Japan, Liechtenstein, Luxembourg, Malaysia, Malta, Monaco, Netherlands, Norway, Singapore, South Korea, Spain, Sweden, Switzerland, Taiwan, UK-British citizen, UK-British national (overseas), USA, and the Vatican. Holders of UK passports which indicate their nationality to be British national (overseas) cannot be processed for an ETA by a travel agent or airline outside Hong Kong. If you do not hold a passport approved for ETA, you will need to apply for a 'label' visa at an Australian diplomatic mission (see *Embassies*, below).

Business ETA and visa
This is available to people intending to come to Australia temporarily to undertake some highly-skilled activities involving very short-term projects or events. This applies only to visits of up to three months.

For people wanting to come to Australia for more than three months, there is a range of temporary residence visas available. Sponsorship from an Australian organisation or prospective employer may be required.

Overstaying your visa
A number of officials and staff from several countries' sporting teams went walkabout after the Sydney Olympic Games in 2000 and overstayed their visas. The country is tempting but if you overstay your visa by so much as a day you will be in trouble and may be refused future entry. Instead, leave the country or get advice from the Department of Immigration (web: www.immi.gov.au).

EMBASSIES
Australian embassies in your country
Australian embassies or High Commissions are widespread:

Canada High Commission, Suite 710, 50 O'Connor St, Ottawa, Ontario K1P 6L2; tel: 613 236 0841; fax: 613 236 4376; web: www.ahc-ottawa.org.
France Embassy, 4 rue Jean Rey, Paris 75724 Cedex 15; tel: 01 4059 3300/2; fax: 01 4059 3310; emailInformation.Paris@dfat.gov.au; web: www.austgov.fr.
Germany Embassy, Friedrichstr 200, Berlin 10117; tel: 88 0088-0; fax: 88 0088-201; web: www.australian-embassy.de.
Ireland Embassy, Fitzwilton House, Wilton Terrace, Dublin 2; tel: 01 676 1517; fax: 01 678 5185; email: austremb.dublin@dfat.gov.au; web: www.australianembassy.ie.
Italy Embassy, Via Alessandria 215, Rome 00198; tel: 06 852 721; fax: 06 852 724 00; email: info-rome@dfat.gov.au, consular-rome@dfat.gov.au, visas-rome@dfat.gov.au; web: www.australian-embassy.it.
Japan Embassy, 2-1-14 Mita, Minato-Ku, Tokyo 108-8361; tel: 03 5232 4111; fax: 03 5232 4149; email: ajfjapan@gol.com; web: www.australia.or.jp.

Netherlands Embassy, Carnegielaan 4, The Hague 2517 KH; tel: 70 310 8200; fax: 70 365 2350; web: www.australian-embassy.nl.
New Zealand High Commission, 72–78 Hobson St, Thorndon, Wellington; tel: 04 473 6411; fax: 04 498 7135; web: www.australia.org.nz.
Spain Embassy, Plaza del Descubridor Diego de Ordas, 3, Madrid 28003; tel: 91 441 9300; fax: 91 442 5362; web: www.ambaustralia.es.
United Kingdom High Commission, Australia House, The Strand, London WC 2B 4LA; tel: 020 7379 4334; fax: 020 7465 8217; web: www.australia.org.uk. Consulate, Melrose House, 69 George St, Edinburgh EH2 2JG; tel: 0131 624 3333; fax: 0131 624 3701; email: william@rox.co.uk; web: www.australia.org.uk.
United States Embassy, 1601 Massachusetts Av, Washington DC NW 20036-2273; tel: 202 797 3000; fax: 202 797 3331; email: library.washington@dfat.gov.au; web: www.austemb.org. Consulate General, 150 East 42nd St, 34th Floor, New York NY 10017-5612; tel: 212 351 6500 (24 hours); fax: 212 351 6501; email: consular@australianyc.org; web: www.australianyc.org. Consulate general, Century Plaza Towers, 19th Floor, 2049 Century Park East, Century City, Los Angeles, CA 900067; tel: 310 229 4800; fax: 310 277 2258; web: www.austemb.org. Consulate, 123 North Wacker Drive, Suite 970, Chicago IL 60606; tel: 312 419 1480; fax: 312 419 1499.

Overseas embassies in Australia

Canada High Commission, Commonwealth Av, Canberra, ACT 2600; tel: 02 6279 4000; fax: 02 6273 3285; web: www.canada.org.au.
France Embassy, 6 Perth Av, Yarralumla, ACT 2600; tel: 02 6216 0100; fax: 02 6216 0127; email: Embassy@france.net.au; web: www.france.net.au.
Germany Embassy, 119 Empire Circuit, Yarralumla, ACT 2600; tel: 02 6270 1911; fax: 6270 1951; email: embgerma@bigpond.net.au; web: www.germanembassy.org.au.
Ireland Embassy, 20 Arkana St, Yarralumla, ACT 2600; tel: 02 6273 3022 or 6273 3201; fax: 02 6273 3741; email: irishemb@cyberone.com.au.
Italy Embassy, 12 Grey St, Deakin, ACT 2600; tel: 02 6273 3333; fax: 02 6273 4223; email: embassy@ambitalia.org.au; web: www.ambitalia.org.au.
Japan Embassy, 112 Empire Circuit, Yarralumla, ACT 2600; tel: 02 6273 3244; fax: 02 6273 1848; email: cultural@japan.org.au; web: www.japan.org.au.
Netherlands Embassy, 120 Empire Circuit, Yarralumla, ACT 2600; tel: 02 6273 3111; fax: 02 6273 3206; email: can@minbuza.nl.
New Zealand High Commission, Commonwealth Av, Canberra, ACT 2600; tel: 02 6270 4211; fax: 02 6273 3194; email: email: nzhccba@austarmetro.com.au.
Spain Embassy, 15 Arkana St, Yarralumla, Act 2600 (PO BOX 9076, Deakin, ACT 2600); tel: 02 6273 3555; fax: 02 6273 3918; email: embespau@mail.mae.es; web: www.embaspain.com.
United Kingdom High Commission, Commonwealth Av, Yarralumla, ACT 2600; tel: 02 6270 6666; fax: 6273 3236; email: information.section@uk.emb.gov.au; web: www.uk.emb.gov.au. There is a UK honorary consul in Tasmania for emergencies only at 1a Brisbane Street, Hobart 7000; tel: 03 6230 3400; fax: 03 6231 1139. Also try the British Consulate General in Melbourne, 17th Floor, 90 Collins Street, Melbourne, VIC 3000; tel: 03 9650 4155; fax: 03 9650 2990; email: bcgmelb1@uk.emb.gov.au.
United States Embassy, Moonah Place, Yarralumla, ACT 2600; tel: 02 6214 5600; fax: 02 6214 5970; email: usiscanb@ozemail.com.au; web: usembassy-australia.state.gov/. US embassy has a consulate in Melbourne at 553 St Kilda Road, 6th Floor, Melbourne, VIC 3004; tel: 03 9526 5900.

IMMIGRATION, CUSTOMS AND QUARANTINE

It has been my experience that immigration officials at all Australian ports of entry are usually extremely pleasant. The Australian Customs and Quarantine officers are also pretty decent, but at the same time very strict. As no international flights reach Tasmania, you will clear Australian immigration and customs in a mainland city, then be directed to your domestic flight if you are connecting straight through. Read the customs and quarantine form carefully and declare anything you are not sure about. You are not permitted to bring in any organic matter, not even airline food or the melted chocolate bar you forgot about in your hand luggage. This also applies to anything made of once-living material – wicker mats, coconut bowls and the like – and if you have been on a farm recently overseas, tell the officers and they'll clean your boots for you. Anglers cannot bring in any live bait and are required to clean their equipment before arrival. Mountain bikers should make sure their vehicles are sparkling before they check them into the hold of the plane.

Australia is almost disease-free and determined to maintain that status. Quarantine service sniffer dogs patrol the baggage claim areas and officers will fine you on the spot if you have not declared a prohibited item. On arrival in Tasmania you will be checked again by quarantine officials and dogs to make sure you are not bringing in anything from elsewhere in Australia that could spread disease or pests (including, for instance, the core of an apple bought at a Sydney market that morning and munched on the plane).

If you are arriving on a cruise ship direct from overseas you will be processed by Customs and Immigration on board as you sail in, and the same rules apply as if you were landing in Sydney by plane from overseas. Likewise for any paying passengers on container vessels. If you are arriving by sea on your own vessel and it is your first Australian port of call, you must notify Customs and Immigration of your intention to enter an Australian port. You must fill out the relevant paperwork, including a crew and guest list and the vessel's name and size. Usually all crews are cleared with the vessel rather than in separate procedures. At the time of writing, Foot and Mouth Disease was still a threat to the UK and some other European nations, and customs and quarantine officers were applying extra diligence. If you have been in an infected area, tell the officers and they will examine your shoes and maybe your trousers. To avoid a delay, have these ready at the top of your luggage to show them.

GETTING THERE AND AWAY
By air
There are no scheduled direct flights between Tasmania and other countries – all international flights arrive on the Australian mainland and connect to domestic services to Tasmania. Flights to and from Australia during high season (December and January) are more expensive and usually booked months in advance. The Australian airline Qantas has daily flights to all main Australian cities from Europe and North America. Most European airlines fly to Australia but not necessarily on their own planes. British Airways and Lauda Air do, but many use Qantas or an Asian airline as a partner. Some Asian carriers fly from Europe to Australia, including Singapore Airlines via Singapore, Thai Airways via Bangkok, Malaysian Airlines (who code share with Virgin) via Kuala Lumpur, and Cathay Pacific via Hong Kong. Others include Air New Zealand via Los Angeles and the South Pacific or Auckland, Emirates via Dubai and Singapore, and Gulf Air. The most direct flight takes 22–23 hours inclusive of a one-hour refuelling stop in Bangkok or Singapore. A traditionally cheaper way of getting to Australia has been on less convenient and longer routes via Japan, or by hopping along with stops in the Middle East, Singapore or Bangkok, and Indonesia or Brunei. This can involve up to 36 hours of travelling inclusive of two or three refuelling stops and plane changes.

LONG-HAUL FLIGHTS
Dr Felicity Nicholson

There is growing evidence, albeit circumstantial, that long-haul air travel increases the risk of developing deep vein thrombosis. This condition is potentially life threatening, but it should be stressed that the danger to the average traveller is slight.

Certain risk factors specific to air travel have been identified. These include immobility, compression of the veins at the back of the knee by the edge of the seat, the decreased air pressure and slightly reduced oxygen in the cabin, and dehydration. Consuming alcohol may exacerbate the situation by increasing fluid loss and encouraging immobility.

In theory everyone is at risk, but those at highest risk are shown below:

- Passengers on journeys of longer than eight hours duration
- People over 40
- People with heart disease
- People with cancer
- People with clotting disorders
- People who have had recent surgery, especially on the legs
- Women who are pregnant, or on the pill or other oestrogen therapy
- People who are very tall (over 6ft/1.8m) or short (under 5ft/1.5m)

A deep vein thrombosis (DVT) is a clot of blood that forms in the leg veins. Symptoms include swelling and pain in the calf or thigh. The skin may feel hot to touch and becomes discoloured (light blue-red). A DVT is not dangerous in

From North America, you can take Qantas, Air New Zealand, United or Air Canada. Non-stop flights from the west coast of North America take 14 hours – add on an hour or two if you touch down to refuel.

A number of airlines fly between the mainland and Tasmania. Hobart is the main gateway, but flights also come into Launceston, Devonport and Burnie/Wynyard.

Qantas is the main carrier, flying from Adelaide, Brisbane, Cairns, Canberra, Darwin, the Gold Coast, Melbourne, Perth and Sydney. Most services are not direct. All fares are returns and are inclusive of taxes. Sydney–Hobart (twice daily) restricted sale fare (no changes allowed) costs around $369.67; 14-day advanced purchase (minimum stay three week nights or Saturday night) is $446.67. Melbourne–Hobart (numerous, daily) restricted return sale fare costs $233.74; 14-day advance purchase is $244.74. Melbourne–Launceston return sale fare costs $233.74; 14-day advance is $290.74. Also daily flights from Sydney and Adelaide to Launceston, and from Melbourne to Devonport and Burnie/Wynyard. Adelaide–Launceston 14-day advance purchase return fares cost around $490.67. Melbourne–Burnie/Wynyard 7–day advance is $376.74. All reservations call 13 13 13 in Australia or book through travel agents or on the website: www.qantas.com.au.

Ansett, Australia's second carrier, was temporarily shut down in September 2001 when it ran into financial turbulence. A rescue package was put together by two Australian businessmen but this did not manage to save the airline. All mainline flights were suspended from midnight on Monday March 4 2002. Flights from the mainland to Tasmania operated by regional airline Kendell are still running. Previous flight prices for these sectors were: Sydney–Hobart (daily via Melbourne) costs from $176 one-way (exclusive of taxes); Melbourne–Hobart (daily) from $88 one-way (exclusive of taxes); Brisbane–Hobart (daily itself, but if a clot breaks down then it may travel to the lungs (pulmonary embolus). Symptoms of a pulmonary embolus (PE) include chest pain, shortness of breath and coughing up small amounts of blood.

Symptoms of a DVT rarely occur during the flight, and typically occur within three days of arrival, although symptoms of a DVT or PE have been reported up to two weeks later.

Anyone who suspects that they have these symptoms should see a doctor immediately as anticoagulation (blood thinning) treatment can be given.

Prevention of DVT

General measures to reduce the risk of thrombosis are shown below. This advice also applies to long train or bus journeys.

- Whilst waiting to board the plane, try to walk around rather than sit
- During the flight drink plenty of water (at least two small glasses every hour)
- Avoid excessive tea, coffee and alcohol
- Perform leg-stretching exercises, such as pointing the toes up and down
- Move around the cabin when practicable

If you fit into the high-risk category (see above) ask your doctor if it is safe to travel. Additional protective measures such as graded compression stockings, aspirin or low molecular weight heparin can be given. No matter how tall you are, where possible request a seat with extra legroom.

via Sydney) $253 one-way (exclusive of taxes). Also daily flights from Melbourne to Burnie/Wynyard (from $214.50 return), Devonport (from $214.50 return) and five flights a week to King Island (from $93.50 return), all exclusive of taxes and all flights on Kendell. Call 13 13 00 in Australia or check www.ansett.com.au for details.

Virgin Blue, Sir Richard Branson's expanding, cut-price airline in Australia, started flying between Melbourne and Launceston in November 2001. Virgin Blue departs from Melbourne every day at 12.20, arriving in Launceston at 13.15. The return departs from Launceston at 13.45 and arrives in Melbourne at 14.45. One-way fare is $77, return $154. Information, price changes, availability and reservations via www.virginblue.com.au or tel: 13 67 89 in Australia.

Smaller services include:

Island Airlines Tasmania (tel: 1 800 645 875 in Australia) which runs scheduled services to Launceston and Flinders Island from Melbourne.

King Island Air (tel: 9580 3777; fax: 9580 7361) operates a scheduled flight to King Island from Moorabbin, 10 miles southeast of Melbourne. Return flights are twice a day from Monday to Friday and once daily on Saturday and Sunday. Charters available.

RegionAir has one scheduled flight between Moorabbin and Flinders Island which runs three or four times a week, and costs $350–400 (tel: 1800 818 455 in Australia; fax: 9580 8955; email: info@regionair.com.au; web: www.regionair.com.au). They also run charters.

Air extras

Australian airports, especially Sydney, burden passengers with tax after tax which are included in your ticket price. It might be useful to add these in to your holiday calculations to avoid a nasty shock on the credit card bill. In November 2001, the taxes were as follows:

Ansett Tax A tax on all international and domestic tickets to cover the losses incurred by Ansett workers after the airline's collapse. Qantas passengers pay $10 one-way or return, Virgin Blue $5.

Insurance Tax Added by all domestic and some international carriers following the terrorist attacks on September 11 2001. Qantas passengers pay $6.50, Virgin Blue $2.50.

Noise Tax Applies to all passengers through Sydney to cover the costs of the airport's noise insulation programme for those living under flight paths. Qantas passengers pay $3.58, Virgin Blue $3.74.

Departure Tax All passengers departing Australia must pay $38 (excluding children under 12).

Passenger Service Charge Sydney airport charges each international arriving and departing airline $17.55 per passenger, and most airlines offset this cost to the passenger (ie: $35 each visit). It does not apply to domestic services.

Security Tax After the September 11 terrorist attacks, all passengers departing Australia on international flights other than from Sydney must now pay. Adelaide charge $1, Brisbane $1.56, Darwin $2.97, Melbourne $1.40, and Perth $0.52.

Domestic Head Tax Passengers are charged between $2.50 and $24 for landing at regional airports (not state capitals).

So if you are arriving from overseas into Sydney and taking a Qantas domestic flight to Hobart, then returning to Sydney to exit Australia you can add roughly $103.26 to your ticket cost (not including the 10% goods and services tax – GST – on basic ticket price).

Flight specialists
From the UK
Airline Network The Trident Centre, Port Way, Ribble Docklands, Preston, Lancs PR2 2QA; tel: 0870 241 0012; fax: 01772 835280; web: www.netflights.com.
Ebookers 34–42 Woburn Place, London WC1H 0TA; tel: 0870 010 7000; web: www.ebookers.com.
Flight Centre 64 Goodge St, London W1P 1FP; tel: 0870 666677 or 08708 999000; web: www.flightcentre.com.
STA Travel (stores nationwide); tel: 08701 600599; web: www.statravel.co.uk.
Trailfinders 194 Kensington High St, London W8 7RG; tel: 020 7938 3939. 254–284 Sauchiehall St, Glasgow G2 3EH; tel: 0141 353 2224. 58 Deansgate, Manchester M3 2FF; tel: 0161 839 6969. 22–24 The Priory, Queensway, Birmingham B4 6BS; tel: 0121 236 1234. 43 Corn St, Bristol BS1 1HQ; tel: 0117 929 9000; web: www.trailfinders.com.

From the US
Airtech 588 Broadway, Suite 204, New York, NY 10012; tel: 1 212 219 7000; email: fly@airtech.com; web: www.airtech.com.
Flight Centre (stores nationwide); tel: 1877 967 5347; web: www.flightcentre.com.
Council Travel national phone reservation centre tel: 1800 226 8624, fax: 617 528 2091; web: www.counciltravel.com.
STA Travel (stores nationwide); tel: 1800 781 4040; web: www.statravel.com.

From Canada
Flight Centre (stores nationwide); tel: 1888 967 5351; web: www.flightcentre.com.
Travel CUTS (stores nationwide); tel: 1866 246 9762; web: www.travelcuts.com.

Above Once found on mainland Australia, the carnivorous Tasmanian devil, *Sarcophilus harrisii*, is now found only in Tasmania (RJ)

Right Footprints of Tasmanian devil in the sand (MB)

Above left Visitors can cuddle wombats and see many other marsupials in the Bonorong Wildlife Park, Brighton (TK)

Above right Found throughout Tasmania and the islands of the Bass Strait, the potoroo, *Potorous tridactylus*, is wholly protected in Tasmania (RJ)

Right The bushtail possum, *Trichosurus vulpecular*, is common throughout bushland Tasmania. This nocturnal marsupial can also be found scampering around suburban backyards (GM)

Below The spotted-tailed quoll, *Dasyurus maculatus*, is often sighted in bushland around the state (TT)

From Australia
Flight Centre (stores nationwide); tel: 13 31 33; web: www.flightcentre.com.
STA Travel (stores nationwide); tel: 1300 360 960; web: www.statravel.com.au.

From New Zealand
Flight Centre (stores nationwide); tel: 0800 243544; web: www.flightcentre.co.nz.

From South Africa
Flight Centre (stores in Johannesburg, Cape Town and Durban); tel: 0860 400747; web: www.flightcentre.co.za.
Student Travel Centre 31 Riebeek St, Cape Town; tel: 021 418 6570; email: capetown@statravel.co.za. 1102 Hilda St, Hatfield, Pretoria; tel: 012 342 5292; email: pretoria@statravel.co.za; web: www.statravel.co.za.

By sea
The *Spirit of Tasmania* vehicle and passenger ferry makes four overnight return voyages per week all year round between Melbourne and Devonport, but will start running daily from September 2002. The trip takes between 13 and 14 hours depending on the conditions, which can be rough. Evening departures are from Melbourne, morning arrivals at Devonport. Going back, boats leave late afternoon, arriving at Melbourne in the early morning. A fourth service runs, dependent on demand. Passengers pay $124–158 each for a dormitory bunk and $270–368 each for a suite one-way, depending on the season (cheaper for pensioners and students). Cars cost an extra $40–55, bicycles $21–27, and motorbikes $30–38. Prices include an evening meal and continental breakfast.

In summer the *Devil Cat* fast vehicle and passenger catamaran makes three six-hour crossings from Melbourne to George Town each week (daily over Christmas and New Year and holiday times). Adult passenger one-way fare is $150–180 (cheaper for pensioners and students); cars cost an extra $40–55 one-way, motorbikes $30–38.

Southern Shipping Company (tel: 03 6356 1753; fax: 03 6356 1956) runs a freight service from Port Welshpool, three hours southeast of Melbourne, to Bridport once a month, but it is pretty rough going as there are no sleeping or dining facilities on board. Return fare costs $98.55.

For full details and special deals tel: 13 20 10 in Australia; email: reservations@tt-line.com.au; or see website: www.tt-line.com.au. A campaign group, the National Sea Highway Action Committee, has been fighting for a decade to get the fares reduced.

Cruise ships
A few cruise ships come into Tasmania but they are few and far between and invariably arrive during summer. Every now and then one leaves for an Antarctic voyage (see *Chapter 15*, page 279) or heads up to Sydney. Specialist cruise agents in your country would be the best to advise on the latest schedules and rates.

HEALTH AND SAFETY
Health and travel clinics
UK
British Airways Travel Clinic and Immunisation Service 156 Regent St, London, W1; tel: 020 7439 9584. This place also sells travellers' supplies and has a branch of Stanford's travel book and map shop. There are now British Airways clinics all around Britain and six in South Africa. To find your nearest one, phone 01276 685040.

MASTA (Medical Advisory Service for Travellers Abroad) Keppel St, London, WC1 7HT; tel: 09068 224100. This is a premium phone line number, charged at 50 pence per minute.
NHS Travel Web: www.fitfortravel.scot.nhs.uk. This website provides country-by-country advice on immunisation and malaria prevention, plus details of recent developments and a list of relevant health organisations.
Nomad Travel Pharmacy and Vaccination Centre 3–4 Wellington Terrace, Turnpike Lane, London N8 0PX; tel: 020 8889 7014.
Thames Medical 157 Waterloo Rd, London SE1 8US; tel: 020 7902 9000. This is a competitively priced, one-stop travel health service. All profits go to their affiliated company InterHealth, which provides health care for overseas workers on Christian projects.
Trailfinders Immunisation Centre 194 Kensington High St, London W8 7RG; tel: 020 7938 3999. Also at 254–284 Sauchiehall St, Glasgow G2 3EH; tel: 0141 353 0066.

USA

Centers for Disease Control 1600 Clifton Rd, Atlanta, GA 30333; tel: 877 FYI TRIP or 800 3111 3435; web: www.cdc.gov/travel. This organisation is the central source of travel information in the USA. Each summer it publishes the invaluable Health Information for International Travel which is available from the Division of Quarantine at the above address.
Connaught Laboratories PO BOX 187, Swiftwater, PA 18370; tel: 1800 822 2463. They will send you a free list of specialist tropical medicine physicians in your state.
IAMAT (International Association for Medical Assistance to Travelers) 736 Center St, Lewiston, NY 14092; tel: 716 754 4883. A non-profit organisation which provides a list of English-speaking doctors abroad.

Australia
TMVC Tel: 1300 658844; web: www.tmvc.com.au. TMVC has 20 clinics in Australia, New Zealand and Thailand including:

Brisbane: Dr Deborah Mills, Qantas Domestic Building, 6th floor, 247 Adelaide St, Brisbane, QLD 4000; tel: 07 3221 9066; fax: 07 3321 7076.
Melbourne: Dr Sonny Lau, 393 Little Bourke St, 2nd floor, Melbourne, VIC 3000; tel: 03 9602 5788; fax: 03 9670 8394.
Sydney: Dr Mandy Hu, Dymocks Building, 7th floor, 428 George St, Sydney, NSW 2000; tel: 02 9221 7133; fax: 02 9221 8401.

South Africa
There are six British Airways travel clinics in South Africa:

Johannesburg, tel: 011 807 3132; *Cape Town*, tel: 021 419 3172; *Durban*, tel: 031 303 2423; *Kynsna*, tel: 044 382 6366; *East London*, tel: 043 743 7471; *Port Elizabeth*, tel: 041 374 7471.

Preparations
Tasmania is frequently compared to England because of its rolling hills and mild climate but in my view this is mainly a false comparison. Even though it has no deadly diseases such as malaria or rabies, every year scores of visitors underestimate this island thinking it to be a gentle, temperate place. Tasmania is wild, unpredictable, has dangerously variable weather patterns and treacherous coastlines. Some of its parks, especially in the southwest, are very remote. Walking and helicopters are the only ways in and out and there are no communications. Mobile phones do not work in most national parks and visitors are reliant on someone going for help or someone back in town realising they are missing – and that can take days.

Guest books are left at all walking lodges, cabins and ranger stations. Always fill in your details and your plans, including any side trips off the main path that you are hoping to do. These could be the most important diary entries you ever make. Also Parks and Wildlife are trialling a scheme whereby walkers can hire an EPIRB (Emergency Position Indicating Radio Beacon) for $10. It is yours for a month. If you have been in a yellow fever country (sub-Saharan Africa and parts of South America) within six days of arriving in Australia, you will need a current yellow fever certificate. Otherwise there are no vaccine requirements.

Dial 000 for the emergency services. It is essential to carry good maps in Tasmania even for the shortest walks and adventures. A full list of the available maps can be found at the Tasmania Information and Land Services Division (Hobart GPO Box 44A, Hobart, TAS 7001; tel in Australia: 1300 368 550; email: webmaster@dpiwe.tas.gov.au; web: www.dpiwe.tas.gov.au). Maps are available from them direct or you could try any of the outdoor adventure stores in Hobart (see *Shopping* section in *Chapter 5*, page 119.)

Bushfires
It is likely you will see a bushfire but the chances are it will be a controlled burn, so do not panic. However, the following information is worth committing to memory.

Bushwalking Check updates on fire bans, especially when total fire bans are in place. On days of total fire ban it is best to postpone a trip into the bush since the risk of fire starting and growing rapidly is extremely high. If you are caught in the bush during a fire, find as clear an area as possible and prepare to shelter there. Do not try to out-run a bush fire as it can travel at up to 50mph. Seek streams or rivers, bare clearings, or large rock outcrops that will break the path of the fire. Avoid places uphill from the direction of the fire or at the crest of a hill. Do not shelter in water tanks above the ground surface. Do your best to cover your skin to protect against radiant heat. Use a long-sleeved shirt and long trousers or a blanket soaked in creek water.

Driving Bush and grass fires often cross roads and highways creating dangerous situations for road users. If you see smoke ahead, play safe by turning around and finding an alternative route. Don't risk getting caught in a bush fire. If you are driving around the state at a particularly dry time, keep several woollen blankets in your car and a supply of water in case you are caught in a bush fire and have to use your car as a refuge.

If you need to shelter in your car:

- Drive your car into a bare, clear area well away from surrounding trees;
- Leave your headlights on;
- Roll up the windows and shelter below window level;
- Cover yourself with blankets as protection from radiant heat;
- Drink water frequently.

It will be a hot and frightening experience but it is safest to remain in the car where there is protection from radiant heat.

Camping It is prohibited to light a camp-fire on a day of total fire ban, or use portable barbecues or gas-fired stoves or fires or barbecues burning solid fuel (wood, charcoal, heat beads). A camp-fire may be lit during the bushfire danger season (October 1 to March 31) provided:

- It is in a permanently constructed fireplace surrounded by ground that is clear of all combustible matter for a distance of at least two metres.

- It is at a site surrounded by ground that is clear of all combustible matter for a distance of three metres.
- You ensure that the fire is completely extinguished before leaving the area.

These regulations also apply to the use of portable gas stoves or barbecues during the bushfire danger season.

It is dangerous to use naked flame inside a tent. Never light a portable stove or barbecue inside a tent. Use an electric torch for lighting.

Caravans Follow the regulations for camp-fires and barbecues during the bushfire danger season and on days of total fire ban. You may not use a portable barbecue outside a caravan during a total fire ban; however, you may use the stove inside the caravan provided due care is taken. Take care with gas cylinders. Be sure they are vented away from the caravan.

When staying in a caravan park, find out if a safe refuge has been designated in case of bushfire and use it when fire threatens. If no refuge area has been designated, decide ahead of time where you will shelter from fire. Brick toilet blocks, stone picnic shelters, or behind concrete walls are safer than inside your caravan.

Smoking During the bushfire danger season, do not drop or throw down any lighted cigarette, match or anything burning. Don't light or carry a lighted cigarette or match within 15m of stacked or standing crops or stubble fields.

Snow

Do not rely on the weather and always prepare for all conditions. It regularly claims lives here. Blizzards can whip in over the mountains, even in mid-summer, with incredible speed, dragging the temperature down to freezing in minutes and causing white-outs. Hypothermia is a real risk.

Avalanches are rare but possible after heavy snow falls and mountaineers should take guidance from national park authorities before setting out. If you do not have an EPIRB and people are searching for you in snow then lay out the brightest clothing you can on the snow to attract the attention of planes and helicopters (but not if it is your warm gear).

Hypothermia

Hypothermia results from prolonged heat loss due to immersion in water or insufficient clothing in cold, wet and windy conditions. It is also prompted by physical exhaustion, hunger and anxiety. The heat loss from wet skin is greater than from dry skin, and wind on unprotected skin increases that heat loss further. Damp, windy conditions, with temperatures less than 6°C, are most dangerous to unprotected survivors. Everyone in the wilds of Tasmania is potentially at risk if not kitted out sufficiently. The onset of hypothermia can be rapid and, in extreme cases, death can occur less than one hour after it begins. But it is hard to recognise. Look for signs of exhaustion, reluctance to engage in any physical effort, irritability and slow reactions. Frequent stumbling is usually a sign, as is slurred speech and maybe swollen lips, hands and feet. The minute you think one of your party might be at risk, stop, pitch a tent and put them inside in a sleeping-bag with as many extra clothes and as much bedding as you have. Brew up some warm drinks (not alcohol – tea is best, with plenty of sugar for energy).

NEVER rub limbs to warm someone you think might have hypothermia or place them near external heat such as a fire. If necessary, join the victim in the sleeping-bag to transfer some of your own heat. Those boating, kayaking or rafting on inland waters should be particularly careful and be aware of the symptoms and effects of hypothermia as the water temperature in lakes and rivers is much lower than the seas. This is of particular importance in the winter when water temperatures can drop as low as 5°C. If the situation is more serious, follow the guidelines from Tasmania's Marine and Safety authority:

- After rescue, first check if the person is breathing. Listen for heart sounds. If the survivor is not breathing, begin artificial respiration. Continue mouth-to-mouth resuscitation until medical advice is available. The heart may be beating very slowly – one or two beats per minute – so check the pulse for a full minute instead of the usual five or ten seconds. Do not compress the chest if a heart beat is present, even if it is very slow. In extreme cases, a sudden movement or blow can stop the heart.
- Prevent further heat loss due to evaporation or exposure.
- Place the survivor next to other people for warmth. Huddling together under covers will promote heat transfer to the victim.
- Avoid unnecessary handling of the person.
- When conscious, give a warm, sweet drink.

For boaters suffering from exposure to cold water:

- Do not wrap in a blanket unless the air temperature is less than the water temperature.
- Do not massage the body or limbs.
- Do not feed solids or liquids to an unconscious survivor.
- Do not give alcohol.
- Do not use a thermal protective aid unless in an open boat and there is no other way to protect a person suffering from hypothermia from cold winds.

Protection from the sun

In summer, the hole in the ozone layer over Antarctica expands and its outer edge gets perilously close to Tasmania's south coast. Follow the Aussie maxim of 'Slip, Slop, Slap': slip on a T-shirt, slop on some sunscreen, slap on a hat, even on cloudy days. Even those of dark complexion would do well to use at least a factor 16 sunblock out here – more if you are fair – and wear a wide-brimmed hat in summer. Take some shades to protect your eyes – the Australian Cancer Council sells pairs with highly reflective surfaces to keep out harmful rays. If you do get burned out on a long walk there is little that can be done unless you have some after-sun creams. It is rare to get prickly heat here, but in hot spells it is not impossible. It manifests itself as a rash, usually on the trunk of the body, and is soothed by relaxing, taking cool showers, dabbing the skin dry and applying talcum powder to the body.

Snakes

All three Tasmanian snakes are venomous and although snake bites are rare, and no-one has died from one for more than 50 years, it is possible, especially with a bite from a tiger snake. Many so-called 'bush first-aid tactics' are useless and can do more harm than good. The only treatment is antivenom; in Tasmania the same one is used to treat bites from all three snakes, so there is no need to try to capture the offending wriggler. It is worth remembering that even a severed snake head can bite before it finally expires.

- Try to keep calm and breath deeply. A tiger snake's fangs are set well back in its head and venom is not always dispensed.

- Prevent movement of the bitten limb by applying a splint.
- Keep the bitten limb BELOW heart height to slow the spread of any venom in the bloodstream.
- If you have a crêpe bandage, bind up as much of the bitten limb as you can but release the bandage every half-hour.
- Seek help and evacuate the victim to a hospital that has antivenom as soon as possible.

NEVER:

- give aspirin (but paracetamol is safe);
- cut or suck the wound;
- apply ice packs;
- apply potassium permanganate.

On the road
Driving or cycling the state's roads is a joy. Traffic is light in towns and scarce in the countryside. However, Tasmania's roads are frequented by animals too. Wallabies and kangaroos feed along their verges at dawn and dusk when drivers should take the foot off the gas and keep their eyes peeled. A collision with a fully grown kangaroo will almost certainly kill the roo, and cause serious damage to your vehicle and possibly to yourself. Also be on the look-out for logging trucks, especially on dirt-roads. They take longer than usual to stop their heavy loads on slippery ground. Cyclists need to take particular care with logging trucks. If you can, hop off and let them rattle past. Hitchhiking is practised by visitors and locals but not advisable. Always try to take a bus. If you have to hitchhike, do so in pairs. Drivers must always stick to the speed limits which certainly, to most Europeans, will seem very slow. It is unlikely you will get above 100km/h (62.5mph) out of town, and more likely be down to 50km/h (31mph) or 40km/h (25mph) in urban areas. Police across Australia are obsessed with catching speeding motorists and believe fining them heavily will deter them from racing around. Unfortunately, the high road-death statistics throughout the nation seem to indicate that this is not the case.

On the water
Always maintain a safe speed and a proper look out. It is also advisable to familiarise yourself with the area each time before attempting any high speed activities. Caution is required in all conditions, and particularly following heavy rain or flooding when floating trees, branches and other debris may be present and can cause serious damage and injury if collision occurs. As waters levels recede, new navigational hazards may be uncovered. All boats in inland waters must carry an anchor, rope and chain, a bailer or bilge pump, personal flotation devices, a fire extinguisher, and oars or auxiliary propulsion.

Safe sex
The sun, the fresh air and the wild open spaces make the most staid traveller feel romantic, but sexually transmitted diseases are a fact of life too. Take condoms or femidoms for protection. Spermicide pessaries can help reduce the risk of transmission. Tasmania is a healthy state in a healthy nation but HIV and Aids do occur here so it's always better safe than sorry.

Women travellers
The chances are that women will be safe pretty much everywhere but lone travellers should assess situations a little more carefully. Even though things are

changing for the better, some parts of Tasmania have retained their pioneer image and the attitude that the man is boss and the women something of a lesser species. This is at odds with the great warmth and friendliness of most Tasmanians. Street crime is low, but women should avoid walking alone after dark in the quieter and less salubrious areas of towns and cities.

Crime

Tasmania is a very safe destination but, as anywhere, keep your valuables in room safes or in secure areas arranged by management at your accommodation.

I have only heard of one theft on the Overland Track but with more and more people doing the walk each year the opportunities are there, although it would be a fit and healthy thief who makes a living from stealing from bushwalkers. You will want to keep your baggage to a minimum on bushwalks anyway, so try to take the compact camera only and leave the heavy, expensive equipment locked up at the hotel.

WHAT TO TAKE FOR THE BUSH
Carrying your gear

If you are moving around Tasmania in a rented vehicle then you would be best to travel with a suitcase or holdall, presuming you are not going to be doing that much carrying other than from airport to vehicle and into hotels. Always lock your baggage when unattended, even in your hotel room or vehicle when you go out for the day. Having ruined my back lugging all manner of cheap, fat suitcases around the world, I cannot now function without one with wheels and an extendable handle. Also, after a recent 22-hour flight back to Sydney from London, I emerged fuzzy-headed to discover that a woman from the Blue Mountains had decided my blue bag was her blue bag and had run off with it. Qantas were excellent but I was still without my clothes and gifts for most of the day, so now I festoon my baggage with all manner of coloured flags and straps to deter the idiots. If you are bushwalking, then you need a rucksack. If you plan to do one-day or two-day walks then carry a medium-sized day pack (about 40–50l), but big enough to fit essential survival supplies. For longer trips, I would recommend a full-sized hiking pack (70–90l) with an internal and adjustable frame. Few packs are fully waterproof so I line mine with a thick survival or 'bivvy' bag. This rather primitive method is often much abused by fellow walkers until the chill of evening has fallen on the campsite and I am the only one wearing dry underwear. Throw in a very light, empty day pack in case you want to do brief side trips up steep valleys – for example, scrambling up Mount Ossa from the Overland Track. Choosing a big hiking pack is an important decision. I usually examine at least seven or eight and try them on with weight before I make a decision. Too small and you'll be tempted to skimp on essential equipment; too big and you'll put so much in it that the walk will be hard work. I also favour bright colours rather than khaki or navy – they are easier for helicopters and rescue teams to spot from the air should the unthinkable happen, and if you use them in politically unstable countries in the future you will not be mistaken for a soldier.

Clothes

Four seasons in one day require four sets of clothes. Even on short walks, go prepared. Several thin layers are warmer than one or two thick layers and clothes must be kept as dry as possible. Don't worry about washing dirty clothes en route. Detergents are not allowed in national parks and it is a terrible fuss anyway; wait until you get back to a hotel and hit the laundry bags. For a five-day hike over high country, but not involving mountaineering, I take four T-shirts (two of which are thermally insulated), a fairly tight (not bulky) jumper made from Polartec material or similar, a really good fleecy jacket with sleeves (from same kind of material), breathable shorts with deep pockets, a thoroughly waterproof over-jacket and trousers, a set of gaiters, and a pair of comfortable, sturdy boots. I swear by a British make called Brasher, and am still wearing the same pair I have had for almost a decade of frequent and sometimes gruelling travel. Take spare walking socks for wet weather and a pair of insulated socks for chilly evenings in the tent. Also, to keep the warmth in after a big evening meal, take a pair of light, long trousers with deep pockets (in which to stash stove lighters, can openers and torches when you are wandering around the campsite). Outdoor or safari-style shirts are an option. Hats are essential. An incredible amount of body heat is lost from the head – something more than 50% – so take a fleecy mountain hat for cold weather and a very light wide-brimmed number to keep the sun off.

Gloves are advisable but not essential unless it is winter. For mountaineering or camping in winter, make sure T-shirts, underwear, socks, gloves and hats are all insulated. A balaclava is advisable, as are over-jackets that are not only thoroughly waterproof but also fleece-lined. Insulated under-trousers or 'long johns' are deeply unflattering but a great comfort when it's below zero on the other side of the canvas. All the usual mountaineering hardware is essential too – ice-picks, ropes, crampons, etc, depending on your mission. If you haven't brought your own gear, any of the specialist mountaineering stores in Hobart are good for advice.

Camping gear

The basics include a stove (gas or solid fuel) with spare fuel supply, lighter (better and safer than matches), multi-purpose knife (with scissors, can-opener, at least two blades, and a nail-file to get rid of blisters and trim toenails causing discomfort), fork and spoon, lightweight but tough bowl and mug, dishcloth and drying-cloth (light and no bigger than a sheet of A4 paper), and headtorch with spare batteries. Sleeping-bags are so sophisticated now that some come with a system of shifting the down in the coat from the bottom of the bag to the top as the temperature drops. I have not tried one but they could be ideal for Tasmania, where one summer evening can be balmy and pleasant while the next can bring freezing conditions. Some have built-in pillows but I find a rolled up T-shirt usually suffices. I also take a very light, heat-reflective 'space blanket' for chilly nights which goes inside the sleeping-bag, but I have a reptilian body-warmth system. A good sleeping-bag means blankets are superfluous, which will save you weight in your pack. One thing I forgot last time I walked the Overland Track was a ground mat. These take up a lot of room but can make the difference between a restless and a peaceful night. I now use an inflatable one that takes up half as much room as my tent in the rucksack. Radios and phones do not work in the bush and a pack of playing cards is the best evening's entertainment. Don't forget the toilet paper!

Medicine

All hikers should take at least one first-aid kit between three people. Go for the best, the one that has won the awards and that costs a bit more. It should have a stitch kit, bandages and tape, plasters, antiseptic cream, antihistamine cream, needles and an intravenous drip kit. If the Australian currency remains at the low level it was when we went to press, you might consider buying one in Hobart and possibly saving some money. Bring sunblock, at least factor 15, and higher if you are fair-skinned or are travelling with children. Also worth considering are mosquito repellent and sting relief, paracetamol, soluble rehydration powders, fungal powder for feet, and anti-inflammatory tablets (I once only made it out of a wilderness area thanks to these quelling pain in a troublesome knee).

Food and drink

Dried food is the way to go. The packs are light and easily packed and they have developed in leaps and bounds over the past few years with better ingredients and flavours. There are plenty in the camping stores of Hobart and other Australian cities, and an increasing number are free from preservatives and additives.

Work on a diet of one big, hot meal a day each evening, a pasta or rice soup for lunch, and snacks and hot drinks two or three times a day. High protein, a decent amount of carbohydrate and low fat is the best mix. Take small packs of nuts and dried fruit for vitamin C, and chocolate blocks and honey and nut bars for energy hits. Take as much water as you feel you can carry, and fill up only at streams you know to be clean (upstream from animal populations and well away from campsites). Pack more tea bags than you would normally need and take a small tub of sugar – they could help stave off hypothermia if the weather closes in.

MONEY

The unit of currency is the Australian dollar, divided into 100 cents. At the time of writing (November 2001), the exchange rates of roughly US$1 = A$2 and £1 = A$2.75 were stable. This is a poor rate for Australians but good for visitors from America and Britain. The rate got steadily worse throughout 2000 until the Australian dollar dropped below the danger mark of US$0.50. The Australian dollar has weakened to such a level that it has been nicknamed the 'Kangarouble'.

All prices in Tasmania are quoted in Australian dollars, as they are throughout this guide. Denominations are $100, $50, $20, $10 and $5, with coins $2, $1, 50¢, 20¢, 10¢ and 5¢.

Travellers' cheques are still the safest and most convenient way of carrying money with you but keep some cash on you as well, especially when you arrive to pay shuttle-buses or cabs. Visitors can expect widespread use of all international credit cards and the presence of ATMs in all towns and cities. Australia also operates a useful system for people who are staying longer and have opened local bank accounts. EFTPOS (Electronic Funds Transfer at Point of Sale) serves the same function as a cheque but using simply a bank card. Local bank accounts can be opened easily with a passport and a small sum but Australian banks are pretty brutal on charges; they actually charge for depositing money as well as withdrawals. The main four banks are ANZ, Commonwealth, National and Westpac. Most ATMs allow use of foreign cards through Maestro or Cirrus links.

A 10% goods and services tax (GST) was introduced throughout Australia in 2001.

GETTING AROUND
By air

In direct contrast to the Australian mainland, air travel around Tasmania is not all that useful. The state is too small and so beautiful that people prefer to stay on the ground and take their time. The exceptions are scenic flights or short hops to the islands in Bass Strait (see *Scenic flights*, page 29).

Tasair Regional Airlines Tel: 1800 062900; web: www.tasair.com.au. Fly from Hobart to Burnie/Wynyard, Hobart to Devonport, Hobart to King Island, Burnie to King Island, and Devonport to King Island.

Island Airlines Tasmania Tel: 1800 645 875; email: bobpratt@bigpond.com.au; web: www.iat.com.au. Flies between Melbourne and Launceston 3 times a week (Mon, Wed, Fri). Also between Launceston and Flinders Island 2–3 times a day, and Launceston–Strahan–Hobart return 3 times a week (Tue, Thu, Sun). And charter flights from Essendon to Strahan.

RegionAir Tel: 1800 818 455; fax: 9580 8955; email: info@regionair.com.au; web: www.regionair.com.au). Runs charters only.

Wilderness Air Strahan Wharf, Strahan, TAS 7468; tel: 6471 7280; fax: 6471 7303; email: wildernessair@tasadventures.com. Run seaplane flights along Ocean Beach and Macquarie Harbour, over Sarah Island and the mouth of the Gordon River, with a stop for a rainforest walk. Departure: 09.00, 10.30, 12.00, 14.00, 15.30 and 17.00 (flights last about 80 minutes). Adult: $132; child (5 to 12 years inclusive): $73; child (3 to 4 years inclusive): $32; infant (up to 3 years): free.

By bus/coach

This is a good and cheap way to get around Tasmania as long as you don't mind working to a timetable and sticking to the main centres. All the main towns are linked and services also run along the east coast from St Helens to Port Arthur, over to Strahan and Zeehan, down to Bruny Island and Cockle Creek, to the far northwest, and into the wilderness area at Scotts Peak Dam. There is a confusing number of operators, some of whom are linked with each other and others who are independent.

A rough sample of one-way fares is: Hobart to Swansea $25–28; Launceston to Hobart $23–25; and Burnie to Smithton $13–16. There are travellers' passes and multiple-trip tickets on offer at various times of the year. Timetables and prices change, so it is always best to check with the companies before you travel.

The following companies offer statewide bus services and/or coach tours:

Tasmanian Redline Coaches (TRC) Tel: 6336 1400; fax: 6334 5685; email: bookings@tasredline.com.au; web: www.tasredline.com.au. Bookings can be made online. Runs services from Hobart to St Helens, Swansea, Bicheno, Launceston, Burnie, Devonport and the Spirit of Tasmania docks; from Launceston to St Helens, Derby, Swansea, Burnie, Smithton, Hobart, Devonport and the Spirit of Tasmania docks; and from Burnie to Smithton and Devonport.

Hobart to Bruny Island Bus Service Tel: 6293 1265. Runs service from Hobart to Bruny three days a week.

Hobart Coaches Tel: 6233 4232; fax: 6272 8770; web: www.metrotas.com.au. Charters and short- and long-break tours for 16–60 people.

TWT's Tassielink Regional Coach Service Tel: 1300 300 520; web: www.tigerline.com.au. Runs services between Hobart and Strahan via Lake St Clair and Queenstown; between Launceston and Strahan via Devonport, Sheffield, Cradle Mountain and Queenstown; between Hobart and Launceston via the Coles Bay turnoff, Bicheno and St Helens; between Hobart and Dover and on to Cockle Creek via Huonville and Geeveston; and between Hobart and Port Arthur via Nubeena. You can buy an Explorer Pass for unlimited travel (around $150 for 7 days, $180 for 10 days, $210 for 14 days, and $250 for 21 days). Some restrictions apply. Buses leave from the Transit Centre at 199 Collins Street. Tigerline (the day coach tours and charter operation part of the business) also runs charters, extended tours, short-break tours, soft adventure tours, history and wilderness tours.

Tassie Getaway Tours Tel: 6431 2466; fax: 6431 4798; mobile: 0419 581800; email: tbrooks@tassie.net.au or james.smith@tassie.net.au. Runs tailor-made, guided charters, from 2–22 people. Based in Burnie and Stanley but operates statewide. Costs depend on accommodation required, ranging from $50–150 a day.

Maxwell's Cradle Mountain-Lake St Clair Taxi and Bus Service Tel/fax: 6492 1431.
Runs services from Devonport and Launceston to Cradle Mountain, Lake St Clair and the
Walls of Jerusalem, as well as operating shuttle services at Cradle Mountain and from Lake
St Clair to Derwent Bridge, Bronte Park and Frenchmans Cap.

Also try **Top Tours** (tel: 6462 1245; fax: 6462 1565; email: toptours@
tasadventures.com) and **Under Down Under** (budget; tel: 6369 5555; fax: 6369
5433; mobile: 015 396958; email: udu@tasadventures.com).

If you can't get up-to-the-minute information from these companies or
Tourism Tasmania, then look out for a tabloid-size free newspaper called
Tasmanian Travelways, available at tourist information centres, which has details of
the latest timetables and fares. (It also has comprehensive lists of accommodation,
restaurants and attractions.)

One valuable tip is to book in advance if you are catching the bus from one end
of the Overland Track. Seats on these services get reserved far in advance. When
booking, let them know what bags you will be carrying as they have a luggage
trailer but it has limited space. Special fares apply for bushwalkers taking a service
to the start of a long-distance walk and the return leg from the other end.

By car

There is no shortage of rental car companies in Tasmania. Self-drive trips are not
the most environmentally friendly way to see the state but certainly the most
convenient. Most roads are sealed and in good condition, although frost damage is
present in some mountainous sections. Many roads in national parks and other
wild areas are unsealed and vary in condition from simply bumpy to impassable by
everything but the toughest 4WD vehicles. Visitors should examine where they
plan to drive and use the specific region chapters of this guide as well as
information from Parks and Wildlife and Tourism Tasmania to work out if they
need 2WD or 4WD. Rental car companies can help too, but they may insist 2WDs
are not taken off-road. You will need to produce a passport, international driving
licence (UK and US licences are accepted), and a credit card to guarantee the car.
For seven days' rental of an economy, manual (stick-shift), two-door compact car
with power steering, air conditioning and unlimited mileage, expect to pay around
$392 inclusive of insurance and GST. Extras include a 2% state government stamp
duty, refuelling costs and levies for pick-ups and drop-offs at airports. Individual
chapters show rental car company listings, but a few are given below. Diesel and
unleaded petrol both fluctuate between $0.85 and $1 per litre.

Autorent Hertz 122 Harrington St, Hobart 7000; tel: 6237 1111; and 58 Paterson St,
Launceston City, Launceston 7250; tel; 6335 1111; fax: 6331 2788. Branches also at
Launceston and Burnie-Wynyard airports, at the Devonport Ferry Terminal, and in
Devonport and Burnie. For all, email: mail@autorent.com.au; web:
www.view.com.au/autorent.

Avis Tasmania 125 Bathurst St, Hobart 7000; tel: 6234 4222; fax: 6234 4190; email:
avishbt@netspace.net.au; and corner of Brisbane and Wellington Streets, Launceston 7250;
tel: 6334 7722; fax: 6334 6260. Branches also at Hobart, Launceston, Devonport and
Burnie-Wynyard airports.

Bargain Car Rentals 189A Harrington St, Hobart 7000; tel: 6234 6959; fax: 6234 6991;
email: bargaincar@telstra.easymail.com.au; and Launceston Airport, Evandale 7212; tel:
6391 8175; email: bargaincar@telstra.easymail.com.au. Branches also at Launceston and
Devonport.

Betta Rentacarz 27 William St, Launceston 7250; tel: 6334 3299; mobile: 0419 123 599;
fax: 6334 1500.

Budget Rent-A-Car 96 Harrington St, Hobart 7000; tel: 6234 5222; fax: 6231 0252; email: reservations@budgettas.com, web: www.budget.com.au; and 138 George St, Launceston 7250; tel: 6391 8566; fax: 6334 1048; email: reservations@budgettas.com. Branches also at Hobart, Launceston, Devonport and Burnie-Wynyard airports, and Devonport ferry terminal.

Cheapa Island Car Rentals 1 Netherby Rd, King Island 7256; tel: 6462 1603; fax: 6462 1603; email: kimotors@kingisland.net.au. King Island only and manual transmission vehicles.

Economy Car Rentals 27 William St, Launceston 7250; tel: 6334 3299; mobile: 0419 132 599; fax: 6334 1500.

Flinders Island Car Rentals Memana Rd, Whitemark, Flinders Island 7255; tel: 6359 2168; fax: 6359 2293. Also try Flinders Island Transport Services Whitemark, Flinders Island 7255; tel: 6359 2060; fax: 6359 2026.

National Advance Car Rentals Hobart MidCity Motor Inn, Hobart 7000; tel: 6224 0822; fax: 6224 0844; email: rentals@advancecars.com.au; web: www.advancecars.com.au; and 32 Cameron St, Launceston 7250; tel: 6391 8000; fax: 6391 8008; email: rentals@advancecars.com.au; web: www.advancecars.com.au . Branches also at Launceston and Devonport airports.

Range/Rent-A-Bug 105 Murray St, Hobart 7000; tel; 6231 0300; mobile: 0417 398 536; fax: 6231 5017; email: rentabug@southcom.com.au; and 5 Murray St, East Devonport 7310; tel: 6427 9034; fax: 6427 9444.

Thrifty Car Rental 11–17 Argyle St, Hobart 7000; tel: 6234 1341; fax: 6231 2475; email: thrifty@tasvacations.com.au; web: www.tasvacations.com.au; and at Launceston Country Club Casino, Prospect Vale, Launceston 7250; tel: 6391 8105; fax: 6391 8482; email: thrifty@tasvacations.com.au; web: www.tasvacations.com.au . Branches also at Hobart, Launceston and Burnie-Wynyard airports, Devonport ferry terminal, Hobart at Sandy Bay, and in Devonport.

By taxi

Good taxi services operate in Tasmania's main centres but there is limited service elsewhere. The average pick-up charge is $2.60, with moving charges around $1.10 per kilometre. If money is no object, try Tasmanian National Tours (tel: 6225 3131; mobile: 0418 127 188; fax: 6225 2445) who run chauffeur-driven cars for day tours. Expect to pay around $55 an hour.

By campervan

The popular **Britz Campervan Rentals** chain opened its first Tasmanian branches in October 2001 in Hobart, Launceston and Devonport. Having spent two weeks in the outback in a Britz HiAce, I can vouch for it as cosy, sturdy and great fun, if a little cramped. It sleeps two adults and two children, but any more is a crowd. Renting a two-berth HiAce with gas stove and fridge in high season (summer) is $112 per day. Rates over Christmas and New Year leap to $156 per day but drop to $69 per day in low season (winter). Insurance costs are fixed all year round at between $25 and $35 a day. All costs are inclusive of Australia's 10% GST. If you pick up and drop off in Launceston or Devonport there is an extra handling charge of $145 as an agent operates these depots. No extra charge for Hobart. Addresses of the offices are as follows:

Launceston office C/o Launceston Tourist Park, Old Bass Highway, Hadspen, 7290.
Hobart office C/o Bowen Park Holiday Village, 673 East Derwent Highway, Risdon, 7015.
Devonport office C/o the Devonport Tourist park, 13–19 Tarleton Street, East Devonport, 7310.

All reservations in Australia, freephone tel: 1800 331 454; email: info@britz.com; web: www.britz.com. The freephone number gives access to all offices.

Also try **Trailmaster** (tel: 1800 651 202; web: www.trailmaster.com.au). **Hertz**, **Bargain** and **Rent-A-Bug** (see *By car* above) also rent campervans and motorhomes.

By bicycle

Cycling is a great way to see Tasmania and help reduce your impact on the environment. A number of companies rent bicycles by the hour, day and week.

Prices range from $15–50 a day for road and mountain bikes, and weekly and longer rates are usually negotiable. Deposits may be asked for and it's better to leave an imprint of your credit card than anything like a passport or cash. Check the bikes thoroughly and make sure they give you a puncture-repair kit. Local bicycle rental places should also have an idea of the local road conditions.

Don't underestimate distances in Tasmania. It is bigger than most people think. St Helens to Scottsdale, for example, looks like a hop but is in fact about 70 miles and with some pretty tough hills en route. Cycling Tasmania takes careful planning. The following companies rent bicycles:

Bicheno Penguin and Adventure Tours Tasman Highway, Bicheno 7215; tel: 6375 1333; fax: 6375 1533.

Bright Water Canoe and Bike Hire 21 Sale St, Tullah 7321; tel: 6473 4165; fax: 6473 4177; email: randbboyle@trump.net.au.

Derwent Bike Hire Regatta Grounds, Queen Domain, Hobart 7000; mobile: 0407 342 918; fax: 6268 6654; email: bikehire@southcom.com.au.

East Lines 28 Cecilia St, St Helens 7216; tel: 03 6376 1720. Also rents golf clubs, sandboards, snorkelling equipment, tennis-rackets and wetsuits.

Lakeside St Clair Wilderness Holidays Derwent Bridge 7140; tel: 6289 1137; mobile: 0417 591 289; fax: 6289 1250; email: lakestclair@trump.net.au; web: www.view.com.au/lakeside. Half-day bicycle hire for $25.00.

Oliver's Performance Sport and Cycle 109 Rooke St, Devonport 7310; tel: 6424 9366; mobile: 0419 551 875; fax: 6424 1244; email: judeoliver@bigpond.com.

Rent A Cycle – Tasmania 36 Thistle St, Launceston 7250; tel: 03 6344 9779; fax: 03 6344 9779.

By motorbike

Motorbikes can be rented through the Tasmanian Visitor Information Network in Launceston; tel: 6336 3133; email: info@gatewaytas.com.au.

By train

The only trains you will find in Tasmania are on scenic railways. The highlight must be the reconstructed Abt Railway which runs through the spectacular rainforest gorges between Queenstown and Strahan. The Abt locomotives use a unique rack-rail system to climb the steep gradients. In the northwest, the Don River Railway runs regular excursions and has a good collection of steam and diesel locos. In the south of the state, the Bush Mill miniature steam railway crosses tall trestle bridges and winds through eucalyptus forest near Port Arthur. See individual chapters for scenic railway details, and contact the Tasmanian Association of Tourist Railways at the Don River Railway (tel: 6424 6335).

By ferry

Services run from Orford to Maria Island; Kettering to Bruny Island; and from Bridport to Flinders Island once a week, but this is dependent on the tide. This ferry sometimes continues on to Port Welshpool on the mainland and has no sleeping quarters or food. See individual chapters for ferry details.

Tasmanian Visitor Information Network

Open seven days a week, the statewide accredited centres in the Tasmanian Visitor Information Network are staffed by people who know the local area first-hand, and can explain the latest information and guide you to the most interesting attractions. See relevant chapters for your nearest TVIN.

ACCOMMODATION

There is a wide variety of accommodation in Tasmania to suit your preferences and budget. You can stay in Australia's oldest continuously licensed hotel, the country's first licensed casino, or even the first watering-hole that Roald Amundsen fell upon after his return from the South Pole. See individual chapters for accommodation listings. It has been my experience in Tasmania that the stars a place is awarded do not automatically make it a better place, but merely indicate it has more facilities. I hand-picked places I found efficient, friendly, clean, bright, and good value for money. Some others came highly recommended and others still have won tourism awards. The odd one or two made all three categories. All accommodation prices are for the rack or walk-in rate and are inclusive of GST unless otherwise stated. Many places offer special rates.

Hotels All main centres have hotels ranging from lavish five-star properties with harbour views, multi-channel televisions, 24-hour room service and spa baths to basic, functional two-stars where you get little more than a bed, towels and soap. In Australia the term 'hotel' can actually mean little more than a dingy pub with rooms, so check first with travel agents or direct with the property from contacts in the relevant chapters of this book. Prices range from $40–105 per double room per night for a 0–2-star hotel; $65–240 per double room per night for a 2–4-star hotel; and $154–330 for 4-star hotel and above. Rooms are slightly more expensive in Hobart.

Wilderness Lodges There are several of these, mainly in more remote and mountainous regions. They have log fires and excellent food, and are romantic and great fun. Definitely worth paying a little more, even if just for one or two nights. Rates can range from $100–300 per double room or apartment per night.

Motels For those on the move with a vehicle there are scores of motels, most of which are fairly basic but quite respectable. You will find the usual world chains here, such as Flag Inns and Best Western. Some call themselves 'resorts' which tends to mean they are in rural or coastal locations and usually have facilities for kids such as a pool and games. Prices range from $60–80 for a 0–2-star motel; $65–90 for a 2–3-star; $80–150 for a 3–4-star (all prices per double room per night).

Guesthouses/B&Bs This is a fun way to see Tasmania. Most are family owned and often very good value for money. You do without the room service and entertainment centres but in return you get individual service, great home-cooked food and often an introduction to a Tasmanian family. A number of guesthouses and B&Bs are in colonial properties. Prices range from $75–200 for bed and breakfast only per double per night. Most provide excellent evening meals for extra, which is an especially good idea in more remote places where even the fish and chip shop shuts at 19.00.

Pub B&Bs Australia has a long tradition in pub accommodation. Some are very basic and cheap and would not suit all, while other pubs' rooms are cosy and warm, and often the establishment does food so you don't have to fish around in a strange place if you have got in late. You might want to check on the live music situation and what time the bar closes to ensure you get some sleep. Prices range from $32–100 per room per night.

Home and farmstays These are especially good for couples and families who want to interact with Tasmanians. A growing number of houses and farms are offering homestays where you eat with your hosts and sometimes help muck in on the farm. Rates are usually favourable (between $50 and $209 per double room per night). The farmstays are especially good for visitors with young children as there are always plenty of animals to see on site.

Camping and motorhome parks The only way to really see the wilderness is to get out there with a tent. There are numerous campsites around Tasmania, many of them in excellent locations. Expect to pay between $8 and $17 for a tent pitch per night, and $30 and $50 per night for a motorhome site with electricity and water hook-ups. Park cabins can be up to $75 each per night. There are communal shower blocks, which are usually in good condition. Certain rental companies have affiliations with campsite chains and you can get discounts when you show up. Ask rental companies for details.

Hostels These are popular with backpackers and those on a budget. They are widespread around the state but again can vary in quality. Think about spending a little more to get a better deal. Often they have dorm beds as well as private rooms, but en-suite facilities are rare. Members of the Youth Hostel Association anywhere in the world can use their membership to get cheaper rooms. Always worth booking your hostel well in advance. Prices range from $12–30 for a single dorm bed, around twice that for a separate double room. A lot of hostels are not much more than roofs over your head, which may be all you need, but it is worth checking whether they provide bed linen and towels.

EATING AND DRINKING

One of Tasmania's great delights is its natural produce. Its climate allows for a wide range of food and drink. Its cheeses and wines are the toast of Sydney's finest restaurants. In fact, the most praised chef in Sydney, Tetsuya Wakuda, insists on as much Tasmanian produce as often as possible for his kitchen.

There are several cheese farms, especially in the north, most of them open for tours and tastings. Tassie cheeses have won awards in the Australian Specialist Cheesemakers' Show. In particular, watch for the names King Island Dairies (especially for blue cheese), Lactos, Mella Lacrum, Ashgrove (try the mature cheddar), Pyengana, Heidi (for Gruyère), and Bothwell (for goat's cheese). Many dairy areas boast homemade cream and ice-cream too.

Asparagus is thick and meaty, and a number of varieties of mushrooms are grown here, including shiitake, oyster and honey brown. The Huon Valley is the place to head for apples, cherries, berries and stone-fruits.

Do not leave Tasmania without tasting leatherwood honey. I pride myself on being a bit of a Winnie the Pooh when it comes to honey and have tried samples in more than 25 countries, and this is the best. Fudge and chocolate truffles are made in Hobart and Launceston (a recommended make is Anvers, especially their pralines, which are divine).

The first Australian cookbook was written in Tasmania in 1860 by Edward Abbott, who was a politician as well as a gourmet. In it, he mentioned with some effervescence the array of Tasmania's game, fresh fruit and vegetables, and its seafood. Seafood is possibly the jewel in Tasmania's culinary crown. Fat, juicy oysters; rich, milky scallops and abalone; fragrant crayfish; delicate blue-eye cod; firm, fleshy tuna; and wakame seaweed – all straight from the cleanest waters on earth. You'll see Atlantic salmon on the menu everywhere. It is fished here, but was originally introduced from the northern hemisphere.

Tasmania's vineyards are winning awards hand over fist. Pipers Brook, near Bridport in the northeast, is the most talked about. It produces a fine pinot noir and chardonnay. European visitors will notice that Australian wines are classed by the grape rather than merely the region. While you may be familiar with requesting a St Emilion in France, here you will need to specify your grape choice – a Ninth Island Pinot, for example. Many vineyards are family owned and offer tours and accommodation.

Tasmania's crystal-clear streams are used to produce some of the finest beers in the southern hemisphere. James Boag's is a personal favourite. The company has been operating since 1881 and little has changed. Its lager beer has a clean and truly refreshing taste. The judges at the Australian International Beer Awards thought so too, and named it as the Grand Champion, beating 425 beers from 100 breweries in 27 countries for the title. The brewery also produces a good, darker, Strongarm Bitter which won a gold medal at the same awards ceremony. You can tour the brewery in Launceston. Cascade is another good one.

Hobart, in particular, is blessed with some first-class restaurants with good food, great service and some innovative chefs. Bring Your Own, or BYO, is one of Australia's best ideas. If only the system operated in the UK and the US to this extent. Any establishment that has BYO allows you to bring your own booze. Some restrict this to wine only, and some rather meanly charge corkage (you pay them to open your bottles). It is always worth checking when booking a table and, if BYO is an option, pick up some wine or beer from a bottle shop on your way there. Pubs often have off-licence sales.

Pubs are often called hotels as they have a few small rooms. They almost all do food, which is mainly good pub grub for lunch and supper. Expect to pay between $9 and $20 for hot main courses, less for salads and sandwiches.

SHOPPING

The first point to remember about shopping in Tasmania is that for every visitor (apart from Australians or New Zealanders, obviously) it is a long way home if you are planning to ship anything. Most antique shops, and the more expensive art and furniture galleries, should have a rough idea of packing and shipping costs. There are quite a few good antique shops, especially in Hobart, but also in Launceston, Devonport and Burnie, as well as in smaller centres such as Latrobe, Evandale, Richmond, Oatlands and Bothwell. Most have a penchant for furniture, which is understandable considering Tasmania's colonial past. The rocking-chairs, writing-desks and card-tables of hundreds of naval officers and settlers all came here with their owners. Others would have taken advantage of the vast expanses of timber and had new ones hewn. The finest Tasmanian-made furniture is undoubtedly from speciality timbers such as Huon pine, myrtle and blackwood. There will be few guests arriving at your home who will be able to match a Huon-pine chest, but do check these tree species are not rare or endangered at the time you are buying. There are a few art and ceramic galleries too with modern works and historic pieces, many from colonial times. The items that interest, and have so far eluded me, are Antarctic memorabilia and antiques – old lantern slides, frost-gnawed boots and the like. Most are probably in the Smithsonian in Washington DC or the

Royal Geographical Society in London but I live in hope that a dusty Hobart antique shop might throw something up one day.

Distance from home might also be a problem when you are perusing shelves laden with fresh Tasmanian produce. This is a garden state, with all manner of delicious chutneys, pastes, sauces and preserves to choose from. My favourite is leatherwood honey, made by hard-working bees gathering nectar from the leatherwood trees in the central and northern mountains. It comes in prettily painted metal jars, and I have not tasted finer.

If you are staying for a while and are in accommodation where you can cook for yourself then take a trip to the Salamanca markets on Saturday mornings from 08.30. There is always a staggering array of fresh produce. The markets are living legends in Hobart. They boast scores of stalls selling jewellery, wooden boxes, incense, scarves, trinkets and hundreds of other things. The large number of arts and crafts shops and galleries around the state, mentioned in the *Arts and entertainment* section on page 57, nearly all sell direct to customers.

If you want to support local conservation, then pop into the Wilderness Society shop on Montpelier Retreat, just off Salamanca Place in Hobart. It sells a wide variety of goods, all with an environmental theme, including some particularly nice soaps. They also have a stall in the Salamanca markets.

Keep all substantial receipts and present them to the GST booth at the airport when you depart from Australia. You will be able to claim back the 10% GST you were charged on those items.

PUBLIC HOLIDAYS AND FESTIVALS
Holidays

January 1	New Year's Day
January 26	Australia Day (celebrates nationhood)
March 4	Eight Hour Day (like Labor Day in the US and May Day in the UK – to celebrate the passing of laws confirming the eight-hour working day)
March/April	Good Friday, Easter Saturday, Sunday, Monday and Tuesday
April 25	Anzac Day (celebrates the loss of Australian and New Zealand troops at Gallipoli)
June 10	Queen's Birthday
December 25	Christmas Day
December 26	Boxing Day

Festivals
January
Taste of Tasmania Food fest in Hobart in early January.
Hobart Summer Festival Runs until February.
Wrest Point King of the Derwent A yacht race, with boats fresh from the Sydney–Hobart classic, usually on January 2.
Great Tasmanian Bike Ride Mid-January.
Tamar Valley Folk Festival A cavalcade of music, dancing and workshops in George Town in mid-January.

February
Tasmazia Lavender Harvest Festival Music and arts at Promised Land near Sheffield in early February to celebrate the lavender harvest.
Herb Fair Herb-growers gather en masse in Cygnet in early February to display their plants.

Australian Wooden Boat Festival Every two years, on Hobart's historic waterfront, hundreds of wooden boats pack Constitution Dock and Sullivans Cove. The next festival is due in 2003.
Festival of the Senses Launceston comes alive for ten days in mid–late February with a festival and food and wine workshops.
Clarendon Road Race A race for penny farthing bicycles near Evandale in late February.

March
Horticultural shows Around the state.
Taste the Harvest Food and wine festival along the banks of the Mersey River in Devonport.
Ten Days on the Island Major arts spectacular across Tasmania from late March every two years.

April
Ten Days on the Island Continues into early April.
Tasmanian Heritage Festival Month-long festival with events statewide.
Spreyton Apple Festival In Spreyton in early April.
Woodchopping Carnival This is a must for those who have never seen it. Make your way to the Pyengana Sports Club in mid-April.

May
Agfest Tasmania's award-winning agricultural fair, with lots of machinery and great food and drink. Early May in Carrick.
Devonport Chrysanthemum Show A traditional flower show in early May.
Tasmanian Symphony Orchestra Federation Ball In Hobart in mid-May.

June
North East Arts and Crafts Exhibition A celebration of products in Scottsdale in early June.
Suncoast Jazz Festival In St Helens in late June.
Tastings @ The Top A food and drink extravaganza at Cradle Mountain Lodge in late June.
The Doll and Bear Fair Great for kids and collectors. At the Boardwalk Gallery, Wrest Point, Hobart, in late June.

July
Royal Tennis Australian Open Women's singles and doubles in Hobart during late July.

August
Tasmanian Rally Car racing in the Styx and Plenty valleys – a leg of the Australian Rally Championship, early August.
Opera Gala Hobart in late August.

September
Blooming Tasmania The launch of a series of statewide events celebrating Tasmania's botanical diversity. Also the annual Open Gardens scheme begins again.
Festival of Dance Launceston in mid-September.
Spring Orchid Show In Hobart in late September.

October

Burnie Show Two-day regional show featuring traditional events, in early October.

Tasmanian Poetry Festival Readings and appreciation in Launceston in early October.

Wynyard Tulip Festival Fields of red and yellow around Wynyard in mid-October.

Derby River Derby A mad race on homemade rafts at Derby in late October.

November

Tasmanian Craft Fair Australia's largest working craft fair, in Deloraine in early November.

The Challenge Classic Car rally along country roads of the northeast in early November.

Tullah Challenge Triathlon in Tullah in mid-November.

December

Lavender in Bloom Majestic lavender fields at the Bridestow Estate Lavender Farm.

Bushranger Festival A period festival with parades, music, arts and displays, in Sorell.

Christmas celebrations Around the state.

Sydney to Hobart Yacht Race Watch the winners sail up the Derwent and then watch Hobart let its hair down. After Boxing Day.

Hobart Summer Festival Begins at end of December and lasts until February.

School holidays

The Australian school year runs from January to December. Christmas holidays last until the second week in February, when term one begins and runs until the last week of May.

After a three-to-four-week break, term two begins in the third week of June and runs until the first week of September. Holidays run for three to four weeks, with term three commencing in the fourth week of September and continuing until the first week of December.

University years have two semesters. The first runs from the third week in February to the first week of July. After three to four weeks off, the second semester begins in the third week of July and runs until the last week of November. There are one-week half-terms in April and late September or early October.

ARTS AND ENTERTAINMENT

Tasmania is bursting with artistic events. It is an incredibly lively place and makes the most of every chance to express itself. It has its own symphony orchestra that performs at the new Federation Hall in Hobart. Operas are also performed, and theatres operate in Hobart and Launceston. Hobart's Theatre Royal is Australia's oldest theatre. The Queen Victoria Museum and Art Gallery at Inveresk in Launceston has just opened a new gallery and industrial art space.

Lots of pubs have live music in the evenings, from solo guitarists trawling through the John Denver back catalogue to emerging bands from Tasmania on their way up (and some on their way back down again). Big acts play at the Derwent Entertainment Centre, just out of town. If street theatre and music are your things, then Salamanca in Hobart is the place to head. Jugglers, acrobats, fire-breathers and all manner of buskers gravitate there.

Come summer, and the events almost invariably take place outdoors, from folk festivals in the woods to a polka band playing in a Hobart courtyard. Hobart has a summer festival which runs from the end of December until February and includes scores of arts events. The most famous arts event, however, is Ten Days on the Island. It always offers a packed programme of leading local, national and international performers from every art form, and is well worth catching. Ten Days on the Island celebrates the artistic talents of island communities from around the world. It is a celebration of the unique characteristics that set island people apart. The biennial festival is a recent addition to Australia's cultural calendar and was first held in 2001 during late March and early April. It is a whole-island celebration, bringing world-famous performers to Tasmania. The event embraces indigenous arts and crafts, music, dance, theatre, visual arts, film, community and fringe events and a Writers' Festival. Performances are held in more than 30 venues around Tasmania. All international artists are from other islands.

The National Trust of Australia (Tasmania) was formed in 1961 and since then has identified, registered and cared for buildings that preserve history and exemplify unusual, interesting and beautiful architecture or design. There is an extensive register of Tasmanian buildings that are noteworthy for various reasons, such as rarity and beauty. If you are a member of the National Trust in your country, bring your card and gain free or reduced-rate entry to many properties. Alternatively, a Tasmanian Heritage Pass will gain you access to all these historic properties for three months (adult: $25; pensioner/concession: $20; accompanied children: free. Contact Head Office, PO Box 711, Launceston, TAS 7250; tel: 6344 6233; fax: 6344 4033; email: nat_trust@vision.net.au; web: www.tased.edu.au/tasonline/nattrust/). The Trust also co-ordinates the annual Tasmanian Heritage Festival, usually in April, which includes a number of festivals, events, tours, walks, exhibitions and activities highlighting Tasmania's heritage.

Craftwork is big in Tasmania. There are wood-turners and metal-workers in every other town and village, and you are likely to see lots of galleries on your travels. Most are more than happy to let you wander around and watch them at work. Markets sell their work regularly, and throughout the year the craftsmen and craftswomen get together to display at bigger fairs and festivals. There is also a fairly prodigious number of jewellers, glassblowers and potters. Of course, you will come across the usual junk, but generally Tasmanian crafts are of a high standard and reasonably priced.

Watch out for sandstone-sculptor, Folko Kooper, in Oatlands; potter, Bill Thomas, in Dodges Ferry; watercolour-painter, Nigel Lazenby, in Sisters Beach; kaleidoscope-maker, Strato Anagnostis, in Bream Creek; artist-jeweller, Phill Mason, in Hobart; ceramic-artist, Derek Smith, in Mangalore; and designer-maker, Mark Bishop, and furniture maker, Toby Muir Wilson, both in Stanley.

The Tasmanian Wood Design Collection often travels to international exhibitions when not on show at home in Launceston. When buying, it pays to check that woods have been used from sustainable sources. Try not to buy any products made from woods that are rare or endangered.

Contemporary design is on display at the Tasmanian Museum and Art Gallery, and Tasmanian photographers run workshops.

PHOTOGRAPHY

Other professional photographers I know say nowhere comes close to Tasmania for photogenic variety, and I tend to agree. You have the brilliant light of the east coast turning the sea a deep ultramarine, and making the granite rocks with the red algae stand out wonderfully in contrast. This is the same intensity of light that drew painters to the south of France. Inland, you have ranges of moody mountains punctuated by lakes, streams and lace-like waterfalls. And in the rural areas of the Huon Valley and the rolling country south of Wynyard there are hidden valleys whose fruit groves are wrapped in mist at dawn. Hobart provides endless opportunities around its pretty harbour, heritage buildings and handsome façades, while the southwest wilderness reveals rich forests, massive cliffs and thunderous seas.

However, this is also one of the most challenging places to take photographs. Such changeable weather means your gear has to be quite varied to handle the different conditions, and you must be able to keep everything dry. Also, if you are photographing in mountainous conditions you need to make sure you can carry everything in and out with you. Heat is rarely a problem for film or equipment in Tasmania but if it is a dry summer, dust might be an issue when driving on dirt-roads. When photographing on beaches, be wary of sand grains in high winds and take a small protective bag or pillowcase to keep your gear safe from sand and salt.

Film

For landscape and people, choose a lower-speed film (50, 64 or 100 ASA). If you have little light, and so lower shutter speed, you will need a tripod. If you are photographing animals, pick a faster film such as 400 or 800. It gives a more grainy picture (which can be atmospheric) but means you've got more chance of snapping your creature in focus and unblurred. Print film is available everywhere but it is harder to get the more specialist lower and higher speeds. Slide film and black-and-white-print film are available from some newsagents and chemists, but you will probably need a photographic shop which you can find only in Hobart and the other main towns. No photographic shops open on Sundays. It is best to stock up before you get to Tasmania and then rely on places here only for emergencies and replacement film. The number of films required is an individual choice. On my last trip I shot 40 rolls in two weeks, which was a bit excessive; perhaps aim to shoot about two films a day. There are a few places that will develop print film but you might want to wait until you get home to get the slides done.

Equipment

If you are using an SLR (single lens reflex) camera, bring one body with a standard zoom lens (35–80 or 50–100) and a long lens (300–400, autofocus if possible) for animal shots. Also bring a polarising filter (essential for the east coast), and a neutral density or tobacco filter for moody shots on the mountains when the weather gets bad. In poor light, I choose fast film rather than a tripod to save space and weight.

If you are using a compact or digital camera you will save yourself a lot of weight and some of these cameras are good enough to produce shots to rival those from an SLR.

If you are flying to Australia via Singapore or Auckland and have time for a stopover, you will find some excellent bargains on equipment. I bought a Nikon F90X with a 28–80 zoom lens in a shop in Singapore for about half the price it would have been in England. It takes some hunting around, however, and you need a full day to compare prices and haggle. New Zealand is also cheap for cameras. Try not to buy in airports as they are not that much cheaper. Sydney and Melbourne are very competitive for camera equipment and have lots of second-hand photographic shops.

Tasmania is also about the best location you can find for using a panoramic camera. If you have one, or a camera that has that function, bring it. A wide shot of the Overland Track from the summit of Mount Ossa makes a wonderful framed memento.

Wet weather protection

A good bag is essential. I prefer canvas, with a tough strap and heavy, floppy lid. If you are bushwalking or camping with SLR equipment, use the inner shell of a camera bag to slide inside your rucksack and pad with clothes or towels. For SLRs, take a few professional, clear slip bags to slip over the camera when shooting or carrying in rain or mist, or, even more importantly, when on the beach on a windy day. Sand and salt have eaten their way through the shutter cushion on two of my cameras in alarmingly short times.

Photographic tips

You will find lots of handy tips relevant to particular destinations in each chapter of *Part Two, The Guide*. On a more general level always take note of the sun's position and try to ensure it's behind you over your right or left shoulder. If you are shooting a portrait, make sure the subject is not staring directly into the sun and squinting. Shadows form on a person's face during the middle of the day when the sun is directly overhead, and you may need to use fill-in flash to equal the light balance. In Australia, I use flash far more during the day than after dark.

Portraits and animal shots are best taken either early in the morning (07.30–10.00) or evening (16.00–19.00). Not only are there far more animals about, grazing and playing, but also the light will be softer and bring out their colours and the textures of their fur or wings. With animals, it's best to try to get a clean background – a mono-colour field for example, or blue ocean or sky. A busy background with lots of trees or buildings will make the eye wander from the subject and detract from the overall picture quality. Also try to ensure the subject fills the frame as much as possible. This can be extremely difficult as many Tasmanian animals and birds are shy, and getting close, even with a long lens, is difficult.

Before taking any shot, quickly check your horizon is horizontal and flit your eyes around all four corners of the frame in the viewfinder to make sure you haven't inadvertently got a Coke can or lamppost sneaking into an otherwise perfect landscape scene. Stand with feet slightly apart, and just before you release the shutter breathe in and out, pressing as you exhale – this will steady you slightly. If you are doing an early-morning shoot, don't have too much caffeine beforehand as it might give you extra camera-shake. When taking shots from a car, cut the engine to reduce camera-shake.

Be sparing with the polarising filter. It is necessary to reduce glare but it can dull photos and make them look as though the camera took them through a pair of sunglasses (which work on the same principle). It is sometimes better to wait an hour or two until the glare softens and use the camera without a filter. Alternatively, use the filter but rotate it so that the shot is not fully polarised. This is especially relevant in snow, which a polariser can turn blue if used to its fullest extent. Where it is brilliant is in taking a shot of a stream or lake when you want to negate all the reflection and see through the surface into the water beneath.

If you get bad weather make the most of it. If the Huon Valley is draped in mist and murk, stick on a tobacco or neutral density filter to emphasise the gloom.

Black-and-white shots can be improved greatly by using a red or yellow filter to increase contrast and make greys into blacks or whites. For mountains, use a higher speed black-and-white film at about 400ASA to give it real grain and moodiness.

Sensitivity

It is always advisable to ask before you take someone's picture, especially someone who you believe might be of Aboriginal descent. It is often taboo for them to be photographed but they will usually agree if asked. Aboriginal sites must also be respected, but the rules vary here. Technically, if you photograph a known sacred Aboriginal site, you should get permission first, and get your pictures checked with an Aboriginal authority before you show them to anyone and certainly if you plan to publish any. But this may not apply to Tasmania. Best to check with the Aboriginal Information Centre in Hobart. You can photograph freely around the harbour, but the occasional submarine or naval vessel pops in and obviously it is wise to be cautious about snapping anything resembling military material.

COMMUNICATIONS AND MEDIA

Tasmania is a modern state in a modern country with excellent communication networks. Phones, faxes, email and internet are prevalent. Australia and New Zealand share a three-pronged plug socket, but with two slanted holes. Anyone travelling from outside the region will need an adaptor, available at electrical shops and travel gadget stores. Voltage is 220–240V.

Telephones

Note *All numbers printed in this guide carry the area code 03 unless otherwise specified. Some 1800 freecall numbers may work from outside Australia; all 6-digit cheap-call numbers (eg: 13 13 13) work inside Australia only.*

Phoning Tasmania from outside Australia Exit dial code from your country, then Australia code of 61, then 3 for Tasmania followed by the number.

Phoning Tasmania from mainland Australia outside Victoria Dial 03, then the number.

Phoning within Tasmania Dial number only.

Phoning from Tasmania overseas Dial 00 11, then the country code, area code minus the 0, then the number (eg: for a central London number, dial 00 11 44 207 000 0000; for a New York City number, 00 11 1 212 000 0000).

If you are using a mobile phone bought and authorised in Australia you can phone as you would if you were in Sydney, Brisbane or Perth. If you are bringing your own mobile from home, check with your company first to see how it can work here and what charges apply.

Television and radio

There are four terrestrial television channels. The ABC (Australian Broadcasting Corporation) is the public service channel, with good news and current affairs shows (evening news at 19.00). SBS (Special Broadcasting Service) carries some advertising and has foreign language shows and also good news and current affairs. Win and Southern Cross are the two wholly commercial stations. Most of the larger hotels have cable and satellite channels too, usually offering at least CNN and BBC World.

Lots of radio stations have sprung up around the state serving all tastes in music and current affairs. If you are a BBC World Service fan, tune to the following stations at varying times of the day:

In Hobart 86.4FM, 92.1FM and ABC News Radio on 729AM

In Wynyard 106.1FM

In Geeveston 93.5FM

Check newspapers for more details.

Newspapers and magazines

Newspapers include the Rupert Murdoch-owned daily *Hobart Mercury*, which covers the city and the south of the state (the Sunday version is the *Sunday Tasmanian*); the *Examiner* for Launceston and the northeast; the *Advocate* in Burnie and the northwest and west. The *Australian* is the only daily national newspaper (it has a Tasmania edition). The weekend version on a Saturday has features, travel and sport supplements. Smaller papers include the *Western Herald*, the *Western Tiers Deloraine* and *Meander Valley News*.

Depending on your air carrier, from the mainland you should get an in-flight magazine with events guides and features, but not always covering Tasmania.

Look out for *40° South*, a glossy quarterly magazine with excellent photography and articles all about Tasmania. There are a number of adventure magazines catering for the outdoor crowd. Try newsagents for *Outdoor Australia*, *Wild*, *Outback*, and *Rock*. Those interested in the arts should get their hands on a free monthly magazine, *Artswatch Tasmania*, which has features about performers and a list of events. Walkers should hunt down copies of *Tasmanian Tramp* which is not a pamphlet detailing how to be a hobo in Hobart but rather is full of walks that are not so well known or are rarely attempted. It is produced by the Hobart Walking Club and is published irregularly.

Internet

There are several internet cafés in Hobart and Launceston and a lesser number in smaller places. The link can be slow, and in summer these are usually swamped with backpackers emailing home for several hours making these frustrating places if you are trying to work. If you can bring your own laptop it will make life easier (if you require the internet for business purposes), but do make sure you employ a global roaming device to be able to dial a local number in Tasmania to get on-line. Otherwise it will require an international call each time you log on and this will cost a small fortune. Check with your internet service provider before you leave home. One helpful internet café is Drifters on Montpelier Retreat, just off Salamanca, where the staff are friendly and there are facilities to scan and email photographs and charts. They also serve good hot chocolate and excellent biscuits.

BUSINESS

Most larger hotels have business and conference facilities but there are nowhere near as many as you would expect in Sydney or Melbourne. If you are using the internet, find out the charges before you log on. The Department of State Development (web: www.dsd.tas.gov.au or the overall website for Business Tasmania: www.bt.tas.gov.au) administers a broad range of business assistance schemes, ranging from 'Getting Started' seminars for small business people to project facilitation services for large-scale investments. If you are bringing your business team to Tasmania for meetings, conferences or exhibitions, try **Team Discovery** (7 Scott Street, Bellerive, Hobart, TAS 7018; tel: 6244 8488; fax: 6244 8477; email: leaders@teamdiscovery.com.au; web: www.teamdiscovery.com.au) for some team-building activities and motivation work. They provide challenging experiences for individuals to experience the benefits of clean air, natural beauty, personal challenge and group achievement.

Programmes range from mentally challenging indoor initiatives to physically active adventure experiences including bushwalking, caving, abseiling, kayaking, rafting, mountain biking and orienteering. Prices on application.

A good place to hold a conference is **Woodstock** (140 Cascade Road, South Hobart, TAS 7004, opposite Cascade Brewery; tel: 6224 1117, fax: 6223 3906; email: woodstock@cub.com.au).

GIVING SOMETHING BACK/LOCAL CHARITIES

There are some good ways to give back to Tasmania if you are staying for more than a month. Your first stop might be the **Wilderness Society** (130 Davey Street, Hobart, TAS 7000; tel: 6224 1550, fax: 6223 5112; web: www.wilderness.org.au/tasmania). Drop into their shop on Montpelier Street or their stall in the Salamanca markets. They stage fund- or awareness-raising events from time to time and are always keen for some support. The organisation is now national but it began here under the watchful eye of Bob Brown, now a Greens senator in the federal parliament. One of the big campaigns is to save the Styx Valley, home to giant eucalyptus trees (see *Chapter 4*).

You might also want to consider becoming a volunteer for **Wildcare Incorporated**, which organises community action for natural and cultural heritage conservation. There is a $20 membership fee which goes directly to help fund the work of the organisation, and you can pick the specific activity and even the exact reserve or area you would most like to work with. Wildcare was recognised nationally for its contribution to conservation and given the Banksia Foundation Environment Award in 2000. For more information, call the chairman Andrew Smith (tel: 6233 2836), or the secretary, Allison Wing (tel: 6233 2185; fax: 6224 0884), visit the Parks and Wildlife department website (www.parks.tas.gov.au) and go to the Wildcare option, or email them direct at wildcare@dpiwe.tas.gov.au. Alternatively, you can write to them at Wildcare Incorporated, GPO Box 44A, Hobart, TAS 7001.

Dusky antechinus

The Natural World

Tasmania is probably the closest to Eden you are likely to find here on earth. If you are not a natural history fanatic when you land, you almost certainly will be by the time you leave, for this country is a treasure trove of geological, geographical, botanical, zoological and oceanic riches. Lush, sheltered valleys of fruit trees and vineyards open on to rolling hillsides carpeted with lavender and poppies. Towering forests of giant eucalyptus trees climb the foothills of sawtooth mountain ranges to wild, semi-alpine scrubland and snow-capped peaks. Tasmania has more than 60 peaks above 915m. To the west lies one of the last surviving (and fully protected) temperate rainforests, a living museum of plants whose history can be traced back to the days of the supercontinent known as Gondwana, 180 million years ago. Offshore are the cleanest seas in the world, a sanctuary for whales, sharks, dolphins, seals and penguins.

Since it became an island 12,000 years ago, species have evolved with few outside influences, and Tasmania now boasts its own unique flora and fauna. If you thought the kangaroo was a bizarre and individual species, wait until you sample some of Tasmania's wildlife. It would give *Jurassic Park* a run for its money. The island boasts a carnivorous marsupial known as a devil that cries in the night like a child being strangled and can devour an entire wallaby carcass in little more than an hour; a trigger plant that uses tiny hammers to slap pollen on to the backs of passing insects which then pollinate neighbouring plants; the tallest hardwood trees on earth; bright-blue freshwater crayfish the size of cats that live in streams halfway up hillsides; a wedge-tailed eagle whose wingspan makes it the biggest bird in Australia; and tiger snakes, some of which have accelerated their evolution in order to almost double in size and therefore be able to catch mutton-birds.

But how did it all begin? Where have these species come from, and how have they survived and flourished here? Why are the beaches of the eastern coast so snowy white? Why is Tasmania so enriched with beauty and natural wonder? For answers we must look first in the bedrock and take a trip back to the time when dinosaurs roamed the earth in the Jurassic era about 180 million years ago, and when Tasmania formed a central part of Gondwana somewhere between the present locations of Antarctica and Australia. And for this we must call on the experts.

GEOLOGY
Tim Ireland, BSc, Hons (Geology) at the University of Tasmania, Hobart
Tasmania contains a greater density of amazing landscapes than perhaps anywhere else in Australia, and it is widely celebrated for its environmental heritage. Its metals and minerals have also made it a stronghold of the Australian mining industry for over a hundred years. Behind every one of those landscapes and every deposit is a curious geological tale which gives an appreciation of both the geological processes important in the evolution of Tasmania and the relations between geology and other natural systems.

Southwestern Tasmania (and the early evolution of the Tasmanian continental fragment)

A billion years ago, the whole of eastern Australia did not exist as continental rock; instead, part of what is now the western United States was continuous with what is now central Australia (evidence for this is the similar uranium-decay age of zircon in sandstones on both continents). That ancient landmass began to stretch and thin and a shallow sea formed in which sandy and silty sediments were deposited. Such a thickness of sediment accumulated over a 300-million-year period that the sediments compacted and partially re-crystallised under their own weight to become cohesive rocks.

The two land masses finally parted company 770 million years ago and the continental rocks responded to the abruptly changed pressure regime by flexing upwards (known in the trade as 'isostatic rebound'). The newly consolidated sedimentary rocks were raised above sea-level. Around 250 million years later, more continental rifting set in and dislocated a small piece of continental rock off the southern extremity of the proto-Australian block.

This small block then suffered a torrid structural fate when oceanic rocks were thrust beneath it from the east (this 'subduction' is similar to, say, the modern descent of the Indian oceanic crust under Indonesia). About 510 million years ago, an arc of volcanic islands, similar to the Tonga-Kermedec volcanic arc in the Pacific, collided with this subduction zone, causing the continental sedimentary rocks to fold, buckle and break, and slabs of crust from in front of the arc were thrust up and over the continent (we call these allochthons). Under the weight of the allochthon sheets and the pressure of collision, the old continental sedimentary rocks re-crystallised to dense, hard and durable quartzite, and the wonderfully named rocks 'gneiss' and 'schist'. Look out for small and rather battered signs pointing to examples of these on the final miles of the road to the Gordon River Dam.

A short and complex period of structural reorganisation along Tasmania's western margin brought metamorphic rocks back to the surface to create an oval-shaped domain known as the Tyennan Nucleus which dominates southwest Tasmania today. The rugged spires of the southwest wilderness are examples of the durability of the metamorphic rocks and rock units. As you walk trails in this area, to Frenchmans Cap or Federation Peak for example, you will notice the extent of re-crystallisation and deformation affecting the rocks. Nearly every boulder contains multiple sets of veins, any primary sedimentary textures have been obliterated, and/or the component minerals have grown parallel to one another in the direction that minimises the stress under which they crystallised.

The rocks are dominated by quartz, feldspar and mica, which have derived from the original sands and silts of the shallow sea. Quartz is resistant to weathering and chemical attack, and soils in the area are distinctively clay-poor (and nutrient-poor), their black-white hue revealing they are made almost entirely of quartz and organic material.

Western Tasmania

The rocks of western Tasmania were formed after the complex collision described above. There are fragments of several allochthonous sheets preserved in the area. These are completely foreign to the volcanic and sedimentary regimes in Tasmania: green silky serpentinite, tough kyanite- and talc-bearing whiteschist, and spotted garnet- and amphibolite-dominated eclogite. The serpentinite began life as molten rock rich in magnesium and contains the chromium oxide mineral chromite, and the rare platinum-group metals osmium and iridium. There are prospectors who still pan tiny grains of a natural alloy of these metals from creeks in the west and from near another serpentinite source at Adamsfield. Rumour has it they sell their findings to NASA.

Other allochthons are exposed in the north along the foreshore at Burnie and along the coast of the Narawntapu National Park. Here the rocks are deformed schist and gneiss that show evidence of up to five separate folding events.

The basis of Tasmania's mining industry is a north–south belt of volcanic rocks that wraps around the western side of the Tyennan Nucleus and is known as the Mount Read Volcanics.

As arc-microcontinent collisions continued about 150 million years ago, subduction briefly reversed and metamorphic rocks were thrust westwards underneath the allochthons. Melting at depth created magmas containing potassium and silica that erupted along a shallow basin which had developed on the suture between the continent and volcanic arc. Some of these eruptions were highly explosive events, and much of the rock today consists of massive beds composed of broken crystals and small fragments of lava. Torn apart by violent gas release at surface, the molten rock fragments welded together again because they were still hot when deposited from turbulent clouds of ash and volcanic gas.

The deposit of sedimentary rocks (composed of fragments of older rocks) followed the end of volcanism about 505 million years ago and a thick 'boulder conglomerate' formed the resistant cap of many mountains in western Tasmania. In still periods during the volcanic period, the heat flow from volcanism caused convection of superheated sea water beneath the seabed. The hot waters leached metals from the pile of volcanic and sedimentary rocks and, when fluids leaked into the sea, cooling and neutralisation caused rapid precipitation of lead, zinc, copper, gold and silver as rich deposits of massive sulphide (think of the 'black smokers' found recently erupting along central ocean ridges and you'll get the idea).

The Rosebery, Hellyer, Hercules and Que River mines all exploited this style of deposit. Tasmania has become such a centre of research into ore-forming systems that the University of Tasmania now includes a Special Research Centre, highly regarded around the world. The multiple copper-gold ore bodies at Mount Lyell put Tasmania on the international mining map in the late 19th century. The moonscape of denuded hills around Queenstown, which is now a tourist attraction, was the combined result of logging and intense acid rain caused by a particular smelting method used at Mount Lyell at the turn of the century.

Recently the mining industry has acknowledged the need for environmental consideration and the rich Henty gold mine near Tullah has received wide acclaim for the minimal impact it has on the local environment.

The lead-zinc deposits of the Zeehan mineral field, and the tin-tungsten mineralisation at Renison, Mount Bischoff and Kara, were created by the intrusion of granites during a later deformation event.

Eastern Tasmania

Fifty million years after the end of volcanism in western Tasmania, the entire region was inundated by the sea and a thick package of sandy and silty sediments was deposited in the east. Around 390 million years ago sediments called the Mathinna Beds were folded, lightly metamorphosed, and shortened by thrusting. During metamorphism, water was expelled from the sediments and leached gold from the rocks. The pressure confining these fluids reduced and gold was deposited as reefs (gold-bearing lodes or veins) like the one at the Beaconsfield Mine. Acidic, metal-rich fluids given up during the crystallisation of granites reacted with their adjacent rocks and deposited a variety of metals, most notably tin (and its accompanying gemstone, topaz). These were mined throughout the 20th century on the Rossarden field. Rare lavas in the northeast contain sapphires which can be washed from the gravel in the Weld and Branxholm rivers.

The crystalline core of eastern Tasmania has since re-emerged and now makes up the mountainous terrain through the Scottsdale area, Mount William National Park, Freycinet, and the headlands at Bicheno. This area is a favourite for rock-climbers because, while the granite is strong, it fractured creating a blocky appearance with large flakes, hollows and pits, generating abundant handholds.

The geography and ecosystems of the east are fundamentally controlled by this geology too. The quartz-rich granite rocks disintegrate to a porous soil which is dominated by the coarse sand favoured by she-oak and banksia plants. They also provide a constant supply of clean sand to the coastal environment which results in the beautiful white-sand beaches for which the area is famed.

Central and southeastern Tasmania

From Maria Island to South Cape, the coastline is dominated by dark column cliffs of a rock known as dolerite, rich in iron-magnesium. Around 180 million years ago (in the Jurassic or dinosaur age), Tasmania was located somewhere in the middle of the Gondwana supercontinent between modern Antarctica and Australia. As Gondwana began to tear apart, melting of the upper mantle just beneath the earth's crust generated large volumes of molten rock that squeezed between layers of sedimentary rock which had been laid down 100 million years earlier and crystallised as sheets up to 500 metres thick.

Because molten rock contracts on cooling, sets of vertical fractures developed perpendicular to the contacts between molten rock and the existing rock. These fractures extend all over the southeastern two-thirds of Tasmania and, because they are hard and crystalline, stand up in topographic relief. The dolerite comprises almost all of the central highlands, including Cradle Mountain and mountains as far distant from each other as Mount Anne in the southwest, Ben Lomond in the east, and Mount Wellington near Hobart.

The last glacial maximum extent occurred just 18,000 years ago, a geological blink of an eye, and the landscape of the central highlands is good evidence that it was covered by ice. The entire highland plateau has been scraped clean of surface rock by the ice, and the mountains of the Walls of Jerusalem area and the Cradle Mountain-Lake St Claire National Park are pillars left standing by the erosive glacial cap.

In places there are polished faces of rock on which multiple parallel grooves have been scoured as the ice dragged rocks across them. Poorly consolidated boulder deposits or 'till', laid down as the ice retreated, occur throughout western Tasmania, and there are perched lakes in the southwest (known as 'cirques' or 'corries') in armchair hollows gouged out by ice.

The sedimentary rocks into which the dolerite intrudes are 200–300 million years old and record the end of a much older and more widespread glacial event. Thickly bedded marine siltstones, such as those at the base of Mount Wellington, were deposited during glacial retreat (the Ferntree Formation) and contain sparse pebbles that have been dropped into a generally quiet, moderate-depth sedimentary environment from icebergs floating above. Many of these sediments are limey, sandy siltstones created near shorelines and preserve a rich marine fauna. On Maria Island, one limestone contains an amazing diversity of shell fossils up to 20cm across, and can only have been deposited in a shallow marine paradise. At higher levels in the strata, marine sediments are mixed with layers of freshwater sediments that include thin coal seams, and record some uplift of the land relative to the sea.

Tasmania has attained its present form due to tectonic reorganisation over the last 30 million years; the Derwent Estuary and the Tasman Peninsula have formed by relative subsidence and uplift along major north/northwest to south/southeast fault lines.

The ramparts of the Great Northern Tiers are the result of faulting in comparatively recent geological history. The structures controlling the Derwent Valley are still active and there have been suggestions that Hobart is at much greater seismic risk than most people perceive. In the late 19th century there were several very large earthquakes (magnitude of more than seven) focused near Flinders Island, and the question that should be asked about future earthquakes in Tasmania is *when* rather than *if* they will occur.

As you travel around Tasmania, keep an eye on the shape of the land, the colours and textures of the rocks, and the nature of the coastline. Everywhere you walk is steeped not just in antiquity but in geological dynamism. On the east coast, pause to consider that the granites have been exhumed by the erosion of overburden which was more than 10km thick. In the south, remember the dolerites are a manifestation of the break-up of Gondwana. And in the west, imagine your best fire-and-brimstone environment of heat, humidity, thick atmosphere and violent volcanism … and you won't be too far from what it was like 500 million years ago!

CLIMATE

Tasmania is blessed with a mild, temperate, maritime climate giving it warm, calm summers and cool, stormy winters, but this is a very simplistic overview. During one day in June, I woke to a frost, had a cup of tea on a northern beach in shorts and a T-shirt, sat in my car a few hours later in a jacket with the heater on and eating a bag of chips for lunch to warm up, and almost drove off the road as a violent hailstorm heralded a wintry dusk at around 17.00. All this in less than 12 hours, during which time I covered less than 250km!

I have walked the Overland Track in late November in glorious spring sunshine and a temperature of 28°C (82°F), gulping handfuls of water from mountain streams and applying sunscreen liberally as the edge of the Antarctic's ozone hole comes dangerously close to Tasmania during summer (see *Protection from the sun*, page 43). A month later, during the Christmas holidays (mid-summer here), blizzards howled in from the west and blocked off the track, stranding scores of walkers. At least one was killed.

The reasons for the frequent and rapid changes in weather are mainly twofold. Firstly, Tasmania is situated between 40° south and 44° south, latitudes known to sailors and land-based Tasmanians as the 'Roaring Forties'. These are areas of particularly turbulent storms and wind patterns. Secondly, Tasmania's geology means the western half of the island is mainly mountainous while the east is much flatter. The prevailing winds from the west and southwest (from the Southern Ocean and Antarctica) are forced up over the mountain ranges and drop their rain on them, leaving little for the eastern half which is subsequently in a 'rain shadow'. Similar rain shadows are noted in the United States, with the Rockies sapping the moisture and the plains states going dry, and in Britain, where Welsh mountains are considerably wetter than the drier plains of Cambridgeshire. Queenstown, near the west coast, can average 2,413mm a year while Triabunna on the east can get barely one-quarter of that (560mm).

Hobart is the second-driest state capital in Australia after Adelaide, which is on the southern edge of the great central deserts of the mainland. This is a fact that comes as a considerable shock to many mainland Australians who firmly believe Hobart to be a permanently dank, gloomy and vaguely unhealthy sort of place somewhere down near the South Pole. In fact its summers are dry and beautiful and its winters often sunny and crisp.

The mean daily temperature range for Hobart varies from between 5.4°C (41.5°F) and 12.5°C (54.5°F) in mid-winter (June to August) to 11.9°C (53°F) and 21.1°C (70°F) in mid-summer (December to February). The capital receives a daily average of four or five hours of sunshine in winter and up to eight hours in summer.

Winter brings lazy days and outdoor festivals across the state, but winter can be magical as well, with snow on the peaks and the chance of seeing the aurora australis, or southern lights. The light show occurs throughout the year but is best seen in winter.

Tasmania is one of the least-polluted islands on earth. For years, scientists at the meteorological base at Cape Grim on the far northeast tip have been recording the cleanest air in the world, and the surrounding seas are virtually pollution-free and crystal clear. This has a lot to do with the fact that when winds and waves hit the west coast of Tasmania they have travelled over the longest stretch of open ocean on the planet – all the way around the Southern Ocean from Patagonia, missing the southern tip of Africa en route.

Nature in Tasmania has blossomed under such meteorologically diverse conditions.

FAUNA
Mammals

Most Tasmanian mammals are covered in fur, all are warm-blooded and feed their young with milk. The Australia region, which includes Tasmania, the mainland, and Papua New Guinea, is the only part of the world where all three of the mammal groups are found. Monotremes are unique to this region. Of all Tasmania's mammals, 34 species are native (19 marsupials, 13 placental mammals and two monotremes).

It is a testament not only to the diversity of this island but also to its strong drive for conservation that almost all of the creatures you are about to meet are wholly protected here. Only the common wombat, common brushtail possum, red-bellied pademelon, red-necked wallaby, and the water rat are partly protected, and there are occasionally culls of Tasmanian devils when they reach pest proportions.

Hunting, stressing, or interfering with any wildlife in Tasmania is an offence, not only in the eyes of the law, but also against the background of this island's precious ecosystem. It is also important not to feed wildlife unless special food is provided in national parks by the rangers for this purpose, and even then not up close. Take this book in one hand and a pair of binoculars in the other and watch from a good distance – even the sweetest possum can gouge out an eye if threatened.

Marsupials

Marsupials are mammals whose young are born in an imperfect state and are then carried and nurtured in a specialised pouch in the female adult known as a 'marsupium'.

Swamp antechinus (*Antechinus minimus*) Head and body are about 13cm long, with a tail of about 8cm. Distinguishable from the dusky antechinus by its smaller size, shorter and rounder snout and its smaller and rounder ears. It is widely seen in Tasmania, especially in the low-lying southern and southwestern regions. It is also found on the islands in Bass Strait and on the rugged block of Maatsuyker Island, south of Tasmania.

With a host of predators, this small marsupial has developed into a particularly active and fast-moving individual, especially when it is feeding. It eats mainly insects and other small animals which it catches predominantly during the early evening. It is relatively tame and is often found in inhabited buildings, where it sneaks to find food and places to nest.

As yet, scientists do not fully understand the breeding habits of the swamp antechinus, but it is believed it limits its breeding to just once a year. The all-important pouch develops during this time, big enough to hold the usual litter of six babies.

Dusky antechinus (*Antechinus swainsonii*) Head and body of between 10 and 16cm, tail is long and pointed and can measure more than half its head and body length. Unlike its swampy cousin, it has a long and pointed snout, larger eyes but similar-sized (small) ears. It has dark brown fur and prominent, large guard hairs. The best way to tell the two apart is probably to remember that the dusky variety has a defined and narrow head that looks separate from its body, whereas the swampy's head is a mere continuation of its main frame.

The dusky antechinus is fairly widespread in Tasmania although it prefers the upland and alpine areas, hiding out in dense foliage. It is also a busy fellow, foraging both day and night for food. Its diet is slightly more varied than that of the swamp antechinus, including lizards and snails, and sometimes grabbing the odd berry. It mates in winter for a short period and the male dies three weeks after the event.

Litters of up to eight young are carried in the pouch for up to eight weeks. Look for nests in tiny holes in the banks of creeks and hollow logs.

White-footed dunnart (*Sminthopsis leucopus*) To the untrained eye, this small mammal resembles a mouse, with a head and body length of little more than 8cm and a tail about the same. It has light grey fur on its back and sides, and is white underneath its body and tail. It has small, white feet, a long, pointed snout, large and rounded ears, and whiskers that point decidedly backwards.

You will stand the best chance of spotting one of these rarely seen creatures in the north and east of Tasmania, including Cradle Mountain and Mount Roland, but also as far south as Orford. Look for it in sparse bushland, where it finds the hollow trees and rotten logs it favours.

It is mainly nocturnal and feeds on insects and other small animals. The young are born in spring (late September and early October), usually eight to the litter.

Spotted-tailed quoll (*Dasyurus macalatus*) A beautifully marked, but sometimes quite vicious, little thing. It has a long body (up to 60cm with a 50cm tail), is usually dark reddish-brown on its back and sides, and pale yellowish-brown underneath. Both body and tail are peppered with its trademark light spots, roughly 0.5cm to 3.5cm in diameter.

Most common in the forests of the west, this quoll is a scavenger, predominantly feeding on carrion. To watch it catch live prey you would question how it has survived, as its movements are anything but deft. It can climb well and has a keen sense of smell.

It is nocturnal and mates from April to July, usually producing litters of five young. Nests are mainly in hollow logs, caves or trees.

Eastern quoll (*Dasyurus viverrinus*) Smaller than its spotted relative at just 40cm with a 25cm tail, this quoll is also spotted on its body but lacks spots on its tail (the best way of distinguishing between the two). It has all but died out on the mainland but is still common in Tasmania.

It favours bushland, and, although mainly a scavenger, it is a more proficient killer than its cousin. It will catch small animals and even go for chickens and ducks.

Mating occurs between mid-May and early June, producing litters of more than eight. Usually, however, only six survive as the female adult has only six nipples with which to feed. This is a secretive species and almost entirely nocturnal.

Tasmanian devil (*Sarcophilus harrisii*) You never forget the first time you hear the blood-curdling scream of a devil. It fills the night air with dread and fascination. This much-maligned creature has its place in folklore as well as natural history, and has earned a reputation as a fearsome beast.

Although only 65–70cm long in the body, with a height at the shoulder of about 30cm, with small ears and a shambling trot, its large head, powerful jaws and perilous teeth (with a bite equal to a crocodile's) are ominous to behold up close.

It is a bad-tempered thing but don't let that put you off. It flees from humans if confronted, although the chances of that happening are small as it has an acute sense of smell and wonderful hearing apparatus which mean it is usually long gone before we show up clumping around in our boots.

Covered in dark brown or black fur, with irregular patches of white on its rump, shoulders and chest, it is found only in Tasmania, its mainland populations having died out. It is found in bushland, sometimes right down to the coast, and even in the outer suburbs of towns. It will rarely attack prey, preferring to gorge on dead meat, and will eat just about anything from grubs to fully grown wallabies. I once watched a posse of five devils tear apart and devour a wallaby carcass in about an hour, near Marrawah on the northwest coast. Everything was consumed, bones and all. Not a jot was left.

The devil is bad-tempered but rarely fights. Instead it will spit and lunge and scratch at a rival who tries to muscle in on a feed. Mating is in March and April, with usually four young making a litter. It is nocturnal and spends the day sleeping off its giant meals slumped in a log, cave, disused burrow, or among the foundations of a raised building.

A wholly protected status means its terrifying howl and fierce reputation will, thankfully, endure.

Southern brown bandicoot (*Isoodon obesulus*) A comically named Tasmanian creature with a body about 40cm in length and a long, pointed snout. It has small feet with claws, and a short, pointed tail which is almost devoid of fur. Its fur is coarse and brown on its back and flanks but white and soft underneath. Like most small mammals it needs good ground cover to remain camouflaged from predators and to forage in relative safety. Both the Tasmanian bandicoot types are mainly nocturnal and gather food (snails and insects and their larvae) in the evening by digging them out of the ground with their sharp claws.

The southern brown breeds in winter for six months, usually giving birth to litters of six offspring. It builds well-concealed nests in dense foliage and will defend its territory savagely (well, savagely for a small shrew-like creature).

Eastern barred bandicoot (*Perameles gunnii*) Same size as its cousin but distinguishable by horizontal stripes across the reddish-brown fur of its rump. Fur is creamy-white underneath and in general much finer and softer all over. Males are larger than females.

The population has all but disappeared on the mainland but thrives in Tasmania, especially in the north where it revels in ground cover and can live relatively harmoniously with its cousin, eating the same foods. It is territorial, however, and males will fight.

It breeds during winter but extends the season into spring and summer when necessary. Litters usually contain five young.

Common wombat (*Vombatus ursinus*) The wombat is usually seen ambling across lonely highways around the state, a black ball of fur on the strip of grey asphalt. It stands about 35cm high at the shoulder and is roughly 80cm long when fully grown. Its fur is coarse and dark brown, sometimes almost black, with faint white tips of the hairs. It has a stocky stance, a broad head and no tail to see.

Apart from road verges which, to its cost, it seems to favour, the wombat can most often be found shuffling around in pasture, satisfying its strictly vegetarian diet of grass, shoots, roots, and cultivated vegetables. It is mainly nocturnal but is quite often seen out in daylight.

So sturdy is the wombat that it has few predators in the wild. It also ranks as Tasmania's only burrowing marsupial, and what a burrower. Its holes have been known to stretch for ten metres underground and have a myriad of entrances. It breeds all year round and produces usually just a single baby.

Possum There are five types of possum in Tasmania. All are nocturnal and most are widespread and live both in trees and on the ground. The rare eastern pygmy-possum (*Cercartetus nanus*) is only found in the western forests and is almost completely arboreal.

The larger common ringtail (*Pseudocheirus peregrinus*) and common brushtail (*Trichosurus vulpecula*) are vegetarians, dining on leaves and flowers, with the latter getting a bad name for itself among farmers and gardeners by having a taste for agricultural crops.

The smaller eastern pygmy-possum and its cousin, the little pygmy-possum (*Carcartetus lepidus*), which is the smallest of the lot, favour insects, spiders, lizards and nectar.

The bigger two breed throughout the year, while the smaller restrict to late winter (September) through to spring and sometimes into summer (January). During cold periods they go into a torpid state like semi-hibernation.

Telling them all apart is not that difficult. The ringtail is 35–40cm long and lean, with a tail almost as long containing splashes of white towards the tip, which is also clearly white. It is almost certain to be up a tree.

The much more common brushtail is bigger and fatter, and more likely to be found on the ground, even in a back garden or public park where it can be quite tame when food is on offer.

Distinguishing between the pygmy varieties is fairly straightforward too. The much more common little has oversized, bat-like ears and a chubby body, whereas the secretive eastern is an altogether sleeker model, with ears in proportion.

For a touch of exotica, take a trip to Bruny Island to seek out the golden possum, which is technically a brushtail but has a beautiful golden colour to its fur.

INVASION OF THE FOX

In October 2001, Tasmania officially lost its fox-free status as evidence was found of at least one specimen that had got in from the mainland. It is thought to have jumped ship on the north coast from a ferry or cargo ship, and there were fears there may be more at large.

The full impact on native wildlife of adding a predator to the food chain will not be known for some years – but it doesn't look good. The lack of such predators is one reason Tasmania's wildlife has survived so successfully while sister species on the mainland have been decimated or even wiped out altogether. **Feral cats** have also affected some populations of smaller mammals and birds.

Sugar glider (*Petaurus breviceps*) Seeing a sugar glider sailing silently through the air from tree to tree is one of the most wondrous sights in Tasmania. To spot one, you need to get out at night and look up as they rarely, if ever, venture down to the ground.

A sugar glider measures about 15cm in length, with a tail the same again. It has thick silver-grey fur and a black stripe down its back. It has a small head with large prominent ears, and flies courtesy of a membrane that stretches between all four limbs and fans out like a parachute when it launches itself from a branch. Flights of 40 metres have been recorded.

It was introduced into Tasmania and is now common in all bush areas and some gardens. It eats nectar, blossoms, insects and shoots, and it nests in tree hollows or sneaks into the odd abandoned ringtail possum nest. Breeding starts in August, with females giving birth to two young.

THE THYLACINE

Extinct or just secretive? The debate rages but it is pretty safe to say the thylacine or Tasmanian tiger is no more. No sightings have been confirmed since the last one died in Hobart Zoo in 1936. The Australian Museum in Sydney is experimenting with DNA extracted from a preserved thylacine foetus to see if it is possible to clone from the dead and re-introduce the species.

The thylacine was a large, dog-like, carnivorous marsupial that inhabited Tasmania and the eastern ranges of the mainland. It had distinctive tiger stripes across its lower back and rump.

For more information we turn to award-winning young writer Keith Millar:

I have stopped somewhere on the Western Tiers, drawn by an ancient thylacine report, in a deserted layby etched from the mist-rIdden forest. I believe in destiny. So I search for an animal thought long-extinct but which still tantalises, with fragments of proof to quesiton its untimely end. Glancing up the track, I wish for a thylacine the szie of a small dog, black stripes running down its back, a stiffly erect, bare tail and a knowing look of survival chiselled into his non-dog-like face. It might come even now, trotting openly toward me. In this primordial and empty land, there is always hope.

But so much rain. Sixteen solid days of it, striking the ground mischievously from every angle. Eventually, at dusk, the constant patter on the camper-van roof ceases. But then my electricity supply inexplicably begins to dim and I steAl outside for a change of darkness. There are noises everywhere – on the ground, in the trees, far away and very, very close. At this irrational moment, I wonder if a black-striped predator is stalking me in the night, all three-foot-six of it. I retire to bed, leaving the possums to their playtime, and my leg continues to bleed from an unsuspected leech. Things can only be better in the morning.

The dawn chorus in Tasmania, noisy, piercing, rasping – and with little hint of soothing or melodic. Indistinct black and grey shapes meld into the sun-starved trees, just as the familiar call of goldfinches sparks an unforced smile. Those few weeks ago, striding from the little plane that had ferried me across the Bass Strait and down the cloud-covered Tamar Valley, all had seemed immediately familiar. Green, fresh and damp, with a hawthorn hedge in November's full bloom and swallows wheeling overhead. But this land deceives you into thinking it is home. Only suddenly do you realise that you are very far away. I notice my emergency telephone still doesn't work, and if the television has four channels, why am I yet to find one? I have no bread to eat. My culinary

If you spy one in the treetops the chances are it will not be alone as it is a social animal, living in groups of seven adults and their young who share the same nest.

Long-nosed potoroo (*Potorous tridactylus*) A member of the kangaroo family, although with short legs and a shrew-like snout. The potoroo is about 40cm long, with a tail up to 30cm and usually white tipped, and dark grey fur on its back and sides with the longer hairs tipped white. Underneath, the fur is a greyish-fawn. Its head is long and pointed, its ears large.

It is common in Tasmania and the islands of Bass Strait. Look for it in low-lying areas of dense, well-watered scrub. It moves on all fours and generally has a distinctive kangaroo-like hop when in a hurry. It eats worms, insects, household

repertoire is entirely based on toast, and this is a real difficulty. Outside, there is an outbreak of spring sunshine, and a fantail flits in and around the nearest bush – precisely what fantails enjoy doing most.

At dusk, animals of all kinds occupy the roads: Bennett's wallabies, pademelons, possums, wombats and, sometimes, a devil, which turns to snarl defiantly at the van, 100 times its size. There is road-kill everywhere. I drive cautiously. Faced with oncoming traffic, a marsupial's instinct is to stand, blink and await evolutionary inspiration. With so much prey, the predatory trot of a thylacine must surely be redundant. I picture it roaming this cold and saturated land. An animal destroyed by early settlers because it could out-pace a sheep and consequently trapped, shot and poisoned into the oblivion of extinction. Alternatively, despite the odds, it is living quietly in the backwoods, a testament to the durability of nature.

That night I walk up a steep track, the light from the van's headlamps partly illuminating the forest edge. And then it happens, right beside me – a strange yelping bark, strong but also plaintive. I quickly turn to face it. Again it calls. This is it. I can feel its eyes boring into me. Surely this is it. Fate! Tingling and promised, somewhere in that tangle of protective deep, dark vegetation. I stand on that track, recovering, long after I sense my quarry has stolen away. Only much later do I remember the horrible truth – boo-book owls can bark, but thylacines never did.

My last day. Down from the hills and into sweet, warm, sunshine and a bird hide, empty except for a basking lizard. I make a note of every swamphen, harrier, egret and swan. On higher ground, between the creeks, an abandoned garden, with Scots pine and thistles, the house and its homesick occupant long gone, and a whistling kite rising above the treetops. I actually cry. If this is failure, there is no one here to judge. I am happy to accept the release.

Launceston airport departure lounge. Black plastic seating, stale air and Tasmania's state flag fluttering in the breeze outside. There has been a new 'tiger' sighting on the road between Queenstown and Strahan. I was there only yesterday. I am reminded of a 70-year-old photograph – a farmer proudly displaying the lifeless form of the last recorded wild thylacine. But I know better. It really is just biding its time, until I return, just around that very corner, caught curious and conclusively in my headlights.

Keith Millar's article won the 2001 travel writing competition which is run annually by Bradt Travel Guides in conjunction with BBC Wildlife Magazine.

scraps, and the odd fungi. The potoroo breeds in early spring and late summer, but some breed throughout the year.

Tasmanian bettong (*Bettongia gaimardi*) Another kangaroo relative, about the same size as the potoroo but with more defined hopping legs and kangaroo-like paws. Hair on the top surface of the tail is long, bushy and at the tip is white. On the head and body the fur is light brown and white underneath. Its face and ears are small and rounded.

It is found in dry, open areas on the edge of low scrubland. It seeks out thick bushes behind which to build a nest with twigs and foliage carried in the curled-up tip of its tail. Believed to be mainly vegetarian. It breeds throughout the year, with females producing two to three young.

Red-bellied pademelon (*Thylogale billardierii*) Dark brown fur with fawn tips covers its short, stout body which is about 50–60cm high. Males are more thickset than females. It has a small head, with short rounded ears and a muzzle, and its tail is short and pointed.

It is common in Tasmania and the islands of Bass Strait, although could now be extinct elsewhere in Australia. You can usually find one grazing in low scrubland and dense forest adjoining good grazing areas. The pademelon is nocturnal and feeds at dusk. It is a timid creature, sticking close to the undergrowth at the edge of open spaces in case it needs to run for cover. Breeding is year-round, but most young seem to be born from April to June.

Bennett's (or red-necked) wallaby (*Macropus rufogriseus*) Those who have not seen kangaroos in the wild could be forgiven for thinking they have spotted one when it is in fact the much smaller, and much more common, wallaby. Their facial features, stance and movements are similar, so size is your best guide.

The wallaby stands about 80cm high, and is covered in dark brown fur, apart from on the back of the neck and the shoulders which are more reddish-brown. It has a small head with obvious, pointed ears and a defined muzzle.

It is vegetarian and can be seen browsing on shrubs and bushes in dense scrubland and eucalyptus forests, usually on its own but sometimes in small groups.

It breeds from late January until July, with most births occurring in the summer months of February and March.

A sub-species exists on Bruny Island known as the painted white wallaby. When I first saw one, at dusk in a paddock next to the Adventure Bay Holiday Village cabin and caravan park, I thought I was staring at a ghost. Its light fur was almost glowing in the gloaming.

Eastern grey (or Forester) kangaroo (*Macropus giganteus*) This is Tasmania's largest land animal. An adult male can reach a standing height of 1.6 metres, females about 1 metre. Both sexes' fur is pale fawnish-grey on the back and side and slightly lighter underneath. Ears are very large and the muzzle rounded. When the female kangaroo is standing, any joeys in its pouch are usually clearly visible. It is a grazer, so look for it in open grassland with patchy woods and open sclerophyll forest in the northeast and northern midlands regions only. Mount William National Park is usually a good bet.

Do not approach a kangaroo, however attractive and gentle it may look. It may be timid initially and hop away, but it can become aggressive if it feels threatened and attack with great force and savage claws.

The Eastern grey is gregarious, spending long periods of time in small groups, resting during the heat of the day and grazing in the evening. Most births are in summer, usually a single joey.

Monotremes

Monotremes are egg-laying mammals. They make up a rare order of mammals with only two species surviving today.

Platypus (*Ornithorhynchus anatinus*) Possibly the most famous of Tasmania's animals, the platypus is a great sight in the wild but one which is not always guaranteed despite the fact that it lives in all freshwater lake and river systems. It is both nocturnal and amphibious, and you are most likely to catch it surfacing and causing gentle ripples on a lake. The locals will tell you the platypus doesn't like rain and not to bother searching unless it's fine, but the only platypus I have ever seen in Tasmania have been in downpours, so it's always worth a try. The Aborigines called it the 'mallingog'; the first settlers thought it was a kind of badger, which is understandable at a distance.

The platypus is a perfect blend of mammal and reptile, laying soft-shelled eggs and possessing venom sacs like a reptile, but also being able to regulate its body temperature and feed its young on milk, both features of mammalian behaviour. It is about 50–57cm long, with short legs and webbed feet and claws. Its jaw is modified into a leathery duck-like bill and two grinding plates replace teeth. Its tail is short and flattened and covered with coarse brown fur. Body fur is darker on the back and sides, and yellowish-brown underneath. Males have poisoned barbs on the insides of their hind legs, almost like spurs.

The best bet for spotting a platypus is to ask a local guide who can point out, from a distance, entrances to the elaborate labyrinth of tunnels built into a river bank that make up its burrow.

It feeds on worms, insect larvae, molluscs and crustaceans, using its bill – which scientists believe can pick up minute electrical impulses emitted from the prey – to locate them. It breeds in early summer, and females lay two to three round, leathery eggs.

Short-beaked echidna (*Tachyglossus aculeatus*) Resembling a flattened porcupine, the echidna is a thrilling animal to spot. I have seen two or three along the boardwalks over the boggy marshes at the southern end of the Overland Track who seemed oblivious to me until they bumped into the toes of my boots and changed direction. They have good hearing and smell but shockingly bad eyesight.

The first view of an echidna that most visitors to Tasmania get is its image on a 5¢ coin. It has a stout, flattened body up to 40cm long and 20cm wide, with short legs, tiny eyes (hence the bad eyesight), sharp claws, a tubular snout with a small mouth at the end, and no visible tail. The body is covered with thick, strong spines up to 4cm in length. It prefers dry, hilly areas and light scrubland, and is common throughout Tasmania and the Bass Strait islands.

The echidna is considered a highly successful animal, living on just ants and termites, of which there are usually several million per hectare. It feeds like an ant-eater by digging a hole in a nest and sticking its tongue in. It protects itself as a porcupine or hedgehog might by rolling into a ball and half-burying itself in the ground.

Usually a single egg is laid and carried in the pouch for ten to 12 days during which time the youngster is fed by milk secreted from glands in the inner walls of the pouch. Once the spines develop, the adult will leave its offspring in a concealed nest during the day.

Placental (bats, rats and mice)

It might come as a shock to know that we humans have a fair amount in common with bats, rats and mice, but it is true that their young, like ours, are nourished

MEGA-FAUNA

In the excellent Tasmanian Museum in Hobart is a particularly fascinating, if disturbing, exhibit. In a room of their own are models of the giant animals that used to inhabit Tasmania. A kangaroo stands almost 3m (8–9ft) tall, and an over-sized Tasmanian devil, weighing up to 30kg, lurks nearby on its haunches.

According to the museum's senior curator of geology, Noel Kemp, gigantism in animals was common on most continents during the Pleistocene era, 1.8 million to 10,000 years ago. There were also snakes, crocodiles and birds, but remains of these animals have not been found. They may not have made it to Tasmania. If they did, it is possible that climatic changes meant they did not last long here.

In Australia, many species of mammals were of a size unmatched by their descendants of today. Their bones and teeth are found as fossils both in Tasmania and on the Australian mainland. There was a marsupial lion and a marsupial tapir that weighed about 300kg. Some were definitely around when humans appeared, so fires would have been about all that kept them at bay. Thankfully, most were herbivorous.

before birth by a placenta in the female's uterus and are then born in a fairly well-developed state.

Bats There are eight varieties in Tasmania, all wholly protected, ranging in size from the large forest eptesicus (*Eptesicus sagittula*) which measures about 9–10cm long, to the lesser long-eared bat (*Nyctophilus geoffroyi*) which is just 4.5cm long. All are nocturnal, insectivorous, fast-flying and can be found throughout Tasmania, although the Gould's wattled bat (*Chalinolobus gouldii*) and chocolate wattled bat (*Chalinolobus morio*) are rare, and the greater long-eared bat (*Nyctophilus timoriensis*) is secretive and has only been sighted in Tasmania in recent years. Some, like the lesser long-eared, are gregarious and favour caves or trees for their colonies, whereas others, like the great pipistrelle (*Falsistrellus tasmaniensis*), are solitary and prefer to dwell in buildings.

We know most about the widespread little forest eptesicus (*Eptesicus vulturnus*) which breeds in early summer, with young being born from late November to mid-December. The young are often carried by the female adults when they go to feed – a way of teaching the young to fly and to hunt on the wing.

The King River eptesicus (*Eptesicus regulus*) is less likely to feed like the other bats at ground level, and instead prefers to catch its meals in the treetops; scientists have even pinpointed the fact that they choose to hunt amid re-grown forests as opposed to mature stands.

Rats There are three varieties in Tasmania: the seafood-eating water-rat (*Hydromys chrysogaster*), which is 40cm long and one of the most widely distributed of all native mammals; the much smaller, vegetarian broad-toothed rat (*Mastacomys fuscus*) which, by contrast, is one of Tasmania's rarest mammals; and the particularly aggressive swamp rat (*Rattus lutreolus*), which is about half the size of the water-rat and favours wet grasslands and alpine heaths.

All have shiny, dark brown fur and most have a white tip to their tail, but the water-rat is the only one with an underbelly of golden orange.

Mice Two types. The long-tailed mouse (*Pseudomys higginsi*) has a body of about 14–17cm and a tail longer than that. It has grey fur on its back and white underneath. It is found only in Tasmania, making it the island state's only endemic rodent. It is omnivorous, eating grasses, seeds, insects and even spiders. The long-tailed breeds from November to April and one or two litters are born with three or four young in each.

The New Holland mouse (*Pseudomys novaehollandiae*) is named after the old label for the great southern continent of Australia, as dubbed by the Dutch. It lies about 8cm long, with a tail shorter than its cousin's. Has only been known about in Tasmania since the mid-1970s, and is found mostly in northern areas of the main island. It eats seeds, leaves and flowers in summer, and insects and other small animals in winter.

Birds

There are hundreds of bird species in Tasmania, enough to keep the keenest bird-watcher happy for months. We have picked out here some of the rare, endemic, significant and interesting varieties. All national parks and reserves have lists of their birds and how, when and where to see them, and fact-sheets on their history and current health.

Birds Australia (tel: 9882 2622; web: www.birdsaustralia.com.au) can help with identification and up-to-date details on all species in Tasmania, as well as across the entire continent

Rare birds

The **orange-bellied parrot** (*Neophema chrysogaster*) is one of the most rewarding sights in Tasmania, but it takes an awful lot of time and effort to spot one. It is on the brink of extinction here, with barely 50 breeding pairs left. This also makes it one of the rarest birds on earth. It stands 20cm long and has bright grass-green plumage, mostly yellow underneath, with a bright orange patch on its belly. It migrates from coastal Victoria and the southeastern regions of South Australia to the southwest wilderness of Tasmania to breed each spring, using Hunter Island and King Island as pit-stops. It usually arrives in early October and leaves again to head north in March or April. This flight across open water is perilous and claims young birds each year.

When trekking in the southwest wilderness, listen for a repeated call of 'zip, zip, zip' and watch for the flash of its orange belly against a grey mountain backdrop. It eats seeds and has a penchant for those of the buttongrass plant which is abundant in the southwest. The parrot will nest in eucalyptus trees that mark the edges of buttongrass plains.

Couples mate for life, which could be one reason their numbers are so low. Also, although the parrot lays six eggs, it usually rears only one or two young. However, habitat-loss through fire and clearance and the introduction of predators (especially feral cats) and of rival seed-eaters like sparrows and finches are thought to be the main reasons for the decline.

The flamboyantly named **forty-spotted pardalote** (*Pardalotus quadragintus*) is one of the smallest and rarest birds in Australia, endemic to Tasmania and now endangered. About 10cm long, with a light olive green and pale yellow body, and with black wings with white dots, it belongs to a group called diamond birds because of their jewel-like appearance.

Look for it in the upper storeys of white gum eucalyptus trees in the Darling Range on Flinders Island, and on Maria and Bruny islands, and on the main island around Tinderbox and Conningham, south of Hobart, and Lime Bay on the Tasman Peninsula. Listen for a soft call as if it is asking 'where, where, where', as opposed to its cousin, the spotted pardalote (*Pardalotus punctatus*), that trills 'me, me' (and has a spotted head). There are only two colonies of more than 100 birds and those are on Bruny and Maria islands. The Tasmania Parks and Wildlife Service can narrow it down for you a bit more. On Maria Island their records show the areas around Bernnachis, Counsel and Four-Mile creeks are best.

The government has set up a recovery programme to assist in managing the habitats and population, and is increasing awareness about the threats to the bird and asking farmers and landowners not to chop down their white gums.

The **swift parrot** (*Lathamus discolor*) is considered to be in a vulnerable position, with fewer than 1,000 pairs reported to be left. They are not year-round dwellers but seasonal visitors, migrating here across Bass Strait to breed in late spring and lay eggs in hollows in tall trees. Listen for a 'clink, clink, clink' when they fly. The **ground parrot** (*Pezoporus wallicus*) is also under threat, which is not that surprising as it spends most of its time on the ground. It is one of only three ground-dwelling birds in the world.

Land birds

There are several honey-eaters. The first three to mention are all endemic.

The **strong-billed honey-eater** (*Melithreptus validirostris*) has green back feathers, a black cap, and a white collar around the back of its neck. You will no doubt hear it before you see it as it is one of the noisier chirrupers in the woods of the island state.

The **black-headed honey-eater** (*Melithreptus affinis*) has a black head and throat with a small, white eye crescent and a shrill whistle. It is a heath and garden bird but is also found in some forests. It makes its nest of grass, hair and fur, and binds it all with strands from a spider's web.

The **yellow-throated honey-eater** (*Lichenostomus flavicollis*) is bigger than the other two with a black face and breast and a bright yellow throat. It makes a number of calls, including a 'tonk, tonk', a 'tchook, tchook' and one that sounds like 'pick-em up'.

The **crescent**, **New Holland** and less common **tawny-crowned honey-eater** all have populations on the mainland too.

Tasmania's (and Australia's) biggest bird is the **wedge-tailed eagle** (*Aquila audax*), a true giant standing more than half a metre (females are bigger than males) and sporting characteristic fur on their legs that makes them look like they are wearing leg warmers. They are marginally bigger than their cousins on the mainland.

They can be seen throughout the island but look most impressive in the central and southwestern mountains and the giant eucalyptus forests of the south. Their nests are large platforms of sticks, bark and eucalyptus leaves (the latter acting as a natural disinfectant to keep the grubs away). They must not be approached under any circumstances as they are wont to abandon them. In flight they soar high, searching for small mammals, marsupials and carrion on the ground, and showing off the distinct wedge shape in their tail feathers.

An Australian favourite is the **laughing kookaburra** (*Dacelo gigas*) which was introduced to Tasmania. It has a large and strong bill, brown and white feathers with pale blue wing patches, and a loud, raucous laugh.

The word kookaburra means alarm clock in many Aboriginal languages and they are well named, as anyone who has camped in Tasmania will tell you. They are easy to spot as they spend a good deal of the day perching on branches waiting to spy their favourite meals of insects, amphibians, small reptiles, and even rodents and other young birds.

The **superb lyrebird** (*Menura superba*) is a wildlife marvel which was also introduced to Tasmania. It is brilliant at mimicking the sounds it hears in its environment, so when you are trekking through a forest and the sound of a chainsaw reaches your ears, think twice before cursing the forestry department – it could be a lyrebird doing an uncanny impression. It does an awfully good kookaburra too.

To get an idea of what it looks like, dig into your pocket and find a 10¢ piece which it shares with Queen Elizabeth II. It is a forest bird, mostly ground-dwelling, as what it boasts in vocal talents it seems to lack in extended flight power. The male uses a series of mounds as territorial markers and as display areas during the breeding season from May to July; however, young males sing and dance all year.

A good place to hear them, and maybe even catch a glimpse, is on the Lyrebird Nature Walk in Mount Field National Park (see *Chapter 7*) on the eastern boundary of the Franklin-Gordon Wild Rivers National Park, where some specimens were released in the 1930s.

When driving in the north of the state through seldom-visited forests, keep an eye out for the large shapes of **yellow-tailed black cockatoos** (*Calyptorhynchus funereus*) in the trees. If you are lucky – as I was one showery afternoon on the C741 dirt-road in the Dazzler Range between Port Sorell and Beaconsfield – three will glide across the road in front of you, squawking and cackling, and then sit on a branch muttering to themselves until you drive on and leave them in peace.

A host of water birds such as **plovers**, **grebes**, **egrets**, **ducks** and **teals**, **stints** and **lapwings** can be seen throughout Tasmania's extensive wetlands. Areas inland in the central Midlands and the Western Tiers leading to the north coast are good, as are the remote swamps and buttongrass plains of the southwest wilderness region. Perhaps the most elegant two are the **black swan** and the **white-faced heron** which can both be seen particularly well on Bruny Island.

Sea birds

Only one species of **penguin** is present on the main island of Tasmania, the little (or fairy) penguin (*Eudyptula minor*). Less than 100 years ago this species was slaughtered for its oil and as food for sealers and whalers. Now it is protected and revered, and is a major draw for ornithologists and tourists alike. It is the world's smallest penguin, standing just 400mm tall, with black and blue-grey markings and silver underneath. It yaps like a puppy but can growl rather ominously when it feels threatened. When on land, it nests under rocks or in burrows using sticks, grass and seaweed, and lays two white eggs. Rookeries can be made up of hundreds of such nests. There are usually one or two hatches per season. The penguin eats pretty much anything marine that it can grab in its beak, including deeper fish, as this tiny bird can dive to a staggering 60m below the waves.

The best spots to see fairy penguins are at Stanley and George Town on the north coast, Bicheno on the east, and King, Flinders and Bruny islands. At Stanley, local resident and B&B operator, Graham Wells (see *Chapter 10*, pages 195 and 197) has built more than 100 nest sites with blocks of stone along the seashore at the foot of the Nut. Scores of penguins have moved in and can be seen scuttling about outside their miniature caves at dusk. Graham even has one nesting in a wooden box in his garden. They have also, rather spookily, moved in to a number of tombs in the beachfront cemetery.

Bruny is another good site as there is an easily accessible rookery on the Neck between the north and south islands where about 100 breeding pairs are resident for part of the year. Here they start to mate in August and lay eggs in September, with chicks hatching in late September or October. The first batch are ready to leave the rookery around Christmas. Any that are left there by February will be in trouble, as that is when adults begin moulting. When this happens they lose their waterproof oily coat and cannot be at sea, and so cannot fish to feed their young. The best viewing times on Bruny are from September to January, and especially at Christmas, when the chicks are about and a lot of feeding is going on. The young sit outside the burrows waiting for their parents to return with the catch of the day.

The parents spend much of the winter at sea on semi-permanent 'rafts', feeding out on the open ocean.

There are a few simple but important points of etiquette for observing penguins which are worth heeding not just for the penguins' benefit, but to maximise your chances of viewing them (see *Minimal impact*, page 90).

The nature reserve of Albatross Island off the northwest coast of Tasmania boasts the largest single **albatross** colony in Australia. There are about 3,000 nesting pairs of **shy albatross** here, revelling in the wild winds that buffet this outcrop. Occasionally albatross are spotted flying off the coasts of the main island but usually out to sea.

Sooty, **wandering**, **grey-headed**, and **black-browed albatross** are all found on sub-Antarctic Macquarie Island, 1,500km southeast of Hobart. The **wandering albatross** was declared endangered in 1995 after numbers here fell dramatically, mainly due to getting caught on the baits of longline tuna fishermen. The island is also home to colonies of **fairy** and **rockhopper** (*Eudyptes chrysocome*) penguins.

The **short-tailed shearwater** (*Puffinus tenuirostris*) or **mutton-bird** is legendary in Tasmania. These birds sustained the Aborigines for centuries, followed by the sealers and whalers (not to mention the oversized snakes of Mount Chappell Islands). The penchant among early settlers on Norfolk Island for eating them prompted an officer in the Royal Marines to dub them the 'flying sheep', from whence came the name mutton-bird. They are migratory, turning up here from September and staying until April. Little was known about their migratory patterns until recently, when it was found that they travel a staggering 10,000 miles each year, up the Pacific coast to the Aleutian Islands off Alaska and then back across the central ocean.

Storm petrels (*Oceanites nereis*) are also present on Tasmania, as well as **Australasian gannets** (*Morus serrator*) and many **gulls**, including the **Pacific** (*Larus pacificus*), **kelp** (*Larus dominicanus*) and **silver** (*Larus novaehollandiae*) varieties. The column-like cliffs, especially of the east coast, are the haunt of the **white-bellied sea eagle**.

Reptiles

There are three species of snake, all venomous. As bad luck would have it – or Darwinian theory – the most common is also the most dangerous. The **tiger snake** (*Notechis ater*) usually grows to more than a metre long. It is dark green or black in colour, of medium thickness and with a slightly flattened body. It is part of the tiger snake family that makes up one of the most feared breeds in Australia, and is said to be one of the most deadly in terms of venom-strength. Walking the Overland Track, I saw seven in four days on the path, and the tail tips of at least another two slinking off into the undergrowth.

Like many snakes, it is rarely aggressive with people but nevertheless it will attack if trodden on or cornered or if its young are threatened. Pay particular attention to where you step during the mating season between February and March when they can be irritable. If you are in dense bushland with no discernible path then carry a stick to strike the ground as you walk and make some noise – snakes usually flee from approaching earth vibrations. For those not used to snakes, a sighting can make their day. Just knowing something so deadly is visible really gets the adrenaline pumping.

Some Bass Strait islands are littered with tiger snakes that have flourished with no predators and plenty of prey. On the Chappell Islands off Flinders Island they have grown alarmingly in size to more than 2m (6ft) on a diet of mutton-birds, and are thought to be evolving by growing hypodermic fangs to increase the effectiveness of their venom.

The **Australian copperhead** (*Austrelaps superba*) is a more slender snake, with rust-brown skin on its back and flanks and pale grey underneath. It is less obvious than the tiger snake, arguably better looking, and rarely seen, although it still has a dangerous bite.

The **white-lipped whipsnake** (*Drysdalia coronides*) is much shorter than the other two – at around 40–50cm and olive-green and grey in colour with paler skin underneath. It has a distinctive white line along the upper part, or lip, of its mouth, and is chiefly nocturnal.

Tasmania has a large number of lizards, mainly **skinks**. They are slender beasts, found sun-baking on rocks and paths and hiding below them during the winter when they retreat to hibernate and reserve energy levels. They can put pregnancies on hold, starting and stopping them depending on the weather. An egg fertilised one summer may not be born until the following summer.

Leathery turtles can be found in the seas around Tasmania although they do not come ashore here. You will have to visit tropical Australia for that.

Amphibians

Tasmania has ten species of **frog**, all of which provide an important link in the food chain. They dine on insects, and are in turn dined upon by many other animals, including kookaburras and snakes.

Three are endemic to Tasmania: the omnipresent **Tasmanian froglet**, the **tree froglet**, which is found only in the western woodlands and forests, and the more scarce **moss froglet**, which lives only in the remote southwest and which was only discovered in 1993 in the Hartz Mountains. Since then it has been spotted in Port Davey and Mount Sprent.

One of the best places for frogs is around Lake Dobson in Mount Field National Park (see *Chapter 7*, page 153) where they call in abundance.

Freshwater fish

There are 36 species of fish and freshwater crustaceans in Tasmania, including three types of trout, eels, perch, lamprey, whitebait, carp, giant freshwater lobster and Tasmanian crayfish.

There are ten species of galaxia, all unique to Tasmania, although the genus is found elsewhere in Australia and the southern hemisphere. **Pedder galaxia** (*Galaxias pedderensis*) is Australia's rarest freshwater fish, found only in Lake Pedder and its tributaries in the southwest. It was reportedly common in the early 1970s before the lake was created for a huge hydro-electricity scheme, but the population fell fast as the waters rose to form the new lake, and not one specimen has been found in this region since 1996. To save the species from extinction, 31 individuals were moved to a nearby lake in 1991–92 and recent surveys by the Inland Fisheries Service have confirmed that a small breeding population has established itself there and is doing well. The species is one of three that are threatened and protected under state and federal legislation.

A cousin is the **climbing galaxias** (*Galaxias brevipinnis*), which has large pectoral and pelvic fins that enable it to climb over rocks in streams. As a result it is found in the upper reaches of rivers beyond the barriers that prevent other species from moving upstream. It is about 20cm long with large fins low on its body.

Marine life

Tasmania's sea life is as rich as that on land, thanks mainly to the pristine waters surrounding it. The Southern Ocean that wraps around Antarctica suffers much less pollution than seas nearer to the world's human populations. **Australian fur seals** frolic in the surf. The male is dark grey-brown and the female more ginger-brown, with hints of silver. The fur seal is found lazing on 'haul-outs' – rocky islands and exposed reefs, especially on the north coast, notably near Stanley, but also on the southeast coast of Bruny Island. It eats cuttlefish, squid, octopus, redbait, mackerel and leather jacket fish. Where there are seals there are usually sharks, and Tasmania has no shortage of them.

White pointers (or Great Whites) and **whalers** cruise the temperate oceans. They are rarely seen on the surface and those keen for an encounter must don scuba-diving gear. Shark attacks are rare in Australian waters but it pays to heed the warnings.

Tasmania is also en route for migrating **whales**. There are regular sightings of southern right, humpback and pilot whales. Southern rights, especially, are seen most often in May and June as they head north to warmer waters to escape the southern winter, and again from September to November as they return. They tend to favour the east coast and often swim right into estuaries and bays. The Derwent estuary at Hobart and Great Oyster Bay have both been visited, but also the Tamar estuary at George Town on the north coast.

There are numerous whale-watching tours available but it is worth checking to see if all of them recognise and follow the environmental code which requires watchers and their vessels to keep a distance (see *Minimal Impact*, page 90).

Bottlenose and common dolphins play off the coast. Again, the wonderful island of Bruny is a good spot from which to watch them.

You are most likely to spot sea dragons while snorkelling in the marine reserves at Governor Island, Tinderbox and Ninepin Point, but if you want to stay on dry land take a visit to Seahorse World at Beauty Point on the north coast (see *Chapter 11*, page 220).

The following fish are all found in Tasmanian waters: southern bluefin tuna, East Australian salmon, flounder, sole, parrotfish, black bream, yellow-eyed mullet, striped trumpeter, blue warehou, bearded rock cod, and squid and octopus. The **giant Tasmanian crab** can grow to 45cm across. It is hard to see unless you are diving, so take a quick tour of the Stanley Fish warehouse in Stanley (see *Chapter 10*, page 197) where they, and some equally vast lobsters, are kept in tanks.

FLORA

Roughly 2,000 native species of flowering plants are known to exist in Tasmania. More than 200 of those are endemic. The origins of many plants can be traced back to the time of Gondwana (at least 100 million years ago) when Tasmania was connected to what are now Antarctica, New Zealand and South America. Similar species have been found in these other regions. However, many species have long since vanished and we know of their existence only through fossils found in Antarctica. Related species still exist, in particular the endemic Tasmanian deciduous **beech** (*Nothofagus gunnii*). Other modern-day plant relatives include **man ferns** (*Dicksonia antarctica*), **myrtle** (*Nothofagus cunninghamii*), **creeping pine** (*Microcachrys tetragona*), **Huon pine** (*Lagarostrobus franklinii*), and **celery-top pine** (*Phyllocladus aspleniifolius*).

At that time Tasmania was also part of the Australian land mass so other species resemble those on mainland Australia.

Botanists split the island up into six distinct climate zones: montane (including alpine and sub-alpine), temperate rainforest, wet sclerophyll (forests with hard, stiff leaves), dry sclerophyll, coastal heath, and wetlands (including river banks).

Some species occur in more than one zone, depending on the soil types which range from deep, well-drained soils in the northwest and northeast or fertile soils

TALL TREES

Arborists are always finding taller trees but these are the current top six:

White gum 89m (292ft) at Evercreech Forest Reserve, about 12 miles southwest of St Helens, east coast.

Swamp gums 96.5m (317ft) unverified reading for one at the Andromeda Reserve recorded in November 2001. Also 88m (289ft) at Andromeda Reserve (it was 99m (325ft) before its top was blown off in 1962), 90m (295ft) at Big Tree Reserve, 88m (289ft) at Lawrence Creek Reserve, and 87m (285ft) at Big Tree Reserve.

Andromeda, Big Tree, and Lawrence Creek reserves are around the Styx Valley region, halfway between New Norfolk and the Lake Gordon-Lake Pedder area.

in the midlands and north, to shallow, acidic and infertile soils in the southwest. Other species are widespread throughout the island. Spring and summer are the best seasons to see Tasmania's flora at its best.

The two **beech** species are also found in New Zealand, New Caledonia, Papua New Guinea and southern South America.

The **deciduous beech** (*Nothofagus gunii*) grows in the western and southern mountain areas, with good examples at Mount Field National Park and Dove Lake at Cradle Mountain. Its crinkle-edged leaves change to red and golden brown in the autumn (April to May). The **myrtle beech** (*Nothofagus cunninghamii*) inhabits wet gullies in rainforests, mainly in the west of the state. There are good examples along the Enchanted Walk at Cradle Mountain and at Russell Falls in Mount Field National Park.

More than 30 **eucalyptus** varieties grow in Tasmania. In the mountains you will see the striking, smooth white bark and yellow and red branches of the **Tasmanian snow gum** (*Eucalyptus coccifera*). The wet sclerophyll forests of the northeast and the central plateau are home to the **gum-top stringybark** or **mountain white gum** (*Eucalyptus delegatensis*). It too has white bark but much rougher than its sub-alpine cousin. It is one of the favoured hardwoods, being sold as mountain ash. The most impressive of all the Tasmanian eucalyptus family is the **swamp gum** or **giant eucalyptus** (*Eucalyptus regnans*) which is the tallest flowering plant in the world, growing to 100m (329ft). The California redwoods beat it, but they are coniferous and do not have flowers.

There is much debate about the logging of these trees (see *Conservation*, page 94). For some great examples, head for the Styx Valley.

In dry sclerophyll is the **blue gum** (*Eucalyptus globulus*) which provides the floral emblem of Tasmania. The **white gum** (*Eucalyptus viminalis*) is also common throughout eastern Tasmania. Both have rough bark collars on their lower trunks, with a smooth white and grey streaked surface extending to the branches and canopy.

The **pines** are the only trees that come close to the height of the eucalypts. Four species are endemic to Tasmania: the **King Billy pine** (*Athrotaxis selanginoides*), found usually on valley slopes, the **pencil pine** (*Sathrotaxis cupressoides*), often growing on the edges of streams, tarns and lakes, the **celery-top pine** (*Phyllocladus aspleniifolius*), which is fairly widespread, and the **Huon pine** (*Lagaros-trobos franklinii*), found in the west and in the valley of the same name, and capable of living for 3,000 years.

BUSH TUCKER

Survival in the wilds can mean a rather dull diet of berries and shoots boiled for ever in questionable river water. In Tasmania, however, bush tucker is gourmet.

The leaves of the **sassafras** tree (*Atherosperma moschatum*) smell like sarsaparilla when crushed, and spice up a cup of bush tea no end.

The sweet-smelling flowers of the **leatherwood** tree (*Eucryphia lucida*) attract bees and are important for the Tasmanian honey industry. You will see car-parks in remote mountain areas half-full of wooden, white apiaries.

Mountain pepper (*Tasmannia lanceolata*) produces berries with a hot, peppery taste that are wonderful to cook with. They add piquancy to sauces and can even be used to make liqueurs.

George Robinson recalled that the Aborigines he spent time with included a wide range of tubers, seeds, fungi, shoots and saps in what must have been a pretty tasty diet, but very few of their recipes and procedures were given to the white settlers. There is a bit of a bush tucker revival happening in Tasmania, with berries, leaves and chutneys on sale in the shops.

If you are walking in sub-alpine heathland and your hands are grubby, seek out the **lemon-scented boronia** (*Boronia citriodora*), a shrub from the orange and lemon family with pink-white flowers from December to March. When crushed, its leaves emit a beautiful lemon scent. It stands less than one metre high and is a favourite with walkers on the Overland Track and on the track to Crater Falls at Cradle Mountain-Lake St Clair National Park.

Orchids are present in lightly forested areas in spring. **Cushion plants** (*Dracophyllum*) are prevalent in mountainous areas, some the size of large beanbags. They have white flowers in spring and summer but grow close to each other for warmth during the winter to prevent their water supplies from freezing. However tempting it may be to flop down on them for a nap, they should not be touched as it can take 30 years for them to recover from one boot mark. Very good examples can be seen on the Overland Track, especially on the climb up Mount Ossa, and between Kitchen Hut and Marions Lookout at Cradle Mountain.

Clumps of **buttongrass** stretch for miles across the lower, flatter, boggy plains between the mountains of the southwestern wilderness. Bushwalkers curse them as they are tricky to walk over without spraining an ankle. Thankfully, the Parks and Wildlife Service has now engaged volunteers to construct boardwalks across some of these areas and other wetlands in the state.

My prize for the most enterprising plant goes to the **trigger plant** (*Stylidium gramini-folium*). When an insect lands and probes inside the flower for nectar it activates the stem, and a hammer-like column rises and strikes the insect, depositing pollen on its back. This is then transferred to the next plant the insect visits and the pollination problem is solved.

A personal floral favourite is the **tree fern** (*Dicksonia antartica*), which also has its historical roots in the mists of time. Fern fossils have been found in Antarctica which unquestionably link the two land masses. Some living species in Tasmania are at least 15 metres tall, and are most often found in shady glens watched over by mighty swamp gums. A good spot to walk through glades of ferns is at Notley Fern Gorge State Reserve, 24km northwest of Launceston. Another is at Hellyer Gorge State Reserve, south of Wynyard. The Murchison Highway (or A10) winds through the gorge, providing one of the most spectacular drives in the state.

Above Hiker on boardwalk on the Overland Track, at Cradle Cirque (MB)

Left More rugged terrain on the Overland Track (MB)

Above left Penguin road sign on Bruny Island (MB)

Above right Goat in shelter (MB)

Below The Cape Barren goose, *Cereopsis novaehollandiae*, can often be seen on Flinders Island. These birds are found on the Bass Strait islands; they rarely enter the water (SL)

National Parks and Conservation

NATIONAL PARKS AND RESERVES

Tasmania is ecologically pristine and diverse. Its natural abundance is aesthetically, scientifically and economically important. More than half of all visitors come to see these natural wonders and most are protected in national parks and reserves. Roughly 24,500km², or 35%, of the total land area is under some protection and managed by the Tasmania Parks and Wildlife Service in 384 parks and reserves (detailed with the relevant sections of *Part Two The Guide*). This is an area bigger than Wales and about the same size as Maryland. Few states or countries can boast such a level of protection.

World Heritage Area

About 14,000km², or 20%, of the island state (the size of Northern Ireland or a little bigger than Connecticut) is protected in a World Heritage Area that was established in 1982 and expanded in 1989. It covers the southwest sector of the state stretching from Cradle Mountain in the north to the Southwest Cape and the islands beyond. It includes the four largest national parks – in descending order, the Southwest, Franklin-Gordon Wild Rivers, Cradle Mountain-Lake St Clair, and Walls of Jerusalem. It also harbours a precious biosphere reserve.

This is one of the last temperate wilderness areas on earth, along with southwest New Zealand and the Los Glaciares region of Argentina. A fair amount is impenetrable and has only been explored by the odd wandering botanist.

There is human history here too in the form of cave paintings dating back at least 23,000 years. The ones in the Ballawinne and Wargata Mina caves are among the earliest ever found. UNESCO officials, debating whether to grant this area World Heritage status, passed it with flying colours after it satisfied more criteria for selection than any of the other 409 World Heritage Areas in the international club, and they include Mount Everest, the Great Wall of China and the Taj Mahal.

National parks

Tasmania's 18 national parks, covering 14,300km², or 21%, of the state, have the same protection as the World Heritage Area. In their own words the Parks and Wildlife department's role in the parks includes measures to

> encourage and provide for tourism, recreational use and enjoyment
> consistent with the conservation of the national park's natural and cultural
> values; to encourage cooperative management programs with Aboriginal
> people in areas of significance to them in a manner consistent with the
> purpose of reservation and the other management objectives; and to
> preserve the natural, primitive and remote character of wilderness areas.

Many of the parks have a well-documented history that describes Aboriginal life and settlement by Europeans in the 19th century, as well as exploration and the

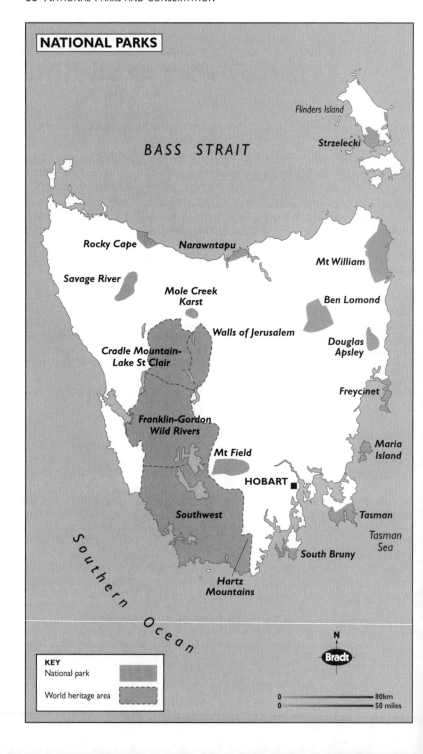

industries that followed it. Some parks contain Aboriginal middens and cave paintings, while others still retain the remains of huts, mines and the rusting debris of long-dead freight railways.

Many later settlers from Europe saw in the pristine areas of Tasmania how their own continent might once have looked before the industrial revolution, and they began to fight to save it from overdevelopment and scarring. They formed walking clubs, where like-minded people could get together with a common goal to enjoy and campaign for the environment. Tasmania's conservation movement was born. A few generations on, their work is clear for all to see in these beautiful national parks.

National parks range in size from compact Rocky Cape National Park, at 3,064 hectares, to the giant Southwest National Park, which covers 608,000 hectares. There are numerous activities on offer, including bushwalking, camping, fishing, boating, and horse-riding. Private operators also use the parks for white-water rafting, rock climbing, abseiling, and trail riding. Each summer a host of seasonal events are staged, including beach-combing, history tours, platypus prowls, penguin-watching, and rock pool hikes. Rangers patrol the parks to help and inform walkers, as well as giving talks on wilderness navigation, minimal impact bushwalking, and identifying flora and fauna.

Reserves

These areas come under different categories and also offer many outdoor activities. They are split into state reserves, conservation areas, game reserves, historic sites and Aboriginal sites, and each have different protection and forms of recreation. There are 55 state reserves, 71 nature reserves and 133 conservation areas which have different levels of protection. Oddly, mining is possible in conservation areas. The Parks and Wildlife Department's brief for all these includes measures to conserve natural biological diversity. Forest reserves are managed by Forestry Tasmania, a former government department and now a private company. All four marine reserves have been created to conserve the island's fascinating and important marine life. These clean seas provide perfect sites for species to breed and also offer great opportunities for tourists to dive in and watch the colourful displays, and for scientists to study behaviour and health. The main marine reserves are along the north of Maria Island (1,500 hectares), Ninepin Point at the mouth of the Huon River (60 hectares), around Governor and Alligator islands off Bicheno (60 hectares), and at Tinderbox, south of Kingston (45 hectares). A marine reserve was declared at Macquarie Island in July 2000 (7,500 hectares). Marine reserves are run jointly by the Parks and Wildlife Service and the Department of Primary Industry and Fisheries who agreed in August 2001 to undertake the identification and selection of new marine-protected areas, including possibly the area around Port Davey and Bathurst Harbour in the far southwest and the Kent group of islands which have been on the agenda for some years.

Walking

Tasmania's national parks, reserves and other areas of outstanding beauty contain more than 2,000km of walking trails. They range from gentle half-hour strolls to waterfalls through tree fern glades and eucalyptus forests to five-day walks along snow-white beaches and gruelling ten-day hikes over barren, testing terrain. Some of the shorter, easier ones can accommodate wheelchairs. Long and short walks are dealt with in detail in their geographically relevant sections, as are official 4WD (four-wheel drive) tracks.

Fees

A fee is charged for entry to all national parks and some reserves, with all monies raised going towards maintenance of the park. Visitors can buy a 24-hour pass for one vehicle and up to eight passengers for $9.90 per vehicle. If you're touring on foot, by bicycle, with a motorbike or as part of a coach tour, you need only pay $3.30 for the same single-day access.

A better deal is to spend $33 on a pass that allows entry for a vehicle and eight passengers to all national parks for two months. Visitors not in cars pay $13.20 each for the same access.

Passes can be bought from the ranger stations or information desks at bigger national parks and from Tasmanian Visitor Information Service. When planning your trip, it might be advisable to ask your travel agent, or any people you are dealing with directly in Tasmania, to get one sorted out for you and your party, so that it is ready when you arrive.

Rules and restrictions

All national parks and reserves have restrictions to help protect these fabulous areas and their flora and fauna from damage by pollution, introduced species or physical destruction. They are worth reading as rangers do patrol the parks and can impose fines on visitors who do not comply with the regulations. For example, lighting a fire in a 'fuel stove only' zone will cost you $5,000.

But there is more you can do to minimise your impact on Tasmania. It takes a little more effort and may involve some unfamiliar behaviour, but it is worth it to keep this wilderness paradise as pristine as possible.

MINIMAL IMPACT

More and more hotels and lodges are producing environmental statements which list how they minimise impact to their surroundings and increase awareness among their guests. Some good examples are at the Bay of Fires and on the Freycinet Peninsula, where lodges have won both state and national awards for environmentally conscious tourism. Sensitive vegetation and Aboriginal middens were avoided when building, and re-vegetation was done with native species. Some lodges clean their showers with vinegar and bicarbonate of soda rather than detergents, standing bush camps operate greywater programmes which remove from national parks every bit of waste, including human waste. Solar energy is used where possible, and much recycling is done.

When booking bush accommodation in Tasmania, ask for environmental statements to see how much your chosen lodge or country hotel does to preserve its natural surroundings.

It has taken years of campaigning and dogged work to preserve Tasmania's wild areas in the beautiful and pristine state they are in today. Tasmania's Parks and Wildlife department and Tourism Tasmania are serious about protecting them for the future and encourage you when out in the wilds to follow their country code. It is probably the strictest set of rules and suggested guidelines you will have come across in a national park or area of outstanding beauty, but the rules are not hard to follow and will greatly improve your enjoyment of the state, and that of your fellow visitors.

Stick to the track

Parts of a number of tracks, especially the long-distance walks in the World Heritage Area, consist of raised boardwalks or 'duckboards' which are superb both for protecting plants and animals, and saving walkers' ankles.

Where there are no duckboards, stay to the middle of the track as much as possible (if it is wide) to limit further trampling of verges. A healthy fear of snakes should be enough to deter most people from straying from the path.

If you have to leave the track to dig a bush toilet (see below, page 92) tread carefully.

If there is no track and you are in a party, do not walk in single file but spread out to minimise damage along one walking line. I have seen walkers trying to create a track where they felt there should be one. It sounds like a good idea to help out your fellow walkers but in fact is illegal and carries a fine. Avoid rare or sensitive vegetation such as sphagnum bogs and cushion plants. No matter how tempting they might be to sit on, they can take up to 30 years to recover from even a boot step. If you plan to walk in a party of more than six, contact the Parks and Wildlife Service first for more information about limiting habitat destruction.

Wildlife care

Do not interfere with, or cause stress to, any wildlife or pick or damage any plants. Do not feed wildlife at all; they have more than enough in this abundant place and it will off-set their natural feeding cycles. They can easily develop diseases such as lumpy jaw which can be fatal, and many animals scratch and bite when grabbing food from human hands. If you find injured wildlife and are within a day's walk of a ranger station, report it when you get there. If the ranger station is in the opposite direction, mention the injury and the animal's location to someone you pass heading that way and get them to report it. However, to be honest, distances are so large out here that the chances are that injured wildlife will not make it; it is a hazard of living in a wilderness area. Never put your own life at risk for an injured animal.

When viewing penguins at night, always wear dark clothing to blend in with your background, stay on any marked tracks or walkways, and ensure your torch is covered by a red filter of some sort. Some tour operators supply them but you can make one very easily with some red cellophane or use a red camera lens filter. Torch light damages their eyes. Also, don't take flash photographs of penguins. The flash bulb is harmful to them, you will scare them off, and – take it from a professional photographer – the pictures never turn out that well anyway unless you've got several flash bulbs strategically placed with trip switches. Wait until daylight or buy a postcard. The rules on approaching wildlife vary, but a distance of at least 500m must be kept from an eagle's nest.

When whale-watching, all craft (including surfboards and kayaks) must keep at least 100m distance. If the whale has a calf, that distance increases to 200m. A strict 'no wake' speed must be adhered to from 300m. Jet skis must not approach closer than 300m at any time and must keep to a no wake speed within 400m. Swimmers must stay 30m away. Aircraft, including *ultralights* and hang-gliders, must not be operated less than 300m from a whale; helicopters are restricted to 400m. Dolphins are faster and less likely to get stressed by human contact but still keep your distance.

It is unlikely you would want to get close to a seal. In the water they are shark magnets and on land can get aggressive. For both these reasons, never get between seals and the water.

Keep it clean

The microscopic root rot fungus, *Phytophthora cinnamomi*, is present in Tasmania and is transmitted in mud or soil and can kill native plants. To help stop its spread, make sure all equipment likely to touch the ground or undergrowth (boots, gaiters, socks, tent-pegs, groundsheets, etc) are clean when you first stride out on a walk, and at the end wash them all, preferably in sea water.

Litter

All visitors to the World Heritage Area and national parks must carry out with them everything they carry in unless they can find waste bins en route; this includes all food, wrappers, condoms, tampons, cigarette butts, etc. A good motto is to leave an area in an even better condition than you found it. There are few, if any, garbage facilities on tracks. If you see litter, by all means curse your irresponsible fellow visitor, but also do the decent thing and pick it up.

Bush toilets

There are composting toilets at cabins and campsites – be sure to throw down a cup of oats afterwards to aid composting. They are provided in a bucket. If toilets are not available, walkers should strictly speaking carry all human waste with them to the nearest one, although this is a big ask for many who might not be used to camping and walking in such pristine areas, so the bush toilet is the next best thing. The bush toilet can be a relatively straightforward procedure on fine days but the arts of balance and poise come into their own in a downpour or blizzard or when confronted with wildlife at an awkward moment. Take your trowel or spade, walk 100m away from any water source and the track or camp ground, dig a hole about half a foot deep, and bury your waste and the toilet paper. This is to reduce the occurrence of the intestinal infection giardiasis that affects all mammals, including humans. In snow, dig down to the ground level and then half a foot further.

Camping

Most campsites on long-distance tracks have wooden cabins that can sleep anything from six to 14 people. If they are full on arrival, pitch your tent in a well-used area – this will limit habitat destruction and the chances are they will be a lot flatter and more comfortable. Some sites have raised wooden platforms with metal hooks to clip guy ropes to which should be used, again to limit harm to the ground. Try to wear sandshoes and limit your movements around the campsite to prevent more ground damage (they are easier on the tired old feet as well). Make one trip to get all water needed for the night, then one trip to wash yourself and your dishes. Finally, have a thorough check of your camping area before you leave in the morning to see you have not inadvertently dropped something.

Cooking

When cooking, always use barbecue or camp-fire sites that are provided. Never light a fire anywhere else. Bushfires spread rapidly through these forests (see *Safety*, page 41). If you do have to light a fire, keep it small (less than one metre square), use only fallen dead wood, and make completely sure it is out before you head for bed or leave the area. At times of high fire danger (usually hot and windy days in summer), do not light fires, even in designated spots. The World Heritage Area and some national parks and other areas have been declared Fuel Stove Only areas. Camp-fires are completely banned and fines apply of up to $5,000. Instead, take with you a gas burner or bush stove; they are much easier to light and cook with, and you will be sitting back and eating your supper a long time before anyone who has opted to scramble around in the undergrowth for firewood. Try to cook on tent platforms or stones as some vegetation has trouble recovering from scalding by pots and stoves. Keep all food covered to keep away flies and boil all stream or lake water for at least five or ten minutes.

Washing and washing-up

This should be done with hot water only and an absolute minimum of detergent, which can harm fish and other water life. You will probably only be a few days' walk from a ranger station or information booth where you can give your pots and pans a good, soapy soak at the end of your hike. Use biodegradable soap for personal washing and try to do without toothpaste (or keep the waste in a small container to dispose of later). Do not wash up or wash your body in streams or lakes but rather take water in buckets and wash 50 metres away, allowing the waste water to be filtered through the earth before it returns to the source.

Mountain biking

Bikers are asked to keep their party size small to minimise impact and to pay particular attention to the cleanliness of their machines. The root rot fungus *Phytophthora cinnamomi* is not above hitching a ride on a patty of mud stuck to a bike pedal, so start the ride with clean equipment and wash it all down again when you finish. Walkers and horse riders have the right of way on shared trails and bikers should stop and wait for them to pass.

Ride only on approved trails, try to keep the wheels in the middle of the track, and avoid riding in very muddy or wet conditions to protect vegetation.

Four-wheel driving

Before you turn the key make sure you have all relevant maps. Notices on track closures can be found in local newspapers but, to be sure, check with local land managers or park rangers. Make sure your vehicle is clean to prevent the spread of root rot fungus. Stick to existing tracks, and use existing entry and exit points when crossing streams and creeks, and when bridges and culverts are not available. Try to avoid tracks with gradients of more than 30° on erodible soils and during wet weather.

Obey track closures and regulatory signs, try to avoid winching from trees (and if necessary use protective padding), and use wheel chains as a last resort only.

On beaches, enter and exit at existing points, stick to damp sand below the high tide mark where there are no nests or scrapes (especially in spring), drive on dunes only when expressly allowed and when you do so avoid vegetated dunes. Recently, a number of tyre-tracks have been found driving right across culturally sensitive and archaeologically important Aboriginal sites, mainly midden collections near shorelines. Most are marked on maps, and drivers are asked to consult these and abide by laws restricting access. Middens are hard to see from behind the wheel but are made up of half-buried piles of seafood shells.

Snorkelling and diving

Marine reserves operate under the same rules as national parks and land reserves. You are welcome to spend as long as you like observing, but collecting or harming any living or dead plants, animals or other natural material is forbidden. Fishing is not allowed in the reserve but usually there are good spots nearby. Garbage, especially plastic, can trap, injure and kill fish and other marine creatures. It is illegal to dump any garbage at sea anywhere in Australia.

Disease free

You will have cleared customs and immigration at your first Australian port of call, even if you were there only long enough to change planes, so you will be familiar with the country's strict quarantine laws. Australia is an almost disease-free continent and the authorities are determined to keep it that way. You may be surprised then to find on arrival in Tasmania that you are checked again by quarantine officials and possibly dogs. Make life easier for them and you by declaring all plants and foodstuffs, including airline or ferry food, and putting it in the bins provided. Anglers must not bring in any live bait and must clean their equipment before arrival.

Follow all the rules and guidelines above. For more information on minimal impact tourism in Tasmania, contact the Parks and Wildlife Service who have brochures (tel: 6233 2669; fax: 6223 8308; email: tracks@dpiwe.tas.gov.au). Drivers should ask for the *Cruisin' without Bruisin'* brochure produced by Parks and Wildlife, Tourism Tasmania and the Tasmanian Recreational Vehicle Association (tel: 6343 0318 or 6244 5290). This has 24 well-described driving trails covering the state and ranging from easy to hard. Trailbikers can get hold of the *Ride Around Tasmania* booklet from Service Tasmania outlets.

CONSERVATION

There is a conservation debate raging in Tasmania that has caught the attention of thousands of Australians and people overseas, and earned the island international headlines. Conservationists want some areas with partial protection reclassified to allow fuller, if not total, protection, predominantly to save forests from logging, and more areas currently not under any protection to be awarded some. They argue that logging, hydro-electric production and mining have already devastated large unprotected areas of beauty and importance so measures should be put in place to ensure this does not happen again.

The forestry industry says it is crucial to the economy of Tasmania and, with almost a quarter of the state fully protected, logging should be allowed to continue at current rates. With almost all of the state's power coming from hydro sources, that industry needs to do little to prove its importance. Mining is virtually finished in Tasmania.

Forestry

The Wilderness Society are campaigning to save several areas of Tasmanian forest. One is the Styx Valley near Maydena, west of Hobart, which is the home of the island's tallest trees. In November 2001 a new record was set with the measurement of a swamp gum (*Eucalyptus regnans*) in the valley's Andromeda Reserve at 96.5m. If verified by forestry officials, it will be the tallest hardwood tree on earth, but its future is in doubt as the reserve has no formal protection.

The Styx Valley is part of a 500km² area of native forest approved for clearing across Tasmania for agriculture and plantations. It is an enclave of the white goshawk, black cockatoo, pygmy-possum, sugar glider, and the threatened wedge-tailed eagle. Fewer than 100 pairs of 'wedgies' are known to survive.

According to Forestry Tasmania it is being logged for sawlogs (24%) and a few veneer logs (1%) but mainly lucrative woodchips (75%) which are exported to Japan. The gums are estimated to be worth more than $275 million in total, and they could almost all vanish as only 15% of the 190km² valley is legally protected.

Loggers chainsaw and remove the largest trees and then drag metal cables through the forest, decapitating everything else. With them die tree ferns, mosses and lichens, their resident fauna, and any as yet unclassified insect species.

The land is then scorched with incendiary devices in preparation for new plantations which are surrounded with poison to kill off displaced wildlife that might try to eat the new shoots. Almost three-quarters of these giant trees have gone since the first British colony on Tasmania was founded 250 years ago. Only 13% of the tallest, oldest trees remain.

The Styx Valley is expected to lose another three square miles of virgin, old-growth forest in the next three years according to Forestry Tasmania.

But the state also has books to balance. It is not rich, and forestry is the second biggest employer in the state in terms of contribution to GDP ($1billion a year), and it employs 6,000 directly and another 20,000 in related industries. The Wilderness Society contest some of these figures. The company says it is promoting sustainable forestry and saving jobs. Both state and national governments back the industry, with the federal government recently giving $110 million to develop exports.

Forestry Tasmania argues that with 35% of Tasmania protected in national parks and reserves and 76% of forests still standing, logging the Styx is a small price to pay. On paper, Forestry Tasmania has admitted 'tall tree biology and tourism values in the Styx area have been recognised for decades'. The company also vows to promote the development of a 'statewide tourism strategy for tall tree appreciation'.

Hydro

Hundreds of square miles of land have been flooded since the 1960s when the Gordon project was begun. The two biggest hydro schemes, Lake Gordon and Lake Pedder, cover about 388km^2 and 259km^2 of land respectively, containing a combined total of almost 12,000 cubic metres of water when full. The Gordon is estimated to hold 27 times the amount of water contained in Sydney Harbour. Lake Pedder was created after a seven-year campaign by environmentalists failed and the area was flooded in 1972.

Both are now in the World Heritage Area but were in unprotected areas when dammed. Another huge lake would now cover the Franklin River Valley if it had not been for the Franklin River blockade.

Mining

Mining takes up less space (there is little opencast) but has resulted in some major environmental destruction and pollution, especially in the west and most notably around Queenstown. Hills that were once densely forested resembled a moonscape after more than two million tonnes of timber were taken to fuel the blast furnaces of the Mount Lyell mine smelters.

Those that were left standing were killed by tonnes of acid rain that fell during a century of toxic emission from the industry.

Water courses downstream are to this day deeply contaminated with heavy metals. Just about every living thing between Queenstown and the mouth of the King River in Macquarie Harbour has suffocated. In 1969–70 the smelters closed and in December 1994, after 101 years of continuous mining, the Mount Lyell Mining and Railway Company closed the mine. A year later, Copper Mines of Tasmania took on the lease and re-opened the mine but its future is probably bleak as the price of copper is not healthy. Tourism is seen by many as a viable and longer-term option. Over time the bare, scarred flanks have become a tourist attraction and recent attempts to replant trees were fiercely contested. Some reports spoke of people tearing out saplings in the middle of the night.

A future in green tourism?

Environmentally responsible tourism might provide some answers. Tourism Tasmania's surveys have found more than half the island's half a million annual

THE FRANKLIN STORY

The central pillar of the conservation movement is Dr Bob Brown, a Green senator to the federal parliament, who has fought both the loggers and the dammers and continues to lobby for tougher environmental laws.

He led a huge protest against the damming of the Franklin River in 1982. The government authority in charge of electricity, the Hydro-Electric Commission (HEC), had planned to dam the river and flood thousands of hectares of forest to create a lake and a hydro plant. Brown and a horde of protestors, including the well-known British botanist and campaigner, Professor David Bellamy, paddled up river from Strahan to blockade the machinery. More than 1,500 people were arrested, including Brown and Bellamy (who spent his birthday in jail), and the huge protest was reported round the world. As a result of the efforts of Brown's Wilderness Society in the Franklin, it became a national campaign organisation and now lobbies on a wide range of issues. Brown takes up the Franklin story...

> After six years of increasing contention, the Labor Premier of Tasmania, Doug Lowe, who wanted to save the Franklin River, was dumped on November 11 1981. In the 'choose your dam site' referendum a month later, 33% of Tasmanians put a defiant 'No Dams' on their ballot papers. The Hydro-Electric Commission's favoured Franklin Dam failed to get a majority vote and the alternative dam site was also rejected. Then the Australian Labor Party whip, Mary Willey, joined Mr Lowe in resigning from Labor and forcing a state election which resulted in a change of government . In May 1982 the bulldozers rolled into the Franklin Valley forests. The Wilderness Society, fearing this outcome, had secretly been planning a peaceful blockade of the dam site in the wilderness forests on the Gordon River, just below its junction with the Franklin. In December, on the day the UNESCO committee in

visitors come primarily to view wildlife in wild places. The industry is growing as the number of operators and activities increases and the volume of visitors rises. Some wild places could now begin to be priced not in terms of their temporary worth to logging but instead in terms of their continued value to nature tourism.

David Bellamy sees this as the way to go. 'Tourism is the world's biggest industry and Tasmania is a major location on the eco-tourism map,' he said.

> Tourists come to see big trees, the biggest in the southern hemisphere, not great piles of woodchips destined to offshore all the profits and all the jobs to Japan. Australia has one of the world's worst records of extinction of mammals and of per capita production of greenhouse gases. At the round of Kyoto deliberations in The Hague it was stated that the carbon store in old growth forests can be used for carbon trading. So for all these reasons the time has come to stop trashing one of Tasmania's key resources.

Currently there are also plans for a major wetlands strategy supported by the state government's Department of Primary Industries, Water and Environment, and Natural Heritage Trust, and this could incorporate tourism. Wetlands are

Paris declared the wilderness a World Heritage Area, the blockade began. Hundreds of citizens from all over Australia (and 50 or so from overseas including Britain, the USA and Germany) descended on 'Greenie Acres', a tent village set up in Strahan. In the ensuing two months, 1,500 were arrested for blocking machinery in the forests or as equipment was barged up river from Strahan. Around 600 were jailed for refusing bail conditions instructing them not to return to the dam site. Hobart's major prison, Risdon, was crammed, enabling wardens to get a pay rise after they threatened strike action. A counter-protest was mounted in the nearby mining city of Queenstown. The arrest of David Bellamy made front-page headlines in Fleet Street. In February the Australian Prime Minister, Malcolm Fraser, whose offer of $500 million to Tasmania to halt the dam was spurned, called a national election. In Australia's biggest ever environmental protest, 15,000 people turned out in Melbourne and 21,000 crammed the streets of Hobart chanting 'NO DAMS' and 'LET THE FRANKLIN RUN FREE!' It was a major national election issue and on March 5 1983 Labor Party leader, Bob Hawke, who had promised to stop the dam, swept to power. The new Tasmanian state government challenged his authority. In July 1983, in a split High Court decision (four judges to three) the federal power to uphold the World Heritage convention was upheld and the dam work (then costing $60 million) was halted forever. Today, Strahan is the one prosperous centre for investment and job creation in western Tasmania. It is dependent on its tourism industry taking 120,000 visitors each year to see the wilderness, which so nearly became a casualty of a dam. And the Franklin River (one of the world's great rafting adventures, with its ancient Huon pines, platypuses, tumbling rapids and magnificent gorges and tributary waterfalls) flows free to the sea.

popular with tourists as they provide such rich environments for birds. It is estimated that about half of Australia's wetlands have been lost since the first settlement of Sydney Cove in 1788. In Tasmania, surveys to date covering about half of the state have reported that 51% of remaining wetlands have been disturbed and 12% severely disturbed. The degradation and loss of wetland areas has directly impacted on biodiversity. In Tasmania, 14 species of freshwater plant, 76 species of freshwater animals and more than 30 riverine plant species are considered threatened.

At sea

In the oceans two major eco-conflicts are flaring. More and more fishing fleets scour these waters each year for tuna and Patagonian toothfish. Some are legal and have catch quotas; many are not and fish indiscriminately. This unregulated or pirate fishing is gradually diminishing species that play essential roles in the ocean food chain and over time could quite seriously upset the ecological balance.

Just as alarming are the whaling fleets. Conservationists, and some governments, have for years been wrangling with the whaling industry to stop all killing and demarcate the Southern Ocean as a whale sanctuary. Australia has been at the forefront of this campaign in recent years. The fleets still come, however, and take a quota of southern right whales each year under the auspices of 'experimental fishing'.

There is also concern that longline fishing for tuna is hurting populations of albatross and other sea birds who inhabit Tasmania and its outer islands, notably Macquarie, 1,500km southeast of Hobart. These giant global travellers (with the widest wingspans in the bird world at around two metres) swoop down on baits laid out for tuna, get snagged on the lines and drown.

Sassafras

Part Two

The Guide

White-footed dunnart

Hobart

Tasmania's capital city lies at the mouth of the Derwent River in the southeast of the state. It is Australia's most southerly capital and one of the most southerly settlements in the world, making it a key base for the Antarctic research community. Its equivalent latitude in the northern hemisphere runs through the Côte d'Azur in the south of France and the Great Lakes of North America, and its population of 194,200 enjoys a mainly mild climate all year with low rainfall. It is the second driest state capital after Adelaide in South Australia, and is is blown clean by some of the freshest winds and waves in the world.

Hobart is protected from big westerly weather systems by Mount Wellington (1,270m) rising behind it and a spit of land called South Arm to the south and east. It is a small city, full of elegant stone cottages and cosy pubs, packed with history and culture, and blessed with good restaurants, cafés, hotels and guesthouses. It makes a perfect centre for a mini-break from the mainland or for exploring the rest of the state on a longer holiday. Tourism here has blossomed and there is almost too much to do, which makes any stay invigorating. In spring, the parks and gardens are full of flowers and the first of many festivals begins. Summer brings long, sunny days, alfresco meals by the harbour and impromptu performances by street entertainers in Salamanca Place. Autumn days can be balmy and pleasant, the trees turn golden yellow and the harbour begins to fill up with returning Antarctic research ships, back in port to sit out the wild winter weather further south. Winter days are usually cool and crisp with keen air and skies of the deepest blue, marred only by storms that blow in from the Southern Ocean with alarming speed.

If you have been in Sydney or Melbourne for any length of time prior to your arrival in Tasmania you will notice a distinct change in pace, a warmth that the big cities sometimes lose in the rush and the crush. Hobartians have time for you, are keen to meet and chat. Most realise how crucial tourism is to Tasmania's economy, but their welcome is also an altruistic one. They are genuinely proud of their home town and keen to share it. Many have strong European family links, mainly with England and Ireland, and, with the steady growth of the Antarctic scientific community, many nationalities are now represented here.

Hobart is a walking city. It is small enough to be able to stroll almost anywhere from your accommodation, which is especially pleasant in the summer evenings when you can wander through the parks and along the harbour and wonder how you are going to break the news to your family and friends back home that you have decided to relocate here permanently. There are plenty of organised walking tours to join to get the full history of the place.

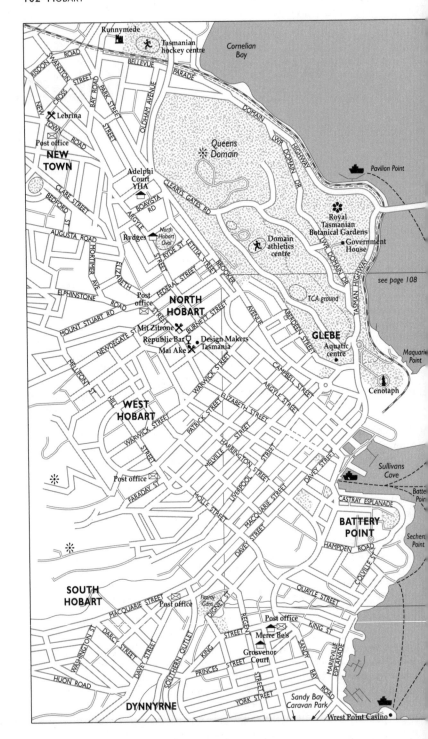

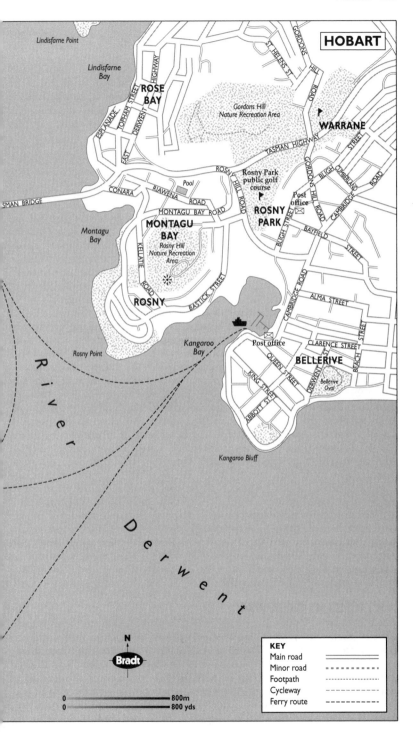

HOBART

Lindisfarne Point

Lindisfarne Bay

ROSE BAY

Gordons Hill Nature Recreation Area

WARRANE

TASMAN HIGHWAY

SMAN BRIDGE

CONARA

RIAWENA

Pool

ROAD

Rosny Park public golf course

Post office

ROSNY PARK

BAYFIELD

MONTAGU BAY ROAD

Montagu Bay

MONTAGU BAY

Rosny Hill Nature Recreation Area

CAMBRIDGE ROAD

ALMA STREET

ROSNY

BASTICK STREET

Rosny Point

Kangaroo Bay

Post office

CLARENCE STREET

BELLERIVE

QUEEN STREET

KING STREET

Bellerive Oval

ABBOTT ST

Kangaroo Bluff

River

Derwent

N

Bradt

KEY
Main road
Minor road
Footpath
Cycleway
Ferry route

0   800m
0   800 yds

Those who know other Australian cities will see a big difference in the look of Hobart. Its aspect is far more English, particularly northern English. Strolling through parts of Battery Point you could almost be in County Durham. There are terraces of solid, stone houses with slate roofs, some in crescents, small parks bordered by black iron railings, and the smell of coal and wood fires. The omnipresent corrugated iron and weatherboard constructions of the mainland are not as prevalent here. The emphasis is more on keeping warmth in rather than out.

But there will always be something to remind you that you are a long way from the northern hemisphere: a rich Aussie accent, a kookaburra calling from a eucalyptus or a glimpse of an Antarctic ice-breaker in the harbour.

HISTORY

Aboriginal people from the nomadic Moomairremener tribe lived near the site of Hobart for centuries before the Europeans arrived. They spent the winter months along the eastern shores of the Derwent River, in the areas around Gellibrand Point, living off shellfish and seaweed, and preparing tools for the coming spring hunting season inland. Later, however, this part of Tasmania would become a bloody battleground as the newly arrived European settlers imposed their might on the native population. Truganini, who died in 1876, was once believed to be the last Tasmanian Aboriginal (see box, page 10). We now know others outlived her on the Bass Strait islands and elsewhere. Their descendants are today's Tasmanian Aborigines.

Hobart was Australia's second colony settlement after Sydney, pre-dating all other cities, and hence has a rich European heritage. Van Diemen's Land had already been spied as a good spot for a tough penal colony for the worst convicts but it was an expedition by George Bass and Matthew Flinders that clinched the deal. They proved it was an island and brought back to Sydney favourable soil and vegetation samples.

The British established the first settlement at Risdon Cove, north of Hobart, in September 1803, claiming the territory for King George III. The colonists comprised 49 people of whom 24 were convicts. Within a year the new governor, Lieutenant-Colonel David Collins, decided another spot closer to the mouth of the Derwent was better than Risdon and he moved the settlement (by now a couple of hundred strong) to the current site of Hobart. The first full shipment of convicts arrived at Sullivans Cove near Hobart in 1804. Although the penal colonies were established outside Hobart, the town had one notorious clink, the Cascades Female Factory, a women's prison established in 1827 on the site of an old brewery. It was built on dank marshes and nicknamed Shadow of Death Valley.

Hobart prospered in the 19th century and became a major southern hemisphere whaling and sealing town, processing hundreds of tonnes of blubber and oil each year. After bans were introduced on those industries, the city's deep-water port became more and more important for exports of wool. More recently, tourism has taken hold in the capital and a total of 277,900 visitors came here in 2000/2001, almost a quarter of them from overseas.

ANTARCTIC GATEWAY

There is an awful lot of science going on in Tasmania and much of this is to do with its geographical position. It is a natural gateway to Antarctica. Some historians argue the first link between Tasmania and Antarctica might not have been thanks to an eminent explorer such as Cook but to the captain of a sealing boat. Captain John Briscoe cruised into Hobart on May 10 1831 on the brig *Tula* with tales of huge seas and an icy coastline. During his southern voyage with the *Tula* and the *Lively*, he named a stretch of ice Enderby Land which is now east of Australia's Mawson Base. Since then several explorers have used Hobart as a base for expeditions south, including Scott and Amundsen. In the late 1830s, Dumont d'Urville's French expedition sailed in the *Astrolabe* and the *Zelee* to the coast of George V Land. In the early 1840s, James Clark Ross took a British expedition in the *Erebus* and the *Terror* to the same coast and on to the Ross Ice Shelf. The Shelf was also reached in 1899 by another British expedition led by Carsten Borchgrerinck in the *Southern Cross*. And, in March 1912, Roald Amundsen's party returned after reaching the South Pole and cabled the news to an excited world from a Hobart post office.

Hobart now probably contains the world's largest and most diverse body of Antarctic research and education. Four organisations, all located in Hobart, are mainly responsible for Antarctic and Southern Ocean research: the Australian Antarctic Division; the University of Tasmania; the Bureau of Meteorology; and the Commonwealth Science and Industrial Research Organisation's (CSIRO) Division of Marine Science. Together with the Australian Geological Survey Organisation (AGSO), they form the Cooperative Research Centre for the Antarctic and Southern Ocean Environment (Antarctic CRC).

The Australian Antarctic Division is the federal government agency which has been responsible for the nation's Antarctic Programme since 1947. It operates four permanent research stations, three on the coast of Eastern Antarctica and one on sub-Antarctic Macquarie Island, from where it carries out its own research, as well as acting as a back-up for other organisations' projects. In its own words, its 'principal aims are to protect the Antarctic environment, to understand the role of Antarctica in the global climate system, to undertake scientific work of practical, economic and national significance, and to maintain the Antarctic Treaty System and enhance Australia's influence within that system'. The University of Tasmania runs the Institute of Antarctic and Southern Ocean Studies (IASOS), a postgraduate teaching and research department with key staff in all the major disciplines. IASOS offers a one-year Graduate Diploma with Honours plus higher research degrees (Master of Science, Master of Arts, PhD). The Bureau of Meteorology aims to improve weather predictions for high southern latitudes. CSIRO's Division of Marine Science explores the Southern Ocean and its currents to determine their influence in global climate. The Antarctic CRC is one of the world's biggest research organisations investigating polar regions. It is an independent organisation established in 1991 to investigate the large-scale interactions of the south polar region with global climate and the environment. Hobart is also the home port for Antarctic supply ships. Both Australia and France have a re-supply and research vessel based here. Australia's bright orange ice-breaker, the *Aurora Australis*, and France's smaller *L'Astrolabe* are in port most of the winter and for short periods between expeditions during the summer.

Seasoned Antarctic expeditioners live in Tasmania providing pre-expedition training in navigation, emergency shelters, first aid, communications, fire-fighting, and search and rescue. The Tasmanian Polar Network provides a single organisation from which a wide range of goods and services, and advice, can be provided to international expeditions.

Hobart is littered with reminders that south from here there is nothing until the frozen continent. There are the interactive displays at Antarctic Adventure, the rich collection of Antarctic memorabilia at the Tasmanian Museum and Art Gallery and Maritime Museum, and at historic sites such as Hadley's Hotel in Murray Street, where Roald Amundsen stayed before his successful journey to the South Pole in 1912. Such reminders can also be found at Franklin Square, where there is detail of the stories behind the 1898–1900 Antarctic Expedition, the first to spend winter on the ice.

GETTING THERE AND AROUND
By air
Qantas fly to Hobart from Adelaide, Brisbane, Cairns, Canberra, Darwin, Gold Coast, Melbourne, Perth or Sydney. Most services are not direct. Sydney–Hobart (twice daily) return fares cost from around $341 for a restricted sale fare (no changes allowed) and $418 for a 14-day advance purchase with a minimum stay (for all fares, add taxes of $28.67). Melbourne–Hobart (numerous, daily) has a restricted sale return fare of $209 and a 14-day advance purchase of $220 (add taxes of $24.74). For all reservations, call 13 13 13 in Australia or book through travel agents or online (web: www.qantas.com.au).

Ansett, Australia's second carrier, was temporarily shut down in September 2001. A rescue package put together by two Australian businessmen did not manage to save the airline. All mainline flights were suspended from midnight on Monday March 4 2002. Flights from the mainland to Tasmania operated by regional airline Kendell are still running. Previous flight prices (all exclusive of taxes) for these sectors were : Sydney–Hobart (daily via Melbourne) costs from $176 one-way; Melbourne–Hobart (daily) from $88 one-way; Brisbane–Hobart (daily via Sydney) $253 one-way. Also daily flights from Melbourne to Burnie/Wynyard (from $214.50 return), Devonport (from $214.50 return) and five flights a week to King Island (from $93.50 return). Call 13 13 00 in Australia or check www.ansett.com.au or www.kendell.com for details.

Island Airlines Tasmania (tel: 1800 645 875; email: bobpratt@bigpond.com.au; web: www.iat.com.au) flies Launceston–Strahan–Hobart return three times a week (Tuesday, Thursday, Sunday).

From the airport
There are plenty of taxis at Hobart airport. Expect to pay around $25 one-way to the city centre. For a cheaper option, catch the Airport Shuttle, a minibus that waits for flights from Sydney, Melbourne and Adelaide and will get you into the city centre in about 15–20 minutes. It costs around $9 one-way or $16 return. Buses wait outside the terminal front entrance. Alternatively, call 1300 653 633 or 6272 6611 to book. Drops off at, and picks up from, most hotels and other points of interest in Hobart. Many rental car companies have bases there for pick-ups and drop-offs.

By sea
The only passenger boats that come in to Hobart are cruise ships and container vessels. All ferries to Tasmania arrive on the north coast.

By road
Hobart is linked with all centres in Tasmania by good sealed roads. By car, the drive between Hobart and Launceston is roughly 2½ hours, Devonport 3½ hours, Strahan 4 hours, and Port Arthur about 1¼ hours. Add half an hour to an hour each for bus times.

Buses and coaches
A number of companies run bus and coach services to and from Hobart.

TWT's Tassielink Regional Coach Service Tel: 1300 300 520; web: www.tigerline.com.au. Runs services between Hobart and most destinations,
Tasmanian Redline Coaches (**TRC**) Tel: 1300 360 000. Offer statewide scheduled bus services from Hobart. Both operate from the Transit Centre at 199 Collins St.
Hobart Coaches 4 Liverpool St; tel: 6234 4077.

See *Getting Around*, page 48, in *Chapter 2* for a full list of statewide bus and coach services.

By cab and limo
The following companies offer taxi and/or limousine services:

Airport Taxi Service Tel: 0500 579 202.
Bass Stretch Limousines Tel: 0418 882 547.
Central Cabs Tel: 131 008.
Chauffeured Cars and Coaches Tel: 6234 9444.
City Cabs Tel: 131 008.
Hobart and Southern Maxi Taxis Tel: 6227 9577.
Limousine Services Tel: 0418 132 535.
Personal Taxi Service Tel: 6224 2242.
Prestige Taxis Tel: 0418 179 202.
Taxi Combined Services Tel: 132 227.

By rental car
The following rental car companies operate in Hobart:

Autorent Hertz 122 Harrington St, Hobart 7000; tel: 6237 1111; email: mail@autorent.com.au.
Avis Tasmania 125 Bathurst St, Hobart 7000; tel: 6234 4222; fax: 6234 4190; email: avishbt@netspace.net.au. Also at Hobart airport.
Bargain Car Rentals 189A Harrington St, Hobart 7000; tel: 6234 6959; fax: 6234 6991; email: bargaincar@telstra.easymail.com.au.
Budget Rent-A-Car 96 Harrington Street, Hobart 7000; tel: 6234 5222; fax: 6231 0252; email: reservations@budgettas.com; web: www.budget.com.au.
Delta Europcar Hobart MidCity Motor Inn, Hobart 7000; tel: 6224 0822; fax: 6224 0844; email: restas@deltaeuropcar.com.au; www.deltaeuropcar.com.au.
Range/Rent-A-Bug 105 Murray St, Hobart 7000; tel: 6231 0300; mobile: 0417 398 536; fax: 6231 5017; email: rentabug@southcom.com.au.
Thrifty Car Rental 11–17 Argyle St, Hobart 7000; tel: 6234 1341; fax: 6231 2475; email: thrifty@tasvacations.com.au; web: www.tasvacations.com.au. And at Hobart airport and Sandy Bay.

By bicycle
Several companies rent bicycles by the hour, day and week. Try **Derwent Bike Hire** (Regatta Grounds, Queen Domain; mobile: 0407 342 918; fax: 6268 6654; email: bikehire@southcom.com.au) and **Cycling Adventures Tasmania** in Salamanca Square (fax: 6244 3251; email: rowanburns@hotmail.com).

WHERE TO STAY
There is a wide selection of accommodation in Hobart, but it scores highest on its mid-range bed and breakfasts which are friendly, homely and reasonable. Most are family owned, so you are assured of lots of information and chatter, and breakfasts that will keep you going until supper. There are some elegant upper-range places too, and some good hostels for those on a budget. A good number of Hobart pubs also offer rooms but check first on the live music situation in case you fancy an early night and end up with the room above the stage.

Upper range
Oakford on the Pier (and **Oakford on Salamanca**) (Elizabeth Street Pier, Hobart, TAS 7000; tel: 1800 620 462 or 6220 6600; fax: 6224 1277; email: sales.hobart@oakford.com or

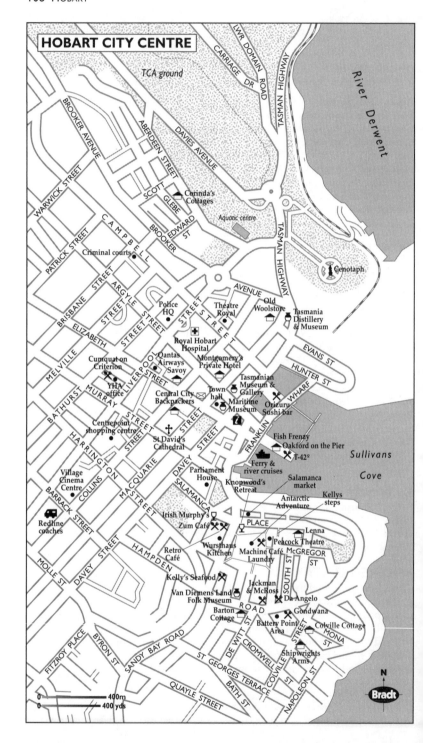

HOBART CITY CENTRE

res.hobart@oakford.com; web: www.oakford.com) is stylish, with probably the best location in town. It is right on the harbour. It offers split-level loft suites. The windows are vast and let in lots of light, and every apartment has views over the water, private laundry and kitchen facilities, air conditioning, stereo and television with free 24-hour in-house films, and mini-bars with Tasmanian wines and produce. There is a gymnasium and sauna, function centre and conference centre, serviced offices, and a café, restaurant and bar. A single-bedroom suite costs around $180 ($220 with balcony), and a family studio $235 ($255 with balcony). The hotel has opened a second property on Salamanca Place which has studio apartments for $165 and a two-bedroom suite for $275.

Moorilla Estate (655 Main Rd, Berriedale, Hobart, TAS 7011; tel: 6277 9900; fax: 6249 4093; email: wine@moorilla.com.au; web: www.moorilla.com.au) has well-appointed, self-contained chalets made from elegant Tasmanian timbers, and sweeping views over the Derwent. There is a museum of antiquities. Chalet for $250.

The Old Woolstore (1 Macquarie St, Hobart, TAS 7004; tel: 1800 814676 or 6235 5355; fax: 6234 9954; email: enquiries@oldwoolstore.com.au; web: www.oldwoolstore.com.au) won the Australian Hotels Association national award for best superior accommodation in 2001. It has 59 suites, 72 studio apartments, 80 single-bedroom apartments, six executive spa apartments and 25 two-bedroom apartments. There are numerous services, and guests get complimentary swimming passes to the Hobart Aquatic Centre and discount gymnasium passes. Apartment from $179–210, single and double; en-suite room $155, single and double; studio apartment $169, single and double.

The **Savoy** (38 Elizabeth St, Hobart, TAS 7000; tel: 6220 2300; fax: 6224 0997; email: savoyhobart@bigpond.com; web: www.savoyhobart.com.au) is in the centre of town and a 10-minute walk from Salamanca Place. It has 24 studio apartments, all with kitchen, spa bath and European furnishings. Each room has independent internet access. There is also a therapeutic bathing centre with spas, sauna, steam room, and massage and beauty treatments. Apartment $255, single and double; studio apartment $208, single and double.

Rydges (corner Argyle and Lewis Sts, Hobart, TAS 7000; tel: 6231 1588; fax: 6231 1916; email: reservations_hobart@rydges.com; web: www.rydges.com/hobart) is a good chain with efficient service and high-quality rooms. Standard suite $185; antique suite $205, (two-bedroom $240); cottage $240; presidential $280.

Moderate

Colville Cottage (32 Mona St, corner Colville St, Battery Point, Hobart, TAS 7004; tel: 6223 6968; fax: 6224 0500; email: colvillecottage@bigpond.com; web: www.colvillecottage.com.au) is an excellent place in a fine location. The mid-Victorian, National Trust-listed, weatherboard house is full of antiques, fireplaces, stained-glass windows and beautiful polished floorboards. All six en-suite rooms are at ground level which is good news for the less able and those who have just staggered off the bus after a long-distance walk with aching feet and a heavy pack. It is roughly a 10–15-minute walk from Salamanca Place and just around the corner from one of the best pubs in Hobart, the Shipwrights Arms. Hosts Louise Gerathy and Carl Hankey provide a friendly welcome and vast breakfasts, and are both mines of information on Hobart. The large number of repeat visitors proves its worth. Rooms cost $130/155 single/double. Winter rate June–August is $105/130, single/double. All rates include a full cooked breakfast daily.

Corinda's Cottages (17 Glebe St, Hobart, TAS 7000; tel: 6234 1590; fax: 6234 2744; email: info@corindascottages.com.au) were built in the 1850s in the grounds of Corinda, a grand Victorian mansion on the register of the National Estate. One was the servants' house and the other the coach-house. Antique furniture, original fittings, and tranquil gardens. A charming stay. Rates on enquiry.

Lenna of Hobart (20 Runnymede St, Battery Point, Hobart, TAS 7004; tel: 1800 030 633 or 6232 3900; fax: 6224 0112; email: admin@ausvillas.com.au or reservations@lenna.com.au) is an Italiante sandstone and brick mansion close to Salamanca Place, built in 1874 by a shipbuilder and member of the Legislative Council of Tasmania, Alexander McGregor. There are 50 en-suite rooms, and views of Mount Wellington and the River Derwent. The hotel has a baby-sitting service, business and convention facilities, and queen-size beds. En-suite rooms $145, single and double.

Grosvenor Court (42 Grosvenor St, Sandy Bay, Hobart, TAS 7005; tel: 6223 3422; fax: 6223 6344; email: grosvenorcourt@bigpond.com; web: www.view.com.au/grosvenor) is a welcoming motel with family apartments within a 15-minute walk of the city centre and Sandy Bay beach. One- and two-bedroom suites available. It is situated in a quiet area near Battery Point and surrounded by heritage properties. One-bedroom suites $119 for a double, two-bedroom suites $159 for a double.

Merre Be's (17 Gregory St, Sandy Bay, Hobart, TAS 7005; tel: 6224 2900; fax: 6224 2911; email: merrebes@bigpond.com.au; web: www.merrebes.com.au), a Victorian house in a quiet street, began life as a family home in 1884. Ground-floor accommodation, phones and faxes, en-suite or spa rooms, and king and queen beds so comfortable it is hard to extricate oneself in the morning. The breakfasts are good and the welcome friendly. $105/110–160 single/double.

Barton Cottage (72 Hampden Rd, Battery Point, Hobart, TAS 7004; tel: 6224 1606; fax: 6224 1282; email: Barton.Cottage@tassie.net.au) is another special colonial bed and breakfast but has a different style and a claim to fame. This one has a corrugated-iron roof and elegant iron tracery over the porch, and is the oldest licensed bed and breakfast in Australia. The house was built for a Captain William Wilson, who arrived here with his father in 1822. Despite being struck by lightning, he became a pioneer of the whaling industry and set up a brewery. I think I prefer him for the latter contribution. Each of the 6 en-suite rooms (including twin, double and family) is non-smoking, and has television, and tea and coffee facilities. Cooked and continental breakfasts are available. Children are welcome and cots are provided on request. Rates on enquiry.

Budget

The **Shipwrights Arms** (29 Trumpeter St, Battery Point, Hobart, TAS 7004; tel: 6223 5551; fax: 6224 8048; email: shippies@southcom.com.au) is arguably the best pub in Hobart and one of the best in Australia. It has taken a stand against the curse of 'pokies' (one-arm bandits or slot-machines) which are omnipresent throughout Australia. The Shippies has no gambling of any sort, nor live music, but it does serve fabulous Guinness, excellent steaks and fish pies. It has a few small, but homely and very reasonable, double rooms (two comfortable bunk-beds) upstairs away from the main bar, and access to a shared kitchen with cereals and milk, coffee and tea provided. There is a distinct nautical theme with photos of yachts in full sail and US navy frigates signed by visiting crews. At the end of the Sydney–Hobart yacht race between Christmas and New Year, the place is heaving with yachties. Rooms from $45–65, single and double.

Adelphi Court YHA (17 Stoke St, New Town, Hobart, TAS 7008; tel: 6228 4829; fax: 6278 2047; email: yhatas@yhatas.org.au) is a little out of town (ten minutes in a cab). It is a quiet place to stay, with two double en-suite rooms, modern heating and electric blankets, and tea and coffee. There is also space for 88 people in dorm and bunkhouse beds. Cooking facilities available. Dorm bed $19/38 single/double; double room $47/58, single/double.

Montgomery's Private Hotel (9 Argyle Street, Hobart, TAS 7000; tel: 6231 2660; fax: 6234 4450; email: engel@southcom.com.au) is in a good location 100 metres from the harbour and near the general post office, museum, bus centre and the main shopping area. There is a tour desk on site for information and reservations. There are 14 double en-suite rooms and space for 36 people in the dorms. Dorm bed $18, single only; en-suite rooms $75–89 single, $85–99 double.

At the **Central City Backpackers** (138 Collins Street, Hobart, TAS 7000; tel: 6224 2404; fax: 6224 2316; email: centralbackpackers@mbox.xom.au; web:

www.centralbackpackers.com.au) guests have use of kitchen, laundry, lounge, and bike and baggage storage. Near shops and attractions. Dorms and bunkhouse sleep 80. Single rooms are available on request. Dorm bed $18–34/$22–42 single/double.

Campsites and caravan parks

Sandy Bay Caravan Park (1 Peel Street, Sandy Bay, Hobart, TAS 7005; tel: 6225 1264) is the only one within walking distance of the city. A 15-minute walk to Salamanca and close to the water. Campervans $44; cabins $66, single and double.

If you have a bicycle then you could park across the Derwent at the **Bowen Park** site (673 East Derwent Highway, East Risdon; tel: 6243 9879) and pedal in each day. Cabins $60–70, single and double.

WHERE TO EAT

There are plenty of places to eat in Hobart, from cheap and cheerful cafés to expensive gourmet restaurants. When booking, check if they are licensed or BYO.

Upper range

At the top end of the scale you have restaurants like **Mit Zitrone** (333 Elizabeth Street; closed Sunday and Monday) which serves modern Australian cuisine (try the braised lamb, and the excellent twice-cooked poached eggs; main courses about $25). At **Gondwana** (Hampton Road and corner of Francis Street, Battery Point) everything is local. Try the seafood laksa, and the wallaby loin smoked in eucalyptus (mains about $25). **Kelly's Seafood Restaurant** (5 Knopwood Street, Battery Point) has great fish and oysters and is open on Sunday nights. **Lebrina** (155 New Town Road, New Town) has oxtail, local anchovies with a garlic and almond mayonnaise, and a superb cheese list (mains about $30).

Moderate

Moderately priced places include **T-42°** on Elizabeth Pier which has arguably the best view of any Hobart eatery. It is on the pier overlooking the harbour and tables spill out onto the waterfront in the summer. The place does great seafood (especially the tuna steaks) and salads and has a good wine list by the glass and bottle. Try a Cape Mentelle shiraz from Western Australia. It attracts locals, as well as the trendy crowd breezing in from Sydney for the weekend and pretending to be famous. Main dishes are about $20–25. **Mai Ake** at 277 Elizabeth Street in North Hobart is a good Thai restaurant. Try the tasty barbecued octopus ($5–8) and the superb Panang curry ($10–15). A glass of port for $4 is good value. If this one is full try the other numerous Thai, Indian, Chinese and Vietnamese places along this part of Elizabeth Street. **The Shipwrights Arms** (29 Trumpeter Street, Battery Point) serves high-quality pub grub. There is a wide menu, with steaks (around $15–20) and a wonderful chowder ($5–8) which is a small meal in itself, and goes well with a pint of Guinness from the bar. For those with a penchant for Japanese food, try the **Orizuru Sushi Bar** (Mures Lower Deck, Victoria Dock, Sullivans Cove) which has main dishes for $17–26 (closed Sunday).

Cafés, bistros and fish and chips

Hobart has embraced café culture. Some of the best places to hang out are the **Machine Café Laundry** at 12 Salamanca Square. There is a young crowd and breakfast is served all day or for as long as your wash takes. In summer, patrons take advantage of the courtyard. **Jackman and McRoss** (57–59 Hampden Road, Battery Point) undoubtedly offers Hobart's finest breakfast experience. The coffee is good and the pie and cake displays are tantalising. Try a frangipane tart. **Retro Café**, on the corner of Salamanca Place and Montpelier Retreat, is a good spot for lavish cooked breakfasts ($10–15) and for people-watching, and good muffins. Just up the road, another favourite among Hobartians is **Zum Café** where the salads are good. You will also find light meals available at **All Bar One** (a bar-bistro in Salamanca Square), **Da Angelo** (Italian eatery at 47 Hampden Road), and the **Republic Bar** (299 Elizabeth Street, North Hobart).

There are scores of places for fish and chips. One of the best is **Fish Frenzy** (Elizabeth Street Pier) where you get fish in brown paper cones for under $10; also try the **fish punts** at the docks where you can buy fresh fish or fish and chips (Shane's and Mako are especially good). **Cumquat on Criterion** (10 Criterion Street) is wonderful for vegetarians and vegans and those on a gluten-free diet or wanting to avoid preservatives. Breakfast of rhubarb risotto, and great laksa.

BARS AND NIGHTSPOTS

Hobart has some of Australia's finest pubs. Its climate leans towards log fires and snugs rather than to the cavernous, dusty bars in the outback or farm towns on the mainland. **Knopwood's Retreat** is possibly the most noticeable pub in town, standing on the corner of Salamanca Place and Montpelier Retreat. On Fridays after 19.00 the place fills up rapidly, and for the rest of the evening it is a fight to get to the bar. Hundreds of drinkers mill around on the pavement and roads outside in the summer. Great if you want to meet people or you are with a crowd, not the best choice for a quiet romantic drink. There is live music upstairs from Knopwood's at **Around Midnight** (open to the early hours but not on Sunday and Monday). Between the two is **Syrup**, a nightclub playing house music. Just up Salamanca Place, away from the water, is **Irish Murphy's** which is similarly popular.

For an easier drink but still with lots of character try the **New Sydney** at 87 Bathurst Street, near the corner of Elizabeth Street. This is one of the better spots for live acts. Hobart has a swinging pub scene with lots of live music. The pubs come alive during the summer festival season but put on singers, solo guitarists and bands during the winter too.

My favourite Hobart pub is the **Shipwrights Arms** (the Shippies to its regulars) at 29 Trumpeter Street in Battery Point where they have banned all gambling (machines and horses) and concentrated their efforts on creating a relaxed atmosphere and pouring what might just be the best pint of Guinness in the southern hemisphere. The pub was built in 1846 and has always been closely linked with the sea. Framed photographs of naval frigates and destroyers cover the walls, some signed by visiting crews. There are also plenty of colourful shots of yachts in full sail. The place is packed between Christmas and New Year when the yacht crews from the Sydney–Hobart race gravitate here. A local by the name of Max Eiszele has been drinking here for 44 years, an achievement that prompted the pub's owners to put in a memorial stained-glass window to honour him. It shows him in his red jumper, jeans, yellow belt and boots. Legend has it that Max thought nothing of putting in 12-hour shifts in the Shippies at least six days a week.

Republic Bar (299 Elizabeth Street, North Hobart) has great live music every night.

The Temple Place (121 Macquarie Street) has live jazz and a separate cigar lounge, and has won state entertainment-venue awards. Out of town to the north is the **Derwent Entertainment Centre** where the bigger bands play.

USEFUL INFORMATION
Tourist information
The **Tasmanian Travel and Information Centre** is on the corner of Davey Street and Elizabeth Street, near Elizabeth Pier (tel: 6230 8233; email: tasbookings@tasvisinfo.com.au).

Open December–April, Monday–Friday 08.30–17.15; Saturday/Sunday 09.00–16.00. May–November daily 09.00–13.00; public holidays 09.00–16.00. Closed Christmas Day. Also tune to 88MHz on the FM band of your radio for tourist bulletins.

Maps and books
One of the best places to pick up detailed maps of Tasmania and its regions, and in particular the long-distance walks, is in the cluster of outdoor equipment shops on Elizabeth Street, between Liverpool Street and Melville Street. These have up-to-date maps and guides essential for bushwalkers. The Tourist Travel and Information Centre on Davey Street also has some maps. Hobart has several bookshops with plenty of histories of the city and the island. One of the widest selections is at the branch of the national chain **Dymocks**, in the Centrepoint Shopping Center (tel: 6231 6656; web: www.dymocks.com.au). Also try the **Hobart Bookshop** (22 Salamanca Place; tel: 6223 1803; fax: 6223 1804) which also has second-hand books and specialises in fiction, poetry and Tasmanian and children's literature. The book and gift shop of the **Tasmanian Museum and Art Gallery** is excellent for natural history and pictorial guides, and the **Wilderness Society Shop** on Montpelier Retreat has a wide range of environmental books.

Post
There are several Australia Post offices in Hobart and all keep strict hours, opening Monday to Friday 09.00–17.00, and closing at weekends and public holidays. Stamps are also available from newsagents and some gift shops. Most larger hotels will post mail for you. Postcard stamps to the UK and the US cost $1; small letters to both cost $1.50.

WHAT TO SEE AND DO
Historical buildings
There are many historical buildings in Hobart – considering its size, possibly a greater density than in any other Australian city. One of the best ways to see them is on a walking tour. You can read up on the buildings in the library or bookshops and either conduct a tour yourself or take advantage of one of the excellent organised walks.

Most walks include a stroll along Hobart's most famous street, **Salamanca Place**, where every Saturday morning the concrete disappears under hundreds of stalls as the markets get under way. You can find pretty much anything here, including a wide range of fresh fruit and vegetables, some of them exotic.

📷 *Photo spot*
The Salamanca Markets are hard to photograph. The background is usually busy and it is hard to get a shot that later looks clear and which highlights one event or person. Walk the markets first to find your subject then return and ask to take a portrait shot. One of the best is a photo of one of the Hmong community, a migrant group who made their way here from Laos and who sell fantastic exotic vegetables. If you can crack a joke you will get a smile that is worth a thousands photos. If your character is shaded by a tarpaulin and consequently has a darker face, use a sheet of

white paper held just under his or her chin to bounce sunlight back up. If your subject is wearing a hat ask him or her to remove it or tilt the head back slightly so light gets under the brim.

The **Battery Point Heritage Walk** (tel: 6223 7570) is organised by the National Trust of Australia and gives a succinct history of old Hobart Town. Your guide will lead you along the sandstone warehouses in Salamanca Place which were once right on the waterfront before land was reclaimed to allow the design of a small park. The walk carries on through Battery Point, one of the oldest parts of the city and the home of some grand mansions and fine cottages and boatyards. The walk includes the Royal Tennis Court, St David's Park and morning tea at St George's Church (on Saturday). Group bookings are available any day except Sunday. Minimum 6 adults. Adult $10; child $2.50 (6–16 years, under 5s free); family $20.

📷 Photo spot

Arthur Circus is a pretty oval-shaped village green in the heart of Battery Point. Spring months are best, when the flowers are in full bloom. Walk down Runnymede Street and head left when you hit the circus, taking your shot looking west. You might be able to get Mount Wellington in the background. Wide angle lens is best but not too wide – say about 28mm. Try not to polarise as this will dull the flowers' colours.

The **Hobart Historic Walk** provides a good all-round history lesson on Hobart. Tours are also given in German, French, Italian, Dutch or Japanese, on request. Adult $17; pensioner and student $15; family $38; child (under 12) free. Tickets can be bought at the Tasmanian Travel and Information Centre on Davey Street. You might also like to try the **Hobart Historic Pub Tour** (tel: 6225 4806; fax: 6225 4807; mobile: 0418 991 767; email: naturtas@netspace.net.au; web: www.naturtas.com.au) which traces a timeline through Tasmania's early history, including colourful stories about the early days of the colony and the fairly major role alcohol played in its evolution. Learn about Bengal rum, the use of alcohol as a bartering tool, smuggling, and illegal brewing. The guides dress up in the garb of a 19th-century wharfie (docker) and there is a drink to be had in each pub. Adults only, $19. There are also a number of **Sandy Bay Historical Walks** (tel: 6223 6703; email: kedwards@trump.net.au). Adult $10; pensioner and student $5; child (5–14 years) $2.50; family $25.

If churches are your buildings of choice then join the **Historic Church Walking Tour** (tel: 6231 4033; fax: 6234 6947; email: office@ citycentre.tas.uca.org.au) and follow a trail around the city for two hours which includes the Scots, Memorial and Wesley Uniting churches built from 1825 to 1870. Tours leave from the Tasmanian Travel Centre on Davey Street at 09.30 every Wednesday, between December 6 and February 28. Adult $5.50; concession $4.40; child $2.50 (includes refreshments).

Runnymede (61 Bay Road, New Town, Hobart, TAS 7008; tel: 6278 1269; fax: 6278 1267; email: nat_trust@vision.net.au; web: www.austnattrust.com.au) is an elegant colonial house overlooking New Town Bay on the River Derwent. It was built around 1836 for Robert Pitcairn, the first lawyer to qualify in the new colony. He became a leading campaigner against convict transportation. A Captain Charles Bayley bought the house in 1864 and named it Runnymede after a favourite ship. The Bayleys lived here for the next 100 years. More recently the National Trust restored and furnished the house to its original elegance. The garden features many historic trees and plants including hellebores. Adult $7.70;

concession $5.50; child free if with adult; family (2 adults, 2 children) $15.40. Open Monday–Friday 10.00–16.30, Saturday/Sunday 12.00–16.30. Closed July, Christmas Day, Good Friday.

The **Penitentiary Chapel** (corner of Brisbane Street and Campbell Street) was designed by John Lee Archer and building started in 1831. It served the adjacent prison barracks and is a rare example of Georgian ecclesiastic architecture in Australia. In 1860 two wings of the building were converted to be used as criminal courts. The chapel was used until 1961 and the courts until 1983. There are underground passages, solitary cells and a yard formerly used for executions. Guided tours operate daily at 10.00, 11.30, 13.00 and 14.30. Special guided tours for parties of ten or more, and evening ghost tours (tel: 6231 0911; email: nat_trust@vision.net.au) are also available. Adult $7.70; concession $5.50; child free if with adult; family (2 adults, 2 children) $15.40. Open daily. Closed Christmas Day, Good Friday.

Museums, galleries and other sights

An excellent first stop for any new visitor to Tasmania is the **Tasmanian Museum and Art Gallery** at 40 Macquarie Street (tel: 6211 4177; fax: 6211 4112; email: tmagmail@tmag.tas.gov.au). The exhibits are informative and exciting and the staff engaging, knowledgeable and helpful. In a couple of hours you will get a wonderful précis of this island's geology, flora and fauna. There is a full history of Tasmania – information about the indigenous culture that existed here for centuries before the Europeans arrived; a solid account of the new colony and its rapid development; plenty of gory detail about the desperate conditions convicts faced in the penal centres; and lots of facts about Hobart's role as an Antarctic research centre, including information on Antarctic expedition equipment. There is a children's discovery area with lots of hands-on devices, and a rather chilling but fascinating room with models of extinct mega-fauna that once roamed the island, including a 9ft-tall kangaroo. There are also regularly changing art exhibitions in the gallery. No admission fee. Open daily 10.00–17.00. Closed Anzac Day, Christmas Day, Good Friday.

Also good is the **Tasmanian Transport Museum** (Anfield Street, Glenorchy, Hobart, TAS 7010; tel: 6272 7721; fax: 6229 7997; email: ttms@bigpond.com). The New Town Railway Station has been rebuilt at the museum and a new platform added. The station master's office and signal room have been retained and restored to their original condition. There are relics and photographs featuring the history of Tasmanian railways, and seven steam locomotives, two operational diesel-electric locomotives, two operational diesel rail cars, six carriages and numerous goods wagons. Anywhere else this would be just another railway museum but Tasmania has not one scheduled train passenger service left so this is a bit of a blast from the past. Adult $6; child (5–16 years) $3. On every first and second Sunday admission fees include a demonstration train ride. Open 13.00–16.30 every Sat/Sun only and public holidays.

The **Maritime Museum of Tasmania** (corner of Davey Street and Argyle Street; tel: 6234 1427; fax: 6234 1419; email: maritimetas@bigpond.com) features scores of maritime artefacts and salty tales. Tasmania's coast is an overcrowded graveyard of hundreds of wrecked ships, and some of their gruesome histories are told here. There is also some good information about early exploration of the island by sea, and the vast influence whaling, sealing and ship building had on Tasmania. Adult $6.60; child (4–16 years) $4, family (2 adults, 2 children) $17, concession $5.50. Open daily 10.00–17.00.

The **Cascade Brewery** (140 Cascade Road South, Hobart, TAS 7000; tel: 6221 8300) is worth a look, and a taste. Tours leave at 09.30 and 13.00 on weekdays and take two hours. Cascade is the beer with the Tasmanian tiger emblem. Adult $8.25; pensioner and student $5.50; child (5–15 years) $1.65. Whisky buffs should head for the **Tasmania Distillery** at Sullivans Cove (2 Macquarie Street, Hobart; tel: 6231 0588; fax: 6231 0590; email: tasdist@southcom.com.au). Adult $5.50; pensioner and student $4.40; child (10–16 years) $2.20.

The **Lady Franklin Gallery** (Lenah Valley Road, Lenah Valley, Hobart, TAS 7008; tel: 6228 2662) was built in 1842 by Lady Jane Franklin, wife of the then colony governor, Sir John Franklin. The building has been refurbished by the Art Society of Tasmania which runs it as a gallery for leading Tasmanian artists. Open Sat/Sun only, 13.30–17.00 summer, 13.00–16.30 winter.

Increasingly Tasmania is gaining recognition for design, especially of furniture. **Design Makers Tasmania** (27 Tasman Street, North Hobart, TAS 7000; tel: 6231 0512; fax: 6231 3470) is a good spot to check out the latest designs. The gallery also houses workshop machinery, kilns and studio space for members. Work designed and made on the premises includes contemporary furniture, ceramics, metals and textiles. Open by appointment.

Antarctic Adventure (Salamanca Square, Hobart, TAS 7000; tel: 6220 8220) is an interactive museum and a good substitute for Antarctica for those who can't get there. Visitors can don protective clothing and experience what sub-zero temperatures feel like with a head wind and thick blizzard. There are some good science exhibits as well as the fun stuff. Adult $16; pensioner $13; child (4–13 years) $8; family (2 adults, 2 children) $40.

Tasmanian National Tours (Wrest Point Casino, Main Foyer, Sandy Bay, Hobart, TAS 7005; tel: 6225 3131; fax: 6225 2445) offer a Mount Nelson and City Sights half-day car tour which includes Mount Nelson and Salamanca Place. Per car, per hour $55. Bookings required.

Performing arts

There are usually quite a few events going on in Hobart, especially during the summer. The **Theatre Royal** is the oldest in Australia and has seasonal programmes, and the symphony orchestra performs at the new Federation Hall. The **Peacock Theatre** off Salamanca also stages performances and has a great outdoor space for bands to play on warm summer evenings. The **Hobart Summer Festival**, which runs each year from December to February, has a fantastically varied programme with lots of free events (check out details on www.hobartcity.com.au). For details on arts in Tasmania, try the state government website's arts section at www.arts.tas.gov.au.

Sports, tours and other outdoor activities

Wellington Park is the nearest outdoor expanse to Hobart. It is a state reserve measuring 18,250 hectares and stretching from Lachlan near Mount Lloyd to Glenorchy and then south to Crabtree and Neika. The park takes in Mount Wellington (1,270m) with its fabulous views over Hobart. It is home to possums, wallabies, pademelons, potoroos, bandicoots, echidna, wombats, native cats, Tasmanian devils and all three types of snake. Platypus and eastern swamp rats can be seen nearer streams and dams. Many native birds use the park all year round including fan-tailed cockatoos, flame robins, honey-eaters and eagles. The mountain was first mapped by European explorers in 1792 when William Bligh named it Table Hill. It went through a number of names as subsequent explorers looked upon it but in 1822 the name Wellington – after the duke and his boots – finally stuck. There are lots of loop walks to the summit and through glades around the lower slopes. All tracks are clearly signposted and they are not strenuous.

Visitors can explore the Lost World boulder cave system and the Yellow Cliffs. If this is your first walk in Tasmania the abundant flora will give you a taste of what is to come further afield. There are at least 500 species of plant including snow daisies, pineapple grass, sphagnum mosses and snow gums.

You can take the **Mount Wellington Shuttle Bus** (tel: 0417 341 804) from Hobart to the summit and begin walks from there, or catch a public bus (Nos 48 and 49 to Fern Tree). For further information on sports and activities see *Specialist Tour Operators* in *Chapter 2*.

Short walk

Mount Wellington (tel: 6238 2855) Distance: 6km return. Time: 3 hours return. Difficulty: easy–moderate.
Along the B64 Huon Road about six or seven miles out of Hobart, just before Fern Tree, take a right-hand turn into Pillinger Drive (the C616) and follow it to The Springs picnic spot. From here you can take the gentle walk to Silver Falls or drive on to The Chalet. The road passes at the base of some towering cliffs. From The Chalet, take the Organ Pipes track around the same base of the cliffs leading to the summit. When the wind blows through the rock formations it is meant to make the sound of ghostly organ pipes. I felt the acoustics need a bit of imagination but the views are stunning. The track leads to a T-junction with the Zig Zag track which will take you to the top. Alternatively start at the Fern Tree shops and walk uphill to Silver Falls and follow any track that takes your fancy. So fresh is the water tumbling down this mountain that locals are known to collect it and carry it back home for drinking.

Detailed maps of Mount Wellington walks are available in walking and outdoor equipment shops and possibly also in the Tourist Information Centre. Like all Tasmania's high country, Mount Wellington can be engulfed in fog, snow or showers in a short space of time. This should not be viewed as a gentle afternoon stroll. While you may not need camping and climbing gear, it is advisable to take waterproof clothing, food, water, and to leave a note at your hotel to let someone know where you are going.

Photo spot
Along this walk on a clear morning when the sun is east you can get a good shot of the Organ Pipes. A 50mm lens will do; reduce the amount of sky you have in the frame to prevent the shot silhouetting the rocks.

Cycling tour
Hobart itself could do with some cycle lanes but outside rush hour the traffic is light enough for you to be able to move around the city with some ease.

If you fancy an adrenaline rush, book in for a **Mount Wellington Downhill Tour** (683 Summerleas Road, Fern Tree, Hobart, TAS 7054; tel: 6239 1080; fax: 6239 1090) where you take a bus to the summit and mount an 18-speed mountain bike for a ride back to town. The ride shoots through forested glades of alpine plants and trees with several stopping and viewing points. Adult $40 (minimum two people).

Photo spot
Go on ahead of your cycling party, find a good wide and gentle sweep of road that faces away from the sun, park up and take an action shot of your friends whizzing past. Use normal-fast speed film (200–400ASA) and focus on a patch of road. When they come past follow their path, keeping them in the centre of the viewfinder and

snapping as you move the camera. It should catch them static with the background blurred, giving a great sense of movement. Make sure you tell them to scream when they see you, to add excitement. You will have to stand a safe distance away so use a 50mm or small zoom lens (50–80mm).

On the water

There are kayak tours that go out on the harbour and cruise around the docks. Watch out for the occasional submarine slinking in to port. **Roaring 40s Ocean Kayaks** (tel: 6267 5000; fax: 6267 5004; email: rfok@ozemail.com.au) set off from Battery Point on a two-hour twilight paddle via the finish line of the Sydney–Hobart Yacht Race and Constitution Dock. **Blackaby's Sea Kayaks** (mobile: 0418 124 072) also run half-day and full-day sea kayak tours up the Derwent River and around the docks. **Derwent River Classic Cruises** (tel: 6224 8288, mobile: 0418 331 002) run a charter boat including a qualified skipper and crew who will take you on a leisurely cruise up the Derwent.

📷 Photo spot

Take a small compact camera with you on the kayak, in a dry bag if possible. Views from the water are rare in Hobart and you can get some interesting angles. Watch for the sun's reflection dancing on the bows of old wooden boats. If the *Aurora Australis* Antarctic supply ship is in dock you are in for a treat. It is bright orange and affords great pictures. Try not to polarise shots of the *Aurora* unless it is extremely bright as it dulls the orange colour. Instead, use a lower-speed film (64ASA) and ensure the orange colour fills the frame. Use a standard 50mm lens so as not to distort the ship's bow lines.

Sydney–Hobart Yacht Race

Sydney hosts the start of the race on Boxing Day, which is always dramatic and beautiful to watch, but Hobart gets the cream. A few days later (depending on the weather in treacherous Bass Strait), this is where the victorious boat sails triumphantly up the Derwent to cheers from the docks and quaysides. This is where the champagne corks are sprung and the partying begins. It is a great occasion and a must for any budding marine photographers.

Royal Hobart Regatta

If you are here in early February the regatta is fun. It comprises four days of races and exhibitions, and the obligatory Tasmanian pastime of eating and drinking fantastic local produce.

Australian Wooden Boat Festival

If you prefer to stay on dry land but not lose the nautical theme then this is for you. It is a highlight in the Hobart calendar, held over three days in early February every two years, and draws big crowds. Boats displayed come in all shapes and sizes from rowing boats, canoes and dinghies to large working and cruising vessels, square-riggers, yachts and steamboats. There is a boat-building competition, a parade of sails, model boat displays, musicians and street theatre, public forums, and demonstrations. The whole waterfront and harbour is a buzz of activity. The next festival is due to be held in 2003.

Australian Rules Football

We would need another guidebook to explain fully the rules of 'Rules' but suffice it to say that to many Australians who live in the south, especially Victoria where the sport was born, it is a religion. Each year in late September the Grand Final takes place in Melbourne (similar to the FA Cup Final in the UK and the Superbowl in America) and a large sector of the population sit, beer in hand, mouths open, willing their team on. It is closest to Gaelic Football and is played on an oval pitch (originating as it did from cricketers trying to keep fit during the winter months on their oval cricket pitches). The players wear jerseys with no sleeves to show off their biceps and regularly get stretchered off after head-on collisions with opponents and team-mates. There are several officials, including those who stand behind the goals looking like traditional English butchers in their white coats and matching trilby hats. It is very fast and very skilful and great fun to watch, even if the rules are perplexing. It is a winter game played from autumn through until September.

📷 *Photo spot*

If you go to see an Australian Rules game, try to get seats to the left or right of the goalposts, looking down the try-line, so you can get a good shot of the umpire in his English butcher's outfit signalling a goal by throwing his hands down by his sides and pointing between the posts. Long lens would be best, say 100–200mm, with some fast film (about 400ASA).

Cricket

Tasmania also has a quite successful state cricket team that plays in the national competition known as the Sheffield Shield and from time to time produces players for the national squad, currently the most successful in the world. The season runs from late September through to around April.

Shopping

It is hard to beat the shops along and around **Salamanca Place** for gifts and Tasmanian specialities. This is good browsing as well as buying territory. However, these are also the main tourist traps so if you are in town for long enough it might pay to price things here first and then double-check prices elsewhere in town. Many shops offer a package-and-shipping service, so if you are about to buy anything big, bulky or precious ask them about their delivery rates first and check on insurance policies too. On Montpelier Retreat is a fantastic deli, the **Wursthaus Kitchen**, with lots of Tasmanian produce – dried pepperberries, bags of lemon myrtle leaves (which make excellent bush tea when you are trekking), chutneys, tapenades, pastes, oils, honeys and drinks. There is a counter decked with cheeses and another with pâtés and meat goods, and plenty of seafood. It is a real Aladdin's cave, great for lunch and for presents.

Good outdoor equipment and clothing stores such as **Paddy Pallins**, **Mountain Design**, **Snowgum**, **Sport and Dive**, and **Jolly Swagman** can be found in a cluster on Elizabeth Street, between Liverpool Street and Melville Street, and **Kathmandu** can be found at Salamanca Square. They also stock a wide variety of dried meals for outdoor activities, maps, books and guides.

Some have items from the classic Australian clothing range of **R M Williams**. So popular are these 'working' clothes that Australians talk about wearing their RMs. Also look out for the good, hard-wearing footwear range, **Blundstones**.

Elizabeth Street and the **Centrepoint Shopping Centre** have more practical shops (clothing and the like).

FURTHER INFORMATION

Find out more from the Hobart Travel and Information Centre on the corner of Davey Street and Elizabeth Street (tel: 6230 8233).

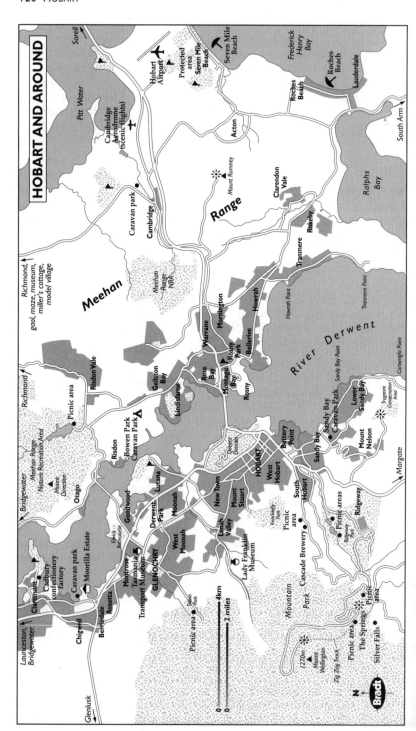

HOBART AND AROUND

Sorell

Pitt Water

Frederick
Henry
Bay

Roches
Beach

Lauderdale

Roches Beach

Seven Mile Beach

Hobart Airport

Protected area

Seven Mile Beach

South Arm

Cambridge Aerodrome (Scenic flights)

Ralphs Bay

Acton

Cambridge

Caravan park

Mount Rumney

Clarendon Vale

Range

Rokeby

Richmond, gaol, maze, museum, miller's cottage, model village

Meehan

Meehan Range NRA

Tramere

Tramere Point

Cartwright Point

Howrah Point

Mornington

Warrane

Howrah

Bellerive

River Derwent

Richmond

Risdon Vale

Geilston Bay

Rose Bay

Montagu Bay

Rosny Park

Sandy Bay Point

Picnic area

Bowen Park Caravan Park

Risdon

Lindisfarne

Rosny

Sandy Bay

Sandy Bay

Caravan Park

Lower Sandy Bay

Trugannini Conservation Area

Margate

Meehan Range Nature Recreation Area

Bridgewater

Mount Direction

Otago

Goodwood

Lutana

Moonah

Queens Domain

New Town

HOBART

West Hobart

Battery Point

South Hobart

Mount Nelson

Launceston, Bridgewater

Glenlusk

Claremont

Cadbury confectionery factory

Caravan park

Moorilla Estate

Berriedale

Rosetta

Chigwell

Elwick Racecourt

Montrose

Tasmania Transport Museum

GLENORCHY

West Moonah

Derwent Park

Lenah Valley

Lady Franklin Museum

Mount Stuart

Knocklofty Park

Picnic area

Cascade Brewery

Ridgeway Park

Picnic areas

Ridgeway

N

1270m

Mount Wellington

Zig Zag Track

Picnic area

The Springs

Silver Falls

Picnic area

Mountain Park

Picnic area

0   2 miles

0   4km

AROUND HOBART

Hobart is a good place to base yourself while exploring its environs. Towns like Richmond and Kingston are a half-hour's drive away, two hours if you are cycling.

Mount Rumney

A couple of Hobartians, who shall remain nameless, had never heard of Mount Rumney (378m) when I asked directions. Maybe this is why when I arrived at the television mast on the summit the small car-park was deserted. Keeping the mast behind you, the view through the light woods of eucalyptus trees is spectacular. You can see right down over the sweep of Seven Mile Beach and across to glistening Pitt Water. I found two maintenance men having a break (or 'smoko') from repairing a fence. One looked out over the vista and said this was the best office view in Tasmania. It is quite hard to find the way up to the mountain. Head east from Hobart on the A3, take the Cambridge turn, double back on to the A3, west this time, and take the first exit where there are signs.

📷 Photo spot

The views from Mount Rumney are excellent for panoramic shots. Otherwise use a slightly wide-standard angle lens (35–50mm) to get a sense of space. The eucalyptus trees on the summit can be used to frame a shot. Use low-speed film if you have a sunny day (64ASA), and use a polariser but turned only halfway round.

Port Arthur Ghost Tour

With a pick up and drop back in Hobart, this fully guided ghost tour (tel: 1300 653 633 or 6229 7465; mobile: 0409 701 221) is handy for those on a tight schedule. Adult $65; concession $55; child (under 16) $50. Open Tuesday, Thursday, Saturday all year. Departure 18.00, return 23.30.

Sea Cats

Just to the north of the city is Risdon, site of the first settlement in Van Diemen's Land. Today it is also famous for its prison and as the berth for the fleet of high speed catamarans known as Incats. These were engineered and developed in Hobart by local man Bob Clifford. One of them holds the record for the fastest crossing of the Atlantic by a passenger vessel. So successful was its design that the Australian navy used them to dash troops across to East Timor during the United Nations operation in 1999. The US armed forces have also shown great interest and at the time of going to press were about to sign a contract to buy some. You can ride on one called the Devil Cat which provides a regular vehicle and passenger ferry service across Bass Strait in summer that takes six hours between Georgetown and Melbourne. You can see the cats lying at their moorings in Prince of Wales Bay from the Bowen Bridge across the Derwent.

Chocolate factory

Chocoholics should make for the Cadbury Factory (tel: 1800 627 367 or 6249 0333; fax: 6249 0334) at Claremont, off the A10 north of Glenorchy. It has been here since 1921, turning out bar after bar, and now offers tours. Adult $11; pensioner $7.50; child $5.50 (4 years and under free); family (2 adults and up to 4 children) $27.50. Tours Monday to Friday 08.00–13.00; closed weekends, public holidays, September.

Richmond

For those on a tight schedule Richmond can be done on a day trip from Hobart, but it is worth staying a night or two in one of the many heritage bed and breakfasts.

Getting there

It can be cycled in a leisurely two hours from Hobart and driven in half an hour. **City Sites Under Lights** (tel: 6235 4353) run day tours from Hobart (not Mondays or Fridays) to Richmond. **Mount Wellington Shuttle Bus** (tel: 0417 341 804) offer a three-hour tour of Richmond twice daily every day for $25. **Tasmanian National Tours** (Wrest Point Casino, Main Foyer, Sandy Bay, Hobart, TAS 7005; tel: 6225 3131; fax: 6225 2445) offer a chauffeur-driven Historic Richmond and Bonorong Wildlife Centre half-day car tour costing $165 per car. Bookings required. Visitors can hold wombats in the Bonorong Wildlife Park.

Where to stay and eat

The town is full of heritage accommodation, bed and breakfast-style, with huge breakfasts and lots of local knowledge and charm. Practically the whole town is National Trust listed. A few to try are as follows:

The **Richmond Arms Hotel** (42 Bridge St, Richmond, TAS 7025; tel: 6260 2109; fax: 6260 2623; email: richmond@tco.asn.au) is a popular sandstone hotel. $99 single and double. Lunches and suppers are good value, with main dishes $15–20.

Richmond Barracks (16 Franklin St, Richmond, TAS 7025; tel: 6260 2453; fax: 6260 2373) was built in 1830 to house officers from the gaol. It was then made into two cottages and is now one building and National Trust listed. $88/121 single/double.

Millhouse on the Bridge (2 Wellington St, Richmond, TAS 7025; tel: 6260 2428; mobile: 0418 580912; fax: 6260 2148; email: millhouse@millhouse.com.au; web: www.millhouse.com.au) was built in 1853 as a steam-driven flour mill and converted into a home in the 1920s by the Australian landscape artist, John Eldershaw. En-suite room $135–160, single and double.

For a touch of luxury and some good food try **Prospect House** (Main Rd, Richmond, TAS 7025; tel: 6260 2207; fax: 6262 2551; email: prosrich@southcom.com.au; web: www.Prospect-House.com.au). Open daily for lunch and dinner (4-course à la carte available) and has accommodation and B&B packages. En-suite rooms $145, single and double; suites $160, single and double.

Tastings and sales on offer at the **Richmond Food and Wine Centre** (27 Bridge St, Richmond, TAS 7025; tel: 6260 2619; fax: 6260 2651; email: richmondwinecentre@hotmail.com).

For ploughman's lunches, Devonshire teas and sweets, try **Ma Foosies** (46 Bridge St, Richmond, TAS 7025; tel: 6260 2412). Open daily. Closed Christmas Day, Boxing Day, Good Friday, last two weeks in July, first two weeks in August.

What to do and see

This is where the Englishness of Tasmania comes alive. I have photographs of Richmond which I could swear were taken in an Oxfordshire Cotswold village. It lies only 15 miles north of Hobart, at the gateway to the Midlands region, and is full of elegant Georgian architecture. Nearly all of Richmond was built during the early 19th century by convicts, a reminder of how useful (if appalling) the convict transportation system was. The authorities wasted no time putting to work the ready supply of free labour. Of particular interest are the graceful arched bridge (said to be the oldest in Australia) over the Coal River and beyond it St Johns Church with its squat stone base and impressive grey steeple.

There are tours around **Richmond Gaol** (37 Bathurst Street, Richmond, TAS 7025; tel: 6260 2127), which was built in 1825 complete with windowless solitary confinement cells measuring just two metres by one metre, torture cells, holding-rooms for chain gangs, and a flogging yard. Adult $3.50; child (6–17 years) $2;

family (2 adults and 2 or more children) $11. There is also a **maze** with tearooms (13 Bridge Street, Richmond, TAS 7025; tel: 6260 2451) open every day. Richmond is best seen on foot strolling past heritage cottages, many of them now operating as bed and breakfasts. You could join a leisurely **Richmond Historical Walking Tour** (tel: 6248 5510; fax: 6248 5510) which lasts just over an hour. Adult $6; student $2; child (6–16 years) $3.

Richmond is also on the Southern Tasmanian Wine Route and sports some of the state's finest **vineyards** to the northwest near Tea Tree and just south of the town. The following all offer free tasting at the cellar door:

Charles Reuben Estate 777 Middle Tea Tree Rd, Tea Tree, TAS 7017; tel/fax: 6268 1702; email: email: chasreuben@eisa.net.com
Morningside Vineyard 711 Middle Tea Tree Rd, Tea Tree, TAS 7017; tel/fax: 6268 1748; email: email: morningside@trump.net.au. By appointment only.
Palmara 1314 Main Rd, Richmond, TAS 70265; tel/fax: 6260 2462

Most vineyards are closed between June and August.

Shopping

Try any (or all) of the antique shops in town for memorabilia. For gifts, try **Richmond Craft & Keepsakes** (50 Bridge Street, Richmond, TAS 7025; tel: 6260 1006; mobile: 0418 385 732; fax: 6260 2648; email: saddco@trump.net.au) which specialises in handcrafted woodwork, forged metalwork and clothing. Open daily 09.30–17.30. At the same address you will find **Saddlers Court Country Style** which has knitwear, clothing, books, accessories and local produce.

Derwent Valley

The valley heads north from Hobart past Glenorchy, Bridgewater and New Norfolk. Upstream it is tranquil. Fields and hop groves sweep away from both banks. They are protected from the weather by lines of poplar trees that act as windbreaks. Like the hop fields of Kent, this valley is dotted with traditional oast-houses. Look out for them particularly around Bushy Park which is now in the biggest hop-growing area of the southern hemisphere thanks to the introduction of hops by William Shoobridge back in 1822. Hops here end up in cans and bottles of Budweiser in the US.

The valley is low-lying and fairly flat so is conducive to cycling tours. Anyone of reasonable fitness could in summer cycle from Hobart north along the western bank of the river to New Norfolk, scoot on a few minutes to Plenty for a sit-down or take-away lunch at the **Salmon Ponds** (tel: 6261 1614; fax: 6261 4485; open daily, call ahead for picnic hamper), then come back along the eastern bank through Bridgewater.

If you are staying in New Norfolk overnight try the National Trust classified, four-star **Glen Derwent** (44 Hamilton Road, New Norfolk, TAS 7140; tel: 6261 3244; fax: 6261 3770; email: glenderwent@glenderwent.com.au; web: glenderwent.com.au). This bed and breakfast is homely and well appointed. En-suite and studio apartment $110–145/$126–166, single/double. The place also has two colonial cottages behind the house.

Rail enthusiasts could contact the **Derwent Valley Railway** (Station Street, New Norfolk, TAS 7140; tel: 6234 6049; fax: 6231 3752) which operates a train ride from New Norfolk to Westerway and a New Norfolk to Mount Field National Park excursion. The train departs from the New Norfolk Railway Station at 10.30. Snacks and refreshments available on the train. The train usually operates on the second Sunday of each month but varies with season and demand. Best to check with the operator. Prices on application. **Classic Rail Tours** (contact via Transport Museum in Glenorchy; tel: 6261 1171; fax: 6261 3872; email: classicrailtours@bigpond.com) run special charters up the valley.

If you are passing through **Lawitta**, across the river from New Norfolk, stop by the Back River Chapel where you will find the grave of the first white woman to set foot on Australian soil. Betty Hackery was a convict on the First Fleet (the term used to describe the first ships to reach the Australian shore from Europe, carrying convicts and some free settlers), which landed at Botany Bay, south of Sydney, on January 19 1788. She later came to Van Diemen's Land in 1807, and was eventually granted land at Back River where she died in August 1856 after a lifetime of momentous memories.

At **Otago Bay** on the eastern shore of the Derwent you can see from the shoreline the remains of the *Otago*, a three-masted iron barque built in Glasgow, Scotland, in 1869. The *Otago*'s main claim to fame is that it was the only command of the novelist Joseph Conrad. The bow rests on the shoreline with the stern lying in about two metres of water. The iron hull has been cut back to the waterline but the bow and stern have been lost.

Tasmanian National Tours (Wrest Point Casino, Main Foyer, Sandy Bay, Hobart, TAS 7005; tel: 6225 3131; mobile: 0418 127 188; fax: 6225 2445) offer a chauffeur-driven Derwent Valley car tour (also to Russell Falls). Each car costs $300. The fee for Mount Field National Park is extra. Bookings required.

Further information
Find out more from the Visitor Information Centre in New Norfolk (Circle Street, New Norfolk, TAS 7140; tel: 6261 3700). Alternatively, write to them c/o Derwent Valley Council (PO Box 595, New Norfolk, TAS 7140).

The Southeast

Beyond Hobart there is not much left of the world. After about 240km the land ends and the turbulent Southern Ocean begins and it is water all the way to Antarctica. You will be reminded of this as you pass through **Kingston** where the Australian Antarctic Division (tel: 6232 3209) has its headquarters. You can drop in to see an exhibition of the work of the AAD, whose brief is to manage Australia's part of the frozen continent, which is considerable.

There is little else to keep you in Kingston and, considering the beautiful Huon Valley and Bruny Island lie to the south, I would press on. If you are stuck here, however, you could try the **Welcome Inn** (Kingston View Drive, Kingston, TAS 7050; tel: 6229 4800) which has good views, some rooms with whirlpool baths and a bistro. En-suite rooms $55–66/$66–77 single/double.

There is a small peninsula of land leading south from Kingston which is worth a visit, for at the tip is one of Tasmania's marine reserves, at **Tinderbox**. These are like national parks, but under water, and this one is excellent as a snorkelling trail has been established with signs detailing plants and fish you are likely to see. There are sandstone platforms and cobbled reefs which harbour many species, including the flamboyant leafy sea-dragon, a kind of sea horse decorated with fans and frills. You will probably need a wetsuit but dip your toe in and see how the temperature feels. The reserve is quite small and protected so there is no big swell. You can also look across the narrows here to Dennes Point, the northernmost tip of Bruny Island.

From Kingston the main A6 runs south past the wonderfully named town of Sandfly and finally drops into the Huon Valley.

GETTING THERE AND AROUND

The main gateway to the Southeast region is from Hobart through Kingston. The main A6 runs right down to Southport, with the B68 branching off to service Cygnet, Woodbridge, Kettering and Margate. From Southport down to Cockle Creek, which is as far south in Australia as you can go by car or bus, the road is rough but not terrible. 2WDs can handle it as long as the weather has been kind but check conditions before you go. If you have a boat on a trailer then there are plenty of ramps to launch it along this coast.

TWT's Tassielink Regional Coach Service (tel: 1300 300 520; web: www.tigerline.com.au) runs bus services between Hobart and Dover and on to Cockle Creek via Huonville and Geeveston. **Hobart Coaches** (tel: 6233 4232; fax: 6272 8770; web: www.metrotas.com.au) also run services from the capital to Woodbridge and Cygnet, as well as to Dover via Huonville and Geeveston but the service is limited and favours weekdays.

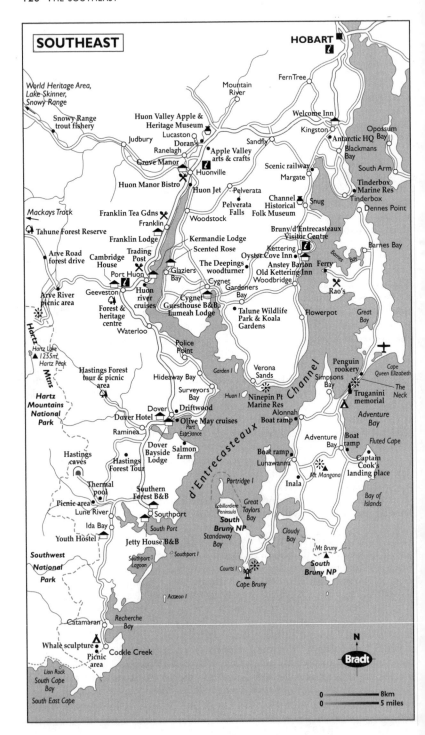

HUONVILLE AND AROUND

Huonville is the fruit capital of Tasmania. In autumn and early winter (May and June) the orchards are carpeted with fallen fruit and the air laced with the heady scent of fermenting apples. It is good to spend a night in this areas as there is a fair amount to see.

The first Europeans to visit this area were the French Rear-Admiral Bruni D'Entrecasteaux and Captain Huon de Kermadec who gave it its name. They explored the Huon River and had friendly meetings with the local Aboriginal people and some sailors even shared meals with them. Early settlers found the land was thickly forested with a pine species that became known as the Huon pine. The region was heavily logged because Huonville was a strategic hauling point where the river was narrow enough to cross. The apples came later but now dominate this valley.

The Huon Valley has a touch of J R R Tolkien about it. Anyone familiar with Bilbo and Frodo Baggins and their beloved Shire might find the similarity too. It is sheltered, gentle and fruitful, but where the land does rise at its edges it does so steeply. Spring and autumn bring mists that settle over the orchards and everything is damp. As you drive through the valley you will see lots of stalls selling in-season fruits. Most operate on an honesty policy – take your fruit and leave your coins.

📷 Photo spot

The orchards here are good at any time of the year. In summer they are green and lush, in autumn laden with fruit and yellowing leaves and wrapped around with mist, winter barren and skeletal, and in spring full of white and pink blossom. Try to get a high vantage point so your feet are level with the tree tops and fill the frame with them, leaving no sky or other background visible. 50mm lens, film varies for the season.

Getting there and around

The main A6 serves this part of the region from Hobart to Kingston, then Huonville and Geeveston. For the towns of Cygnet, Woodbridge, Kettering and Margate take the B68 turnoff. **TWT's Tassielink Regional Coach Service** (tel: 1300 300 520; web: www.tigerline.com.au) will carry you between Hobart, Huonville and Geeveston. **Hobart Coaches** (tel: 6233 4232) run between Hobart and Woodbridge, Cygnet, Huonville and Geeveston.

Where to stay and eat

Grove Manor (Crabtree Rd, Grove, Huonville, TAS 7109; tel: 6266 4227; fax: 6266 4223; email: grovemanor@tassie.net.au) is an elegant property built in 1880 between two rivers. It has three spacious en-suite rooms and an English garden. Evening meals available. $70–90/$140–160 single/double.

For good water views, head just south of Huonville along the west bank of the river. In Franklin, try **Franklin Lodge** (Main Road, Franklin, TAS 7113; tel: 6266 3506; fax: 6266 3731; email: franklinlodge@primus.com.au; web: www.franklinlodge.com.au) a heritage B&B overlooking the Huon River. Heritage listed and has 4 en-suite rooms. $117/126 single/double.

At Port Huon, try **Kermandie Lodge** (Huon Highway, Port Huon, TAS 7116; tel: 6297 1110; fax: 6297 1710) which has self-contained villa units. There is a fitness centre near by with a gymnasium, sauna, pool and squash court. Villas have barbecues so you can carbonise your own catch of the day. En-suite room $77–86, single and double; apartment $88–105, single and double.

In Geeveston, **Cambridge House** (Huon Highway, Geeveston, TAS 7116; tel: 6297 1561; mobile: 0417 129 442) is a good bet. It was built in 1870 for John Geeves, a member of the family that founded the town, overlooking the Kermandie River. It retains many original features and is classified by the National Trust and listed by the Heritage Council. A guest lounge and breakfast room on the ground floor provides a relaxing atmosphere, with an open fire, and a Huon pine and blackwood staircase leads to accommodation with shared bathroom facilities. $50–65/$70–85 single/double.

There is not a huge array of restaurants and cafés in the Southeast region and, with all the fresh produce available and a number of self-contained accommodation options, the best bets are to opt for the evening meal provided by your hosts or cater for yourself.

Alternatively, try the **Huon Manor Bistro** (1 Short Street, Huonville, TAS 7109; tel: 6264 1311) Lunch is served daily but the bistro is closed for supper on Wednesday and Sunday. Light lunches $8.50, main supper dishes from $15.

The **Franklin Tea Gardens** (Main Rd, Franklin, TAS 7116; tel: 6266 3533) has a BYO café for light snacks, or try the **Port Huon Trading Post** (Huon Highway, Port Huon, TAS 7116; tel: 6297 1495).

What to see and do

To the north of Huonville, near Grove, is the **Huon Valley Apple and Heritage Museum** (tel: 6266 4345; fax: 6266 4109) where you can learn everything you ever wanted to know about apples, including how to peel them. They say as many as 500 different apple varieties grow here. Open daily September to May 09.00–17.00; June and August 10.00–16.00; closed July, Christmas Day.

Just down the road is **Apple Valley Arts and Crafts** (tel: 6264 1844; fax: 6264 2869; email: jbhurd@ozemail.com.au) which has a very useful information map outside and lots of produce, books and postcards inside. Open daily December to April 09.30–17.30, May to November 10.00–17.00; closed Christmas Day, Good Friday.

Up Pages Road, off the highway, is **Doran's Jam Factory** (tel: 6266 4377; fax: 6266 4636; email: dorans@tassie.net.au; web: www.ontas.com.au/dorans) with some delicious concoctions. Open daily from 10.00; closed Christmas Day, Good Friday.

For thrill-seekers, **Huon Jet** (The Esplanade, Huonville (on the B68); tel: 6264 1838 or 6223 1164 after work hours; fax: 6264 1031; email: huonjet@tassie.net.au) take passengers on a 35-minute jet boat ride up the tree-lined river with good views and high speeds. Open daily. Adult $50; seniors $45; child (3-16 years) $32.

Or glide up the river in a more leisurely fashion with **Huon River Cruises** (Huon Highway, Port Huon, TAS 7116; tel: 6297 0078; minimum two people). Cruises leave the marina at 11.00 and 14.00 and include a history of the river and a visit to an Atlantic salmon farm. Open daily. Prices on enquiry.

Huonville Market (Websters car-park on Cool Store Road) sells bric-a-brac, fruit and vegetables and arts and crafts. Open 10.00–14.00 on the second and fourth Sunday of every month. Admission free.

Anglers should head inland up the C619 to Judbury and on to the **Snowy Range Trout Fishery** (Little Denison River heading towards Lake Skinner; tel: 6266 0243; fax: 6266 0000; email: Snowy.Range@Bigpond.com; web: www.snowyrangetrout.com.au) where stream-fed waterways are stocked with fish from 300g to 3kg. You can hire rods and no fishing licences are required. There is also a forest drive. Open daily from 09.00; closed July. Adult $4; child $2; and you pay for what you catch.

Check out the list of **rafting** companies (see *Specialist Tour Operators*, page 28) to see which runs trips along the Picton River east of Geeveston.

There are lots of homegrown arts and crafts places throughout the valley specialising in wood products.

For a history of commercial forestry check out the **Geeveston Forest and Heritage Centre** on Church Street (tel: 6297 1836; fax: 6297 1839; web:

www.forestandheritagecentre.com.au). If you are planning on heading further south to the Hastings Forest, this centre provides audio cassettes for self-guided tours. Open daily 10.00–16.30; closed Christmas Day. Adult $5; concession $4; child $3; family $15.

Early October is the time for apple blossom and in early November the region holds its annual Agricultural Show.

Walks and forest drives

From Huonville, at the end of the C619 beyond the Snowy Range Trout Fishery, is a 3–4-hour walk up to Lake Skinner. It is medium to hard going through rainforest to sub-alpine areas. Longer walks into the Snowy Range and to Nevada Peak are possible but take much longer and walkers should be more experienced and well prepared for all weathers.

East of Huonville at Pelverata is a nice walk to the falls. After a good rainfall the water cascades over the lip and drops 80 metres. The walk is moderately difficult and there are some scree slopes nearer to the falls.

From Geeveston, head west to discover a number of walks. A recent addition to the region is the **Tahune Forest AirWalk and Visitor Centre** (at the end of the C631; tel: 6297 0068; web: www.forestrytas.com.au). This is a fascinating structure that allows visitors to walk for about a third of a mile through the canopy of the forest along a platform raised more than 40 metres off the ground. Forestry Tasmania who operate this forest reserve confirm the construction of the AirWalk was done in accordance with the highest environmental standards but that should not stop environmentally aware visitors asking guides exactly what was done to protect the ecology during building. There are also some short trails through the woods from the picnic area. Tickets for the AirWalk are also on sale in Geeveston, at the Forest and Heritage Centre on Church Street. Open daily. Adult $8; child $5; family $25 (2 adults, 2 children).

📷 Photo spot

Make the most of your height at the AirWalk but using a long lens to isolate a eucalyptus crown, preferably with no background other than a blue sky. 100–300mm lens and 100–200ASA film.

Experienced walkers start out from Tahune along **Mackays Track** which leads deep into the Southwest National Park. It is possible to follow that track and a couple of others it joins right out to Port Davey, but this is about the toughest walking possible in Tasmania and it can take up to two weeks if the weather closes in. Peak fitness and rigorous planning are required.

Geeveston is also a good base for exploring the foothills of the **Hartz Mountains**. Head out along the C631 and branch off left just after the Arve River Picnic Area. You will pass through the gates of the Hartz Mountains National Park and so you require a parks pass. The views are spectacular and in spring and summer the alpine wildflowers add real colour. If driving is more your thing then from Geeveston you can take the 60km Arve Forest Drive which will take you through working forests which still harbour a few mighty swamp gums (or *Eucalyptus regnans*). Watch out for logging trucks.

HARTZ MOUNTAINS NATIONAL PARK

The park (tel: 6264 8460) covers 7,250 hectares and varies in altitude from 160 metres above sea level at the Picton River to its highest point at Hartz Peak (1,255 metres). This point gives excellent views westward over the seemingly endless forests of the southwest wilderness. As you pass the park gates you are also entering the World Heritage Area yet you are still only 52 miles from Hobart.

The sedimentary rocks at lower altitudes in the south are among the oldest in the park, formed between 355 and 180 million years ago as lake beds were laid down. The range of mountains that form the backbone of the Hartz are dolerite which was intruded into the earth's outer crust roughly 165 million years ago when the former supercontinent Gondwana was breaking up. Several ice ages have sculpted this park, tearing out hollows or cirques where tarns now lie, and cutting U-shaped valleys and craggy peaks.

Due to the variation in altitude, the park sports a fairly wide diversity of flora and fauna. The three dominant forms of vegetation are wet eucalyptus forest, mixed forest with stringybark gums, and rainforest with myrtle, sassafras, leatherwood and native laurel common in the understoreys. At lower levels in spring and summer you will notice the bright red waratahs blooming in understorey heaths.

Nearer the higher altitudes, the trees are shorter and more sturdy to withstand the harsher elements and sub-alpine plants and shrubs begin appearing. There are snow gums up here which can have quite obvious red sap bleeding from their veins. Also yellow gums and varnished gums. Between these trees watch for butcherbirds, beautiful firetails, finches, striated pardalotes, honey-eaters, tits, wrens and flame robins. In the open skies you may get lucky and spot a goshawk hunting.

Many resident invertebrates are believed to be descendants with extremely long lineages going back to Gondwana. This is also home to one of the world's most recently discovered species. The moss froglet was unknown until a specimen was found here in 1992. It spends all its life out of water. You will hear many frog calls as you walk the tracks in the park.

This park is significant for descendants of Aboriginal people as these were probably once the wallaby hunting grounds of the Mellukerdee people of the Huon Valley. It was named Scenic Reserve in 1939 and became part of the huge World Heritage Area 50 years later.

The mountains are named after a range in Bavaria and were one of the first areas of Tasmania to become popular with bushwalkers. This was thanks mainly to the Geeves family who settled in what is now Geeveston and, being keen explorers, cut the first track up to the Hartz Range. However, tragedy struck the family on November 27 1897 when two of them died of hypothermia after a blizzard engulfed their party. They did not know it at the time but they were within a five-minute walk of the protection and warmth of the Hartz Hut. Late November is summer here and these men were fairly experienced walkers and knew this terrain – another reminder of the potential brutality of the elements in this part of the world.

There are no camping facilities in the park but it is allowed provided tents are pitched at least 500m away from a road and usual national park camping rules are adhered to.

Short walks
Waratah Lookout
Distance: 200 metres return. Time: 5 minutes return. Difficulty: easy.

This is the easiest walk, up a gravel track to a lookout from a car-park on the Hartz Road near Keogh Falls, less than a mile inside the park. The views are good looking east over the Huon Valley to the Wellington Range. In the foreground of your view is old growth myrtle forest. There are toilets, picnic facilities, a gas barbecue and drinking water at the car-park.

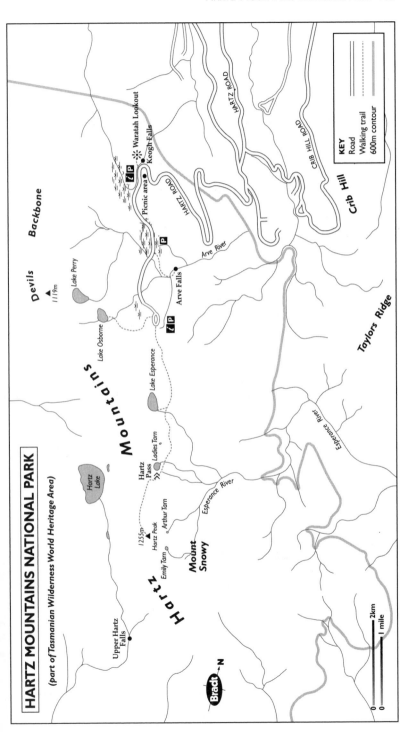

HARTZ MOUNTAINS NATIONAL PARK

(part of Tasmanian Wilderness World Heritage Area)

KEY
Road
Walking trail
600m contour

Devils   Backbone

▲ 1119m

Lake Perry

Lake Osborne

Mountains

Hartz Lake

1255m ▲
Hartz Peak

Emily Tarn   Arthur Tarn

Mount Snowy

Esperance River

Lake Esperance

Ladies Tarn

Hartz Pass

Upper Hartz Falls

Hartz

N   Bradt

0   2km
0   1 mile

Waratah Lookout ☀
Keogh Falls ●

Picnic area

HARTZ ROAD

Arve River

Arve Falls ●

HARTZ ROAD

HARTZ ROAD

CRIB HILL ROAD

Crib Hill

Taylors Ridge

Esperance River

Arve Falls

Distance: 800 metres return. Time: 30 minutes return. Difficulty: easy.
This clear path follows the Arve River through stands of snowgums to the edge of a plateau where the falls drop. Informative signs along the way let you know details of the flora.

Lake Osborne

Distance: 1.6km return. Time: 45 minutes return. Difficulty: easy to moderate
This path leads from the loop at the end of the Hartz Road. It climbs gently through glades of myrtles, sassafras and pandani to this pretty lake. In the distance you should be able to see some large boulders dotting the landscape known as the Devil's Marbles, which were dumped here having been carried from the higher country by glaciers. Signs along the track tell the story of this area's evolution.

Lake Esperance

Distance: 2km return. Time: 2 hours return. Difficulty: easy to moderate.
Be aware that weather can change rapidly here so check forecasts and take a day pack with extra clothes and waterproofs and some emergency rations (chocolate and flask of tea). The other track from the end of the Hartz Road leads to this lake. The path climbs gently into a higher altitude vegetation belt where you will see cushion plants and King Billy pines. Currawong birds frequent the woods around the lake. Look out for the memorial to Sydney and Arthur Geeves, two of the famous local family who came a cropper here in a blizzard in 1897.

Day walks
Hartz Peak

Distance: 6–8km return from car-park. Time: 5-6 hours return. Difficulty: easy to moderate but becoming hard (fit and experienced walkers only) and climbing to 1,255m.
Weather can change rapidly here so check forecasts and take full emergency kit (food, water, clothing and waterproofs, tent). Path beyond Hartz Pass can be faint, steep and very difficult, treacherous in bad weather. Please sign the walker registration book.

From the car-park at the end of the Hartz Road follow the Lake Esperance track but continue on to Ladies Tarn and then tackle Hartz Pass. You will see the rugged silhouette of Federation Peak (1,224m) on the horizon almost due west. This is an excellent test walk for anyone planning to take on the Overland, South Coast or other long distance tracks.

Further information

Contact the Huonville and Geeveston Travel and Information Centre (tel: 6264 1838; email: huonville@tasvisinfo.com.au; or tel: 6297 1836; email: geeveston@tasvisinfo.com.au). Look out for the book *Family Bushwalks in Tasmania's Huon Valley* in bookstores and visitor centres.

CYGNET TO KETTERING

This is one of the most tranquil parts of Tasmania with rolling countryside, fruit farms, quiet inlets and some fabulous views west to the Hartz Mountains and east to Bruny Island. It is tempting to contemplate scooting over to Bruny Island for a few hours as part of this tour but you will be disappointed if you rush it. Bruny's beauty is stunning and it is bigger than people think so it needs at least a full day, if not two or three, to see it properly. You might want to bed down in

Kettering for the night and catch an early ferry the next day (tel: 6273 6725 for ferry sailings and costs).

Where to stay and eat

The **Cygnet Guesthouse B&B** (20 Mary St, Cygnet, TAS 7112; tel: 6295 0080; fax: 6295 1905) is a National Trust listed, former Edwardian bank with elegant blackwood staircase and wall panels. Afternoon teas provided. All standard rooms are en suite. $110/115 single/double.

The Scented Rose (1338 Cygnet Coast Rd, Glaziers Bay, TAS 7109; tel: 6295 1816; fax: 6295 0492; email: scentedrose@optusnet.com.au) is a romantic, luxury retreat for 1 couple only. There are Liberty and Laura Ashley fabrics and high ceilings decorated in art nouveau metalwork. The Edwardian house has 3 acres of gardens with fine rose borders and good views across the river to the Hartz Mountains. $180 single and double.

For another luxury stay, try **Anstey Barton** (82 Ferry Rd, Kettering, TAS 7155; tel: 6267 4199; fax: 6267 4433; email: anstey_barton@bigpond.com.au; web: www.anstey-barton.com.au, a sandstone mansion built in 1824 in the Midlands and later dismantled and moved south to sit in 15 acres of gardens and parkland with great views of the D'Entrecasteaux Channel and Bruny Island. In the tariff is champagne on arrival, pre-dinner drinks and canapés, Tasmanian wines with dinner and a half-day sail on a yacht. After dinner you can play billiards or take a guided moonlit nature walk into the forest. There are 3 en-suite rooms, $300/600 single/double.

More reasonable is the **Old Kettering Inn** (Ferry Rd, Kettering, TAS 7155; tel: 6267 4426; fax: 6267 4884; email ebaldwin@rezitech.com.au). This waterfront guesthouse, built in 1894, has only one suite (sleeps family of three). Dinghy and fishing gear are provided, evening meal on request or use of barbecue provided. There are log fires and water views, and the house is 100 metres from the Bruny Island Ferry. $85/98 single/double. Also try the **Lumeah Lodge** (Lot 22, Crooked Tree Point, Cygnet, TAS 7112; tel: 6295 0980; fax: 6295 0998) $83/93 single/double, and the **Oyster Cove Inn** (1 Ferry Rd, Oyster Cove, Kettering, TAS 7155; tel: 6267 4446; fax: 6267 4330; email: oyster.cove@tassie.net.au), a popular pub built around 1890 with good views over the bay. The owner has restored an original botanical garden. $38–60/$60–90 single/double. The Oyster Cove Inn does food and snacks daily.

The **Mermaid Café** (tel: 1800 676 740) at the ferry terminal and visitor centre does light lunches and cakes. Open daily 09.00–17.00.

Apart from that, restaurants are not prevalent so eating at your accommodation or self-catering is advisable.

What to see and do

There is an award-winning **Channel Historical Folk Museum** in Lower Snug (tel: 6267 9169) which gives a good overview of this region's past. Open 10.00–16.00; closed Wednesday. Admission charge.

Further north in Margate is a **scenic railway** (Margate Train, 1567 Channel Highway; tel: 6267 2545; fax: 6225 2423) where there are gift shops, an antique warehouse and an espresso café. Open daily 09.30–17.00. Ticket charge. Market every Sunday 09.30–17.00.

You can go **sea kayaking** from Kettering into the D'Entrecasteaux Channel (Roaring 40s, Oyster Cove Marina, Kettering; tel: 6267 5000; fax: 6267 5004; email: rfok@ozemail.com.au). The sea kayaking centre provides day tours, twilight paddles, kayak rentals and sales.

Boats are available for charter for diving, fishing or cruising expeditions in the channel, up the Huon River, across to Bruny Island and down to the south coast on a fast nine-metre vessel (tel: 6297 1510; email: f.franken@tassie.net.au; web: www.seachangecharters.com.au).

At Gardners Bay, just inland from Cygent along the C627, is the **Talune Wildlife Park and Koala Gardens** (tel: 6295 1775; fax: 6295 0818; email: wombat@talune.com.au; web: www.talune.com.au). Koalas are out of their natural habitat here as they are strictly a mainland species. The park also has Tasmanian devils. Open daily 09.30–17.00. Adult $7; children $2.50; family $16.50 (2 adults, 2 children).

Cygnet hosts the popular **Huon Valley Folk and Music Festival** every year in early January which is worth a look, but accommodation is hard to find at that time. **Port Cygnet** hosts a market selling organic vegetables and fruits, arts and crafts and the like at 56 Mary Street. Open first and third Friday each month, 14.00–17.00 May–September; 14.00–21.00 October–April.

Ninepin Point Marine Reserve (tel: 6264 8460) is an excellent place to swim, snorkel and dive. It is an unusual ecosystem as cold, nutrient-rich sea water from the Southern Ocean is overlaid with tannin-rich fresh water from the Huon River. The water is tea-coloured and reduces the light filtering through which allows the growth of an amazing variety of sea life not normally found so close to the surface. This reserve alone has recorded more than 100 different species of seaweed. Bring a wetsuit and treat the reserve as you would a national park. Everything is protected.

The **Deepings Woodturner** (118 Nicholls Rivulet Road, Nicholls Rivulet, TAS 7112; tel: 6295 1398; fax: 6295 0498; email: deepings@trump.net.au; web: www.deepingsdolls.com) is Adrian Hunt. He makes upright wooden figurines and his studio is very popular. There is a small fee charged for coach parties and reservations are required. Open daily Monday–Friday 09.00–17.00, Sunday 12.00–17.00 (longer hours in summer); closed Christmas Day, Good Friday.

Further information
Contact the Kettering Travel and Information Centre (tel: 6267 4494; email: kettering@tasvisinfo.com.au) at the ferry terminal which has helpful staff, a café and a wealth of information booklets. Definitely worth a quick look before you head to Bruny.

BRUNY ISLAND
I have to admit some bias here as Bruny captivated me on my first visit. It is ravishingly beautiful, wild and windswept, has important Aboriginal significance with several shoreline midden sites, harbours excellent bird and animal life, and offers the chance of spotting whales and dolphins. Its human population is around 600 and those involved in the tourism and conservation industries are committed, charming and helpful. I would give it at least two full days of your time if you are driving and twice that if on a bicycle. Bruny is split into north and south islands which are joined by a thin strip of land covered in high sand dunes called The Neck. North Bruny consists of open farmland and pockets of eucalyptus forest while South Bruny has high rugged cliffs, rainforests and grassy headlands and is almost all either state forest or national park.

Getting there and around
The only way to get to Bruny is by boat. The *Mirambeena* ferry (tel: 6273 6725) runs from Kettering on the mainland and takes roughly 20 minutes. There are daily sailings about once an hour from 07.00–18.30 and a return ticket for a car costs around $20, more on public holidays. If you are using your own boat or one

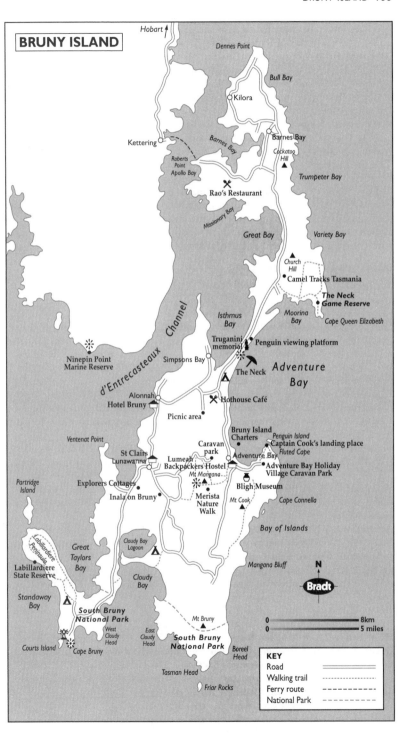

BRUNY ISLAND

Hobart

Dennes Point

Bull Bay

Kilora

Barnes Bay

Kettering

Barnes Bay

Cockatoo Hill

Roberts Point
Apollo Bay

Trumpeter Bay

Rao's Restaurant

Missionary Bay

Great Bay

Variety Bay

Church Hill

Camel Tracks Tasmania

The Neck Game Reserve

Isthmus Bay

Moorina Bay

Cape Queen Elizabeth

Ninepin Point Marine Reserve

Simpsons Bay

Truganini memorial

Penguin viewing platform

The Neck

Adventure Bay

Alonnah
Hotel Bruny

Hothouse Café

Picnic area

Bruny Island Charters

Penguin Island

Captain Cook's landing place

Fluted Cape

Ventenat Point

Caravan park

Adventure Bay

St Clairs
Lunawanna

Lumeah
Backpackers Hostel

Mt Mangana

Adventure Bay Holiday Village Caravan Park

Partridge Island

Explorers Cottages

Inala on Bruny

Merista Nature Walk

Bligh Museum

Mt Cook

Cape Connella

Bay of Islands

Labillardiere Peninsula

Great Taylors Bay

Cloudy Bay Lagoon

Mangana Bluff

N

Bradt

Labillardiere State Reserve

Standaway Bay

Cloudy Bay

South Bruny National Park

West Cloudy Head

East Cloudy Head

Mt Bruny

South Bruny National Park

Boreel Head

0   8km
0   5 miles

Courts Island

Cape Bruny

Tasman Head

Friar Rocks

KEY
Road
Walking trail
Ferry route
National Park

you have rented or chartered there are boat ramps at Barnes Bay and Dennes Point on North Bruny, and at Simpsons Bay, Alonnah, Lunawanna and Adventure Bay on South Bruny. From Hobart to the ferry is a good hour's drive and 10–15 minutes are needed to buy tickets from the visitor centre right by the boat and drive on. The *Mirambeena* docks at Roberts Point north of Apollo Bay on North Bruny (toilets here) and a good road leads all the way south to Lunawanna, with a branch to Adventure Bay. Sections are gravel but still passable with a 2WD at slower speed. A gravel road continues to the lighthouse at Cape Bruny. If you have a 4WD you will be able to take the lesser rough roads with ease. All roads are passable on a bicycle with care. Look out for wildlife crossing signs on the road. The **Lumeah Hostel** at Adventure Bay (tel: 6293 1265) offers return transport between it and Hobart for $35 (bikes carried free).

Depending on your accommodation, it is probably a good idea to bring provisions with you to Bruny as there are only one or two restaurants and cafés and shops are scarce. Also pick up all brochures and other information you might need at the visitor centre for the island which is at the ferry terminal in Kettering. Petrol and services at Alonnah and Adventure Bay.

Where to stay and eat

St Clairs (Lunawanna, Bruny Island, TAS 7150; tel: 6293 1300; fax: 6293 1299; email: getaway@stclairs.com; web: www.stclairs.com) is a self-contained seaside cottage for a couple. There are wide verandahs and lawns which attract possums, wallabies, parrots, black cockatoos and occasionally a 40-spotted pardalote. It has its own foreshore, private jetty and moorings, and a fishing dinghy with outboard motor is available. Cook-your-own breakfasts provided, supper can be arranged for $33 each extra. $165 for one night for a couple (includes cook-your-own breakfast and champagne on arrival); $150 per night for two or more nights; $900 for one week (seventh night free).

Explorers Cottages (PO Box 25, Margate, TAS 7054; tel/fax: 6293 1465; email: info@experiencetas.com.au) on Lighthouse Road, Lunawanna, are charming and cosy self-contained 2-bedroom cottages run (at present) by local eco-tourism operator Rob Pennicott (see *What to see and do*, page 139). Rates on enquiry.

Inala Guesthouse (Cloudy Bay Rd, Bruny Island, TAS 7150; tel: 6293 1217; mobile: 0418 124 934; email: inala@inalabruny.com.au; web: www.inalabruny.com.au). A good, homely, self-contained place in a gentle valley run by biologist and bird expert, Dr Tonia Cochrane (see *What to see and do*, page 139), who gives a percentage of her earnings to a conservation fund for environmental projects on the island. Rates by arrangement.

Adventure Bay Holiday Village (Adventure Bay, TAS 7150; tel: 6293 1270; fax: 6293 1485) is an up-market caravan park just behind the dunes by the beach. This is a good spot with several self-contained cabin and cottages, on-site vans, powered sites and camping pitches. It is right at the western end of the bay with forested hills rising up behind. At dusk you might spot one of Tasmania's rare white wallabies standing ghost-like in a paddock. There is a laundry, plenty of games for wet days, and some facilities for disabled visitors. Cabins and cottages from $50–95; on-site vans $32 double (no bedding); powered sites $14 double (child $4); camping $12 double (child $4).

Hotel Bruny (Bruny Main Rd, Bruny Island, TAS 7150; tel: 6293 1148) at Alonnah has 2 en-suite rooms which are quite basic, but it is fine for a night or two. Locals will tell you this is the southernmost pub in Australia but there is a bit of a squabble between Hotel Bruny and the Dover Hotel over on the mainland. If you have a GPS with you then you might be able to settle the argument once and for all. $40/70 single/double.

Lumeah Backpackers Hostel (Adventure Bay, Bruny Island, TAS 7150; tel: 6293 1265) has dorms and double rooms, offers tours, provides transport, rental of bikes, tents and kayaks, and can even rustle up a massage for aching muscles. Dorm bed $20 per person; double room $53; whole hostel $264 for 18 people.

The Hothouse Café (46 Adventure Bay Rd, Bruny Island, TAS 7150; tel: 6293 1131; email: hotcafe@morella-island.com.au; web: www.morella-island.com.au) does good coffee and light meals as well as seafood suppers. Open daily from 10.00. Bookings essential after 17.30. There is also some first-class accommodation (see same website).

Rao's Restaurant (360 Lennon Rd, Bruny Island, TAS 7150; tel/fax: 6260 6444) is near the ferry terminal on North Bruny and serves Italian food and Tasmanian wines. There are log fires and good waterfront views. There is also a bar with Tasmanian wines for sale. Open daily 10.00–late for morning and afternoon tea, lunch and supper (take-away available). Bookings after 17.30.

What to see and do
Wildlife

Bruny's wildlife is superb and the main draw for most visitors. Hundreds of fairy penguins nest in the dunes along The Neck. There is a sturdy wooden staircase leading to the top of the dunes which provides good access and viewing but allows the penguins to go about their business unflustered. Courtship begins in August followed by mating, and the first batch of chicks hatch in September and October. Viewing is best from October to early January when most penguins are on land with their young (see *Minimal Impact*, page 91). For much of the rest of the year they are at sea. Most young have hatched and are ready to leave the nest burrows by Christmas. This is the optimum viewing time as young wait outside the burrows for their parents returning from the open ocean where they will have dived to as deep as 60 metres to fish. Any chicks still here in February are in trouble because that is when parents begin to moult and temporarily lose their oily waterproof feathers and so cannot fish for their offspring. There are about 100 breeding pairs of penguins at The Neck, making it possibly the best place in Tasmania to watch these birds.

More than 1,000 Australian fur seals play in the waters off the southeast coast of Bruny Island. They use the rocky shoreline of Friar Island as a 'haul-out' or kind of social gathering. These are nearly all males as the females organise their own private get-togethers on the islands of Bass Strait. Males are dark grey-brown and females a gingery-brown with hints of silver. To see the seals you need to get yourself on a boat.

The southeast coast of Bruny Island is also on the migration route for humpback and southern right whales as they head north each autumn (April and May) for warmer waters and south again in spring (October and November). Watch out also for bottlenose and common dolphin, who can frolic here all year round.

There are scores of sea birds that call Bruny home. Look out for cormorants, storm petrels, shy albatross, Australasian gannets, oystercatchers, Pacific and kelp gulls and sea eagles who nest high on the cliffs. In the calmer waters of Isthmus Bay on the western side of The Neck are black swans. The overall bird count for Bruny according to the Parks and Wildlife department is around 115 species of which the majority are here year-round and several are endemic to Tasmania (tel: 6293 1408 for a full list or drop in at the Alonnah Council Chambers).

Bruny's mammals include echidnas, feral cats, eastern quolls (they love the garbage bins at the ferry terminal at Roberts Point), pademelons, possums and wallabies but there are very few Tasmanian devils or wombats. If you are lucky around the eastern end of Adventure Bay and in the hillsides en route to Fluted Cape you might spot a white wallaby – a sub species unique to Bruny and much lighter than other wallabies. All three types of snake are here.

Walks outside South Bruny National Park

There are good short walks at Nebrasca Beach and Bligh's Point, both off the Killora Road near Dennes Point on the north island.

Cape Queen Elizabeth Distance: 6–8km return. Time: 3–4 hours return. Difficulty: easy.

For this beautiful stroll through the northern section of The Neck Game Reserve drive south down the main B66 and shortly after a turn-off on your left signed for camel treks there is another stopping place. A track leading off is marked. Follow this as it skirts the edge of a lagoon and leads to the snow-white sands of Moorina Bay, which makes a good spot for hunting for mysterious animal and bird tracks. A side-track then leads on to the cape with the Hound's Tooth rock jutting up just off shore. There are great views south to The Neck and Adventure Bay. Return by retracing your steps.

Mavista Nature Walk Distance: 1km return. Time: 30–50 minutes. Difficulty: Easy.

Picturesque walk that leads from Resolution Road at the back of Adventure Bay through a fern glade next to Water Fall Creek. Watch for wallabies, and echidnas.

Mount Mangana Distance: 1–2km return. Time: 1–2 hours. Difficulty: easy to moderate.

The walk is straightforward but climbs to 571m. The track begins on the south side of the Coolangatta Road, halfway between Lunawanna and Adventure Bay. It wanders through rainforest, fern glades and eucalyptus stands until it reaches the summit which is the highest point on Bruny Island, offering stunning views in all directions. Keep an eye out for snakes on the path warming up on hot days.

Swimming and surfing

The sheltered bays like Adventure Bay and Jetty Beach are good for swimming as they are protected from the mighty swell that can crash into the Bruny coastline. The waters here are pretty cold though so you might not want to set your heart on a swimming holiday on Bruny. If you see a solitary boat in a harbour with some lines leading from it into the water it means an abalone diver is at work or someone is spearfishing – both can attract sharks and so these are two good reasons for not going for a dip. Shark attacks are very rare in Australian waters but Great Whites do cruise these waters so check with the locals on the safety angle. Surfers should head for Cloudy Bay where the breaks are terrific. A big southerly swell will have you staring open-mouthed at some of the most powerful and perfectly crafted waves in the world. Wetsuits essential.

Truganini memorial

Truganini was thought to be the last Tasmanian full-blood Aboriginal until very recently when it was discovered some had outlived her. She was born here in 1803, daughter of the local chief Mangana of the Nuenonne tribe. She survived the Flinders Island settlement (see *History*, page 8) and was later moved to Oyster Cove. Truganini ended her days living in Hobart until her death in 1876. Not until 1976 did she get a proper burial when her ashes were scattered in the D'Entrecasteaux Channel between the mainland and her beloved Bruny. As you take the ferry across, pause for a minute to contemplate her place in history and to mourn the rapid destruction of her race that she witnessed. A small plaque to her stands at the top of the wooden steps at the penguin breeding grounds on The Neck.

Tours

The Bruny D'Entrecasteaux Visitor Centre by the ferry terminal in Kettering (tel: 6267 4494; fax: 6297 4266; email: enquiries@tasmaniaholiday.com; web: www.tasmaniaholiday.com) has a Bruny Island Self Drive Tour leaflet with detailed instructions on how to see the island at your own pace. But in my opinion your best bet is to contact two local eco-experts for accommodation and tours.

Rob Pennicott runs **Bruny Island Charters** (PO Box 25 Margate, TAS 7054; tel/fax: 6293 1465; email: info@experiencetas.com.au). He organises land-based and sea-based tours to order in the South Bruny National Park. He picks up from hotels as far away as Hobart or will collect passengers from the ferry. He takes them to view penguins on The Neck, seals at Friar Island, whales and dolphins off the coast, and birds everywhere. A full-day tour including a Hobart pick-up, scenic tour to Bruny, five-hour eco-cruise, all food and wine and return is included. Rates on enquiry. At the time of writing Rob runs the Explorers Cottages at Lunawanna but was contemplating selling them.

He is one of a number of operators in Tasmania who have focused on environmentally sensitive tourism. He discourages the use of flash photography when viewing penguins after dark and tries to ensure all torches are covered in red cellophane to protect the birds' eyes. He sticks to the distance rules when observing wildlife on land and sea, and he re-designed his boat to create less pollution and noise. As a result he is one of only five people in Tasmania to be accredited as running a fully approved eco-tourism operation.

Dr Tonia Cochrane operates **Inala Nature Tours** (Cloudy Bay Road, Bruny Island, TAS 7150; tel: 6293 1217; mobile: 0418 124 934; email: inala@inalabruny.com.au; web: www.inala.com.au) and is a biologist and bird expert who often works with Rob and his guests. She runs half-day tours taking nature walks up Mount Mangana to find tree ferns and waratahs, along stretches of wild coastline looking for rare hooded plovers, and to see firetail finches and towering gum trees around her own property. There are also evening tours to see penguins, possums and pademelons, and night tours to spot the masked owl flying under a starry sky. Tonia has spent a lot of time in Antarctica as a krill specialist and puts on an excellent slide show on the frozen continent for guests staying at her Inala Guesthouse. Tour prices on application.

Between them they know pretty much all of Bruny's wildlife secrets. They told me that, while much of Tasmania is under tourism development, Bruny is still 'very raw'.

Also try **Active Holidays Kelly's Lookout** for tours (212 Main Road, Dennes Point; tel: 6260 6466; mobile: 0427 054 494; fax: 6260 6456; email: kellyslookout@aol.com). They run day cruises, fishing and yachting days, cycling tours, camel treks, sea kayaking to Iron Pot islet off the northern tip, wildlife watching, bushwalking, diving, and scenic flights over the islands. They also provide evening meals.

The Lumeah Hostel in Adventure Bay (tel: 6293 1265) also offers day tours of the island from around $50 each.

Adventure Bay

Captain Tobias Furneaux landed here after losing touch with his famous comrade James Cook in heavy seas during a voyage on February 8 1773. Furneaux's ship was the *Adventure*. It was another four years before Cook landed here with the *Resolution* and *Discovery*. His crew compared weapons with the Aborigines who were terrified by the white men's muskets but the meetings were peaceful. Cook stayed here on at least three further occasions, as did Lieutenant William Bligh before heading for Tahiti in the *Bounty* in 1788. Penguin Island was Bligh's last landfall before the famous mutiny. Bligh came back here, however, in 1792 with the *Providence* and *Assistant* and spent two weeks with the Aboriginal people.

The excellent **Bligh Museum of Pacific Exploration** (876 Main Road, Adventure Bay, TAS 7150; tel: 6293 1117; mobile: 0414 922 527; fax: 6225 1081; email: jontan@southcom.com.au) has good information on the various landings here between 1772 and 1808. There are historical maps, documents and paintings. Open daily 09.00–17.00; closed Christmas Day, Boxing Day, Good Friday. Adult $4; child $2; family $10 (2 adults, 2 or more children).

Adventure Bay is a good swimming beach as it faces north and so is protected from the mighty swell that rolls in to this coastline. However, check with the locals on the shark situation. Three white pointers (Great Whites) were caught in the bay in a 12-month period spanning late 2000 and early 2001. This is also a good spot for dolphin watching.

SOUTH BRUNY NATIONAL PARK

The park (tel: 6293 1419) covers 5,059 hectares in two main sections of South Bruny Island and also Partridge Island, The Friars off Tasman Head, most of the east coast and Fluted Cape, Grass Point and Penguin Island near Adventure Bay. It was declared a national park in 1996 and includes towering dolerite cliffs and rocky shorelines broken by sandy sweeps of beach. Plant communities along cliffs are sparse and hardy turning to heaths further inland, then eucalyptus scrub and forest. Pademelons, potoroos, wallabies and possums are common, as are shearwaters (mutton-birds) and penguins. Tasmanian devils and wombats have also been reported.

In 1835 three ships were wrecked in D'Entrecasteaux Channel and it was recommended that a lighthouse be built at Cape Bruny. The lighthouse cost £2,500, was built by convicts and has kept vigil since 1838. This is one of Tasmania's premier spots for seeing albatross. Guided tours are available by prior arrangement and for a maximum of five adults or six people if children are included. Contact Cape Bruny Lighthouse, PO Box 1, Alonnah, TAS 7150; tel: 6298 3114. Open daily 10.00–16.00. Adult $10; concession $5; child $2; family $20.

From the lighthouse, look due south and on a clear day you should be able to make out the rock stack of Pedra Blanca about 48km off the coast which is home to a shy albatross colony. Beyond and to one side of it is the faint stack of Eddystone Rock but you might need binoculars for that. Beyond these stacks there lies 2,500km of open ocean until Antarctica.

📷 Photo spot
From the lighthouse is a wonderful seascape due south. Use a wide-angle lens and 64–100ASA film and on a cloudy day wait for the sun to break through and form patches of silver on the water. A long lens (300mm) might capture the lines of swell if it is big enough.

Short walks
Grass Point and Penguin Island
Distance: 2km return. Time: 1–2 hours return. Difficulty: moderate to hard.
Starting at the eastern end of Adventure Bay beach the clearly defined track leads along the coast to the point from where Penguin Island is visible.

Fluted Cape
Distance: 4–5km. Time: 3 hours. Difficulty: hard.
This is a stunning walk but not for the faint-hearted. It is a loop track. You can take the existing walk to Grass Point (see above) and then head on round the cliffs or

take the track through the woods and uphill to the cliffs which then leads round north to Grass Point. Both are signposted and fairly clear to follow. This section is much harder than the Grass Point track however: there are some big cliffs up to 276m (some of the tallest in Australia) and the track gets quite tricky in places. It is breathtaking to be up there on a windy day with the waves pounding in far below your feet. Watch for sea eagles.

Day walks
Labillardiere Peninsula
Distance: 12–14km. Time: 6–7 hours. Difficulty: moderate (but long so take food and water)
This loop walk starts at Jetty Beach from where there are signs. The track hugs the coast for almost its entire length with great seascape views. Watch for whales and dolphins on the surface and sea eagles and albatross in the sky. There is a short cut loop less than 1km from the start which is signposted and provides an optional 1½-hour walk.

Cloudy Bay Beach Walk
This walk is easy and as long as you want to make it. Start at Whalebone Point at the end of the C644 and walk right around to Cloudy Bay Cabin at the southern end of the beach or west to the entrance to the lagoon. This is one of the best surf beaches but it is a little rough for swimming.

📷 Photo spot
This is a good beach for isolating a piece of driftwood or whale bone or similar and making that your focus, allowing the beach to stretch away on all sides and become blurred. 50mm lens and 64–100ASA film.

Further information
Contact the Kettering Travel and Information Centre (tel: 6267 4494; email: kettering@tasvisinfo.com.au) at the ferry terminal which has helpful staff, a café and a wealth of information booklets. Definitely worth a quick look before you head to Bruny.

FAR SOUTH
South of Geeveston lie some of the most lonely stretches of Tasmania outside the national parks. The A6 to Dover runs along the eastern edge of the Southern Forests with small tracks leading out to the coast at the mouth of the Huon River at the D'Entrecasteaux Channel. On to Southport the settlements thin out and the facilities become more scarce. Once you pass Southport everything becomes 'southerly'. In Lune River you will find the most southerly post office and youth hostel. The final dirt track south from Lune River is Australia's most southerly road leading to Australia's most southerly settlement at Cockle Creek which harbours Australia's most southerly residence. There are walks, caves, thermal pools, and a beautiful coastline. The pace is slow and the surroundings tranquil. Everything south is ocean to Macquarie Island and Antarctica and everything west right around the coast to Strahan is forest and heathland, impenetrable save by hardy walkers and light planes.

Getting there and around
By car, head south from Geeveston on the A6 to just north of Southport, take a right turn on to the C635 then left on to the C636 which becomes a dirt track

immediately. Follow this through Lune River and on to Catamaran and finally Cockle Creek. **TWT's Tassielink Regional Coach Service** (tel: 1300 300 520; web: www.tigerline.com.au) runs bus services between Hobart and Dover and on to Cockle Creek via Huonville and Geeveston. **Hobart Coaches** (tel: 6231 4077) also run services from the capital to Woodbridge and Cygnet, and also to Dover via Huonville and Geeveston but the service is limited and favours weekdays. If you have a boat and a trailer there are boat ramps at Police Point, Dover, Southport and Catamaran on Recherche Bay.

Where to stay and eat

Dover Bayside Lodge (Bayview Road, Dover, TAS 7117; tel/fax: 6298 1788) is a four-star place with good views over the bay, a dining-room and lawn golf. Four en-suite rooms, one standard and one suite. En-suite $75–98, single and double. Standard $65/75, single/double.

Driftwood (Bayview Road, Dover, TAS 7117; tel: 6298 1441; fax: 6298 1401; email: driftwood@tassie.net.au; web: www.farsouth.com.au/driftwood) has four self-contained double and family studios, the Beach House and the Cove House both overlooking Port Esperance. Apartment $130/130–170, single/double. Studio apartment $99/99–130, single/double.

Dover Hotel (Main Road, Dover, TAS 7117; tel: 6298 1210; fax: 6298 1504; email: Doverhotel@bigpond.com.au) is a hotel, motel, B&B and a pub rolled in to one. It has standard and en-suite rooms and apartment units, pub food and its own airstrip. Standard double room $70, en-suite $90, apartment $110.

Southern Forest B&B (30 Jager Road, Southport, TAS 7109; tel: 6298 3306; fax: 6298 3306; email: glaus@telstra.easymail.com.au) is a cosy place close to beaches and fishing spots. Serves afternoon teas. $45–60/$75–80, single/double.

The **Jetty House B&B** (Huon Highway, Southport, TAS 7109; tel/fax: 6298 3139; email: jettyhouse@telstra.easymail.com.au) is a colonial home dating back to 1875 with log fires and a games room for wild and wet days, and cosy evenings. It is opposite a white-sand beach and also serves afternoon teas. Standard room $55–60/85–90, single/double.

Lune River YHA and Backpackers Hostel, Australia's southernmost youth hostel, burned down in late 2001. The place was popular with travellers and walkers and used to hold excellent full moon feasts with home-baked pizzas and seafood smorgasbords. It was also extremely convenient budget accommodation at one of Tasmania's extremities. Contact the YHA in Australia for updates: (web: www.yha.com.au). There are **camping areas** at Cockle Creek for those beginning or finishing the South Coast Track but no facilities.

For food other than at your accommodation, your best bet is the Dover Hotel (see above listing) for good pub grub and snacks. Alternatively bring all your provisions down here with you or stock up at Dover with food, water, petrol and any other essentials.

What to see and do

There are some majestic **sea views** from vantage spots around Police Point, especially at Roaring Bay, Hideaway Bay, Desolation Bay, Surveyors Bay and Huon Point. Access between these places is mainly on a dirt-road which is passable with 2WD provided the weather has not been atrocious.

Dover grew fat on the profits from the timber industry when Huon pine was the wood of choice. Now it is a fishing village and regional tourist centre. You can hop aboard the **Olive May** (Dover Cruise Office, Bay View Road (A6), Dover; tel: 6298 1062), a former trading ship built of Huon pine, for a tour to oyster and salmon farms. Also available for fishing and sailing cruises including the run over to Partridge Island in South Bruny National Park. Open daily September–May 09.00–18.00.

Dover is the southern tip of the **Tasmanian Trail**, a long distance, multi-purpose recreational trail north to Devonport, covering 480km. See *Chapter 11* for full details and trace the route on the Parks and Wildlife Service website (web: www.parks.tas.gov.au).

South of Dover, a dirt-road leads right from the A6 near Raminea and on to the **Hastings Forest Picnic Area**. The drive along forestry roads is pleasant and passes stands of mighty Huon pine and eucalyptus. It is about 10km to the picnic area on the banks of the Esperance River. There are toilets, short signed walks, and some disabled access. The Forest and Heritage Centre in Geeveston provides audio cassettes for self-guided tours of the Hastings Forest.

South of Dover and west of Southport are the **Hastings Caves and Thermal Springs** (tel: 6298 3209) which are definitely worth a look. In the heart of a wild forest you can tour a dolomite cave with good formations, and a geothermal spring with pools to bathe in. The water is a steady 28°C all year and there's a special pool for children. There is also a good visitor centre and café, and a short walk where platypus have been seen. Open all year. Prices on application.

A little further south at Lune River is the 7km **Ida Bay Railway** (tel: 6223 5893), the only stretch of original 2ft-narrow gauge railway left in Tasmania. There were once hundreds of miles of it. Three original 1940s locomotives run along the line with a 1936 steam locomotive for special days. Several passenger carriages date from the 1890s and are among the earliest of their kind in Australia. From Lune River it travels through light bush to the shores of Ida Bay, passing the site of the original town of Ida Bay, its wharf and grave yard. The views are charming and the line ends at Deep Hole Bay, a secluded, mile-long swimming beach accessible only by rail. There are short, signed bush walks to the King George V monument where a convict ship sank with a huge loss of life. Open daily December 26 to Easter, Sunday only for rest of year (departures 12.00, 14.00, 16.00); closed Christmas Day. Adult $12; child $6 (under 16 years); family $30 (2 adults, 4 children).

Short walks in the Southwest National Park
Fishers Point
Distance: 5km return. Time: 2–3 hours return. Difficulty: easy.
Also starting in Cockle Creek, this walk takes you northeast along the southern edge to Recherche Bay and Fishers Point. The going is easy and the views marvellous over the bay and across to the southern limits of Bruny Island. Cape Bruny should be visible on a clear day.

Day walks in the Southwest National Park
South Cape Bay
Distance: 10km return. Time: 4–5 hours return. Difficulty: moderate (but long so take waterproofs, extra clothing, food and water).
The walk starts at Cockle Creek. It is well signed. This is the start of Tasmania's famous South Coast Track which ends at Melaleuca in the heart of the World Heritage Area. As you head south to the cape you may be overtaken by intrepid hikers with towering packs who are setting out on a week-long journey into the wilderness, or passed in the opposite direction by others who are nearing the end of their South Coast Track experience and probably looking and smelling pretty rotten. This part of the track is almost all on duckboards over buttongrass plains which makes it straightforward and pleasant. The views as you approach South

Cape Bay are spectacular and you will want to spend some time on the beach drinking in the atmosphere and looking out for a washed up whale bone. Return the same way.

📷 *Photo spot*

The sign for the start of the South Coast Walk makes a good marker photo, one to prove you were there. Take from a 45° angle with the arrow to the track pointing in to the centre of the frame, and preferably a walker or two with big packs taking their first few strides along it. Wide angle lens and 100–200ASA film.

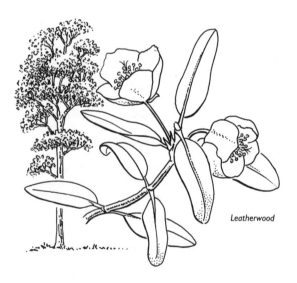

Leatherwood

The Southwest

The southwest is the Tasmania of picture books and of vivid accounts by early explorers. It is inhospitable, dangerous and beautiful. It takes up almost one-quarter of the state and is one of the few places where nature has been left to run completely at will. In an area of roughly 14,000km^2 there is only one sealed road, a few gravel tracks, one or two long-distance walking trails, and an airstrip for a light plane. The rest is virtually inaccessible. It is all within national parks and a World Heritage Area. I am always encouraged by being here as it shows what can be done when people are allowed to fight to protect an environment.

This area's protection was not won easily, however, and it took determined campaigns to secure its freedom from loggers and hydro-electric schemes. Green party senator Bob Brown explains the background to one such campaign in *Chapter 4* (see page 96).

It is scientifically significant as one of only a tiny number of temperate wilderness rainforests left on earth. It contains several mountain ranges all over 1,000m high, deep valleys and highland lakes cut by glaciers during the last ice age, and trees more than a thousand years old. It also harbours a biosphere reserve and mighty swamp gums, the tallest flowering plants on earth and second only in the tall tree race to the California redwoods. But it has been saved too for purely aesthetic reasons and simply because it is there. Its protected status sets a precedent. The example of this wilderness can be employed worldwide to further protect areas.

There is evidence of human habitation stretching back many thousands of years in more than 50 caves, some of which contain some of the earliest cave paintings known anywhere in the world. Having satisfied more criteria for selection than any other World Heritage Area, it was placed on the World Heritage List by UNESCO in 1982, with the Hartz Mountains being added in 1989. It joined several other World Heritage properties in Australia, including the Great Barrier Reef, Lord Howe Island group, Kakadu National Park and Uluru National Park both in the Northern Territory, and Shark Bay in Western Australia.

The wilderness covered in this chapter begins south of the A10 cross-country road from Hobart to Strahan (although the WHA extends north of this up to and including Cradle Mountain-Lake St Clair National Park; see *Chapter 9*, page 177). It extends down to the south and southwest coasts and east to include the Hartz Mountains due south of Hobart, its southeastern extremity being the South Cape. I have also included Mount Field National Park in this section due to its proximity to the WHA and its fabulous flora and fauna that will give people a taste of what is to come further west. And also the Styx Valley which is afforded no protection and is in fact being logged and is now the focus of a major campaign to halt its destruction (see *Conservation*, page 94).

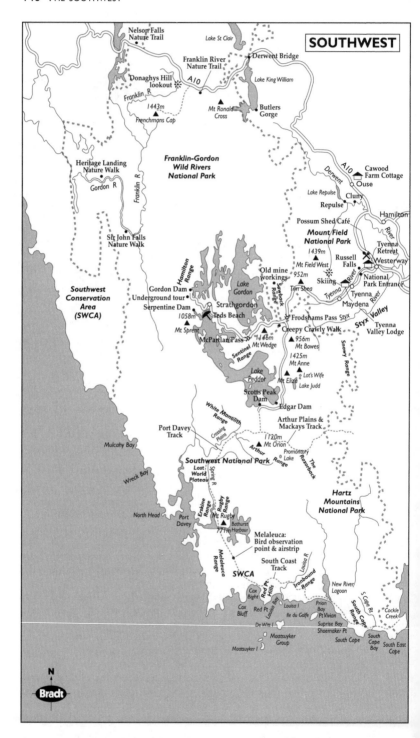

WORLD HERITAGE AREA

About 14,000km² or 20% of the island state (the size of Northern Ireland or a little bigger than Connecticut) is protected in a World Heritage Area that was established in 1982 and expanded in 1989. It covers the southwest sector of the state stretching from Cradle Mountain in the north to the Southwest Cape and the islands beyond. It includes the four largest national parks – in descending order the Southwest, Franklin-Gordon Wild Rivers, Cradle Mountain-Lake St Clair, and Walls of Jerusalem (see *Chapter 9*, page 188). It also harbours a precious biosphere reserve.

This is one of the last temperate wilderness areas on earth and a fair amount of it is impenetrable and has only been explored by the odd wandering botanist.

There is human history here, too, in the form of ancient cave paintings. The ones in the Ballawinne and Wargata Mina caves are among the earliest ever found.

UNESCO officials debating whether to grant this area World Heritage status passed it with flying colours after it satisfied more criteria for selection than any of the other 409 World Heritage Areas in the international club, and they include Mount Everest, the Great Wall of China and the Taj Mahal.

When you walk in to the wilderness area you need to be prepared for at least a ten-day trek, often in harsh and unpredictable conditions. Its position facing the Southern Ocean means it takes the brunt of the wicked weather that these seas regularly throw up. Gales and blizzards are commonplace year round. Winter brings days of persistent, sheeting rain that lashes the forests. It is impossible to get an impression of the scale of this place and just how far you can look without seeing a single man-made object unless you are here, and even then it takes some effort. Visitors are awe-struck to the extent that some consider it too difficult to embark on a trip into this natural expanse. We are so conditioned to contact with fellow humans, or at least the odd telephone booth or power line, that when all this is taken from us we panic. If you have the time and the right equipment then get out there and tackle the southwest. It might just change your life.

GETTING THERE AND AROUND
By air

There are some scenic flights in to the far southwest that drop off or pick up walkers. Par Avion (tel: 6248 5390; fax: 6248 51177; email: paravion@tassie.net.au; web: www.paravion.com) fly two-hour flights twice daily from Hobart over the southwest wilderness with stops for lunch and the option of camping overnight. They also operate one-way flights to or from Hobart for bushwalkers doing tracks in the southwest and can arrange food drops for walkers out there for the long haul.

By road

The only ways in by road are from the A10 Hobart to Strahan road (Lyell Highway) or on the B61 from Westerway in the Derwent Valley, a sealed but windy road that runs for 100km right through the heart of the WHA to Gordon River Dam. This road may well be impassable in winter. Half way along is a turning on to a gravel road that leads south for 40km to Scotts Peak Dam where some long-distance walks begin. Most bus companies run between Hobart and Strahan (see *Getting Around* section in *Chapter 4*) and can drop off at spots along the way. **TWT's Tassielink Regional Coach Service** (tel: 1300 300 520; web: www.tigerline.com.au) also runs services to Mount Field National Park and Scotts Peak Dam but the latter is subject to demand.

By bicycle
Cyclists should give themselves a good two days from Westerway to Gordon River Dam or Scotts Peak Dam. The rough road to Scotts Peak might be too much for some cyclists and some bikes so it is best to check conditions before you depart Westerway.

By sea
The only service is from Strahan up the Gordon River past Sarah Island to Sir John Falls (see *Chapter 8*, *West Coast*). Going further afield around the coastline you would have to charter your own boat (see *Getting Around* section in *Chapter 2*) to get around to Port Davey (landing sites are limited).

By raft
There are rafting tours down the Franklin from put-ins along the Lyell Highway. **Rafting Tasmania** (PO Box 403, Sandy Bay, TAS 7006; tel: 6239 1080; fax: 6239 1090; email: raftingtas@ozemail.com.au) runs four-day and seven-day trips as well as a longer ten-day one. All equipment is supplied and meals are prepared by your guide at camps on longer tours. Leave Hobart by bus and transfer to 4WD. The climb to the river is quite strenuous, but a spectacular gorge with waterfalls, rainforest and rapids is the reward. On the final day, join the Gordon River and paddle the final few kilometres to Sir Johns Falls. Early in the morning the tour boards a yacht to cruise to Macquarie Harbour and Strahan. A bus returns to Hobart early in the evening. Rates on enquiry.

The Wild Way
The Lyell Highway is also known as the Wild Way. Tasmania's South Regional Tourism Association has compiled a helpful brochure on the history and main features of the route between Hobart and Strahan. It is well worth getting hold of a copy. It also mentions off-road drives and short walks from the main road. Ask at the Visitor Travel and Information Centres in Hobart, New Norfolk, Queenstown or Strahan.

WHERE TO STAY AND EAT
As you might imagine, this region is not going to offer the fattest accommodation and dining section in the book. Chances are your bed will be under canvas and your meal cooked by yourself on a camping stove. The exception is Mount Field National Park:

Russell Falls Holiday Cottages (Lake Dobson Road, National Park, TAS 7140; tel: 6288 1198) are quite good. There are four self-contained cottages with single or double bedrooms. Bed linen is not provided but is for hire. $60/77, single/double.
The National Park Hotel (Gordon River Road, National Park, TAS 7140; tel: 6288 1103) has seven standard rooms including some with queen-size beds, and serves big breakfasts and pub food in the evenings. $37/65, single/double.
The **Mount Field YHA** (tel: 6288 1369; fax: 6234 7422; web: www.yha.com.au) is just

outside the park, shortly west of the entrance on the main road. It has five rooms sleeping a total of 23 people. Standard room $15/30, single/double.

Mount Field Visitor Services Caravan Park (66 Lake Dobson Road, National Park, TAS 7140; tel: 6288 1526; fax: 6288 1207; email: mountfield@vision.net.au) has 26 campsites for a total of 52 people and 14 serviced sites for 42 people. Caravans, tents and campervans welcome. It is a peaceful spot by the banks of the Tyenna River. Campsite $5/10, single/double; serviced site $7/14, single/double.

Near by, in the small valley town of Maydena is the superb **Tyenna Valley Lodge** (Junee Road, Maydena, TAS 7140; tel: 6288 2293; fax: 6288 2166; email: info@tvlodge.com; web: www.tvlodge.com) which has self-contained units and budget B&B rooms. Tours can be arranged. Check website for rates.

Just outside Mount Field is **Tyenna Retreat** (c/o PO Westerway, TAS 7140; tel: 6288 1552; mobile: 0419 307 623; web: www.travelways.com.au) which is a country property with accommodation for four people. Fly-fishing trout tours arranged on request. $75–95 double.

An option along the A10 is **Cawood Farm Cottage** at Ouse (tel: 6287 1499; fax: 6287 1489) where you get a small farmhouse to yourself with log fires, breakfast provisions, queen-sized bed, television and a phone. Cawood is a National Trust classified property dating from 1824 and set on a 700-hectare working farm.

Apart from the Mount Field National Park headquarters, bistro and shop, the National Park Hotel and the Cockatoo Café at the Tyenna Valley Lodge in Maydena, food is scarce out here so stock up at one of the convenience stores in the lovely little town of Westerway. The main store and petrol station is full of provisions and there is a toilet out the back. Almost opposite is one of Tasmania's best-kept secrets, the **Possum Shed** café (tel: 6288 1477). It serves light snacks, hearty meals including lots of vegetarian food (main dishes $10–12) and fabulous Devonshire teas. The owners, Alison and Tony, are charming and will tell you how to spot platypus in the Tyenna River running at the side of the café on its way to join the Derwent. You can arrange tours from here and hire fishing gear and there is an excellent gift shop with locally made goods. Open September–May, Wednesday–Friday 09.30–17.30, Saturday 12.00–18.00, Sunday 10.00–18.00. Phone for winter hours.

STYX VALLEY

This valley just east of Mount Field National Park is not protected. The logging firms want to use it to produce veneer logs and woodchip which is exported to Japan. The environmentalists want to get it protected as a national park and market it to tourists. At the centre of the battle are the mighty swamp gums (*Eucalyptus regnans*) which are the tallest flowering plants on earth. As we go to press, news comes through that a new measurement of one of these floral giants topped 96 metres (316ft), a new record if verified by the forestry authorities. They are, however, not the tallest trees – that accolade belongs to the California redwoods which are conifers (softwoods) while the gums are hardwoods (so flowering plants technically). If you are in Hobart near the Wrest Point Casino look up to the roof and imagine about another 5–6metres (15–20ft) on top of that and you'll get an idea of the height. Better still, call the Wilderness Society and get in there to see them for yourselves (130 Davey Street, Hobart, TAS 7100; tel: 6224 1550; mobile: 0412 875 294; web: www.wilderness.org.au/tasmania). Tours start at the office at 09.00 and return at 18.00. Adult $20, children by donation. Bring raincoat, hat, boots, lunch, water and swimming gear for a dip in the creek.

MEET A TASMANIAN: AMANDA SULLY (FOREST ACTIVIST, FORMER NATURE GUIDE)

Amanda Sully has campaigned to save the forests of Tasmania, especially the giant swamp gums in the Styx Valley, for several years primarily with the Wilderness Society.

'You'd never believe I used to be a futures broker working for Swiss Bank in the City of London would you,' Amanda said as she scrambled down the bank of a stream in the Styx Valley to throw some cold water on her face.

I was earning £60,000 a year and gave it all up for this. It was a good decision. You can't get this freedom and this beautiful forest in the City of London. But then you don't get logging companies there either apart from any that might be on the stock exchange. It was wonderful to come back here and get involved in a job that gets me out into the forests all the time. I used to guide for the Parks and Wildlife Service and I love exploring new parts of the forest. I've taken a few trails off the main logging roads and just headed into the bush to see what I can find. Every now and then you come across a secret river or small clearing where you sit down and wait for the wildlife to come to you. And then you see another giant tree, taller than the last one. The problem here is that these trees could all go. These fabulous giant eucalyptus could all be chopped down because this valley has no protection. It's right on the edge of the World Heritage Area and there are some patches called reserves but in reality they have no protection.

We stopped them building a logging road recently because an eagle's nest just to the side of the path of the road was disturbed. Since then the eagles have not returned. These birds are rare – we think there are only 100 breeding pairs left here – so that kind of disturbance is very damaging. Tasmania's forests are being destroyed and replaced by plantations or agriculture at a horrific rate when they could be used for many years as tourism revenue. Think of the amount of money that the state could get from tourists coming in here in controlled groups causing minimal impact year after year after year – that's got to make more economic sense than the tree being used once for woodchips.

📷 Photo spot

It is very hard to photograph tall trees as you are shooting into the sky so they nearly always over- or under-expose. So best to get a high vantage point and shoot horizontally at the crown of a tree whose base starts way down the hill. Long lens for detailed tree crowns, and 100–200ASA film. You may also want to document the destruction from logging here.

MOUNT FIELD NATIONAL PARK

This park (tel: 6288 1149) covers 16,265 hectares of beautiful high country about an hour's drive west of Hobart. This is one of the two oldest national parks (Freycinet is the other) and was highly valued early on and declared a nature reserve as far back as 1885, becoming a park in 1917. It was, and still is, noted for its wild bush habitats, tiny lakes or tarns carved by glaciers during the last ice age, and cascading waterfalls including the graceful Russell Falls, a major tourist attraction. Vegetation is a mix of rainforest, pandani groves, alpine moorlands and eucalyptus stands including snow gums, cider gums and some mighty swamp gums. This abundant and varied vegetation makes the perfect home for pademelons, potoroos, wallabies, wombats, brush-tailed possums and Tasmanian devils. There are platypus in the lakes at the top of the park, and several species of frog hiding out among the pandani plants. There are numerous birds including the great mimic, the lyrebird. Mount Field has had human inhabitants too, however. The Pangerninghe band of the Big River tribe lived here and traded freely with other bands. It is thought they favoured trade with the Aborigines further west who gave them Darwin glass obtained from a meteor crater near Queenstown to make tools. Mount Field was named after Barron Field, an early judge of the supreme court of New South Wales and Van Diemen's Land, who was a keen naturalist. Its dense cover made it ideal for bushrangers to hide out here in the 1840s. In 1922, people began testing out the ponds and lakes as ice-skating rinks and the place became Tasmania's first winter sports centre. The Ski Club of Tasmania was founded four years later and the first hut was built at Twilight Tarn (the original still stands). A new visitor centre features interpretation displays, a shop and a bistro. Access to the highland areas is via the Lake Dobson Road which climbs for 16km through a succession of types of forest to reach Lake Dobson and its tracks.

WHAT TO SEE AND DO
Bushwalking
As this is the main attraction of this region it gets its own section here. Great care should be taken in this part of Tasmania conducting all walks. You are a long way from assistance and services and a simple thing such as a sprained ankle can escalate into much bigger problems when this isolation is taken into account.

We shall start in Mount Field National Park (park fees apply). All high level walks are subject to snow and ice from April to September and skis and/or snowshoes might be required (check with Parks and Wildlife Department). Detailed maps are needed for all higher level walks. Remember to pick up walk brochures at the park headquarters.

Short walks in Mount Field National Park
Russell Falls
Distance: 1km return. Time: 30 minutes return. Difficulty: easy (disabled access). Russell Falls is one of Tasmania's most popular spots. The falls are graceful and set in a perfect setting with tree ferns and rainforest all around. The walk is easy, signposted, and the track on one side of the creek has been sealed for disabled visitors and families with strollers. It begins at the back of the park headquarters and leads through glades of eucalyptus and myrtles.

Tall Trees Walk
Distance: 1km return. Time: 30 minutes return. Difficulty: easy.
This walk starts at a small car-park about 3km up the Lake Dobson Road from the park headquarters. You can walk through magnificent glades of giant swamp gums. Ask at the park headquarters about using a clinometer on your walk – this device measures the height of trees and the ones you are walking past are some of the tallest in the world.

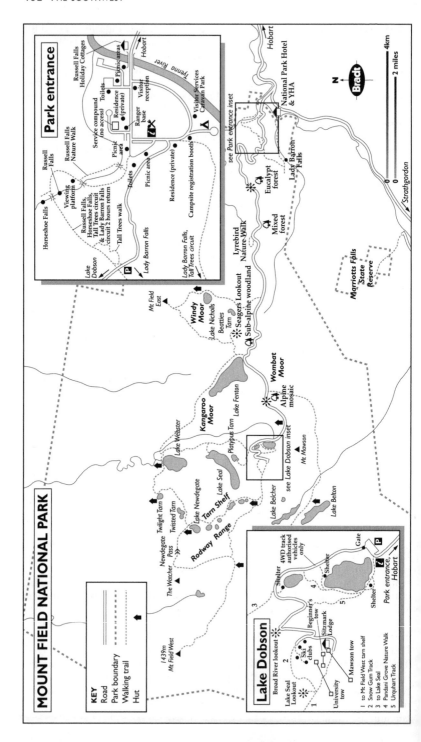

MOUNT FIELD NATIONAL PARK

KEY
Road
Park boundary
Walking trail
Hut

Park entrance

Russell Falls Holiday Cottages
Hobart
Tyenna River
Picnic areas
Service compound (no access)
Residence (private)
Visitor reception
Ranger base
Visitor Services Caravan Park
Toilets
Residence (private)
Campsite registration booth
Russell Falls Nature Walk
Russell Falls
Horseshoe Falls
Viewing platform
Picnic area
Picnic area
Toilets
Russell Falls, Horseshoe Falls, Tall Trees circuit & Lady Barron Falls circuit 2 hours return
Russell Falls, Horseshoe Falls, Tall Trees circuit
Tall Trees walk
Lake Dobson
Lady Barron Falls
Lady Barron Falls, Tall Trees circuit

see Park entrance inset

Lady Barron Falls
Eucalypt forest
Mixed forest
Lyrebird Nature Walk
Sub-alpine woodland
Seagers Lookout
Marriotts Falls State Reserve

National Park Hotel & YHA
Strathgordon

N
Bradt
0   2 miles
0   4km

Mt Field East
Windy Moor
Lake Nicholls
Beatties Tarn

Kangaroo Moor
Lake Webster
Lake Fenton
Wombat Moor
Alpine mosaic
Platypus Tarn

Twilight Tarn
Twisted Tarn
Newdegate Pass
Lake Newdegate
Tarn Shelf
Lake Seal
Mt Mawson
see Lake Dobson inset

The Watcher
Rodway Range

Lake Belcher
Lake Belton

1439m
Mt Field West

Lake Dobson

Broad River lookout
Lake Seal Lookout
Ski clubs
Beginner's tow
Sitzmark Lodge
Mawson tow
University tow
to Mt Field West tarn shelf
Snow Gum Track
to Lake Seal
Pandani Grove Nature Walk
Urquhart Track

1 to Mt Field West tarn shelf
2 Snow Gum Track
3 to Lake Seal
4 Pandani Grove Nature Walk
5 Urquhart Track

Shelter
4WD track authorised vehicles only
Shelter
Shelter
Gate
Shelter
Park entrance, Hobart

Lady Barron Falls Circuit

Distance: 5km return. Time: 2 hours return. Difficulty: easy to moderate.

Start at the back of the park headquarters and complete the walk to Russell Falls then follow signs to Horseshoe Falls just up river. Cross the bridge here and head on to Lady Barron Falls before following the path back to the campsite registration booth.

Lyrebird Nature Walk

Distance: 800m return. Time: 20 minutes return. Difficulty: easy.

About 7km up the Lake Dobson Road from the park headquarters are signs on the right for this walk and a small car-park. You are walking here through mixed forest types with native laurels, sassafras, woolly tea-tree and kangaroo ferns. Watch out for wombats, brush-tailed possums and Tasmanian devils, and at dusk for pademelons and Bennett's wallabies. Birds include the raucous yellow-tailed black cockatoo and the olive whistler, but the main prize here is the fantastic lyrebird. These birds are superb mimics so a number of the calls you are hearing might be from a cheeky lyrebird trying to fool you. It also does an excellent rendition of a chainsaw, apparently.

Pandani Grove Nature Walk

Distance: 3km. Time: 1 hour. Difficulty: moderate (exposed area over 1,000m high so warm clothes needed).

This walk starts from the car-park at Lake Dobson and skirts the lake. There are several examples of trees and plants that are adept at living in areas of extreme climate change. This spot, which can be freezing cold in the morning, becomes sunny and warm by the afternoon. Look out for pencil pine, snow gum and pineapple grass. Pygmy-possums and little pygmy-possums are present here as are platypus, but you have to be rigid still and silent to see one. Keep an eye on the sky too for this is wedge-tailed eagle country. A number of frogs inhabit these upland areas and have mastered the art of copying other creatures' calls. If you hear a duck's quack it is probably the call of a Tasmanian tree frog, while a lamb's bleat signals the presence of a Tasmanian froglet. The brown froglet has cleverly disguised its call to sound like the rusty door hinge creaking open. This walk is named after the pandani plant (*Richea pandanifolia*) which is one of the tallest heath plants in the world. It closely resembles the fronds of the pandanus palm and also looks like an overgrown household yucca plant. Pandani plants grow so big that they eventually topple over and the seeds have to start all over again. When you are near the bridge on this walk have a sniff for the fragrant lemon-scented boronia.

Lake Nicholls

Distance: 6km. Time: 2 hours return. Difficulty: moderate.

A signpost on the right, about 9km up the Lake Dobson Road from the park headquarters, marks the start of this track which climbs steadily through woods and heathland to reach Lake Nicholls. In winter you will find the lake frozen but not enough to take the weight of even a child. Return the same way or go on to Mount Field East (see *Long walks*, page 155).

Seagers Lookout

Distance: 6km. Time: 2 hours return. Difficulty: moderate (steep).

About 11km up the Lake Dobson Road, at the eastern tip of Lake Fenton, are signs for a path that heads uphill steeply and then swings right to Seagers Lookout for fabulous views east and northeast to the Derwent Valley and southwest to the wilderness area. Return the same way or continue on to Mount Field East or Kangaroo Moor (see *Long walks*, page 155).

Snow Gum Track to Lake Seal Lookout

Distance: 6km. Time: 2 hours return. Difficulty: moderate.
At the very top of Lake Dobson Road, next to the ski club buildings, is the start of this delightful walk which affords excellent views over Lake Seal and the Broad River valley below. Here are some good examples of snow gums, as the walk's name would suggest. Return the same way or continue to Mount Field West and/or Tarn Shelf (see *Long walks*, page 155, and *Start of Tarn Shelf*, below).

Start of Tarn Shelf

Distance: 6km. Time: 3 hours return. Difficulty: moderate.
Begin at either the ski club buildings and first walk the Snow Gum Track, or at the Sitzmark Lodge and walk past the ski tow-lines, then take a right at the Rodway Hut. The walk links a number of small tarns all gouged out of the rock by the last ice age. Walk as far as you want and come back the same way. I have not walked it in autumn but the colours of the deciduous beech are said to be spectacular.

Near Mount Field National Park try:

Marriotts Falls

Distance: 1–2km return. Time: 2 hours return. Difficulty: moderate to hard.
You can reach the turn-off for the falls by road from Tyenna, which leads over the river to a small car-park. Follow the signs on foot. This is a deceptively rough track which gets steep in places and follows a creek. At its end are some beautiful waterfalls that make the scramble all worthwhile.

Day walks in Mount Field National Park
Mount Field East Circuit

Distance: 10–12km return. Time: 5 hours return. Difficulty: moderate.
Begin at one of two signs along the Lake Dobson Road, one about 9km from the park headquarters and the other another 2km beyond that. Both are fairly easy going. The first leads past Lake Nicholls (see *Short walks*, page 153) which is a pretty spot for a cup of tea and sit down. The other heads up past Seagers Lookout (see *Short walks*, page 153) and up over the aptly named Windy Moor. The final ascent of Mount Field East is steep and can be a bit of a scramble. Great views.

Lake Fenton to Lake Webster via Kangaroo Moor

Distance: 10–12km return. Time: 5 hours return. Difficulty: moderate.
Begin at a sign about 11km up the Lake Dobson Road from the park headquarters and head along the northern banks of Lake Fenton (pop up to Seagers Lookout if you have the time and energy). This straightforward path leads on to Kangaroo Moor and Lake Webster where there is a hut. You can return the same way or drop down via Lake Seal and Platypus Tarn to the road at Eagle Tarn about 1km from the ski base at the top of the road. Or, for a longer walk, continue to Twilight Tarn (hut), Twisted Tarn and Lake Newdegate (hut) and on even further if you want (see *Long-distance walks*, page 155).

Lake Belcher

Distance: 12km return. Time: 6 hours return. Difficulty: moderate
Start from a sign on the left about 13km up the Lake Dobson Road from the park

headquarters at Wombat Moor and follow over alpine heathland a straightforward path to the lake (hut). This area is usually pretty boggy so take care not to twist an ankle and try not or disturb cushion plants or alpine flowers. Return the same way.

Tarn Shelf Circuit

Distance: 12km return. Time: 6 hours return. Difficulty: moderate.
Follow directions for *Start of Tarn Shelf* (see *Short walks*, page 154) past the Rodway Hut but continue to Lake Newdegate (hut), through the Newdegate Pass and down to K Col (hut) before heading back on the ridge track along the Rodway Range. Or, at Lake Newdegate, turn right and head past Twisted Tarn and Twilight Tarn (hut) to Lake Webster (hut) then down via Lake Seal and Platypus Tarn to the road about 1km down from the ski club buildings. Fantastic views on either route.

Mount Field West

Distance: 16km. Time: 8 hours. Difficulty: moderate but long.
This is the longest day walk at Mount Field and it needs good weather unless you are an experienced hill walker. Start at the ski club buildings and walk first the Snow Gum Track (see *Short walks*, page 154) or at the Sitzmark Lodge and take the track across the ski tow-lines. Then, on past Rodway Hut and follow the ridge track along the Rodway Range to K Col (hut) which leads on west to the summit which, at 1,439m, is the highest peak in the park. If you are here in winter it is possible to ski this walk.

Long-distance walks in Mount Field National Park

Only one, really, which is not challenging but is a combination of several of the ones above. Again you can do as much as you like. Begin at the sign for the Seagers Lookout track about 11km along Lake Dobson Road, follow it up past Lake Fenton and over Kangaroo Moor to Lake Webster. If you have started in the afternoon then you might want to settle here for the night. There is a hut. Continue on to Twilight Tarn (hut), Twisted Tarn and Lake Newdegate (hut) which is a pleasant place to stop for a rest. From here, take the path through Newdegate Pass and around to K Col (hut) where you could pause for your second night. Day three would see you ascend Mount Field West by lunchtime and be back at the ski base easily by dusk. As with all long-distance walks, take all adequate precautions and provisions (see *Chapter 2*'s sections on *Health and Safety* and *What to Take*).

📷 Photo spot

The pencil pines around Lake Dobson are very photogenic shapes and are perfect frame-fillers. Make them take up about half the frame and have a border of the lake and background mountains. If you are here in winter, bring some black and white film to take atmospheric shots of the ski tows in mist and snow.

FRANKLIN-GORDON WILD RIVERS NATIONAL PARK

This park (tel: 6471 2511) is vast, covering 440,000 hectares, and is full of glorious scenery with forested valleys, fast-flowing rivers, deep and narrow gorges and mountains sculpted by glaciers (most notably Frenchmans Cap at 1,443 metres). Other rivers include the Olga and the Denison, and mountains are grouped in the King William, Engineer, and Prince of Wales ranges. The park borders two huge areas of water: Macquarie Harbour on the west coast heading out to Strahan, and the artificial Lake Gordon to the south.

Vegetation is mainly cool temperate rainforest fed by more than 2,500mm of rain per year. This is one of only three remaining temperate wilderness areas in the southern hemisphere and provides an undisturbed environment for hundreds of plant species, many of which are endangered or rare. The bottom storey of the rainforests are made up of exotic tree ferns and, on the ground, smaller fern bushes and mosses.

Drier areas (about 500mm per year) are cloaked in eucalyptus forests and large areas of buttongrass plains. At higher altitude, parts of the park alpine vegetation is common. A wide variety of wildlife lives in this park including broad-toothed and long-tailed mice, the King River vespadelus, lesser long-eared bat, Bennett's wallabies, pademelons, potoroos, little-pygmy and eastern pygmy and ringtail possums, wombats, bandicoots, marsupial mice, Tasmanian devils, eastern and spotted quolls, echidna and platypus. Birds you are likely to see include swamp quail, falcons, goshawks, honey-eaters, thornbills, scrubtits, scrub wrens, flame and pink robins, wedge-tailed eagles, swallows and martins, teal and cormorants, and even the occasional sea eagle.

Aboriginal people were living in these areas many thousands of years ago and there are cave paintings and middens to prove the fact. They cleared the land with fire to make it easier to hunt their prey. Several sights in this park are sacred to Aboriginal people.

In the 1820s the Huon pine industry began to grow and more and more Europeans entered the area. The western gold rush brought prospectors in the 1850s and the first path into the wilderness, the Linda Track, was cut. The first part of the future park was protected in 1908 with the proclamation of the Lower Gordon Crown Land Reserve. In 1932 the cross-country Lyell Highway was opened and 50 years later three national parks – the Franklin-Gordon, the Southwest and the Cradle Mountain-Lake St Clair – were placed on the World Heritage List. In 1983 the damming of the Franklin was stopped after a historic victory by conservationists, more than 1,400 of whom were arrested during the blockade.

Short walks in the Franklin-Gordon Wild Rivers National Park

There are several walks that can be done from car-parks along the Lyell Highway. There are four as you head west from Derwent Bridge to Queenstown.

Franklin River Nature Walk

Distance: 1km return. Time: 30 minutes return. Difficulty: easy.
This is a pleasant stroll along a nature trail at the spot where the Lyell Highway crosses the Franklin, about 25km west of Derwent Bridge. Here it is little more than a stream and it is hard to imagine the mighty force it becomes by the time it pours into the Gordon and heads for the coast.

Frenchmans Cap Start

Distance: 1km return. Time: 30 minutes return. Difficulty: easy.
Watch out for the signs only a few kilometres on from the nature trail (above) and on the left. This is the beginning of a favourite long-distance walk (see *Long-distance walks*, page 157). This first section is simple and only enters the forest a short way. I have seen wedge-tailed eagles here.

Donaghys Hill Lookout

Distance: 2km return. Time: 50 minutes return. Difficulty: easy to moderate.
About another 2 or 3km on from the start of the Frenchmans Cap Walk you will see a sign on the left. This is a great spot to get to for sunset but I mistimed it and ended up stumbling back to the car after dusk which was not so much fun.

🐚 Photo spot

A great spot for a classic sunset photo over the western ranges. Sunsets are only really spectacular on cloudy days when the moisture in the clouds disperses the sun's rays, the sky is broken up by their irregular shapes, and the clouds themselves are kissed pink and red. Check the weather forecast and wait for a cloud front to roll in if you can. 100ASA (no faster), wide angle or 50mm lens, and point right at the setting sun so your foreground goes into full silhouette.

Nelson Falls

Distance: 1km return. Time: 30 minutes return. Difficulty: easy.

At the very western edge of the World Heritage Area is a short walk to some beautiful 30m-high falls on the Nelson River. About 25km east of Queenstown in the Victoria Pass (west of Lake Burbury) look for a car-park on the north side of the road (right if heading west). The walk wanders through forest thick with birdsong and fragrant with fresh scents.

Long-distance walks in the Franklin-Gordon Wild Rivers National Park

Frenchmans Cap

Distance: 46km return. Time: 3–5 days return. Difficulty: hard. Altitude: up to 1,443m.

Before you go Start on Lyell Highway about 18km west of Derwent Bridge (south side of the road). This is one of the most stunning walks in Tasmania but is rarely walked. About 700 people walk the track each year, nearly all these from December to March. One reason is that it is tough, considerably harder than the Overland Track and a world away from the relatively easy stroll of the South Coast Track. Parks and Wildlife classify this as a T2 track (web: www.parks.tas.gov.au) which means the surface may be rough and muddy for long sections (especially the Lodden Plains) and it may be steep in places. All walkers must carry a tent and emergency provisions and wear adequate clothing (see *Chapter 2*'s *Health and Safety* and *What to Take* sections). Walkers will also need fuel stoves as the entire track is within a Fuel Stove Only area. Bushfires have twice devastated this area in recent years. In 1980 a camp-fire at Lake Vera caused more than 6,000 hectares of the park to be burned to a crisp.

Recommended camping locations are: Franklin River, just before you cross it; Loddon River; Philps Creek (the first crossing); Lake Vera (on the track and just after crossing the bridge near the hut); and Lake Tahune (up an overgrown track from the hut towards the lake which veers a little to the left).

All water along the track is safe to drink and both huts have tanks for collection of rainwater. Modern composting toilets have been installed near both huts.

The track is free of *Phytophthora* but, to prevent infecting this area, your boots and all gear that comes in contact with the soil should be cleaned of any mud or dirt prior to your walk. There's a wash-down station about 20 minutes from the start of the walk. Please use it.

Stepping out The car-park is about 200m from the start of the track and some vehicles left here have been vandalised, so do not leave any valuables inside. You could leave your vehicle at the bigger, more popular car-parks at Lake St Clair and get a private operator to take you the rest of the way. Try the bus companies mentioned in *Chapter 2*'s *Getting Around* section.

The track wanders up through forests, over bogs and heaths of buttongrass, past glacially formed lakes, through craggy and remote valleys, and ends with a breathtaking ascent of the peak. The first section climbs to a saddle before crossing the Loddon Plains and reaching Lake Vera which is fringed with Huon pines and makes a good place to camp. There is a camping area and a hut here with wooden bunks (no mattresses) which can sleep 20 people at a push. There are no stoves or cooking utensils. Or you could press on through the dramatic Barron Pass to reach Lake Tahune where there is another camping area and hut that sleeps 16. It is tucked below the towering and ominous Frenchmans crags. The ascent of the white quartzite dome of the Cap is an easy day's hike from Tahune, but you must wait for clear weather.

Further information

More information is available from the Parks and Wildlife Service (Franklin-Lower Gordon Wild Rivers, Queenstown, TAS 7467; tel: 6471 2511). The Queenstown Office is open Monday–Friday 09.00–17.00 and has up-to-date information on the Frenchmans Cap Track. Frenchmans Cap map and notes cost $9 and are available from Service Tasmania (tel: 1300 135 513; email: sthelp@dpac.tas.gov.au).

Tasmanian Expeditions (110 George Street, Launceston, TAS 7250; tel: 6334 3477; mobile: 6334 0427; fax: 6334 3463; email: info@tas-ex.com; web: www.tas-ex.com) run seven-day tours of the Upper Franklin and Frenchmans Cap (including a day walk through mountain wilderness to Frenchmans Cap for panoramic views and white-water rafting.

Craclair (tel/fax: 6242 7833; email: craclair@southcom.com.au; web: www.southcom.com.au/~craclair) run seven-day tours of Pine Valley or Frenchmans Cap for $1,195 (including all equipment, food, transport, accommodation and park fees).

SOUTHWEST NATIONAL PARK

This is the largest national park (tel: 6288 1283) in Tasmania, covering 6,080km², and forms the remote southern part of the Tasmanian Wilderness World Heritage Area. Access is either by the B61 or A10, or at the southern end via Cockle Creek at the end of the A6 and C635. It has many majestic peaks, knife-edge ridges and densely forested valleys, interspersed with buttongrass plains with peaty soil up to three metres (10ft) thick. The south coast has magnificent, sweeping beaches and there is a large natural inlet at Port Davey. As walkers head west along the South Coast Track they are walking over older and older rocks. Those between Cockle Creek and South Cape Bay are 200 million years old, around Surprise Bay they date back 450 million years, Maatsuyker's are 7,600 million years old, and finally north of Port Davey they stretch back one billion years, making them the oldest rocks in Tasmania. The seldom-seen cliffs have been smashed and ground away by the pounding of the waves and have formed gulleys, blowholes, stacks and arches.

The vegetation is predominantly virgin temperate rainforest, with giant eucalyptus (or swamp gums), rare stands of Huon pine, unique buttongrass moorlands, and miles and miles of scrub with banksia, tea-tree and orchids. November and December are popular with visitors coming to see the white flowers of the blossoming heartberry. In the Ironbound Range in the far south there are daisies, pineapple grass, myrtles and leatherwood.

The moors harbour frogs, yabbies, swamp rats, wombats, tiger snakes and jack jumpers – large ants that give a painful bite. In the Ironbound Range there are freshwater shrimps – relics of Gondwana – and skinks that live on moths, beetles and flies. Bird life is prolific. Watch for spinebills, honey-eaters, thornbills, scrub

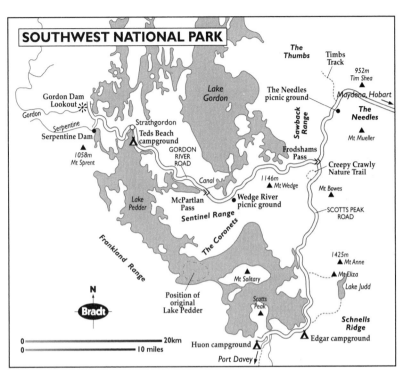

wrens, fantails, pink robins, Richard's pipits, martins, kingfishers (a relative of the kookaburra), white-throated needle-tails, owls, blue-winged parrots, green rosellas, plovers and swamp quails. Albatrosses are often seen. The rarest of the lot is the orange-bellied parrot (see *Birds* section in *Chapter 3*, page 78) which can be found on the buttongrass plains around Melaleuca.

Several hundred Aboriginal people from the southwest and southeast tribes braved this bleak and remote place thousands of years ago – in fact the South Coast Track follows a traditional trading route. They hunted on the moorlands and collected seafood from the shallows. They also went to sea in bark canoes to hunt seabirds and seals. The remains of large middens are still obvious along the coast.

Later the Europeans came. Matthew Flinders sailed past here in 1798 when circumnavigating the island. He was less than impressed with the southwest which he described thus: 'The mountains ... are the most dismal that can be imagined. The eye ranges over these peaks with astonishment and horror.' And with that he ordered his crew to hoist all the sails to get clear from their sight as quickly as possible. Who would have thought they would become a major tourist attraction 200 years later. A succession of men walked through this region, part-bravado and part-exploration for the greater good no doubt. One party had to eat its dog to survive. George Robinson was one of the first, coming through in 1830 along the south coast, up what is now the Port Davey Track, and then heading for the west coast and north to Cape Sorell. Pretty impressive considering his equipment would have been more primitive than we have today – and no GPS to guide him.

The park was declared in 1976 and then became part of the larger World Heritage Area in 1982.

Short walks in the Southwest National Park

There are several walks that can be done from car-parks along the B61 between Mount Field and the Gordon River Dam.

Timbs Track

Distance: 10km return. Time: 4 hours return. Difficulty: easy.

About 20km west of Maydena are signs on the right-hand side of the road for Timbs Track. The track is often muddy and winds through tall rainforest trees (myrtles mainly) and tree ferns, as well as scrub land populated by tea-tree bushes and buttongrass. Snakes seem to favour this path so keep your eyes open and carry a stick. They usually clear off when they hear something larger than themselves approaching but take care anyway. After about 4km the path reaches the Florentine River which can be crossed by a cable. Aboriginal people once hunted kangaroos across these parts of the wilderness and in caves near by they left behind charred remains of their prey and some stone tools.

Creepy Crawly Nature Trail

Distance: 1km return. Time: 20 minutes return. Difficulty: easy.

This is a gem of a track. It starts about 3km along the Scotts Peak Road after the turn-off from the main B61. Very easy walking on duckboards and great fun. The excellent signing gives good information about plants and insects that live here. There are trees with 'trousers' of moss around their trunks. If you have difficulty bending or cannot cope with too many steps then take it slowly. Although the steps are easy there are almost 200 of them.

From Huon Campground

Distance: 3km return. Time: 2 hours return. Difficulty: moderate.

Start from the campground following the Port Davey Track sign and head up to Junction Creek. This is the northern end of the Port Davey Track and it winds through mixed vegetation with rainforest, scrub and moorland species. After the end of the forest the track becomes harder and muddier and the real walking begins, so this is where the short walkers turn around and head back for some tea and biscuits by the lake.

Day walks in the Southwest National Park

Two from Scotts Peak Road:

Eliza Plateau

Distance: 12km return. Time: 6 hours return. Difficulty: moderate to hard.

About 20km down the road, at Condominium Creek, is a sign on the left. The track takes a long, steep climb up an exposed ridge along an often muddy and awkward track. Just before the plateau is a shelter and toilet. Mount Eliza's summit is reached only after a steep scramble over some large boulders. This track requires walkers to be pretty fit and agile.

Lake Judd

Distance: 14km return. Time: 8 hours return. Difficulty: hard.

Start at Red Tape Creek about 30km along Scotts Peak Road. Follow the foot track to the Anne River (cable crossing) then make your way across what is usually a very muddy and uncomfortable buttongrass plain for at least 2km to an unmarked junction of tracks. Take the left fork, wade the river as you head for the lake. Fit and experienced walkers only, and do not attempt in bad weather.

Long-distance walks in the Southwest National Park

There is a track that begins at Tahune, west of Geeveston (see *Chapter 6*, page 129) and heads up into the wilderness. It continues for roughly the next 90–100km over rough and remote terrain (some of it almost requiring mountaineering skills) to the western end of Bathurst Harbour in the far southwest. On the other side of this narrow gap of water a track continues along the south coast for about 70–80km to the South Cape and civilisation once more at Cockle Creek. This huge loop is really the amalgamation of four tracks: Mackays, Arthur Plains, Port Davey, and the South Coast. This is the toughest walking possible in Tasmania. Even highly experienced walkers and climbers get into difficulties here. Conditions are extremely changeable and testing. Help is a long way away and walkers can be stranded for several days before they are found … if they are found. The reason little is found of walkers who perish in the wilderness is that the animals here (notably Tasmanian devils) are expert at recycling every bit of carrion they find. Detailed planning is required to stay alive and avoid becoming one of their meals.

Of course you do not have to do the whole lot. In fact the Parks and Wildlife people and emergency services would probably rather you did not. These tracks are all walkable individually, but some need transport planning unless you want to retrace your steps on the return.

Mackays and Arthur Plains are rarely walked and full details and maps must be obtained from the Parks and Wildlife Service (134 Macquarie Street, Hobart, TAS 7000; tel: 6233 6191; email: ParksEnquiries@dpiwe.tas.gov.au). Roughly, though, Mackays Track begins at the end of a gravel road just beyond the Tahune Forest Reserve in part of the Southwest Conservation Area. It follows the Huon River north of Mount Picton (1,327m) to its junction with the Anne River, and on to the Cracroft River where it veers right and heads into the Arthur Range and becomes the Arthur Plains Track. That alone will take about two to three days in good weather (one-way), more if it is raining or snowing (and it usually is). The peaks to the south of the Arthur Plains Track are between 1,120m (Mount Orion) to 1,160m (West Portal) which will give you an idea of the altitude you are dealing with. This whole area is snow-covered for much of the winter and certain times of the year such as October are not advised for walking as blizzards can whip in during the space of less than an hour. The Arthur Plains Track leads on west approximately another 15km to a junction, Junction Creek. This is crucial to locate on the map as it leads down to the end of the dirt-road at Scotts Peak Dam. It is a vital escape route for walkers on the high ground who need to get down in a hurry and find help. A bus service visits Scotts Peak and there are campgrounds and water and, more importantly, other people to raise an alarm. If you are walking in fine weather then take a side jaunt to Scotts Peak which is on the shores of Lake Pedder and offers a beautiful outlook. Allow five hours to get there and back to Junction Creek. From here, west lies the Port Davey Track.

Getting in there Bus and plane companies provide transport services to the southwest (see section on *Getting Around* in *Chapter 2*). Private vehicles may be left at Scotts Peak or at Cockle Creek, but some vehicles parked in remote locations have been robbed or vandalised.

📷 Photo spot

The plane coming in to land or taking off is often dramatic as it provides a splash of man-made colour in an otherwise naturally green landscape. If you find out the flight times and get a slightly higher vantage point you will get the best shot. Check your background too – nice and simple is best, like a grey mountain range, blue ocean or a plain green-brown buttongrass meadow. Long lens zoom (100–300mm) and 200–400ASA film, unless very bright sunlight in which case use 64–100ASA.

Port Davey Track

Before you go This offers 70km of the most challenging and exhilarating walking anywhere in the world. It lies entirely within the Southwest National Park and runs from the end of the Scotts Peak Road to the shores of Bathurst Harbour and (on the other side of the water) on to the northern end of the airstrip at Melaleuca. There are some very steep and awkwardly muddy sections. Only about 200 walk this track each year and almost all those between December and March. Most take between four and five days to complete the walk (one-way) but as there are no roads to Melaleuca, walkers must either fly out or walk out along the South Coast Track which meets the Port Davey Track here.

The Southwest National Park is primarily a wilderness area. The only huts on this circuit are at Melaleuca. All overnight walkers must carry a tent and fuel stove and groups of less than six people are recommended as campsites can become overcrowded. The recommended campsites after the Huon Campground are Junction Creek, Crossing River, Spring River, Bathurst Narrows and Melaleuca. Running water along the track is safe to drink. What looks like a source of fresh water on a map may turn out to be brackish if it is close enough to the sea. A composting toilet has been installed at Scotts Peak and there is a pit toilet at Melaleuca.

Phytophthora cinnamomi exists at Scotts Peak, Melaleuca and other locations on the track so clean all equipment likely to come into contact with the soil before you step out and along the way where you find wash-down stations.

The Parks and Wildlife Service do not even say there are detailed maps to cover the region in depth. Check with them and take all information they can give. Compass, EPIRB and full emergency equipment and rations are essential on this walk (see *Health and Safety* and *What to Take* sections in *Chapter 2*). If you can take a GPS then do so.

Stepping out At Scotts Peak the track starts next to the Huon Campground. It continues to a junction from where the Arthur Plains Track heads east to Tahune (allow about four days) and the Port Davey continues west and south to Melaleuca (allow about four days). You will be walking mainly over buttongrass plains, peat bogs and rocky outcrops. You will pass Mount Hesperus (1,097m) and should get stunning views of the southwest coast from the plains leading to the Lost World Plateau. Never was an area so appropriately named. The track follows Spring River south, and when Bakers Ridge is on your left and the Erskine Range ahead you are on the home straight down to the water's edge. However, do remember after landing on the other side that Melaleuca is another 8–10km further on.

Further information

More information from the Parks and Wildlife Service (134 Macquarie Street, Hobart, TAS 7000; tel: 6233 6191; email: ParksEnquiries@dpiwe.tas.gov.au; or Huonville Office, 24 Main Road, Huonville, TAS 7109; tel: 6264 8460; fax: 6264 8473). For maps and notes contact Service Tasmania (tel: 1300 135 513; email: sthelp@dpac.tas.gov.au; web: www.servicetasmania.tas.gov.au).

South Coast Track

Despite its position, at the southern edge of the world, this track is actually not difficult, but it is long and requires some walking experience and detailed planning. It is also subject to the worst weather in Tasmania, which is really saying something. It runs for 85km between Cockle Creek in the east and Melaleuca in the far southwest. About 2,000 people walk the track each year, with about 1,500 visiting from December to March. Most people take about six to eight days to complete it (one-way) but longer if they are beach fanatics because these ones are as clean and as seductive as you are likely to find. Much of the track is on duckboard to protect the vegetation but where it is not it may be rough and muddy for long stretches.

Walkers traverse two mountain ranges, wade several rivers, cross a lagoon by dinghy, negotiate many swampy plains and wander remote and lonely wilderness beaches.

This is not a loop track so if you don't want to retrace your steps you have two options: fly out by light plane from Melaleuca or continue across Bathurst Harbour and tackle the Port Davey Track north (see above, page 162). Tourism Tasmania and Parks and Wildlife are encouraging people to fly *in* to Melaleuca and walk *out* to avoid weary walkers not making flights they have booked for the end of their walk.

This is primarily a wilderness area so the only huts on the track are at Melaleuca where very basic accommodation for 20 people is provided in two huts. Water and mattresses are available but there are no cooking facilities. Along the track you will find good campsites in forests or in shelter behind beaches. Recommended campsites are at Melaleuca, Point Eric, Louisa River, Deadmans Bay, New River Lagoon boat crossing, Surprise Bay, Granite Beach (east), South Cape Rivulet and Cockle Creek. All walkers must carry a tent and fuel stove and groups of less than six people are recommended as campsites can become overcrowded.

Most of the coast is exposed to cold, wet, southerly winds. Rain falls on average every second day during summer and more often in other seasons. The Ironbound Range rises to 900m, where the weather changes rapidly. A warm sunny day quickly gives way to high winds, hail, sleet and snow, even in summer. Walkers should be fit and prepared for long days on their feet (up to ten hours) as there are no campsites on the Ironbounds. In heavy seas and high tides some rocky sections of the track can be unexpectedly inundated by ocean waves. Take particular care at Granite Beach and the unnamed bluff on the eastern beach at Cox Bight.

Also, do not cross South Cape Rivulet, the Louisa River or Faraway Creek when they are running high. Walkers must use a small boat at New River Lagoon. Extreme caution is needed when making these crossings, particularly in windy weather or if there are tidal surges. You should carry a couple of days' extra food to allow for delays.

When walking on beaches, please be aware that you are sharing the beach with shore-nesting birds such as the endangered fairy tern and the rare little tern, and walk well below the high-tide mark. Shorebirds nest from early September to late March.

Bushfires have damaged parts of the Southwest National Park. Please carry and use a fuel stove. A Fuel Stove Only Area has been declared over the whole of the Ironbound Range due to the sensitive alpine vegetation and along the section of track from Cockle Creek to South Cape Rivulet. *Phytophthora cinnamomi* exists at Melaleuca and other locations on the track, so clean all equipment likely to come into contact with the soil before you step out and along the way where you find wash-down stations.

Running water along the track is safe to drink but what looks like a fresh water source on the map may be brackish if it is close enough to the sea.

Either way you walk the South Coast Track, you are following an ancient route used by Tasmanian Aborigines centuries before. Let us say you fly in and walk out to Cockle Creek. From Melaleuca you will head towards Cox Bight and then across the Red Point Hills. The track leads you to the Louisa River (see *Pre-European history* section of *Chapter 1*) and on through the Ironbound Range past Havelock Bluff and around Prion Bay. Off the coast are the fabulous rock stacks of the Maatsuyker group of islands. At New River Lagoon you need to hop on the dinghy to cross, but only when safe. From there walk to Surprise Bay and on around South Cape Bay and out to Cockle Creek.

Further information

More information from the Parks and Wildlife Service (134 Macquarie Street, Hobart, TAS 7000; tel: 6233 6191; email: ParksEnquiries@ dpiwe.tas.gov.au, or Huonville Office, 24 Main Road, Huonville, TAS 7109; tel: 6264 8460; fax: 6264 8473). For maps and notes contact Service Tasmania (tel: 1300 135 513; email: email: sthelp@dpac.tas.gov.au; web: www.servicetasmania.tas.gov.au).

Tasmanian Expeditions (110 George Street, Launceston, TAS 7250; tel: 6334 3477; fax: 6334 3463; email: info@tas-ex.com; web: www.tas-ex.com) run nine-day tours of the South Coast Track. On average walkers cover 10–12km (6½–7½ miles) a day with packs initially weighing up to 20kg when full of food. Previous backpacking experience is an advantage. $1,380 per person (includes experienced guides, group camping equipment, park fees, transfers, eight nights' accommodation, all meals).

WHAT ELSE TO SEE AND DO IN THE SOUTHWEST REGION

White-water rafting

Rafting the Franklin River is one of the greatest pleasures in Tasmania and the trick is not to rush it. Try to take a full one-week or two-week trip if possible. The put-in is actually in the Collingwood River, where it crosses the A10 Lyell Highway, and from there it is a mix of genteel floating down lazy parts of rivers, lying back and gazing up at the passing canopy of leaves, and high-octane adventure riding the rapids. If the river is in flood then the fun really starts and some rapids have to be missed as they are simply too dangerous. Camps are on the riverbanks and only when you pluck your gear from the dry bags do you know if they have served their purpose or whether your night will be ruined by having to crawl into a soggy sleeping-bag and blanket. This area is so wild that the sound of car engines has never been heard here and wildlife is incredibly tame. Quolls and platypus are seen quite regularly. The river rafts head down the Franklin to its confluence with the Gordon and then down that bigger river to the top of the Sir John Falls.

Rafting Tasmania (tel: 6239 1080; fax: 6239 1090; email: raftingtas@tasadventures.com) and **Tasmanian Expeditions** (110 George Street, Launceston, TAS 7250; tel: 6334 3477; fax: 6334 3463; email: info@tas-ex.com; web: www.tas-ex.com) run Franklin River rafting trips. Prices for Tasmanian Expeditions: seven-day $1,445 per person; 11-day $1,990 per person (includes experienced guides, emergency radio, transfers, camping and rafting equipment, all meals from lunch on day one to lunch on day seven, wetsuits and park fees).

Scenic flights

A number of local airlines fly light planes on scenic flights over the southwest wilderness. See *Specialist Tour Operators* in *Chapter 2* for details.

Gordon River Dam

At the end of the B61 is Gordon River Dam, an impressive 140m (460ft) wall of concrete holding back millions of gallons of water that now make up Lake Gordon, the biggest in the state. The valleys at the back of the dam were flooded to fuel the hydro-electric generating programme here. There is an excellent visitor centre with friendly, helpful staff and lots of maps and diagrams that detail the scheme and the geography of the region. You can walk down the 100-odd metal steps and along the top of the dam for free or pay **Aardvark Adventures** (tel/fax: 6249 4098; mobile: 0408 127714; email: aardvark@tasadventures.com) to join one of their exhilarating abseils from the top.

If you wish to take a photograph, it is hard to get the right angle as the dam is large and awkwardly shaped to fit the viewfinder and you are too close to it, so use a wide-angle lens and take from halfway up the metal steps which should give some sense of scale.

Aboriginal caves
The only way to see the caves at Kutikina is on a rafting trip. They are way up in the wilderness along the Franklin River. Aboriginal people inhabited these caves around the time of the last ice age and hunted kangaroo and wallaby on the open plains. (See *Rafting* section above and *Pre-European History* section in *Chapter 1*.)

Scenic drives
Basically, anything along the A10 Lyell Highway, the B61 road to Gordon, and Scotts Peak Road is spectacular. If you want to get further into the woods, try the forest drives in Mount Field National Park.

Skiing
During the winter months Mount Field runs a small ski centre (tel: 6288 1149) at the top of the Lake Dobson Road.

Fishing
Some of the best fishing is found in the Southwest National Park. Trout fishing is allowed in both Gordon and Pedder Lakes but using artificial lures only, and it is restricted to the months between August and April (licence required from Inland Fisheries Commission). Fishing is not permitted in any river or stream leading into these lakes. A popular fishing site with a boat launch is Teds Beach, about 4km (2½ miles) before Strathgordon on the B61. Another good site is the Edgar Dam area, 30km (19 miles) along the Scotts Peak Road, just before Scotts Peak itself. Boats can be hired at Strathgordon.

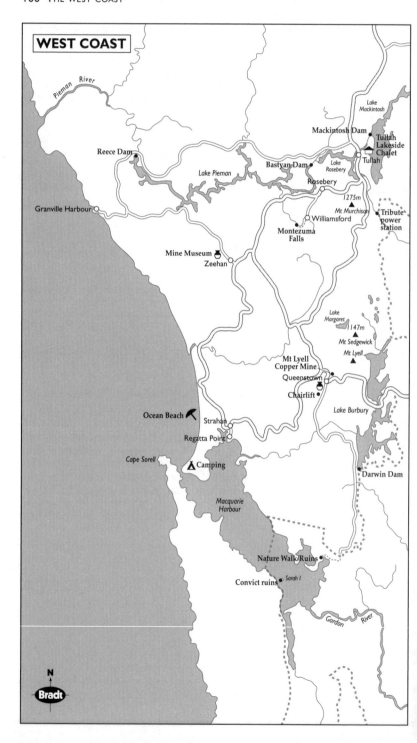

WEST COAST

Pieman River

Reece Dam

Lake Mackintosh

Mackintosh Dam

Tullah
Lakeside
Chalet

Bastyan Dam

Lake Rosebery

Tullah

Lake Pieman

Rosebery

Granville Harbour

1275m
Mt Murchison ▲

Williamsford

Montezuma
Falls

Tribute
power
station

Mine Museum
Zeehan

Lake Margaret

1147m
Mt Sedgewick ▲

Mt Lyell ▲

Mt Lyell
Copper Mine

Queenstown

Chairlift

Lake Burbury

Ocean Beach

Strahan

Regatta Point

Cape Sorell

Camping

Darwin Dam

Macquarie Harbour

Nature Walk/Ruins

Convict ruins   *Sarah I*

Gordon River

N

Bradt

The West Coast

This chapter deals with the central west coast from Macquarie Harbour north to Lake Pieman and inland as far as the boundary with the World Heritage Area. It is a small area but one full of history, interest and beauty. Aboriginal people lived here thousands of years ago and were the first to mine the country, although they found only ochre with which they daubed their bodies and caves. Some of the oldest cave paintings in Australia at Kutikina (see *Chapter 7 The Southwest*) were daubed with ochre from mines at Queenstown. This was the southern most limit of the land of the Tommeginer people who were one of the eight bands of the northwest coast tribes. They moved nomadically around their territory between Macquarie Harbour and Table Cape near Wynyard, following the seasons. Middens along this coast have revealed their varied diet of seals, fish, birds and small mammals, which they cooked with ferns, tubers of lilies and grass tree pith. In summer they could catch mutton-birds and elephant seals in bark canoes off the coast with tools. They survived the wild weather by making cloaks from possum skin.

The first European to see Tasmania, the Dutch explorer Abel Janszoon Tasman, caught his first glimpse of the island off this coastline in 1642. It is believed he named two peaks on the horizon after his ships, Mount Heemskirk and Mount Zeehan. Its remoteness was always going to be a draw for the European authorities, who were seeking hideous places to send their prisoners, and the first penal colony was built here in 1822 on a rock in Macquarie Harbour known as Sarah Island. The very name sent shivers of fear up the spines of all those sentenced to transportation from Britain to Van Diemen's Land. Inmates were treated appallingly and the conditions were dire.

This coast became crucial to the rest of the colony in the late 19th century when prospectors found valuable silver, lead, zinc and copper deposits. Such was the lust for easy money that much of the environment was degraded as they hacked the stuff out of the ground. Chemical processes to purify it before export produced poisonous gases which killed plants and animals in their fall-out zones.

The devastation can still be seen, especially at Queenstown, which has made a tourist attraction out of its moonscape. The early deposits had to go out by rail north as there was no way through the mountains to Hobart at that time. This rugged environment tested the best engineers. Today there are memories of the mining industry in abandoned and refurbished railways, and working and tourist mines. While its poorer neighbour Queenstown tried to shake off its image as a filthy mining town, the pretty coastal town of Strahan thrived on tourism. Today the two centres make very different, but in a way complementary, places to see.

QUEENSTOWN

'Queenie' is a remarkably resilient place and well worth a short stop. Its history, like most mining towns, is one blessed with riches and blighted with slump and pollution. In 1883 three prospectors, Mick and Bill McDonough and Steve Karlsson, hacked their way through the dense foliage up Conglomerate Creek valley and descended into the Vale of Chimouni (now Linda Valley) where they found an ironstone outcrop. They thought it was the source of the gold flecks they had panned further down the creek and that it would give up great big nuggets to make them rich. They were right, as the rock offered about two ounces of gold per tonne, but what the miners did not take notice of at first was that the copper deposits lying in the same rock were much bigger and in the long run more lucrative. A rich silver seam was also found near by around 1893 which lasted only two years but boosted the flagging fortunes of the fledgling Mount Lyell Mining and Railway Company. Copper was king here, however, from 1896 to 1922. A revolutionary pyritic smelting process was pioneered which was later used worldwide, and Queenstown flourished with more than 5,000 inhabitants, about 15 hotels and numerous companies scrabbling in the dirt for wealth.

The industry took its toll on the environment. More than two million tonnes of timber were taken from the surrounding forests to fuel the blast furnaces and those forests that were left standing were killed by tonnes of acid rain from the smelters. Water courses downstream are to this day deeply contaminated with heavy metals. Just about every living thing between Queenstown and the mouth of the King River in Macquarie Harbour suffocated.

In 1969–70 the smelters closed and in December 1994, after 101 years of continuous mining, the Mount Lyell Mining and Railway Company closed the mine. A year later, Copper Mines of Tasmania took on the lease and re-opened the mine but its future is probably bleak as the price of copper is not healthy. Tourism is seen by many as a viable and longer-term option.

📷 Photo spot

Queenstown pubs make good shots, especially at dusk in summer when the lights are coming on and the first few evening drinkers are walking in through the doors. Try a few in the town to get the right angle and try to limit foreground and background clutter like cars and streetlamps and waste-paper bins. 400ASA film for dusk and a grain finish, and a long lens so you can shoot from across the street and no-one going in or out of the pub will challenge you.

Getting there

By air

Island Airlines Tasmania (tel: 1800 645 875; email: bobpratt@bigpond.com.au; web: www.iat.com.au) flies Launceston–Strahan–Hobart return three times a week (Tuesday, Thursday, Sunday). And charter flights from Essendon to Strahan.

By road

From Hobart, take the A10 Lyell Highway through the World Heritage Area and drop down through the West Coast Range into the town. Try to arrive before dark to see the amazing landscape as the road leaves the lush forests and emerges into a barren wasteland of nude hills and yellow, stained valleys. From one of the world's most pristine and heavily protected regions to one of the most polluted and desecrated. It is quite a shock. From Strahan take the B24 and from Zeehan and Rosebery in the north drive in on the A10. Most bus companies run to Queenstown (see *Getting Around* section of *Chapter 2*).

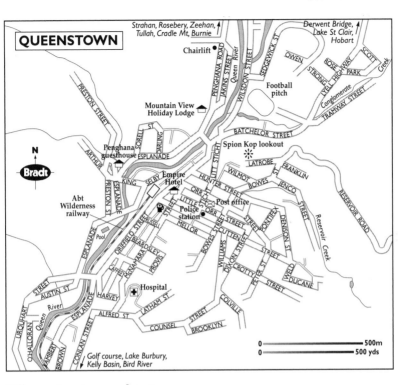

Where to stay and eat

There is really only one place I would recommend staying in Queenstown and that is the old mine manager's house up on a hill, now known as **Penghana Guesthouse** (32 The Esplanade, Queenstown, TAS 7467; tel: 6471 2560; fax: 6471 1535). It was built in 1898 for the first general manager of the Mount Lyell company, Robert Sticht, who was a noted American metallurgist, and named after the first small mining settlement near here which was lost to fire in 1896. It is made of locally made bricks with lofty ceilings and a rare guillotine door in the master bedroom. It took a great effort on behalf of the miners to build, lugging everything up the hill. The class structure was alive and well in Queenstown, with the manager living on top of his hill with relatively fresh air and servants, while the miners coughed down in the polluted streets of the town. There is a lounge, a study and library, and in the ballroom a full-size billiard table. I have been in winter and it was cosy and welcoming. There are four en-suite rooms ($110–132, single and double) and one standard room ($110–132, single and double), $165 for family of four.

If you are on a budget, try the **Mountain View Holiday Lodge Motel** (1 Penghana Road, Queenstown, TAS 7467; tel: 6471 1163; fax: 6471 1306) which used to be the Mount Lyell Company's 'singlemens' quarters. It is fairly basic with dorms ($12/24 single/double) and 28 en-suite rooms ($45/60 single/double).

Eating is a problem in Queenstown. The Penghana does evening meals on request which is your best bet. The Mountain View has a BYO bistro, barbecue facilities and a camper's kitchen. Otherwise there are one or two pubs and fast food places but only as a last resort.

What to see and do

The main new attraction is the restored **Abt Wilderness Railway** (Queenstown Station, Queenstown, TAS 7467; tel: 6471 1700; fax: 6471 2415; email: qstation@southcom.com.au) which now runs the length of its original track. It is Australia's only rack and pinion railway, built in 1896 to haul iron ore to Strahan where it could be transferred a few miles north to the early smelters near Zeehan. Before the Lyell Highway opened in the early 1930s, this 35km railway was the only transport link with the rest of Tasmania, and the world. With the demise of mining in Queenstown the line closed in 1963, but the railway's heritage society would not let it die. For more than a decade from 1990 they worked to restore it and have it reopened as a memorial to the industry and as a tourist attraction. As we go to press, they have achieved their goal with the line opening fully to passengers. The trip takes about 1½ hours and runs through some stunning scenery, over 40 bridges and climbs (or descends), more than 200m up gradients of 1:16, passing historic settlements and abandoned mining camps. Carefully restored and decorated carriages are pulled by a steam locomotive, and passengers get a thorough and interesting commentary about the technical aspects and history of the railway and a potted version of the history of mining in the area (including the pollution). Open daily, departures from Queenstown 09.30, 13.00 and 16.00. Adult $32 (2 adults $62); senior citizens $29; children $12 (4–14 years); family (2 adults, 2 children) $75; group discount 20% (20+). All prices refer to return fares.

There are also **copper mine tours** run by Lyell Tours (Empire Hotel, Queenstown, TAS 7467; tel: 6471 2388; fax: 6471 2222). They organise 2½-hour underground trips to watch the mine at work extracting silver, gold and copper bearing. Tours every weekday (Saturday and Sunday by arrangement) for $55 each; one hour surface tours (daily at 09.15 and 16.30). Adult $13.20; child $7.20 (under 16 years). Also a half-day Bird River rainforest tour (daily from October–May 08.30, by arrangement June–September). Adult $69; child $44 (under 16 years).

The site of the three diggers' **iron blow** is back up the A10 east. Look for a signed side-road quite near the top.

A short drive south of the town through Lynchford and past the John Butters hydro-electric plant will afford views over Lake Burbury which was created for a hydro scheme.

Short walk
Kelly Basin
Distance: 8km return. Time: 4 hours return. Difficulty: moderate.
By car, head south through Queenstown past the Empire Hotel and take a left into Russell Street, then right into McNamara and follow this until it turns into Conlan Street and leads you out of town and onto the Mount Jukes road. Continue for about 30 minutes until you see a right-hand turn for the Bird River walking track. There are picnic tables near the start of the walk but no toilets. The signed track follows the route of the former railway line to Kelly Basin. There are remains of a once thriving town in the lush undergrowth. 1,000 people once lived here. Some sections of this walk can get muddy as the rainfall here is frequent and heavy.

STRAHAN
So close to Queenstown yet a world away, Strahan is a pretty place on a tranquil harbour. The place is obsessed with boats and there are numerous cruises available on all manner of craft. Everyone will tell you about The Ship That Never Was. It is protected from the wild Southern Ocean by a thin stretch of land at the back of Ocean Beach. Ocean Beach is one of those areas of sand that looks like it has been

used in a number of romantic films where the girl finally gets her boy or the boy finally loses the girl and decides to wander into the sea to drown himself. There are several fine places to stay and some pleasant local walks, but Strahan is best when you have no deadlines.

Getting there and around
By air
Island Airlines Tasmania (tel: 1 800 645 875) runs the only scheduled service from Hobart to Strahan.

Wilderness Air (Strahan Wharf, Strahan, TAS 7468; tel: 6471 7280; fax: 6471 7303; email: wildernessair@tasadventures.com) run seaplane flights along Ocean Beach and Macquarie Harbour over Sarah Island and the mouth of the Gordon River with a stop for a rainforest walk. Departure 09.00, 10.30, 12.00, 14.00, 15.30 and 17.00 (flights last about 80 minutes). Adult $132; child (5 to 12 years inclusive) $73; child (3 to 4 years inclusive) $32; infant (up to 3 years) free. Office on waterfront.

Seair Adventure Charters (The Esplanade, Strahan, TAS 7468; tel: 6471 7718; fax: 6442 3208; web: www.seairac.com.au) offer plane flights over Queenstown, Lake Burbury, Frenchmans Cap, Franklin and Gordon rivers, Macquarie Harbour and Ocean Beach, or to Cradle Mountain and the Overland Track, passing Frenchmans Cap and Lake Burbury on the return. By helicopter fly over dense forests of the King River Gorge. 45-minute flight to Frenchmans Cap, Franklin/Gordon rivers: adult $110; child (under 12 years) $55. 65-minute flight Cradle Mountain-Lake St Clair World Heritage Area: adult $160. Helicopter flight to Teepookana Forest: adult $125; child (under 12 years) $65. Helicopter to Frenchmans Cap, Franklin and Gordon rivers: adult $110; child (under 12 years) $55. Helicopter to Cradle Mountain and Lake St Clair: adult $160; child (under 12 years) $88.

By road
From Queenstown, take the picturesque B24 for about 40km. From Zeehan, take the stunning drive down the B27 which has great views of local mountains and east to the World Heritage Area. In a car, expect to spend about five hours driving non-stop between Hobart and Strahan. Bus companies serve Strahan from Hobart and the north (see *Getting Around* section of *Chapter 2*). Buses arrive and depart form the visitor centre on the waterfront. Buses take more than eight hours to complete the drive between Hobart and Strahan.

By sea
You would have to charter your own boat (see *Getting Around* section of *Chapter 2*).

Where to stay and eat
The best in town is **Franklin Manor** (The Esplanade, Strahan, TAS 7468; tel: 6471 7311, fax: 6471 7267; email: Franklinmanor@bigpond.com; web: www.franklinmanor.com.au), a luxury small hotel with superb rooms, good service and a warm atmosphere. There are several indulgences including a bedroom with a log fire which is ready made for your arrival with piles more eucalyptus logs to burn, spa baths, and a fabulous award-winning restaurant. The hotel runs an honesty policy with its bar and serves huge and delicious breakfasts (extra $9–16 each). It is a must-stay. There are 18 rooms, including two executive deluxes with open fires. Standard room $143, single and double; deluxe room $175, single and double; stable cottage $175, single and double; executive deluxe $206, single and double.

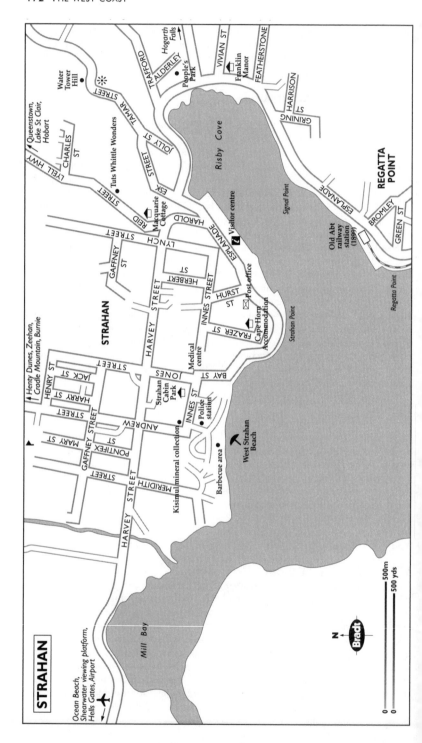

📷 Photo spot

The Franklin Manor is one of the most photogenic buildings in Tasmania and deserves a few shots in your album. The best shot is the one from about 20 yards up the driveway, and another good one is with the piles of logs tumbling out of the log shed at the top car-park. 100ASA film and 50mm lens.

If you want to rent a cottage, try **Macquarie Cottage** (5 Reid Street, Strahan, TAS 7468; tel/fax: 6471 7028) which is yours for $100–130/$130–160, single/double.

Also try **Cape Horn Accommodation** (3 Frazer Street, Strahan, TAS 7468; tel/fax: 6471 7169) which offers an apartment for $65–95, single and double, and a studio apartment for $60–75, single and double. Light breakfasts extra $3 each.

Campers and caravaners should have a look at **Strahan Cabin Park** (corner of Innes Street and Jones Street, Strahan, TAS 7278; tel: 6471 7442; fax: 6471 7278) which is well laid out and whose cabins have attractive window boxes. Rates by enquiry.

Eat at **Franklin Manor** if possible. Otherwise, evening meals at **Hamers Hotel** on the Esplanade are good (especially the seafood). Main dishes about $15–$20 but Strahan tends to eat early. I went one night and everything was gone by 20.00.

Banjo's Bakehouse (tel: 6471 7794), just up The Esplanade, has standard pizzas for $10–12, and the Strahan Bakery does sandwiches and cakes.

What to see and do

Sarah Island Historic Site (tel: 6471 7122) covers six hectares within Macquarie Harbour and became a penal site in 1822. It was notorious for the appalling treatment its convicts suffered and the dreadful conditions in which they lived. They were used as slave labour to build boats from Huon pine. In town the **visitor centre** has good displays and lots of local information and details of tours to Sarah Island and elsewhere in this region. The centre also hosts Tasmania's longest running play, *The Ship That Never Was*, which is based on a real event of 1834 when the last ship built at Sarah Island was about to sail for the new prison at Port Arthur but was hijacked by a group of ten convict shipwrights.

Walking and beachcombing on **Ocean Beach** is a joy. The sand sweeps north for several miles but beware this is a mutton-bird breeding colony every August when the place is swamped with thousands of birds. On these remote west coast beaches it is always best to walk below the hide tide line in case you disturb birds nesting in the dry sand and dunes. This beach is dangerous for swimming, however, as several severe rips have been noted offshore and there is usually a strong undertow. Further north are the Henty Dunes. The road to them from the main B27 is hard to find. It took me several drives past before I found a way in, so ask a local before you leave town where the best entry is.

For **sea kayaking** see *Specialist Tour Operators* section in *Chapter 2*. For harbour and river cruises try the following:

World Heritage Cruises (Esplanade, Strahan, TAS 7468; tel: 6471 7174; fax: 6471 7431; email: worldheritagecruises@tassie.net.au; web: www.worldheritagecruises. com.au) run trips up the Gordon River on a catamaran from Strahan through Hells Gates (entrance to Macquarie Harbour), visiting a trout and salmon farm en route to Sarah Island where passengers can explore the ruins. Then to Heritage Landing for rainforest walk to see 2,000 year old Huon pine. Full-day cruises daily, excluding Christmas Day. Adult $55; child (5–14 years) $25; family (2 adults, 3 children) $150. Half-day cruise October 1–April 30 inclusive. Adult $50, child (5-14 years) $22. Lunch extra.

Gordon River Cruises (Strahan Wharf, Strahan, TAS 7468; tel: 6471 4300; fax: 6471 4317; email: grc@strahanvillage.com.au; web: www.strahanvillage.com.au) also run several trips up river. Rates on enquiry.

If you want to charter a yacht, try **West Coast Yacht Charters** (Strahan Wharf, Strahan, TAS 7468; tel: 6471 7422; fax: 6471 8033; email: wcyc@tassie.net.au) who organise a host of tours and fishing and dinner cruises.

For handicrafts, visit **Strahan Woodworks** on The Esplanade. Open daily 08.00–17.30. Admission free.

Short walk around Strahan
Hogarth Falls
Distance: 3km return. Time: 1 hour return. Difficulty: easy.
The walk begins in the People's Park as you head around the Esplanade, midway between the wharf area and Regatta Point. There are no facilities in the park but public toilets are about 1.5km (1 mile) away in the wharf area. This is an easy, signed walk along a pretty flat track, but there is some flowing water so keep an eye on children.

Further information
More information from the Strahan Visitor and Information Centre (tel: 6471 7622; email: strahan@tasvisinfo.com).

ZEEHAN AND ROSEBERY
These two mining towns have a history of toil and turmoil. Now the miners have all but left and the two towns are quiet and rely mainly on passing tourists for income. They are places you are likely to see en route somewhere else but take an hour or two to stock up on provisions (though get petrol in Strahan as some petrol stations in quieter parts of this region close on Sundays) and have a quick look around.

Getting there and around
Zeehan is on the B27, about 36km south of Rosebery and 46km north of Strahan, and south of the junction with the A10. Rosebery is on the A10, 55km north of Queenstown. Nearby Tullah is also on the A10. Buses service all three towns, stopping at Marina's Coffee Shop on Main Road in Zeehan, at Mackrell's Milkbar in Rosebery, and at the BP Service Station in Tullah. From Zeehan, the C249 heads north for 50km to picturesque Corinna on the Pieman River. You will need a 4WD but this is a way of getting to the northwest away from the crowds.

Where to stay and eat
With Strahan to the south and beautiful countryside further north, I would not recommend staying here for a night. Instead push on and enjoy better views elsewhere. There are several shops and a pub or two in these towns for sandwiches and snacks. If you want to stay, pick the **Tullah Lakeside Chalet** (Farrell Street, Tullah, TAS 7321; tel: 6473 4121; fax: 6473 4130; web: www.melanka.com) which has good views. Or there are several miner's cottages in Rosebery to rent (try one at 12 Karlson Street).

What to see and do
The **West Coast Pioneers Memorial Museum** (Main Street, Zeehan, TAS 7469; tel: 6471 6225; fax: 6471 6650) is worth a look to get a good history of mining

in the region. The discovery of tin deposits at Mount Bischoff in 1871 started an influx of prospectors, and by the turn of the century this area was like California after the gold rush with dozens of lively towns. There are old photographs and a complete range of ore and mineral samples. Open daily October 1–March 31 08.30–18.00; April 1–September 30 08.30–17.00; closed Christmas Day, Good Friday. Adult $5.50; senior citizen and student $3.30; child (up to 17 years) $3.30; family $11.

On the way into Rosebery from the south look for signs to the **Montezuma Falls** which is an hour or two walk from the car-park. There is a tour of the surface area of the **Rosebery Mine** (tel: 6473 1247; fax: 6473 1444) which extracts zinc.

In Tullah, visit the **Wee Georgie Wood Steam Railway** (tel: 6473 2228; fax: 6473 1400; email: drakea@pasminco.com.au), a 600mm-gauge (2ft) 1921 steam locomotive that operates on the short Farrell Tramway, which opened between the then isolated mining township of Tullah and Farrell Siding, some 9.6km away on the Emu Bay Railway in 1909. Open times on enquiry. Adult $4; senior citizen $2; child $1; family $8.

If you want to go riding or boating, check in at **Tullah Horseback and Boat Tours** (Mackintosh Track, Tullah, TAS 7321; tel: 6473 4289; email: pielark94@hotmail.com) who have plenty of horseback and boat tours, and a two-day pioneer adventure trail ride. Rates on enquiry.

A number of companies **rent bicycles** by the hour, day and week. Try **Bright Water Canoe and Bike Hire** (21 Sale Street, Tullah, TAS 7321; tel: 6473 4165; fax: 6473 4177; email: randbboyle@trump.net.au). Rates on enquiry.

Eastern grey kangaroo

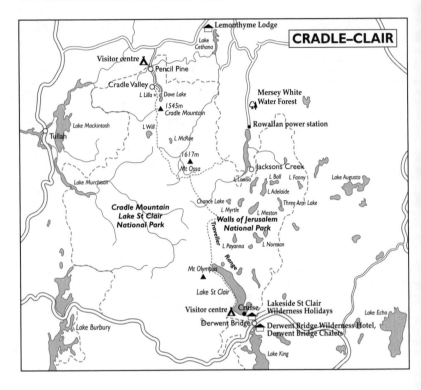

CRADLE–CLAIR

Lemonthyme Lodge

Lake Cethana

Visitor centre
Pencil Pine

Cradle Valley

L Lilla   Dove Lake

1545m
Cradle Mountain

Lake Mackintosh

L Will

Tullah

L McRae

1617m
Mt Ossa

Mersey White
Water Forest

Rowallan power station

Jacksons Creek

L Louisa   L Ball   L Fanny   Lake Augusta

L Adelaide

Lake Murchison

Chance Lake   Three Arm Lake

**Cradle Mountain
Lake St Clair
National Park**

L Myrtle   L Meston

**Walls of Jerusalem
National Park**

L Payanna   L Norman

Traveller

Mt Olympus

Range

Lake St Clair

Visitor centre   Cruise

Derwent Bridge

Lake Burbury

Lakeside St Clair
Wilderness Holidays

Lake Echo

Derwent Bridge Wilderness Hotel,
Derwent Bridge Chalets

Lake King

Cradle Mountain and Lake St Clair

Cradle Mountain-Lake St Clair National Park and the Walls of Jerusalem National Park are both part of the World Heritage Area. Cradle-Clair (as it is abbreviated) is the most accessible of the big parks and contains the Overland Track, Tasmania's most popular and famous walking track from which numerous other side-tracks spread. This track is still the one favoured by most overseas visitors to the island. This region is slightly more forgiving than the southwest wilderness but these are still wild and rugged places. You are more likely to encounter tourists in the Cradle-Clair region but the distances are big enough and the terrain rough enough to ensure you have a good amount of space to yourself. Public holidays and school holidays are particularly busy in these parks so if you can avoid those times all the better. The Walls of Jerusalem is remote and seldom visited.

CRADLE MOUNTAIN-LAKE ST CLAIR NATIONAL PARK

This park (Cradle tel: 6492 1133, Lake St Clair tel: 6289 1172 or 1115) is one of the biggest, covering 161,000 hectares and including some of the state's highest country. The park extends from Pencil Pine Creek in the north near Cradle Mountain to Derwent Bride south of Lake St Clair on the A10 Lyell Highway. It is famous for its lakes, peaks, rainforest, moorland and peat bogs. Tasmania's highest peak is here – Mount Ossa at 1,617m – and the central southwest mountains are from 700–1,000 million years old. Sediments laid down back then have been folded and super-heated to form quartzite and schist in mountains such as Frenchmans Cap (see *Geology* section in *Chapter 3*). The summits of peaks like Mount Ossa and Precipitous Bluff and others in their vicinity look like a giant's building blocks – this is the broken remains of a dolerite plateau. Walking around Dove Lake you cannot help but notice the great gouge that was taken out on the northern side of Cradle Mountain to form the scree slopes and the lake itself. This was all done by glaciers which have torn apart this region on three major occasions during the last two million years. Dove Lake, along with Wilks and Crater lakes, were all carved by moving glaciers that could have been up to 200m thick. The mounds in the valleys are the rock debris the glaciers dumped (the moraine). Lake St Clair at the park's southern entrance is the deepest in Australia at 190m and is the source of the River Derwent.

As you climb through the climate zones you will pass through rainforest, eucalyptus forest, buttongrass plains and heaths, and finally alpine meadows and moorland. During spring and summer the meadows are full of colour, while autumn brings rich reds and yellows to the deciduous beech trees. On the sides of myrtle trees and some sphagnum moss plants grows a fungus called myrtle orange which is a relic of Gondwana that chooses only these plants and which can hold up to 50 times its own weight in water.

On the lower slopes, wallabies, wombats, pademelons, brushtail and pygmy-possums and Tasmanian devils can be seen. In fact, despite the number of walkers along this track many are remarkably tame. You will also see Tasmanian thornbills, dusky robins, wedge-tailed eagles and currawongs. If you are very lucky and wait patiently at the shores of lakes Will and Windermere you might catch sight of a prehistoric-looking fish called a galaxias which is about 20cm long and has large fins fitted low on its body which enable it to climb up rocks on to land.

Aborigines lived here for thousands of years, moving with the seasons and hunting on the higher ground in summer. Archaeologists have found remnants of campsites in the central highlands, and some were believed to have been living in the Cradle Mountain area as recently as the 1830s.

In 1910, an Austrian, Gustav Weindorfer, climbed Cradle Mountain and vowed to protect this region. He and his wife Kate built a home here and for a decade fought for environmental recognition. In 1922, his dream was realised and an area from Cradle Mountain to Lake St Clair was proclaimed a scenic reserve. It was included in the World Heritage Area in 1982.

Getting there and around
By air
Seair Adventures Charters (tel: 6492 1132; fax: 6442 3208; email: seaair@bigpond.com.au; web: www.seairac.com.au) run scenic flights from the Cradle Mountain airstrip. A 25-minute Cradle Mountain flight costs $95 each, a 50-minute one, including Lake St Clair, is $125, with a child (under 12 years) paying $65. Helicopter flights: adult $135; child (under 12 years) $70.

By road
The north of Cradle-Clair is served by the C132 and the south by the A10 and a side-road to Derwent Bridge. The Walls of Jerusalem park is reached by the B12, C171 and C172. Most buses, and lots of tour operators, go to Cradle Mountain and Lake St Clair (see *Getting Around* section of *Chapter 2*) but few if any to Walls of Jerusalem. The visitor centre at Lake St Clair is about five hours on a bus from Hobart, about three from Strahan. Cradle Mountain is about a 3½-hour drive by bus from Launceston, 1½ hours from Devonport and 4½ hours from Strahan. It is a full-day's journey on at least two buses from Hobart. Private charters can be arranged. Try **TWT's Tassielink Regional Coach Service** (tel: 1300 300 520; web: www.tigerline.com.au) and **Maxwell's Coaches** (tel: 6492 1431).

Where to stay and eat
Cradle Mountain is a year-round destination and most of the accommodation is centred around the village of Cradle Mountain just outside the national park. The lodges are particularly romantic in winter. **Cradle Mountain Lodge** (PO Box 153, Sheffield, TAS 7306; tel: 6492 1303; fax: 6492 1309; email: cradle.mountain@poresorts.com; web: www.poresorts.com) has a large central lodge and several cabins in the woods. Log fires, sauna and massage, and good food. Apartment $186–299, single/double. About 16km (10 miles) northeast in a captivatingly beautiful valley is **Lemonthyme Lodge** (Dolcoath Rd off Cradle Mountain Rd, Moina, TAS 7306; tel: 6492 1112; fax: 6492 1113; email: lemonthyme@trump.net.au; web: www.lemonthyme.com.au) which has won several awards including an environmental one. It is quite small, with four apartments, 18 en-suite rooms and eight standard rooms. Standard room $99/110, single/double; apartment $210–225, single and double; en-suite room $199–299, single and double.

📷 Photo spot

This lodge is photogenic at dawn. Ask the staff the best vantage point as there are several, and get up about an hour before the sun clears the hills. Check the weather the night before to see if there is fog or mist predicted – this bathes the lodge in a ghostly early light. If you have an overcast day, wait until the light picks up enough to hand-hold your camera, but then apply a neutral density or tobacco filter to accentuate the scene's moodiness. Standard 50mm lens is fine.

You could also try the **Cradle Mountain Wilderness Village** (Cradle Mountain Road, Cradle Mountain, TAS 7306; tel: 6492 1018; fax: 6492 1076; email: info@cradlevillage.com.au; web: www.cradlevillage.com.au) in the Cradle Mountain township which has 25 apartments for $160–170, single/double.

Highlanders (3876 Cradle Mountain Road, Cradle Mountain, TAS 7306; tel: 6492 1116; fax: 6492 1188; email: cradle.mt@bigpond.com.au; web: www.cradlehighlander.com.au) offers self-contained cabins. Two have corner spa baths (mineral spa baths available and mineral water is on tap). All cabins have continental breakfast provisions, the spa cabins also have cooked breakfast provisions (bacon & eggs). $100–175, single anddouble.

The **Cradle Mountain Tourist Park and Campground** (PO Box 10, Wilmot, TAS 7310; tel: 6492 1395; fax: 6492 1438; web: www.cosycabins.com) has 37 camping sites ($8–10 single, $16–20 double), 2 dorms ($20–22 single, $55–60 double), and 22 park cabins ($75–95 single/double).

Cradle Chalet Boutique Luxury Lodge (1422 Cradle Mountain Road, Moina, TAS 7306; tel: 6492 1401; fax: 6492 1144; email: cradlechalet@winnet.com.au; web: www.cradlechalet.com.au) has eight en-suite rooms and is about a 20-minute drive from Cradle Mountain park entrance. En-suite room $168–188, single and double.

Food outlets are scarce here apart from the **Cradle Mountain Café/Bistro** (also marked on some maps as the Cradle Wilderness Café) opposite the campground, and at the lodges. Bring all food if camping.

In the south at Lake St Clair there is the same arrangement. A cluster of accommodation exists at Derwent Bridge where the A10 meets the side-road that leads into the southern reaches of the park. The **Derwent Bridge Wilderness Hotel** (Lyell Highway, Derwent Bridge, TAS 7140; tel: 6289 1144; fax: 6289 1173) has 39 dorm and bunkhouse spaces and 7 standard rooms. If you have been fishing the chef will cook your catch for you. There are log fires and a cosy bar and usually lots of steaming walkers just arrived after a week on the Overland Track, and full of stories. Dorm bed $23/45, single/double; standard room $85–105, single and double.

Lakeside St Clair Wilderness Holidays (Derwent Bridge, TAS 7140; tel: 6289 1137; fax: 6289 1250; email: lakestclair@trump.net.au; web: www.view.com.au/lakeside) is right at the end of the lake and offers six apartments ($97–150/132–184 single/double), 20 camping sites ($12/17 single/double), 8 dorm or bunkhouse spaces ($25–30/$50–60 single/double), and 8 serviced sites ($15/20 single/double). There is a campers' kitchen too. You could also try **Derwent Bridge Chalets** (Private Bay 4444, New Norfolk, TAS 7140; tel: 6289 1000; fax: 6289 1230; email: 4chalets@h130.aone.net.au; web: www.troutwalks.com.au) which does continental breakfasts.

There is food at the above where not self-catering and at the **Lake St Clair Visitor Centre,** but again it is best to remember this is wilderness and restaurants and cafés are scarce, so bring with you as much as possible.

If Lake St Clair marks the end of your Overland Track walk I would recommend getting in early after your last night in a hut or tent and catching the bus from the visitor centre straight back to Hobart. The place is picturesque and fine for a night but there is nothing like rolling into a cosy Battery Point B&B, having a piping hot bath and healing your blisters and then stepping out for a superb Hobart fish dinner.

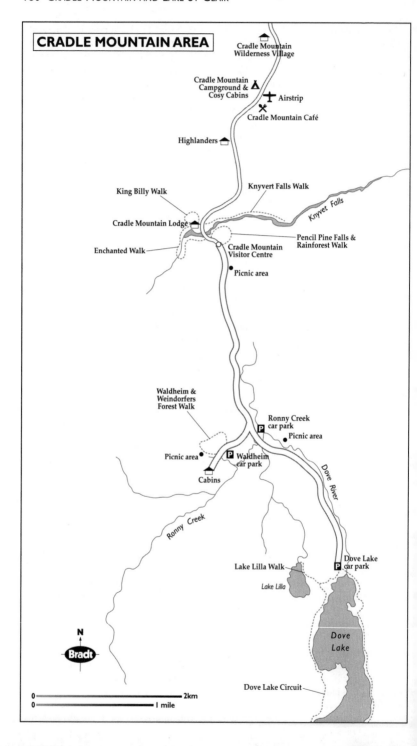

If you really want to stay in style while walking the Overland Track and price is no barrier, then contact **Cradle Mountain Huts** (tel: 6331 2006; fax: 6331 5525; email: info@cradlehuts.com.au; web: www.cradlehuts.com.au) who operate five luxurious huts (the only private ones allowed in the park) which are well hidden from the main track and have to be seen to be believed. They are like mini-hotels in the wilderness: warm, comfortable and decorated with art work and rugs. Pure luxury. The same company operates the fantastic Bay of Fires walk (see *Chapter 12 The Northeast*).

What to see and do
The **Overland Track** is the big thing (see section below, page 183) but there are plenty of shorter walks and lake cruises also.

Short walks at Cradle Mountain
All these walks are well signed and some are suitable for wheelchairs and strollers.

Pencil Pine Falls and Rainforest Walk
Distance: 700m return. Time: 30 minutes return. Difficulty: easy.
This circular walk starts inside the excellent visitor centre and can be accessed by wheelchairs and strollers. It follows a flat path.

Enchanted Walk
Distance: 700m return. Time: 30 minutes return. Difficulty: easy.
Start this loop track at the park entrance and look for the Great Short Walks sign (the W with the boot print). The first half is flat and can be done by those in wheelchairs or with strollers. The rest is a little less even but still easy.

Knyvert Falls Walk
Distance: 1.6km return. Time: 1 hour return. Difficulty: easy.
Start opposite the Cradle Mountain Lodge and walk along the north bank of Pine Creek to the falls, then back the same way. Watch for platypus here.

King Billy Walk
Distance: 700m return. Time: 30 minutes return. Difficulty: easy.
This starts actually at Cradle Mountain Lodge and does a short loop to the north. It is a good one to do before breakfast to get the scent of the pines.

Waldheim and Weindorfers Forest Walk
Distance: 700m return. Time: 30 minutes return. Difficulty: easy.
For this one you will have to walk or drive the 5.5km to the Waldheim car-park where it begins. It is a fine short, loop walk with Cradle Mountain as a magnificent backdrop.

Dove Lake Circuit
Distance: 6km return. Time: 2 hours return. Difficulty: easy.
This is a beautiful walk around a stunning glassy lake. Follow the very first few steps of the Overland Track but then, as it begins to climb, you head around on the flat and keep to the edge of the lake. The path is well marked and circumnavigates the lake to bring you back to the car-park.

Lake Lilla Walk
Distance: 1km return. Time: 30 minutes return. Difficulty: easy.
From the car-park at Dove Lake go west to a T-junction in the path and take the

right fork to Lake Lilla and return the same way. Or you can add this on to your Dove Lake Circuit (see above).

Cradle Mountain day walk
Summit of Cradle Mountain
Distance: 9km return from Waldheim car-park. Time: 8 hours return. Difficulty: moderate. Altitude: 1,545m.

Take day pack with emergency provisions, overnight clothing gear and a good large-scale map. Fit and agile walkers only. Set off from the northern tip of Dove Lake and head up the first 3km of the Overland Track. This is the steepest and toughest bit of the entire Overland, with one section above Dove Lake involving the use of a permanent banister chain and some rather bruising work on your knees. You ascend rapidly and get fabulous views back over the valley and north to the Middlesex Plains and the beginning of the northwest region of Tasmania. Break off from the Overland when you get to an emergency shelter. You will have passed Lake Hanson and Twisted Lakes in the valley to your left (east). The Overland heads south and you veer right to the west of the bluff ahead. After about 2km, a path leads off to the left which will take you to the summit. It is steep. Retrace your steps to return to the car-park or take one of the other two return tracks via Kitchen Hut or Marions Lookout. These are obvious on the map and the ground.

Short walks at Lake St Clair
Lake Clair
Distance: 2.4km return to 4.7km return depending on track chosen. Time: 40 minutes to 1½ hours depending on your tracks chosen. Difficulty: all three walks are easy.

Start at Lake St Clair Visitor Centre after taking the C193 from the A10 Lyell Highway.

There are three short walks here. The shortest is 2.4km return which can be extended by combining it with either one or two additional walks. At their longest, these walks combine to form a 4.7km figure-of-eight loop. All tracks are signed and flat.

Lake St Clair day walks
Echo Point
Distance: 8km one-way. Time: 4–5 hours one-way. Difficulty: moderate.

The first hut on the Overland Track (or the last if you are doing it north–south) is on the western shore of the lake at a tranquil spot. There is a beach and wild forests on one side and the lake's silvery surface on the other, with the Traveller Range of mountains climbing behind it. Take the ferry from Cynthia Bay up to Echo Point and then walk back through lush rainforest along an even but rough track. I did this at the end of the Overland Track and it took at least four hours. Or you could walk north and get the ferry back. Check all ferry sailing times with the Lake St Clair Visitor Centre (tel: 6289 1137).

Mt Rufus
Distance: 15km return. Time: 7 hours return. Difficulty: moderate to hard.

This walk begins at the Lake St Clair Visitor Centre and climbs moderately 400m in height over roughly 5km on a good path, then gets steeper for the pull up to Mount Rufus at 1,416m. Follow the ridge northwest for about 1km (about half a mile) and the path heads down again to Forgotten and Shadow lakes next to each other, curves to the right (southeast) and heads back to the start at Cynthia Bay.

Above Gladstone Police Station (MB)

Right Old School House at Bicheno, now part of the Gaolhouse B&B (MB)

Above left Sunset at North East Cape (MB)

Above right Eddystone Lighthouse, Mount William National Park (MB)

Right Boats at Convict Station, Taranna, on Little Norfolk Bay on the Tasman Peninsula (MB)

Lake St Clair long-distance walk
Cuvier Valley
Distance: 28km return. Time: 2–3 days return. Difficulty: moderate.

This walks starts at the Lake St Clair Visitor Centre and heads inland and northwest on the signed Cuvier Valley Track, with the Cuvier River on your left. You are almost parallel to the Overland Track but on the other side of the Mount Olympus and Seven Apostles range. After 11km you will come to two campsites, one on either side of Lake Petrarch, which makes a good spot for the night. The next decent night stop is 6 or 7km further on at the Narcissus Hut. The track hugs the northern contours of Mount Olympus, passing through Byron Gap, where you get good views up the Narcissus Valley where the Overland Track leads. Then you come round to the top of the lake and make your way back to the start along the lakeshore, stopping if you wish in the cosy but tiny Echo Point Hut (room for 8 at a tight squeeze). Or you can pick up the ferry from Narcissus Hut or Echo Point.

Further information
Lakeside St Clair Wilderness Holidays (tel: 6289 1137; mobile: 0417 591 289; fax: 6289 1250; email: lakestclair@trump.net.au; web: www.view.com.au/lakeside) rent out bicycles and dinghies. Half-day bicycle hire $25; half-day dinghy hire $54; full-day dinghy hire $90; two-hour canoe hire $25; four-hour canoe hire $50.

Cruises up Lake St Clair from Cynthia Bay vary – check times and prices with the Lake St Clair Visitor Centre or the national park (tel: 6289 1137).

OVERLAND TRACK
Distance: about 85km. Time: 5–7 days. Difficulty: moderate to hard. Altitude 1,000–1,300m for most of the way but up to 1,617m at Mount Ossa.

The very least you will need for this walk is a full pack of upland clothing, provisions, a tent, a large-scale map and a compass. Expect to spend at least five days and nights on the track. Those who do the track often have a preferred direction to walk. Some say the views are better heading north while others swear southward is easier on the legs. For anyone tackling this for the first time it makes little difference. Both routes will offer fabulous views, great excitement, a personal fitness challenge and some interesting and often friendly wildlife. I have only walked it north to south so that is what I will recount here.

Day one
It begins at Cradle Mountain. Try to get a ride to the northern tip of Dove Lake where there is a walkers' registration book and information panel. Sign the book and continue to sign in at any hut that has one, leaving your details, party size and walking intentions for the next few days. This information could save your life if the weather closes in or disaster strikes further down the track. Starting on the track by 13.00 is adequate in the summer months and in good weather conditions but earlier start times are advised in times of poor weather and from April to November. In winter, daylight hours are reduced to between 07.30 and 16.45 and snow can make the track impassable.

Your first day's walk is arguably your toughest. The path up the side of Dove Lake is rocky and steep, involving some minor mountaineering at one point where a permanent chain banister has been put in with which to haul yourself up. The views from the top are stunning, right back up the valley and out on to the Middlesex Plains. The path splits at an emergency shelter. Right (southwest) will take you around the western side of Cradle Mountain (including the summit scramble) and left (south) leads east of the mountain and brings you to a good hut for the night. Dove Lake to Scott Kilvert Hut is four hours.

📷 Photo spot
This hut looks very picturesque as you approach from Cradle Mountain and has a good background of green vegetation to isolate it. It looks OK when there are people there too, but approach quietly so they do not see you and start waving when you get your camera out. Woodsmoke coming from the chimney is the icing on the cake. Standard 50mm lens is fine.

A further option is to push on up a steep slope (lightly wooded and home to blue-winged parrots and rosellas) to a saddle called Cradle Cirque, following the path west to meet the track that came around the western side of Cradle Mountain and then on south and down into a Waterfall Valley where there are some good, popular huts (some new ones there now too, I think) and a campground. Dove Lake to Waterfall Valley Hut is about six hours. You can take a side trek up to Barn Bluff if you feel the urge – the views are spectacular. It is about another three hours return from the main track and has a steep summit, so leave any big packs at the base.

📷 Photo spot
As you descend from Cradle Cirque into Waterfall Valley you will get one of the great Tasmanian panorama shots with cushion plants either side, low scrub ahead and the duckboard track winding down. Beyond, as far as the lens can see, is wilderness. Ask a walking pal to walk on and snap when they get to a good distance that makes them look very small in this vast landscape. 50mm lens or wide angle to increase sense of space.

Day two
Walk south through peaty heath and eucalyptus scrub and mainly over duckboarding through Waterfall Valley and out onto a lonely, bare plateau. Watch for tiger snakes and listen for song birds. Windermere Hut turns up after only about three or four hours' walk from Waterfall Valley and there you need to sit down, have an energy bar and make a decision. If you have less than seven hours of daylight left or the weather looks ominous or you are tiring, stay here. If you are fit and the sun is still high, press on. Your next camping spot and hut are a good six hours away. The walking is easy but the path gets rocky and criss-crossed with roots. It passes over bogs, rocky outcrops, small pockets of elfin woodland with small twisted and gnarled trees. A welcome stream occurs at Pelion Creek with the cleanest natural water I have ever seen or tasted. The campsite marked at Frog Flats is often not an option as for most of the year it is at best damp and at worst waterlogged so keep going to Pelion Hut, which is a great place to stay. The hut is usually riddled with mice but it is warm and good for communal cooking and meeting fellow walkers. There is also an old hut about 1km back down the track which serves as an overflow when it gets busy.

Wildlife at Pelion
I had the worst night of sleep here but did not care as it was so comical. Two possums fell on to the crown of my dome tent and proceeded to tear each other's fur out right outside the entrance. As the moon rose it silhouetted a fat wombat on the canvas, making it look alarmingly large, and finally at dawn a wedge-tailed eagle in the tree above me began to issue forth the most blood-curdling cry. I was washed, fed and on the go by 07.00.

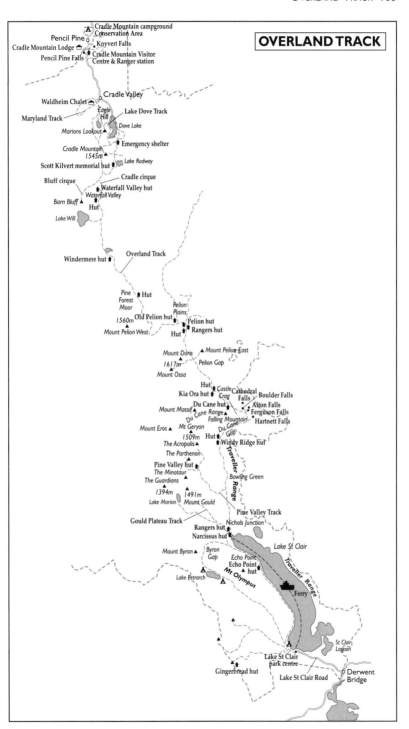

OVERLAND TRACK

Day three

From Pelion you embark on a slow and steady climb (about two hours) through forests to a low, flat saddle at Pelion Gap. There is a big duckboard platform here where people leave their packs and nip up Mount Ossa.

Side-track

The climb from Pelion Gap to the top of Mount Ossa is really a three-hour trek with a final steep ascent (hands and knees) and a rocky and awkward summit. There are alpine plants and tremendous views but do not even bother if the summit is in cloud. I found snow patches at the top in early December but the temperature was about 25°C, the air clear and my views were in every direction for many miles.

From Pelion Gap to the Kia Ora Hut is about another hour or two. This is a spacious hut with good duckboard platforms to pitch tents, divided from each other for some privacy by small eucalyptus stands. The view at dawn over the marshes to Cathedral Mountain (1,378m) is breathtaking. Song birds and wombats are prevalent. There is a stream near by with small waterfalls and a swimming hole. The water is icy.

📷 Photo spot

Take a camera with you up Mount Ossa, but a light one. If there is snow up there it will play havoc with a compact camera's internal light meter, resulting in underexposed shots, so to avoid massive sunlight reflection try to shoot away from snow and not while you are standing in a small drift. There are superb shots from the top, of a companion sitting upon one of the granite pillar rocks, but the drop-offs are treacherous so take great care. You will find cushion plants and beautiful white flowers on the lower slopes that make good close-ups. 50mm lens if you are taking your SLR.

Day four

A big day this, walking southeast from Kia Ora and rounding the lower slopes of Castle Crag (1,482m) through thick woodland.

Side-track

There are two short and easy paths up to the Ferguson and Hartnett Falls (about 30 minutes return). I saw a fair few tiger snakes in these woods. Soon you come into eucalyptus stands as you pass Windy Ridge Hut. There were reports of mice infestations here but I saw no evidence of this. There is a food chamber in the hut which you should use. Then on past some impressively high, but not giant, eucalyptus and past Bowling Green campsite which, like Frog Flats, is usually waterlogged.

Side-track

About 2km beyond this is a side-track, the Pine Valley Track, which leads up Cephissus Creek to a hut. From there walkers can attempt the Acropolis, a steep but rewarding pull up to the 1,471m summit, or up to Cyane Lake. Both return the same way to Pine Valley Hut. A fairly fit student walker from Iowa that I met had walked the valley tracks in a day but most of us would need two. However, this track has become so popular recently that the Parks and Wildlife people are asking walkers to leave it alone for a few years for the vegetation to recover. Bed tonight is at Narcissus Hut at the northern tip of Lake St Clair (from where you can phone for the ferry to pick you up the next morning; tel: 6289 1137).

Side-track

From Narcissus Hut you can take a track northwest past a marsh which then splits into two: the Gould Plateau Track is the steeper but shorter, leading up to the plateau with good views to Mount Gould, whereas the Lake Marion Track wanders gently on to the lake itself which is in a natural amphitheatre at about 1,000m.

Alternatively, push on another 5km to a tiny but fabulously positioned hut at Echo Point. It sleeps eight at a squeeze but the view over the lake is majestic. There is a beach where possums and wombats play.

📷 Photo spot

Echo Point Hut is well photographed and for good reason. It is small and on a beautiful spot right on the lake shore with the glass-like waters of Lake St Clair for a backdrop. Best shots are from the path as you walk in to the hut from the north. Try to stand two packs up neatly by the entrance to give a sense of scale and adventure. 50mm lens fine.

Day five

This is the home straight. The walk out to Cynthia Bay at the southern end of Lake St Clair is pretty and fairly easy, but the path can be littered with roots and there are tiger snakes here too. If you are catching an early bus back to Hobart from the visitor centre then start at dawn and you will get the best of the wildlife. I began at 06.00. The dew made the forests smell like a branch of the Body Shop, full of peppermint and lemon and cinnamon. I saw Bennett's wallabies lurking behind tree ferns, their ears pricked and their eyes watching me as I passed. A wombat hardly made an effort to get out of the way until I was within striking distance. It is about 8km from Echo Point to the visitor centre.

Another option, if you have stayed at Narcissus Hut, is to take a lesser-known track away from the lakeside and around the western side of Mount Olympus. This is the Cuvier Valley Track (see *Lake St Clair long-distance walk*, page 183).

Several thousand walkers do the Overland Track each year, mainly from December to April and especially in January, when as many as 40 walkers set out on the track each day. *The Cradle Mountain-Lake St Clair Map and Notes* (1:100 000 Tasmap) is invaluable and can be ordered from the Parks and Wildlife Service (web: www.parks.tas.gov.au) or bought from outdoor shops (see *Shopping* section in *Chapter 2*). Also try to get hold of *The Overland Track – A Walkers Notebook* which is a popular pocket-sized booklet with notes on the ecology and history of the area, helpful snippets of information for walkers, and illustrations of flora and fauna likely to be seen along the track. Available at visitor centres at both ends of the track.

Further information

Cradle Mountain parks office Cradle Mountain, PO Box 20, Sheffield, TAS 7306; tel: 6492 1133; fax: 6492 1120

Lake St Clair parks office Field Centres, Lake St Clair, Derwent Bridge, TAS 7140; tel: 6289 1172; fax: 6289 1227

Parks and Wildlife Service Hobart HQ 134 Macquarie St, Hobart, TAS 7000; tel: 6233 6191; email: ParksEnquiries@dpiwe.tas.gov

Parks and Wildlife Service Launceston HQ Prospect Offices, Bass Highway, South Launceston, TAS 7249; tel: 6336 5312

If you want to go with an organised tour, try **Craclair Walking Holidays** (tel/fax: 6242 7833; email: craclair@southcom.com.au; web: www.southcom.com.au/

~craclair) who explore the alpine lakes and peaks, tall forests and open moors along the track. Tours walk an average distance of 10km each day with professional guides. Tours include transport, meals, accommodation, park fees and equipment. 8 days $1,220 each; 10 days $1,545 each.

Alternatively, try **Tasmanian Expeditions** (110 George Street, Launceston, TAS 7250; tel: 6334 3477; fax: 6334 3463; email: info@tas-ex.com; web: www.tas-ex.com) who run a six-day trek into Cradle Mountain and the Walls of Jerusalem. six-day trek $980 per person (includes experienced guides, group camping equipment, park fees, transfers, five nights accommodation (2 cabins, 3 camping), all meals to lunch on day six).

WALLS OF JERUSALEM NATIONAL PARK

This is one of the lesser known parks (tel: 6363 5182) in Tasmania but of stunning beauty and well worth exploring. It lies to the southwest of the Great Western Tiers and east of Cradle Mountain-Lake St Clair National Park. The park covers about 51,000 hectares. The land was heavily glaciated, a process which left it pock-marked with a myriad of lakes, waterfalls and streams. Most of this area is covered with bogs and sedgelands, bolster moors and heaths; also grasslands, herbfields and woodlands where ancient pencil pines are the predominant species. In the grasslands you will find snow daisies and some patches of pineapple grass. There are steep mountains that create natural amphitheatres where protected sub-alpine plants grow. Many, like cushion plants, are rare and protected. On the lower, more sheltered slopes are snow gums and yellow gums, and in the north and west, where the rainfall is heavier, you will find pockets of montane rainforest and stands of conifers. These conifers were badly damaged by bushfires in 1960 and 1961. Rockier areas are the place to look for alpine water ferns, club moss and Tasmanian cress.

The bleakness of this park has required its animals to adapt to survive. Wallabies, pademelons, wombats and both brush-tail and ring-tail possums exist but their fur is thicker than that of their relatives in less harsh parts. The dusky antechinus, echidna and platypus are also present in the Walls of Jerusalem, as are Tasmanian devils, echidna, eastern quoll and rats, again with denser coats.

You will probably be free from snakes in winter when they hibernate, but summer brings forth the tiger and the white-lipped varieties, so watch where you step. There are several frogs, lots of skinks and lizards and a wide range of birds, including eastern spinebills, flame robins, blue-winged parrots, skylarks in summer and, much higher, falcons and wedge-tailed eagles looking for a meal. Less than 100 years ago you stood a good chance of spotting a Tasmanian tiger skulking along the edge of a stand of pencil pines. The hardy Aborigines even populated these bleak uplands, although admittedly only in summer and then mainly for hunting.

A lot of the biblical names were suggested by a Launceston solicitor, Reg Hall, who loved this park and came here often. It was declared a national park in 1981. There is nowhere to stay or eat so you must bring in all provisions and, as this is part of the World Heritage Area, you must take everything out again when you leave.

Getting there

This park is reached only by taking the C138 from Mole Creek and then the C171 to the Rowallan hydro-electric power station. There is a rough track that goes beyond this, down the eastern side of Lake Rowallan to Jacksons Creek, which is suitable only for 4WD and even this can be tricky if the weather has been bad and the ruts are big.

Long-distance walk in Walls of Jerusalem National Park

Distance: from 20km–32km return. Time: 2–5 days return. Difficulty: moderate to hard (fit, experienced walkers only). Altitude: up to 1,200m.

There are really only three tracks, so walkers can use one to go up and then have a choice of two to come down.

From Jacksons Creek, a driveable track (Mersey Forest Road) leads almost due south for 3km to Chapter Lake and Grid Falls which are impressive after heavy rain. The track continues south-southeast to Cloister Lagoon at about 1,000m altitude, over Mayfield Flats to a T-junction. A few hundred yards left (northeast) is a hut. This is about 10km from Jacksons Creek in total. The track goes on another 2 or 3km southwest to Lake Artemis, but that is about it for obvious paths in the park. If the weather is good you will have fabulous views over the lake-dotted park. Southeast you are looking over the Mountains of Jupiter, due south to Mount Spirling and west about 10 or 12km to the Traveller Range, past which the Overland Track runs. It is here, particularly, you are likely to see the famous pencil pines for which this park is known – the tree is the park's floral emblem. From here most walkers need to return to the hut and then either retrace their steps via Cloister Lagoon and Grid Falls or take one of two alternative tracks. One leads northeast to the western shore of Lake Meston. Halfway along this shore you will find a building. It is not a cosy hut in the Cradle Mountain sense, but it can provide shelter in bad weather. Another track leads off to the left (north-northwest) just beyond it which will take you to the west of Mount Rogoona (1,350m) past Lake Myrtle and Lake Bill and down a fairly steep descent to the Mersey Forest Road. The main path continues down the shore of Lake Meston and is longer. It skirts the eastern shore of Lake Adelaide and on to Trapper's Hut before dropping down fairly steeply to Lake Rowallan about 5km south of Rowallan power station. There is also a hut right on the lake side.

Sketch maps are available from park offices but walkers must get hold of a good large-scale (1:100,000 series) map. The Cradle Mountain-Lake St Clair one just about includes all the tracks.

📷 Photo spot

A good shot is to isolate a pencil pine with nothing behind it but lonely moorland, making it look like the last tree on earth. If you have bad weather, capitalise on that by adding a neutral density or tobacco filter to make the surroundings look even grimmer than they really are. 50mm lens fine or wide angle.

Further information

If you want to go with an organised tour, try **Tasmanian Expeditions** (110 George Street, Launceston, TAS 7250; tel: 6334 3477; fax: 6334 3463; email: info@tas-ex.com; web: www.tas-ex.com) who run a 6-day trek into Cradle Mountain and the Walls of Jerusalem. In the Walls of Jerusalem, they backpack to the main plateau and set up base camp. Day walks visit the top of the West Wall (at 1,250m), which provides panoramic views over the Central Highlands to the west coast. The trip ends with a return to Launceston. Six-day trek $980 per person (includes experienced guides, group camping equipment, park fees, transfers, 5 nights accommodation (2 cabins, 3 camping), all meals up to lunch on day six).

Alternatively, try **Craclair Walking Holidays** (tel/fax: 6242 7833; email: craclair@southcom.com.au; web: www.southcom.com.au/~craclair) who do 5-day treks through the park for $875 each. Tours include all equipment, food, transport, accommodation and park fees.

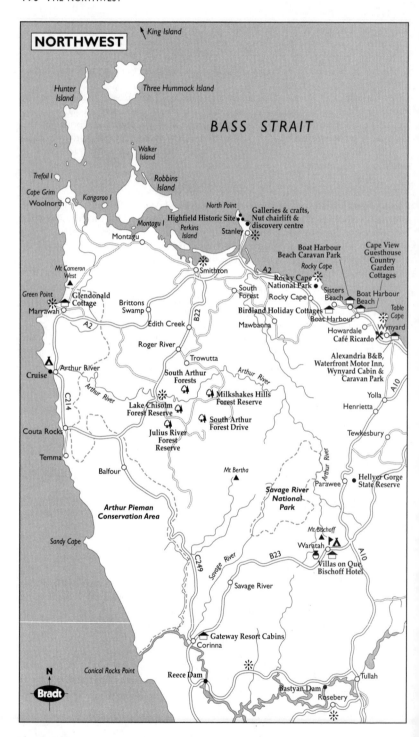

The Northwest

This chapter looks at the northwest corner, north of Lake Pieman and west of the A10 (Murchison Highway). Much of the interior and west coast is impenetrable, so we will concentrate on the southern part across to the coast, the north coast and far northwest, and the islands, including King Island. The climate is milder in this part of Tasmania and wildlife is abundant all year round. There are historical buildings in Stanley, Wynyard and on King Island as well as some excellent Aboriginal sites. King Island in the Bass Strait is famous for its cheese from cows grazed on super-thick grass. Fewer people head up to the northwest which is a shame as there is lots to see and do and some charming B&Bs to stay in. Throw in some giant crabs, some Tasmanian devils, a wind farm and the cleanest air measurements on the planet, and you have a superb tourism destination for the environmentally aware traveller.

GETTING THERE AND AROUND (MAINLAND)
By air
There is an airport at Wynyard that also serves Burnie.

Qantas have flights between Melbourne and Burnie/Wynyard. Call 13 13 13 in Australia or check website: www.qantas.com.au.

Kendell have flights between Melbourne and Burnie/Wynyard. Check website: www.ansett.com.au or www.kendell.com.au for details.

Tasair Regional Airlines (tel: 1800 062900; web: www.tasair.com.au) fly between Hobart and Burnie/Wynyard, King Island and Burnie/Wynyard, and Devonport and King Island.

By car
From the south, take the A10 north through Hellyer Gorge to Wynyard, pick up the A2 Bass Highway and head west. From the west, continue along the A1 coast road to Wynyard and on to Stanley and Smithton.

The following rental car companies operate here.

Autorent Hertz Tel: 6335 1111; fax: 6331 2788; email: mail@autorent.com.au
Avis Tasmania Tel: 6334 7722; fax: 6334 6260; email: avishbt@netspace.net.au
Budget Rent-A-Car Tel: 6391 8566; fax: 6334 1048; email: reservations@budgettas.com; web: www.budget.com.au
Thrifty Car Rental Tel: 6234 1341; fax: 6231 2475; email: thrifty@tasvacations.com.au; web: www.tasvacations.com.au

All have branches at Burnie/Wynyard airport in Wynyard.

By bus/coach

Tasmanian Redline Coaches (tel: 1300 360 000 or 6336 1446) run services from Hobart to Burnie and from Launceston to Burnie and Smithton.

WARATAH TO THE PIEMAN RIVER

A lot of this area is pretty much unexplored territory. It is mainly forested, although logging is going on here so more and more bald patches appear each year. It was once an important tin-mining site and now an iron ore mine still functions. There are no official roads into the area, only some side-roads and dirt tracks that skirt its edges. Part of it was made a national park just before we went to press. So new is it, that I could not find any detailed information on its flora and fauna, but the Parks and Wildlife Service might well have some written up by now. Conservationists are campaigning for more to be protected, maybe all the way across to the Arthur Pieman Conservation Area that stretches along the coast. It makes for a day or two of wild scenery and isolation. Very few tourists enter this area, instead choosing to head on north or south to more popular attractions.

Waratah township began in 1871 when James Smith discovered the Mount Bischoff Tin Ore body. A mine was opened in 1888, with an investment capital of $58,000, and paid dividends of $2 million. So rich was this town it had electric light before most of the rest of Tasmania; even the church was illuminated.

Where to stay and eat

Extremely limited in both departments. If you have a campervan or are travelling with a tent then you will be fine – you can park in a layby off the B23 road to Savage River or there are powered sites and camp pitches at the **Waratah campsite** (Main Road, Waratah, TAS 7321; tel: 6439 7100; fax: 6439 7101; email: warwyn@bigpoind.com.au). Tent site from $6; powered site $11.

In Waratah, check out **Villas on Que** (47 Que Street, Waratah, TAS 7321; tel: 6439 1214) which has 2 self-contained, 2-bedroom units. $70 per night, $250 per week. It does not seem to be open all year, however. The **Bischoff Hotel** (Main Street, Waratah, TAS 7321; tel: 6439 1188) has some rooms and does pub dinners.

Otherwise the nearest permanent accommodation is at Tullah, 50km south of Waratah, or the farming country the same distance north towards Wynyard, or, if you have a 4WD, down near the coast at Corinna.

Waratah has a good country **general store** open seven days a week with fruit, ice-cream, groceries and even the odd newspaper. At the first intersection in Waratah is a **BP Roadhouse** with petrol and snacks – it won first prize a few years ago in a state competition to find the best hamburger. There is also a local butcher.

In Corinna, there is only the **Getaway Resort Cabins** (tel: 6446 1170; fax: 6446 1180) which go for $70 single/double per night with a weekly rate available. There is a small charge for bed linen, and no petrol or grocery shops so bring all your provisions with you and enough petrol to get out to Zeehan (55km) or Waratah (72km).

What to see and do

The **Waratah Museum** in the centre of town has a photo gallery, minerals and other memories of when it was a boom town in the 1890s and sitting on top of the richest tin mine in the world. There is an audio presentation in the Philosopher's Hut (named after James Smith, who discovered the tin ore and was known as 'the Philosopher'), and a replica of an old miner's hut. If the museum is closed, try the council chambers opposite for the key (weekdays) or, at weekends, try the caretaker who lives in the white house between the roadhouse and St James Church.

There is good **trout fishing** in the extensive dam system around here (see *Specialist Tour Operators* in *Chapter 2* for fishing tour operators).

A **self-drive tour** has been produced in a small guide which is available at the municipal offices on Smith Street, at the roadhouse or at tourist information booths elsewhere in this region (try the one just south of the junction of the A10 and B23) where there are also toilets and local information.

The **Waratah Falls** are by the bridge over the Waratah River, but are better viewed from a vantage point a few hundred metres along Main Street.

The 50km scenic drive to **Savage River** is beautiful if you ignore the occasional bald patch of hillside where a forest once stood. Wombats are common here, ambling across the road, so take it easy. The road gets windy in places, with some hairpin turns, but is sealed all the way. To the north lies the newly instated **Savage River National Park**. There is no access to the park at the present time. The drive takes about two hours return.

There is nothing at Savage River but the iron ore mine and some workers' huts. No accommodation, shops or facilities.

If you are heading further south to Corinna (about another 25km) you will need a 4WD vehicle from Savage River onwards. The road is rough and rutted and not good after bad weather.

Corinna consists of just a few buildings and is a perfect getaway, especially in the busy summer season. The main attraction is the 4-hour **Pieman River Cruise** (tel: 6446 1170; fax: 6446 1180) on the *MV Arcadia II*, a historic boat made from Huon pine. The cruise includes morning tea. In summer the boat also makes an afternoon trip. Book ahead. Adult $33; child (5 to 15 years) $16; child under 5 free.

The banks of the Pieman River from upstream of Corinna at the Reece Dam right down to its mouth at the ocean at Hardwicke Bay are in a **state reserve**. From here, with a 4WD, you can take the twisting C249 dirt-road north right up to Arthur River through the Arthur Pieman Conservation Area, but come prepared – it is remote and there are no services of any kind.

ARTHUR PIEMAN CONSERVATION AREA

This area (tel: 6457 1225) covers 96,950 hectares of rugged mountains and mile after mile of thundering beaches. There is virtually no access except by the difficult C249 dirt-road which is well inland. However, there are one or two campsites and boating facilities on beaches at the northern end of the area. Superb for Tasmanian devils and Aboriginal middens, as this was a key hunting ground for the tribes who roamed the northwest.

🎋 *Photo spot*

On wild-weather days the C249 looks like the road to the end of the earth. Capitalise on this by sheltering at the side of your vehicle and shooting a good windy and rutted stretch full of puddles with nothing but wild forest and lashing rain in the background. Use higher speed films (400ASA best) and a wide-angle lens to accentuate space and isolation. A neutral density or tobacco filter will intensify the gloom.

NORTH AND NORTHWEST COASTS

Beautiful, fascinating and packed with history, this region is worth at least four days of your trip. It is not as crowded as elsewhere in the state as most visitors tend to concentrate their time in more popular areas such as Cradle Mountain and the east coast. There is a stunning national park at Rocky Cape with Aboriginal sites and great views over Bass Strait. There are good swimming beaches at Boat

Harbour and Sisters Beach. Inland are rolling hills and good dairy country with cheese farms and state reserves. There is a dramatic fern gully and a rocky beach where Tasmanian devils roam. The remoteness of the coast around Marrawah is delightful and romantic, with some of the biggest waves in Australia pounding the rocks.

Southern approaches

The best way to enter the northwest region is by the A10 Murchison Highway from the south. You will drive up through **Hellyer Gorge State Reserve**, a wonderful small area with ravines covered in tree ferns, some several metres high. There are two short walks from the car-park – the 10-minute River Walk and the 15-minute Old Myrtle Forest Walk – each through fern glades which are cool on a hot day and mysterious and vaguely prehistoric when the mists are down or the weather is dark and brooding. The road then rises again and you get your first views of Bass Strait. As I drove this road one autumn day I came over a rise somewhere around the little farm settlement of Henrietta and looked down over small green fields broken irregularly by clumps of untouched coniferous and deciduous woodland. It all looked familiar, like an English shire, but from the past rather than the present. It resembled a wood-block print or dreamy watercolour of Warwickshire or Dorset circa 1800. It was like Thomas Hardy's Wessex, a view which is hard to find in England any more. The road drops down to the town of Wynyard.

📷 Photo spot

Two here: one is the Hellyer Gorge. Tree fern glades are hard to capture on film as the light differences are huge with a dark green understorey and brilliant sunlight filtering through the fronds. Use a 100ASA film and standard lens and try to shoot in either very bright clearings or actually underneath a tree fern, standing by the trunk. That way the camera will be able to adjust more to lighter or darker scenes without the contrast. The easiest shot here is to look up from under a tree fern and take a silhouette of the umbrella fronds. Shots look professional but are easy.

The second is the lovely rural scene from Henrietta and around. Standard lens and film and no fancy stuff but just check the edges of your viewfinder before you snap to make sure there is not a Coke can in one corner to ruin the ambience.

WYNYARD TO STANLEY

Wynyard is quiet and has some facilities. It is a holiday spot for many Tasmanians and mainlanders. It may be your gateway town as there is an airport here with flights from the mainland (see *Getting to Tasmania* and *Getting Around* sections in *Chapter 2*). Those keen on making the most of their time to see flora and fauna in Tasmania's wilder areas, however, will probably not spend long here.

Where to stay and eat
Wynyard

I would recommend resting your head further west at Boat Harbour, Table Cape or Stanley. However, if you are staying for the night, try **Alexandria B&B** (1 Table Cape Road, Wynyard, TAS 7325; tel: 6442 4411; mobile: 0409 314 300; fax: 6442 4424; email: alexandria@ozemail.com.au; web: www.ozemail.com.au/~alexandria) which has five en-suite rooms for $99–100/$120–130 single/double. There is a pool and views over the Inglis River. The **Waterfront Motor Inn** (adjacent to the wharf, 1 Goldie Street, Wynyard, TAS 7325; tel: 6442 2351; fax: 6442 3749; email: thewaterfront@bigpond.com) has 25 rooms with water views (all ground-floor accommodation). En-suite rooms $72/85–90 single/double. The **Wynyard Cabin and Caravan Park** (30B, Old Bass Highway, Wynyard, TAS 7325; tel: 6442 1998) has a good location on the beach looking out toward Table Cape. On-site vans $31/42, single/double; cabins $53/64, single/double; powered sites $12–16; dorm spaces $17/31, single/double. The town has several restaurants and cafés. Italian food is available at **Café Ricardo** (89a Inglis Street; tel: 6442 1755), which is open every night for supper and Monday to Friday for lunch. Full listings of accommodation and eateries can be found at the visitor centre (corner of Goldie Street and Hogg Street; tel: 6442 4143) or Tasmanian travel and information centres in bigger towns and cities.

Table Cape

Try **Skyescape** at Skye (282 Tollymore Rd, Table Cape, TAS 7325; tel: 6442 1876; fax: 6442 4118; email: skyescape@bigpond.com.au) which has a stunning position right on the cliff top. There are two suites for $140–215/$170–250, single/double. There are nature trails and plentiful wildlife, including bandicoots and echidnas, quolls and wallabies, as well as sea eagles cruising the cliffs and sometimes dolphins and whales offshore. This is one of the best properties on the north coast.

Boat Harbour

Lots of places to stay but they book up quickly for the summer months. Try the **Cape View Guest House** (64 Strawberry Lane, Boat Harbour, TAS 7321; tel/fax: 6445 1273) on a 10-acre property with good views but only two rooms. En-suite $60/95, single/double; suite $80/120, single/double. Or **Country Garden Cottages** (15 Port Rd, Boat Harbour, TAS 7321; tel: 6445 1233; fax: 6445 1019) which has charming hosts and makes a lovely spot for a relaxing couple of days. Fishing and golf available. Rates on enquiry. It is hard to beat the location of the **Boat Harbour Beach Caravan Park** (tel: 6445 1253; fax: 6445 1248) which is on the sand in a great swimming bay protected by a rocky spit. Holiday house $100; cabin $65; on-site van $30; powered site $12; tent site $8. There is a general store at Boat Harbour with fuel, newspaper, provisions and good fish and chips for $5.

Sisters Beach

The order of the day seems to be rented beach homes. I drove around several times but could not find one B&B. Try **Birdland Holiday Cottages** (off Banksia Ave; tel: 6445 1471). Rates on enquiry.

Stanley

Best place in town is **Hanlon House** (6 Marshall St, Stanley, TAS 7331; tel: 6458 1149; fax: 6458 1257; email: hanlon.house@tassie.net.au; web: www.tassie.net.au/hanlonhouse) which is run by Graham and Maxine Wells, who are welcoming and extremely knowledgeable about their town (Graham is a penguin guru). This building was the original Catholic presbytery built in 1904, and has been restored and looks great inside. Evening meals are available. En-suite $100–130/$121–166, single/double. If you are eating out in Stanley, give **Cable Station** a go (tel: 6458 1312; fax: 6458 2009). It is attached to a guesthouse right on the coast on the way to North Point and is licensed. At the Nut is the **Nut Rock Café** (in the Nut Reserve at the base of the Nut; tel: 6458 1186) for light lunches and snacks. There are excellent lobster sandwiches. In town is **Hursey Seafood Restaurant** (2 Alexander Terrace; tel: 6458 1103) with live fish and crustaceans their specialities. Open only for dinner.

Marrawah

Where the main A2 ends is the self-contained **Glendonald Cottage** ($95 for cottage, sleeps 5, washing-machine and drier, wood heater) rented out by Geoff King, a local landowner and Tasmanian devil expert (RA 27520, Bass Highway, Marrawah, TAS 7330;

tel/fax: 6457 1191; email: jonesking@tassie.net.au). It makes a great stay when incorporated with one of Geoff's twilight tours. Otherwise your nearest evening meal is back in Stanley.

What to see and do
Wynyard
The **Wynyard Information Centre** (corner of Goldie Street and Hogg Street; tel: 6442 4143; email: wynyard@tasvisinfo.com.au) has devised brochures detailing some excellent short tours, but most highlights are out of town. There is fishing galore along this coast and plenty of local operators who will take you out and lend you equipment (usually with 24 hours' notice). You might try Mark Newman at **Dive Sight Charters** (212 Port Road, Boat Harbour, TAS 7321; tel: 6445 1444; mobile: 0419 534 572; fax: 6445 1505; email: divesight@winnet.com.au), who run fishing and diving tours.

If you are here in late September or early–mid-October you are in for a treat as the sloping fields of this north coast are painted with thousands of **tulips**. Table Cape is the place to be. **Van Diemen Quality Bulbs** (363 Lighthouse Road, Wynyard, TAS 7325; tel: 6442 2012; fax: 6442 2582) has a spectacular display every year. Farm open from 10.00–16.30 daily during the flowering season (September–mid-October). It is another reminder of the great diversity of flora and fauna on this relatively small island.

Beyond the tulip fields stands the whitewashed **Table Cape Lighthouse** which was opened for business on August 1 1888 with a light crafted by the Chance Brothers in Birmingham, England, which shone a beam which reached 19 nautical miles. The Chance Brothers' factory must have been buzzing for the latter half of the 19th century as it seems most lights in this part of the world bear their makers' plaque.

Boat Harbour, Sisters Beach and Rocky Cape
These are small, pretty seaside places with good swimming and surfing beaches which are ideal for afternoon strolls or a dip.

Rocky Cape makes a wonderful half-day visit with a walk to the lighthouse and along the paths through scrub to Aboriginal caves (see *Rocky Cape National Park* section below).

Stanley
Stanley has been welcoming tourists for decades but it might not be anything but a small fishing village without two things – its telephonic claim to fame and its Nut.

It was from a building on the coast (now the Cable Station guesthouse and restaurant) that the first telephone transmission was made to the mainland in 1936, linking Tasmania to the world. Stanley is rightly proud of its vital role in international communications. The station ceased transmitting in 1967 but the Cable Station has retained a lot of the equipment which is fascinating to see, but you might have to stay a night.

The Nut is a volcanic plug rising to 150m and making an imposing mark on the otherwise flat and gentle coastline. It is now in a 59-hectare state reserve (tel: 6458 1100) but easily accessible. You can walk up it or take a chair lift (tel: 6458 1286). There are seal-watching trips from Stanley that cruise around the base of the Nut to watch for Australian fur seals sunning themselves on rocky outcrops.

For **tours** in the Stanley region, some with an environmental flavour, try the local operators **Stanley Seal Cruises and Sea Charters** (tel: 6458 1312), **Wilderness to**

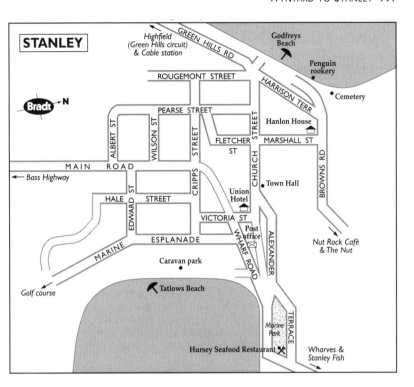

West Coast Tours (tel/fax Bernard Atkins: 6458 2038; mobile: 0417 593 158; email: batkins@tassie.net.au; web: www.tassie.net.au/~batkins), and **Stanley and Beyond Eco Tours and Charters** (tel: 0418 143 099; email: james.smith@tassie.net.au).

But the best eco-tour is free if you are staying at Hanlon House. Ask the owner Graham Wells to take you on a night hike to the **penguin rookery** about 300 yards away, just beyond the graveyard. Graham has created more than 100 small caves using blocks of stone for the little penguins to use and they have flocked here. Remember to cover your torch with some red cellophane and do not take any flash photographs as bright lights can damage the penguins' eyes. Some of the penguins are even using old tombs that have moved over the years and left suitable holes for them to squeeze into.

Stanley was also the base for the Van Diemen's Land Company who began life here in a stately stone house called **Highfield** on the hill outside the town. Today it is on the heritage trail and can be visited. Check with tourist information offices for opening times.

Before you leave Stanley take a quick tour of the **Stanley Fish** warehouse to see the giant crabs up close (tel: 6458 1227; mobile: 0409 959 337; fax: 6458 1190; email: stanleyfish@craigmostyn.com.au; web: www.craigmostyn.com.au). Tours at 10.00 and 14.30, bookings essential.

Marrawah

There is one excellent reason for coming all the way out to this wild coast, other than the fact it is one of the most beautiful, thrilling and deserted spots in Tasmania. Local farmer Geoff King (RA 27520, Bass Highway, Marrawah, TAS 7330; tel/fax: 6457 1191; email: jonesking@tassie.net.au) owns land here and is

MEET A TASMANIAN: GEOFF KING (FARMER, CONSERVATIONIST, DEVIL GUIDE)

Geoff King's large, coarse hands are those of a man who has spent his life on the land. His family arrived more than 120 years ago and the land has been in their possession almost ever since. But now he is fighting to protect it, its wildlife and its Aboriginal heritage. 'I've got 200 acres here and another 860 further south,' he said as we bumped along in his ute from the farmstead to the coast.

> My family first came here in 1880 when they started driving cattle from Stanley down to Queenstown. This land was one of the patches they chose to stop and rest cattle on. It was pretty well watered and had good grass so it was an ideal spot in some ways.

But Geoff has pulled out of some of the family farming that he used to share with his brother.

> I wanted to move further towards conservation of the land and concentrate on low-impact schemes to protect it in some way and I realised that 'people' was the answer. There is some really good wildlife on the land and some important Aboriginal sites but I am finding 4WD tracks over the foreshore between the sea and my property, and sometimes over the middens themselves. It is hard to stop people driving over here when you're not out here watching all the time.

> I now run small tours with a maximum of eight people but I'd prefer four or less to be honest. We take all our food to the hut and take everything back out again when we've finished watching the devils.

> One of the most important spots out here is the site of one of George Robinson's camps as he went around gathering Aborigines to take to Flinders Island for the settlement there. I've been reading Robinson's journal entries for when he stayed here and his descriptions of the view, and from that I've identified the spot almost exactly.

This land is important to Geoff but not just because of the family sentiments.

> Some important animals use this area, like wedge-tailed eagles, wallabies and the devils. They rely on its wildness, and the Aboriginal people who once lived here and all the middens and sites they left – their descendants must feel those are important to them and part of their history – and then you look out to sea and think there's nothing out there all the way to Argentina. It's pretty incredible so it's worth trying to protect.

committed to preserving it as a refuge for wildlife. To demonstrate its worth he has lured hundreds of visitors out here, including several wildlife film crews from around the world, to see **Tasmanian devils**. He takes a maximum of eight people bouncing over the grassy hillocks with a wallaby carcass strapped to the back of his ute, to create a scent trail and get the devils interested. He reaches the shoreline where rocks are speckled with red algae and the waves can get huge. If you took a direct line west from here, the first landfall would be the Patagonian coastline of Argentina, round about the Golfo San Matias to be precise. In a shack at the back of the pebbly beach, Geoff sets up two lights and a baby intercom (the kind parents use to hear their child from another room) and guests watch from inside the shack out of the wind through a large window. 'Just wait for the first crunch,' says Geoff. Within minutes during my visit a devil showed up and began ripping the carcass to pieces. In an hour, after five devils had fought over the meat, there was nothing left, not a hair nor a bone. It was one of the most amazing experiences and is a must-do. He offers salad and lamb chops which you cook in the shack (although it is surprising how quickly some people lose their appetites when watching the devils dining ferociously just feet away).

📷 Photo spot
The pebbly beach at Marrawah is majestic at sunset, so ask Geoff to get you there about an hour before so you can scout out the best position (probably looking south). There is red algae on the rocks here too which glows in the final hour of sunlight. The pebbles make an interesting foreground. Use a wide-angle lens and 64–100ASA, 200ASA if you are shooting as the sun sinks.

Other activities in the region
From Marrawah, a bumpy 4WD track heads south to the Arthur River where you can take a river cruise (4 Gardiner Street, Arthur River, TAS 7330; tel: 6457 1288; fax: 6457 1288; or c/o Jetty, Arthur River Heads, Arthur River, TAS 7330; tel: 6457 1158; fax: 6457 1332; email: arthurcruises@tasadventures.com; web: www.tasadventures.com/arthurcruises). Around $50 per adult, exact prices on enquiry.

Two **craft galleries** to visit in this region are **Touchwood Craft Gallery** (31 Church Street in Stanley; tel: 6458 1348). Open daily 09.30–18.00. Admission free.

And the **Stanley Artworks Studio Gallery** (Van Dieman Land Company Store, 16 Wharf Road, Stanley; tel: 6458 2000). Open daily October–May 10.00–18.00. Adult $2, child free.

Three **markets** to catch are the **Highfield Indoor Market** at Highfield Historic Site (open first Saturday in October–April 09.00–14.00), the **Smithton Market** (Uniting Church Hall, Goldie Street, Smithton; open last Saturday of each month excluding January or February 09.00–13.00), and the **Wynyard Old Theatre Market** (Goldie Street off Moore Street in Wynyard; open January–September and November every third Sunday 09.00–15.00. In October it is part of the Tulip Festival, in December open second and third Sunday). Highfield Historic Site now has summer evening lantern tours.

Short walks
Noel Jago Walk at Wynyard
Distance: 2km return. Time: 45 minutes return. Difficulty: easy.

Leave west Wynyard via the Oldina Road, go south 4km, and turn right into Nursery Road which takes you to the Oldina Forest Reserve. It is part of a state forest and has pines and eucalyptus. There are toilets, a children's play area and places for barbecues and picnics. Within the forest there are mountain bike and horse riding trails. Walk starts at a small picnic spot at the end of Blackfish Creek Road about 2km from the forest reserve. There are several species of fern, some tall eucalyptus and platypus in the creek.

The Nut at Stanley
Distance: 1km return. Time: 1 hour return. Difficulty: easy.
Start by the chair lift and follow the easy and obvious path to the top for great views
and a good lunch spot. Return the same way or take the chair lift down.

ROCKY CAPE NATIONAL PARK
The smallest national park (tel: 6452 4998) at just 3,064 hectares, but striking and
fascinating. It is on the north coast between Wynyard and Stanley and boasts a
rugged coastline with small, sheltered beaches and backed by hills that afford good
views over Bass Strait. The rocks are Proterozoic (1,200 million to 700 million
years old), with quartzite the most dominant.

Vegetation is largely banksia, with heathland and woodland plants growing on
the hills behind the coast. Along the coast itself you will find the more salt-resistant
plants like velvet bush and salt bush, sea box and ice plants. Wind is another factor
the flora here has to contend with. Plants that grow tall in the rest of Tasmania, like
she-oak and sweet wattle, here are squat, staying low to survive the gales.

Spring is best for the woodland wildflowers, which create carpets of colour.
There are bright red Christmas bells and fuchsias and a host of species that might
be new to many visitors – guinea flowers, dusty miller, milkmaids, fringe myrtle,
paperbark and stringybark gum trees, west coast peppermint and boronia. About 50
species of orchids are found in the woods, as are examples of *Banksia serrata*, the
only ones in Tasmania.

The park is home to Bennett's wallabies, possums, wombats, bandicoots,
echidnas, frogs and lizards, but snakes seem to be rare (mind where you walk all
the same). Birds include sea eagles, cormorants, gulls and terns, oystercatchers,
black cockatoos, ground parrots and green rosellas.

The park has special significance for Aboriginal people and as we go to press there
is a campaign to have it, or parts of it, given back to descendants. Rocky Cape's
ancient midden sites provide the most complete record of Aboriginal coastal life in
Australia yet found. Aboriginal people visit sacred sites in the park quite often to
perform ceremonies so it is worth checking before your visit with the park
authorities (telephone number above) where you should and should not walk.

Ancient people crossing the Bassian Plain land bridge from the mainland would
have seen these towering cliffs from some miles off and would have had to scale
them to continue their journey. This was the land of the Rarrerloihener band from
the northern tribe and they called this area Tang Dim Mer. Archaeologists have
found midden sites in some caves as deep as six metres containing thousands of
years of neatly sedimented history and telling us much about their way of life before
the Europeans first landed. They ate fish, shellfish and seals, small land animals,
grass trees and bracken ferns. Some younger layers of earth show the diet changed
about 3,500 years ago and they stopped eating fish. They used tools made of animal
bone, some of which have been dated to between 8,000 and 3,500 year ago.

More recently the cape was named by Matthew Flinders and George Bass on
their circumnavigation of the island. A cattle track ran through here from 1828
which was used a couple of years later by George Robinson and his experimental
party possibly as they headed from Cape Grim to Flinders Island. From 1840,
postmen used the track as part of their rounds.

Activities
The park's shoreline is full of rock pools which make for a good day exploring
exotic seaweeds, anemones and starfish. The best swimming beaches are Sisters
Beach, Forwards Beach and Anniversary Bay. Diving off the coast is superb, but

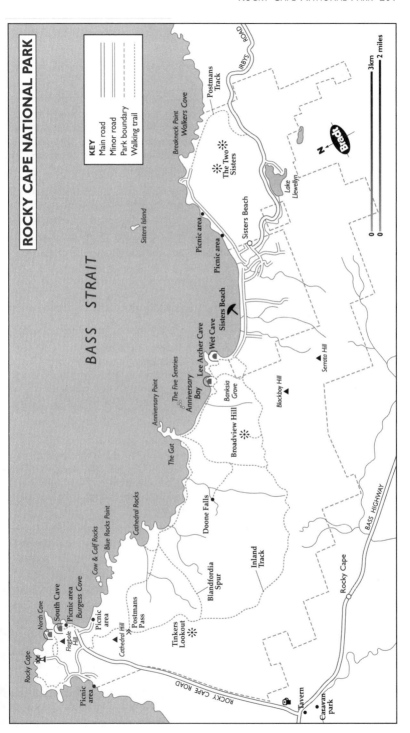

ROCKY CAPE NATIONAL PARK

KEY
Main road
Minor road
Park boundary
Walking trail

BASS STRAIT

Rocky Cape
North Cove
South Cave
Picnic area
Burgess Cove
Flagpole Hill
Cathedral Hill
Picnic area
Postmans Pass
Cow & Calf Rocks
Blue Rocks Point
Cathedral Rocks
The Gut
Anniversary Point
The Five Sentries
Anniversary Bay
Lee Archer Cave
Wet Cave
Banksia Grove
Broadview Hill
Sisters Beach
Picnic area
Picnic area
Sisters Beach
Sisters Island
Breakneck Point
Walkers Cove
Postmans Track
The Two Sisters
Lake Llewellyn
Blackboy Hill
Serrata Hill
Doone Falls
Blandfordia Spur
Inland Track
Tinkers Lookout
Picnic area
Rocky Cape
ROCKY CAPE ROAD
BASS HIGHWAY
Tavern
Caravan park
IRBYS ROAD

N
Beach

0   3km
0   2 miles

not for beginners. Undertows and rips are common in certain parts and it is best to go with a guide.

Short walks
North Cave and the Lighthouse
Distance: 1km return. Time: 30 minutes return. Difficulty: easy
You can drive to the lighthouse or stop a few hundred metres before it where there is a small layby. This is where the walking track to North Cave begins. It runs east through heath plants for about 500m and then climbs briefly to the cave entrance. Retrace your steps and wander up to the lighthouse for good views and an information sign about coastal environment and the wreck of the SS *Southern Cross* that ran aground on a reef in 1889.

South Cave
Distance: 1km return. Time: 30 minutes return. Difficulty: easy.
From the car-park at Burgess Cove, where there are some picnic areas, take the track north to the cave entrance. The debris of thousands of years is obvious and there are informative signs.

Caves Circuit
Distance: 2km return. Time: 1 hour return. Difficulty: easy with some steep sections and rockpools.
Marked track starts at the Sisters Beach boat ramp and heads inland into heath scrub where giant banksia grow. Take a path heading right back towards the coast and Lee Archer Cave. There is a platform to keep the midden from being disturbed. The path heads east and drops quite sharply to Wet Cave which, as you might imagine, has water in it. From here you can return to the beach over the rockpools.

Postmans Track
Distance: 12km return. Time: 2–3 hours return. Difficulty: easy.
Start at the eastern end of Sisters Beach and follow the road and the coastline past two picnic spots to Breakneck Point. Then the track begins and skirts the Two Sisters hills going past Walkers Cove. It rounds the eastern end of the hills and heads downhill to another road. Take a right and follow the road to Lake Llewellyn for a rest and then head back to Sisters Beach.

Rocky Cape Circuit Walk
Distance: 12km. Time: 2–3 hours return. Difficulty: easy.
Start just south of Flagpole Hill where a track leads of the Rocky Cape Road up Cathedral Hill. Follow this over Postmans Pass and up to Tinkers Lookout which affords 360° views. Shortly after the lookout, take a left down Blandfordia Spur to Cathedral Rocks on the coast, which is a good place for a rest and a cup of tea. Onward again northwest, back up to Postmans Pass, and retrace steps over Cathedral Hill to the road.

Longer option From Tinkers Lookout walkers can continue along the Inland Track which runs for about 5km over Broadview Hill and down to Sisters Beach. The adventurous should then head along the coastline northwest to Cathedral Rocks. This is a pretty tough section as most of it is over rocks and boulders. For this longer option leave at least a whole day, wear good boots and take a day pack with clothes, waterproofs, food and water.

Longer stays

If you have more time in this region, take the back roads south of Smithton up into the **South Arthur Forests**. There are three superb forest reserves – Milkshakes Hills, Lake Chisholm and Julius River – and a forest drive. They are seldom visited but hold stands of giant eucalyptus and tree ferns, and buttongrass plains and grasslands on the higher ground. If you have a good large-scale map and a compass then trek off into the woods, but take a day pack with emergency rations and equipment and more if you are walking in winter.

You can also make an appointment to go and see the scientists at **Cape Grim**. It is here that measurements have consistently been recorded over the past decade proving it has the cleanest air in the world (although this is under debate now, I believe, after an increase in particulates was found in some more recent readings). Do not visit independently as this is private grazing land for sheep and cattle, the only remaining property of the Van Diemen's Land Company, which is still going after 175 years.

THE HUNTER ISLAND GROUP

Off the northwest coast are the four main islands of the Hunter Group: Robbins, Hunter, Three Hummock and King. The first three are close to the coast but King is about 100km off, about halfway between Tasmania and the mainland. It is also much bigger. The islands are crucial as a stop-off for migrating birds, most notably mutton-birds.

King Island is absolutely fascinating. It has had a wild and chequered career, being the graveyard of hundreds of ships and thousands of their passengers, and also the slaughterhouse for an entire elephant seal population that once thrived here on the rocks on the sheltered eastern shore. Thanks to a post-war soldier re-settlement scheme it now supports a population of almost 2,000 people, with several industries and a full calendar of social events. It has one or two excellent restaurants and is noted for its cheese, beef and tourism.

Hunter Island is privately owned and a mutton-bird reserve, and as we go to press access is not possible. Three Hummock Island is a nature reserve with fabulous flora and mysterious Aboriginal rock carvings. Only one tour operator – Rob Alliston – is allowed in to run environmentally sensitive trips with small groups (see pages 204 and 207 for details).

Robbins Island and its islet, Walker, is owned by the Hammond brothers (John and Keith), cattle ranchers who are delicately testing the tourism waters through an operator, Simon Cubit, who has taken the first horse-riding group on to the island (see pages 204 and 207 for details). It, too, supports a big mutton-bird colony.

Getting there and around and tour operators
King Island

Access is by plane. **Kendell** fly regularly to King Island from Melbourne (tel: 13 13 00 in Melbourne, 6462 1322 in Currie). **King Island Airlines** (tel: 9580 3777) fly from Moorabbin (Victoria). **Tasair Regional Airlines** (tel: 1800 062900; web: www.tasair.com.au) fly from Hobart, Burnie/Wynyard and Devonport. The following operators run tours in King Island:

King Island Coach Tours 95 Main St, King Island, TAS 7256; tel: 6462 1138; fax: 6462 1563; email: ann@kingislandgem.com.au; web: www.kingislandgem.com.au

King Island Dive Charters Main St, King Island, TAS 7256; tel: 6461 1133; fax: 6461 1293; email: king.island.dive@bigfoot.com; web: www.divecharter.to/kingisland

King Island Trail Rides Heddles Rd, King Island, TAS 7256; tel: 6463 1147; fax: 6463 1151

Top Tours 13 Main St, King Island, TAS 7256; tel: 6462 1245; fax: 6462 1565; email: toptours@tasadventures.com

King Island also has some transport rental companies:

Cheapa Island Car Rentals 1 Netherby Rd, King Island, TAS 7256; tel: 6462 1603; fax: 6462 1603; email: kimotors@kingisland.net.au. Has only manual transmission vehicles.
The Trend Edward St, Currie, TAS 7256; tel: 6462 1360. Rents bicycles.

Three Hummock Island
Access is by light plane charters from Smithton (**Becker Aviation**; tel: 0408 503100) for $117 return each if three people travel, and from Burnie/Wynyard (**Seair Adventures**; tel: 6442 1220; fax: 6442 3208; email: seaair@bigpond.com.au; web: www.seairac.com.au) for $136 return each if five people travel. There is little point going unless with tour operator Rob Alliston (**Three Hummock Island Escape**; tel/fax 6452 1554; mobile: 0428 521554; email: threehummock@tasadventures.com).

Robbins Island
Access by horse only. Occasional treks for small groups being planned. Contact Simon Cubit (**Riding High**; tel: 6248 6281; fax: 6248 1300; email: simon@ridinghigh.com.au; web: www.ridinghigh.com.au) for latest information.

King Island
Where to stay and eat
The Fishermans Cottage (7 Edward St, Currie, King Island, TAS 7256; tel/fax: 9580 1188; mobile: 0417 335 995) is a 3-bedroom cottage that sleeps 6. $595 for 2-night minimum stay. Each additional night is $240 for the entire cottage. Special rates for 5 and 7 night stays. Bring all provisions.
Baudins Holiday Apartments (The Esplanade, King Island, TAS 7256; tel/fax: 6461 1110; email: baudins@kingisland.net.au; web: www.kingisland.rog/baudins.htm) is on the beach at Naracoopa with great views of Sea Elephant Bay and Councillor Island. Self-contained Cedar Cottages with lounge and fully equipped kitchen. Single and 2-bedroom cottages available, each with own balcony. Studio apartment $99–121/$110–154, single/double. There's a licensed restaurant here with good food.
Boomerang by the Sea (Golf Club Road, King Island, TAS 7256; tel: 6462 1288; fax: 6462 1607; email: kiboomerang@kingisland.net.au; web: www.bythesea.com.au) offers breathtaking views over the sea and the golf course. The motel is 5 minutes' walk from the centre of the town and has 1 apartment ($110 single and double) and 16 en-suite rooms ($88/110 single/double). The licensed restaurant has good food and 270° views over the ocean (tel: 6462 1288; email: judy@bythesea.com.au). Closed Sunday evenings May–October.

What to see and do
The excellent **King Island Museum** in Currie is a good place to start, to get a potted history of the place. Open daily 14.00–16.00; closed July–September. Admission adult $2. It is housed in a former lighthouse keeper's cottage and has many nautical exhibits, which forms a theme for your stay. Everything here is inextricably linked to the sea. Once Matthew Flinders and George Bass discovered Van Diemen's Land was an island (in 1798) mariners rejoiced as this cut the journey time from England to Sydney, saving money. But there was a catch. These are among the roughest waterways in the world. They have claimed over a hundred ships and swallowed thousands of souls around King Island alone

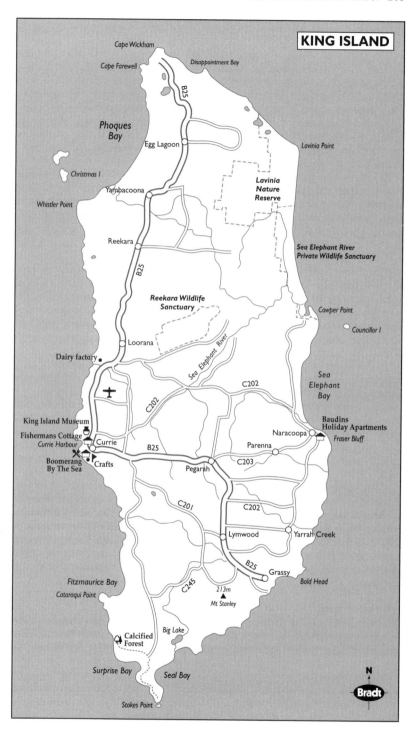

KING ISLAND

Cape Wickham
Cape Farewell
Disappointment Bay
B25

Phoques
Bay

Egg Lagoon
Lavinia Point

Christmas I

Yambacoona

Whistler Point

Lavinia
Nature
Reserve

Reekara

Sea Elephant River
Private Wildlife
Sanctuary

B25

Reekara Wildlife
Sanctuary

Loorana

Cowper Point

Councillor I

Dairy factory

Sea Elephant River

Sea
Elephant
Bay

C202

C202

King Island Museum
Fishermans Cottage
Currie Harbour

Currie
B25

C201

Pegarah

Baudins
Holiday Apartments
Naracoopa
Fraser Bluff

Parenna

Boomerang
By The Sea

Crafts

C203

C201

C202

Fitzmaurice Bay
Cataraqui Point

Lymwood
Yarrah Creek

B25
Grassy
Bold Head

C245

213m
Mt Stanley

Big Lake

Calcified
Forest

Surprise Bay
Seal Bay

Stokes Point

N

Bradt

(hundreds more in the Furneaux Group to the east). There are more than 60 wrecks just offshore.

The *Cataraqui* is one of them. On the night of August 3 1845 this 710-tonne barque was approaching the strait with 367 free settlers from England and Ireland, a crew of 42, and a cargo of slate for Melbourne. Bad weather had pushed the ship south and she smashed against the rocks on the southwest coast of King Island. Only eight crew and a lone passenger, Solomon Brown, survived. The Straits' policeman buried more than 340 bodies in large graves and was rewarded by the government for his efforts. In 1995 a permanent information marker was placed near the historic grave site and at a point overlooking the wreck's location. Some items from the wreck are in the museum in Currie.

Another amazing wreck tale is that of the 616-tonne, fully rigged *Brahmin*, that was smashed against a reef off the west coast at midnight on May 21 1854 en route from Gravesend to Sydney. Some passengers and crew managed to launch the lifeboat at dawn but more were drowned before the rest made it to shore. They then had to survive five months (in winter) on King Island and were rescued only by yet another wreck, that of the *Waterwitch*. A small boat was tossed ashore which two of the *Brahmin*'s crew used to row to Melbourne for help. The *Brahmin* site was rediscovered in 1976 on the west coast by three local divers. They were led to the site by the presence of artefact material scattered along the shoreline and the known location of the survivors' camp. The site of the *Brahmin* is difficult to locate and you are best to dive with a local operator. Some material is in the museum. Australia is full of these stories of irrefutable courage and strength of human spirit by its first settlers, with Tasmania making a major contribution.

In the south of the island is the **Calcified Forest**, petrified trunks of trees thought to be more than 25 million years old. They are clearly visible from a viewing spot.

King Island is noted for its delicious cheeses, notably the brie and the blue, and there is nowhere better to taste them than at the **King Island Dairy** (tel: 9421 0155; fax: 9421 0166; web: www.kidairy.com.au) eight kilometres north of Currie. It is about the purest cheese you will ever eat. The island is pollution-free and the grass of such a high quality that no chemicals, feed supplements or stock growth additives are used.

There are **events** year-round. In November a golf tournament and school fair, horse racing from December to January, the King Island Show on the first Tuesday in March, live theatre and the Queenscliff to Grassy yacht race also in March, mutton-bird season in April and pheasant season in June. Descendants Weekend is especially fun. Descendants of shipwrecked survivors, lighthouse keepers, rescuers and shipping pioneers are invited every November to attend to commemorate the island's maritime history. The 2002 event will also mark the 200th anniversary of the island's sovereignty to the British Empire.

📷 Photo spot
The island is famous for dairy produce, so try to get a shot of a cow munching away in a field with nothing but the wild ocean behind her. The cow should fill about one-quarter of the frame and not be paying you any attention. 100ASA, 50mm lens.

Outdoor activities
King Island has good walks, horseback trails, dive sites and nature spotting. Transport on the island is sporadic, so a bicycle is probably a good choice (see *Getting there and around* section, page 204) or you could join one of the many tours.

There are two nature reserves (Lavinia, and New Year and Christmas islands), two private wildlife sanctuaries (Sea Elephant River and Reekara), two state reserves at Seal Rocks and Kentford Forest, and a protected area surrounding the Calcified Forest.

A French scientific expedition spent two weeks at what they named Sea Elephant Bay in 1802. Their accounts speak of hundreds of elephant seals, as do the logs of a party of English sealers who had been camped there for a year slaughtering them for their oils. One of the French party feared the worst and he was right, for by 1805 the entire population had been killed.

Lavinia Nature Reserve (tel: 6461 1157) is excellent for nature study as it contains many coastal vegetation types, wetlands such as Lake Martha Lavinia and the Sea Elephant River estuary, and part of the habitat of the endangered orange-bellied parrot.

For diving, try **King Island Dive Charters** (Main Street, King Island, TAS 7256; tel: 6461 1133; fax: 6461 1293; email: king.island.dove@bigfoot.com; web: www.divecharter.to/kingisland) with wreck dives and night dives available. Marine life includes giant southern rock lobsters, sponged and gorgonian fans, zoanthids and pink jewel anemones.

Further information
For **more information** tap up the island's excellent website: www.kingisland.net.au.

Three Hummock Island and Robbins Island
All accommodation and food is organised through tour operators Rob Alliston and Simon Cubit, mentioned above.

What to see and do
Three Hummock Island Wonderful wildlife on this 18,000 acre island, including 700 or 800 Forester kangaroos, pademelons, three species of possum and 80 species of bird including shy albatross (at sea) and mutton-birds. The flora is a great draw as it includes five species of rare greenhood orchid. Whales pass occasionally. The first European to see the island, the naturalist E D Atkinson, called it a 'miniature continent of exceeding beauty'. There are unusual Aboriginal petroglyphs carved in granite and depicting an unrecognisable animal. They are thought to be 8,000-4,000 years old. The only way on to the island is through tour operator Rob Alliston, who moved there when he was four years old and lives there with his family. Accommodation is in a lodge that sleeps ten in single or double rooms with panoramic views. Meals can be part of the package, or visitors can take guided or self-guided bushwalks and camp out (camping gear is for hire). Rob runs an amphibious craft called a 'larc' which can access remote beaches. Half-day tour: adult $60.50. Full-day tour: adult $99. Sea kayaks and mountain bikes for use of tour members. See page 204 for contact details.

Robbins Island This island is still in the fledgling stage of tourism, but owner John Hammond is keen to allow small groups in on horseback. It is possible to cross from the northwest coast at low tide (2ft of water). The island is a bird-spotter's dream. There are white-breasted sea eagles, pelicans, mutton-birds, and the odd and rare orange-bellied parrot migrating back north for the winter. There are wallabies too, and wide open beaches to let the horses gallop free. The cook on a recent trial tour led by operator Simon Cubit, of Riding High, was an Aboriginal descendant who told the guests stories her relatives passed down about their life in Tasmania. All enquiries to Simon Cubit (see page 204 for contact details). One to watch.

📷 *Photo spot*

A superb shot would be the riders heading across the water to the island at low tide. Be slightly behind them and about 50 yards to one side, so they are walking away from you across and to the middle of the back of your frame. If you find the sun directly in front of you, use it to silhouette the riders. You could add a starburst filter to give the water and the sun sparkle. 64–100ASA, wide angle and 50mm lens (use both if you have them).

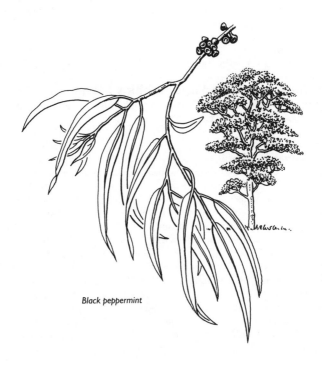

Black peppermint

North Central

11

This region covers the central north coast from Somerset west to the Tamar River, and the Great Western Tiers, the mountain range stretching from Mole Creek west to Lake Sorell and forming the northern escarpment of the central plateau. This is rich agricultural land, excellent for dairy production and mainly north-facing so favoured by fruit farmers and vineyards. There are several gardens open to the public. The coast is busy with industry and a cargo port at Burnie and the ferry passenger terminal at Devonport. You probably won't want to linger too long here for it is lacking in wildlife and wild scenery, but the towns might make a base for a night or two from where to go exploring. There are two national parks; both are excellent and for different reasons. This is one of the older established parts of the state so there are many historic buildings, especially in the west of the region from Deloraine and Westbury through to Launceston.

GETTING THERE AND AROUND
By air
Confusingly, Burnie airport is actually in Wynyard and called Burnie/Wynyard airport (see *Getting there and around* section of *Chapter 10*). Devonport has its own airport with daily flights from Melbourne on Qantas and Kendell (see *Getting there and away* in *Chapter 2*).

By sea
Passengers on the *Spirit of Tasmania* car ferry come in to, and leave from, Devonport (see *Getting there and away* in *Chapter 2*).

By bus
Tasmanian Redline Coaches (**TRC**) (tel: 6336 1446) run services from Hobart to Devonport (and the *Spirit of Tasmania* docks) and Burnie; from Launceston to Devonport (and the *Spirit of Tasmania* docks) and on to Burnie and Smithton.

TWT's Tassielink Regional Coach Service (tel: 1300 300 520; web: www.tigerline.com.au) runs services between Launceston and Strahan via Devonport, Sheffield and Gowrie Park.

Maxwell's (tel/fax: 6492 1431) run services from Devonport and Launceston to Cradle Mountain and Walls of Jerusalem.

By car
The main A1, A5 and A10 roads all run from Hobart to the north coast – A1 and A5 through the Midlands, A10 across to Queenstown and north to Somerset. The following rental car companies operate here:

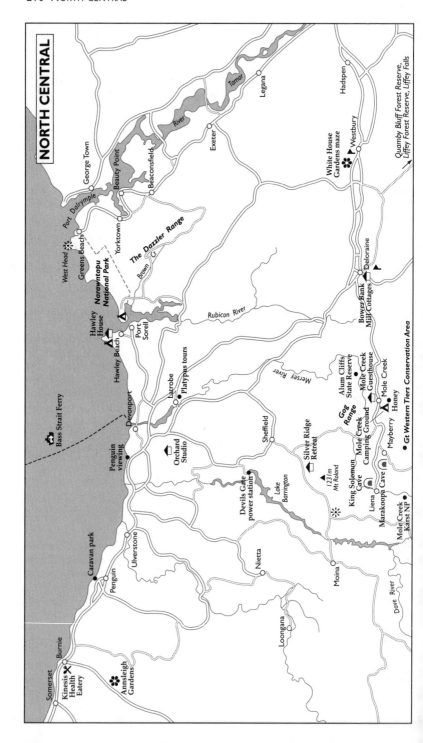

NORTH CENTRAL

Autorent Hertz Tel: 6335 1111; fax: 6331 2788; email: mail@autorent.com.au. At Burnie/Wynyard airport, at the Devonport Ferry Terminal, and in Devonport and Burnie.

Avis Tasmania Tel: 6334 7722; fax: 6334 6260; email: avishbt@netspace.net.au. At Devonport and Burnie/Wynyard airports.

Budget Rent-A-Car Tel: 6391 8566; fax: 6334 1048; email: reservations@budgettas.com; web: www.budget.com.au. At Devonport and Burnie/Wynyard airports and Devonport ferry terminal.

Thrifty Car Rental Tel: 6391 8105; fax: 6391 8482; email: thrifty@tasvacations.com.au; web: www.tasvacations.com.au). At Burnie/Wynyard airport, Devonport ferry terminal and in Devonport.

By bicycle

Olivers Performance Sport and Cycle (109 Rooke Street Mall, Devonport, TAS 7310; tel: 6424 9366; mobile: 0419 551 875; fax: 6424 1244; email: judeoliver@bigpond.com) rent 'Trek' mountain bikes in four sizes. Half-day, daily and weekly rates, and one-way rentals. Hire includes helmet, lock and repair kit, racks and panniers.

NORTH CENTRAL COAST

This is the commercial centre of Tasmania and I would estimate not more than two days are needed to travel its length and get somewhere more scenic for the night. At Burnie is a cargo port that ships out the $700 million worth of metals and minerals the island exports each year. Burnie has had it rough, with industries closing and unemployment rising, but things have taken an upturn. The local tourism board thinks the town is through the worst and is predicting steady growth in the future. Some formerly toxic sites are winning awards for re-vegetation and cleanliness. There is quite a lot of wildlife in and around the town, especially platypus, azure kingfishers and some penguins, and the town runs a wildlife interpretation project. Penguin is a sleepy little place that is good for a sandwich stop and maybe a quick wildlife interpretation tour. There are public toilets by the local tourist office opposite the waterfront. It was named by local botanist Ronald C Gunn. In 1975, the human population was 5,000 and the penguins numbered 3,800. Devonport, on the Mersey River, is Tasmania's third-largest centre, with its economy focused on its port. It is not a tourist town so much as a tourist transit town for those hopping on or off the *Spirit of Tasmania* ferry to the mainland. East to the Tamar is a stretch of picturesque coast with good beaches, beautiful forests and a stunning national park at Narawntapu. There is also a pioneering seahorse farm at Beauty Point.

Where to stay
Burnie

Glen Osborne House B&B (9 Aileen Crescent (off Mount Street), Burnie, TAS 7320; tel: 6431 9866; fax: 6431 4354) is the best, a heritage building dating to 1885 with period decorations and furniture and surrounded by two acres of gardens. En-suite room $80–90/$110–120, single/double.

Or you could try **Weller's Inn** (36 Queen Street, Burnie, TAS 7320; tel: 6431 1088; fax: 6431 6480; email: wellersinn@vision.net.au), which has en-suite rooms for $104–48, single and double, and a restaurant.

The **Chancellor Inn** (139 Wilson Street, Burnie, TAS 7320; tel: 6431 4455; fax: 6431 1026: email: ciburnie@southcom.au) is not bad. En-suite room $95–115, single and double.

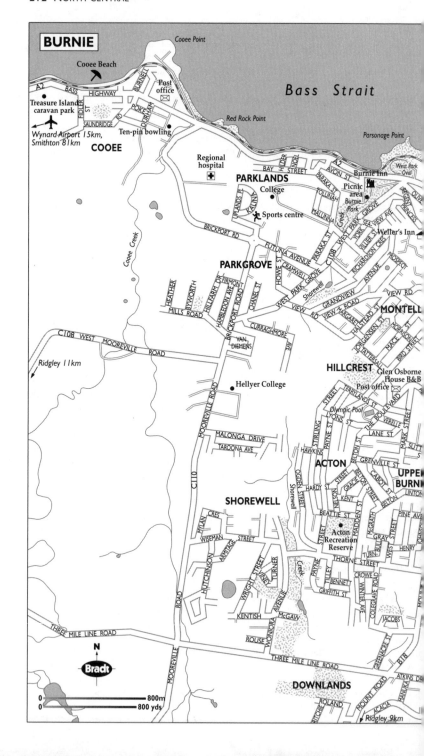

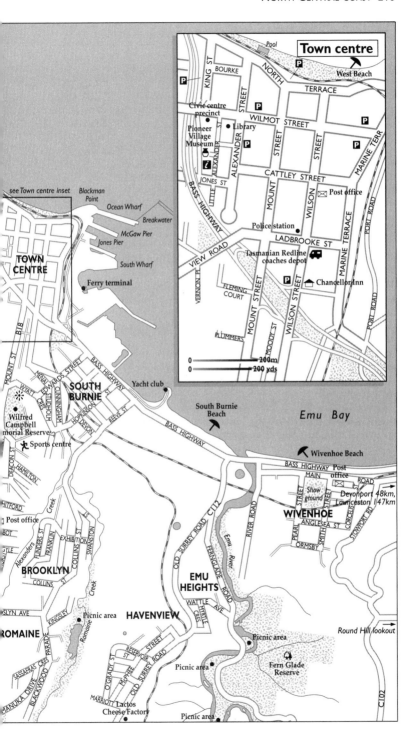

Town centre

Pool

West Beach

KING ST

BOURKE

NORTH

TERRACE

Civic centre precinct

WILMOT STREET

Pioneer Village Museum

Library

ALEXANDER

STREET

STREET

STREET

MARINE TERR

CATTLEY STREET

JONES ST

MOUNT

WILSON

Post office

see Town centre inset

Blackman Point

Ocean Wharf

Breakwater

McGaw Pier

Jones Pier

South Wharf

BASS HIGHWAY

VIEW ROAD

Police station

LADBROOKE ST

MARINE TERRACE

PORT ROAD

Tasmanian Redline coaches depot

VERNON PL

FLEMING COURT

MOUNT STREET

WILSON STREET

Chancellor Inn

TOWN CENTRE

Ferry terminal

PLUMMERS

MOODY ST

0   200m
0   200 yds

B18

MOUNT ST

MENAI

EDWARDS STREET

STIDOLPH

CUNNINGHAM

WYATT

CRAIGHOLM

BASS HIGHWAY

SOUTH BURNIE

HOPKINSON

DEVON

REEVE ST

Yacht club

South Burnie Beach

Emu Bay

Wilfred Campbell Memorial Reserve

Sports centre

BASS HIGHWAY

Wivenhoe Beach

DEACON ST

HAMILTON

BASS HIGHWAY Post office

MAIN ROAD

Devonport 48km, Launceston 147km

WHITFORD

BOT

Post office

Alexanders

FLINDERS ST

FRANKLIN

EXHIBITION

COLLINS ST

SWANSTON

STREET

RIVER ROAD

CI12

Show ground

STREET

PEARL

SMITH STREET

CORCELLIS

STONYPORT RD

WIVENHOE

ANGLESEA ST

ORMSBY

BROOKLYN

COLLINS

Creek

EMU HEIGHTS

Emu River

FERNGLADE ROAD

SLYN AVE

KINGSLEY

Picnic area

HAVENVIEW

WATTLE AVE

MYRTLE CRES

ROMAINE

Romaine Creek

RESERVOIR STREET

ST

Picnic area

Round Hill lookout

SASSAFRAS CRES

BLACKWOOD

MANUKA DRIVE

O'GRADY ST

McPHEE ST

OLD SURREY ROAD

MARRIOTT

Lactos Cheese Factory

Picnic area

Fern Glade Reserve

Picnic area

CI02

The **Treasure Island Caravan Park** (253 Bass Highway, Cooee, Burnie, TAS 7320; tel: 6431 1925; fax: 6431 1753; email: oceanview@southcom.com.au) is convenient and well landscaped. Tent sites $9/14, single/double; serviced sites $14/16, single/double; on-site vans $35/42, single/double; cabins $58/63, single/double.

Devonport

Try **Orchard Studio** (48 Lakeside Rd, Eugenana, Devonport, TAS 7310; tel: 6427 3118), about 10km south of town. It is next to the Tasmanian Arboretum and in the middle of an organic orchard which supplies cherries, plums and apples to speciality stores on the mainland. There are fruits and juices galore in season. The accommodation consists of a downstairs apartment (double bed, bathroom/shower, kitchenette and television) and an upstairs reading room with balcony views across the orchard, lake and arboretum. Good value for $65–75, single and double.

In town check out the imposing, Victorian **McFie Manor** (44 McFie St, Devonport, TAS 7310; tel: 6424 1719; fax: 6424 8766) which has 6 en-suite rooms for $83/100, single/double, and a pleasant verandah.

Keswick by the River (2 James St, Devonport, TAS 7310; tel: 6424 3745; mobile: 0412 651 868; email: elaine@southcom.com.au) is set in a lovely garden of maples and clematis. Maximum two people in one apartment. $100, single and double.

The **Argosy Motor Inn** (221 Tarleton St, East Devonport, TAS 7310; tel: 6427 8872: fax: 6427 9819; email: argosy@tasparkside.com.au) has 37 en-suite rooms $70–110/$75–116, single/double.

Hawley Beach

A real treat along the coast is the wonderful, if slightly crazy, country hotel **Hawley House** (Hawley Beach, TAS 7307; tel: 6428 6221; fax: 6428 6844; email: hero@hawleyhousetas.com; web: www.hawleyhousetas.com), owned and run by self-confessed eccentric, Simon Houghton. Expect the unexpected and do not take anything too seriously. The house is a beautiful Victorian Gothic home, classified by the National Trust in 1878 and with a few additions by the owner (there is a bath on the roof for warm moonlit nights). The English water gardens are delightful and beyond them is a nature reserve. Simon runs the house, a small vineyard, and campaigns for animal rights. His place is an animal sanctuary and even has a chapel for use by non-humans. There are migratory birds landing on the foreshore, peacocks on the lawn and a cockatoo called Alfred (Hitchcockatoo). The restaurant serves good food and Simon's extremely palatable wine. When you get in touch you send an email to one of the Alsatians, Hero. Some rooms are in the main house, others in beautifully converted stables. Apartment $165, single/double; en-suite room $100/155–180, single and double.

📷 Photo spot

If you ask Hawley House's owner nicely he might let you climb up on the roof to take a shot of the bathtub up there. Use a wide-angle lens to place it in the foreground and the wide expanses of the Bass Strait coastline beyond. Sure to be a conversation starter this one. Use 100ASA or 200ASA film. If you have a tobacco-graded filter this will be good to give the sky an atmospheric 'nicotine-stained' look.

Where to eat

Burnie and Devonport's restaurants are not inspiring, so try to pick accommodation offering evening meals otherwise you might be left with a buffet of fast food choices. An exception in Burnie is the **Kinesis Health Eatery** (53 Mount Street, Burnie) which serves excellent, mainly vegetarian, main meals for $8. Open daily until 18.00, later on Friday.

In Devonport, the **Formby pub** (tel: 6424 1601), on a road of the same name, has been recommended for bar meals but I did not try it myself, or give Hawley House a call to see if you can have dinner there.

What to see and do

If you are staying in Burnie for a day or two pay a visit to the **Travel and Information Centre** (Civic Centre Precinct, Little Alexander Street; tel: 6434 6111; email: travel@burnie.net). Open Monday–Friday 08.00–17.00; Saturday, Sunday, public holidays 13.30–16.30. Closed Christmas Day, Boxing Day, Good Friday.

To take a **Wildlife Interpretation Tour**, contact William Walker (tel: 6435 7205; mobile: 0438 357 205; email: wagwalker@bigpond.com). The **Pioneer Village Museum** (Little Alexander Street; tel: 6430 5746; fax: 6434 6123) is worth a look too. Adult $6; concession $4.50; child (under 16) $2.50. Open weekdays 09.00–17.00; weekends and public holidays 13.30–16.30. Closed Christmas Day, Boxing Day, Good Friday.

The **Burnie Regional Art Gallery** (Civic Centre in Wilmot Street; tel: 6431 5918; fax: 6431 4114; email: gallery@burnie.net) has more than 20 exhibitions a year and is home to one of the finest collections in Tasmania of Australian contemporary art on paper. Open weekdays 09.00–17.00; Saturday and Sunday 13.30–16.30. Closed Christmas Day, Good Friday.

Inland from Burnie is a notable English-style **garden** at Annsleigh on the B18 south of town (tel/fax: 6435 7229; mobile: 0419 333 381; email: annsleighgardens@telstra.easymail.com.au). Adult $4.50; child (under 14 years) free; group of 20 or more $4 each. Open September–May 09.00–17.00.

Up the Old Surrey Road, south of Burnie, is the **Lactos Cheese Factory** (tel: 6431 2566; fax: 6431 2647) which produces some delicious varieties and is generous in its tasting sessions. Open Monday–Friday 09.00–17.00; weekends and public holidays 10.00–16.00. Closed Christmas Day, Boxing Day, Good Friday.

As we go to press, a new **penguin viewing platform** is being built in Burnie.

A day in Devonport can be spent at two locations. The very good **Tiagarra Aboriginal Centre** (Mersey Bluff; tel: 6424 8250; mobile: 0418 516 336; fax: 6427 0506; email: tiagarra@southcom.com.au) holds a collection of rare rock engravings, some of which are interpreted. It is in a prominent position right out near the lighthouse at Mersey Bluff (access via Bluff Road) and there is a short track to see some more carvings on the bluff itself. Adult $3.30; concession $2.20; child (6–16 years) $2.20. Open daily 09.00–17.00. Closed Christmas Day, Good Friday.

Also head for the **Don River Railway** (Forth Main Road, Don, Devonport, TAS 7310; tel/fax: 6424 6335) in the village of Don, about 5km west on the Bass Highway. The steam locomotive train leaves Don Village Station for Coles Beach daily, winding along the banks of the picturesque Don River. There is lots of railway memorabilia en route. Spend as much time as you like here and take a later train back. Adult $7; child (under 16 years) $4; family (2 adults, 2 children) $18. Open daily 10.00–16.00. Closed Christmas Day, Good Friday.

Devonport Travel and Information Centre (92 Formby Road; tel: 6424 8176; email: tourism@dcc.tas.gov.au). Open daily 09.00–17.00. Closed Christmas Day, Good Friday.

In **Latrobe**, Ron Hedditch (tel: 6426 1774) can organise a **platypus tour**. He and his two brothers in a Landcare group (an environmental cooperative) have developed a good walk around a lake just out of town on the edge of the Warrawee Forest Reserve and put in disabled access for wheelchairs. The platypus are plentiful.

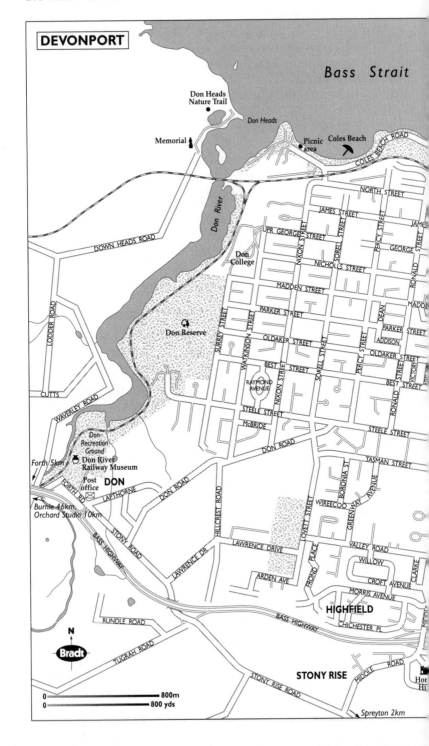

DEVONPORT

Bass Strait

Don Heads
Nature Trail

Don Heads

Memorial

Picnic area

Coles Beach

COLES BEACH ROAD

NORTH STREET

JAMES STREET

JAMES

UPR GEORGE STREET

NIXON STREET

SORELL STREET

PERCY STREET

GEORGE

RONALD STREET

Don River

NICHOLLS STREET

Don College

MADDEN STREET

MADDE

PARKER STREET

DEAN

PARKER STREET

SURREY STREET

WATKINSON STREET

OLDAKER STREET

PERCY STREET

ADDISON

OLDAKER STREET

DOWN HEADS ROAD

LODDER ROAD

Don Reserve

BEST STREET

SORELL STREET

RONALD STREET

VICTORIA

BEST STREET

RAYMOND AVENUE

NIXON STREET

STEELE STREET

CUTTS

WAVERLEY ROAD

McBRIDE

STEELE STREET

DON ROAD

TASMAN STREET

Don Recreation Ground

Don River Railway Museum

Forth 5km

Post office

DON

FORTH RD

LAPTHORNE

DON ROAD

HILLCREST ROAD

LOVETT STREET

WIREECOO

BORONIA ST

GREENWAY

AVENUE

Burnie 46km, Orchard Studio 10km

STONY ROAD

LAWRENCE DR

LAWRENCE DRIVE

VALLEY ROAD

WILLOW

CLARKE

ARDEN AVE

FROND PLACE

CROFT AVENUE

MORRIS AVENUE

BASS HIGHWAY

RUNDLE ROAD

HIGHFIELD

CHICHESTER PL

N

Bradt

TUGRAH ROAD

STONY RISE

MIDDLE ROAD

Hor Hi

0   800m
0   800 yds

STONY RISE ROAD

Spreyton 2km

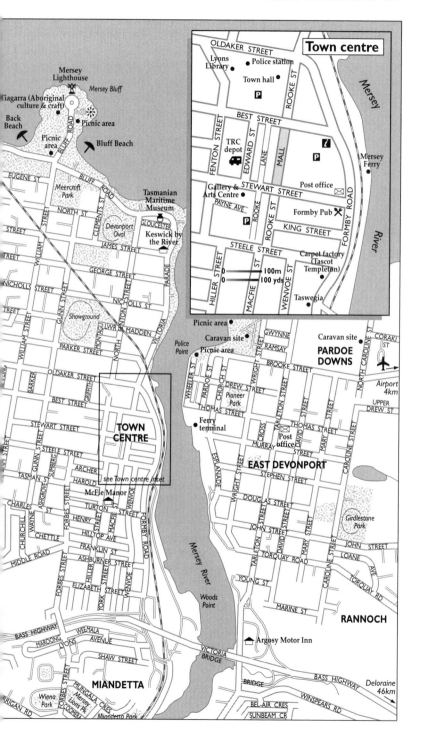

The Tasmanian Trail

This is a long-distance, multi-purpose recreational trail from Devonport to Dover, covering 480km. It is soft adventure, ideal for walkers, mountain bikers and horse riders, using forestry roads and fire breaks, back roads and occasionally going through private land. Almost the entire trail is on an already marked track of some sort and there is no wilderness trekking or bush-bashing.

It offers a wonderfully rounded recreational, cultural and historical experience for the traveller and stands to help some places that would otherwise not benefit by tourism dollars. You can trace the route on the Parks and Wildlife Service website (www.parks.tas.gov.au). *The Tasmanian Trail Guide Book* gives users detailed information for following the trail and is an essential companion. The trail is divided into 30km sections and there are tips on planning and safety. There are notes and maps and vital advice on creating minimal impact as you travel. Available from the Parks and Wildlife Service. You can also join the Tasmanian Trail Association (PO Box 99, Sandy Bay, Hobart, TAS 7005; email: tastrail@dpiwe.tas.gov.au).

NARAWNTAPU NATIONAL PARK

This was formerly Asbestos Range National Park and its Aboriginal name still has to make it on to a number of maps of Tasmania. Narawntapu (tel: 6428 6277) covers 4,349 hectares (10,746 acres) on the north coast, west of the mouth of the River Tamar.

It contains open forest, coastal vegetation, heathlands and two stunning beaches, Bakers and Badgers. It makes a great day out from Launceston or Devonport and a good stop on a trans-Tassie tour. If you come in spring you will see wildflowers carpeting the heaths and the silver banksia out in force. Comparatively few visitors makes this one of the better parks for viewing wildlife. As you approach the main entrance watch out for Bennett's wallabies and occasionally a Forester kangaroo feeding in the open. Narawntapu is a bird lover's delight too, with more than 80 species and a good hide close to the lagoon.

This area was part of territory of the northern Aboriginal tribe whose patch extended across to Burnie and inland about 30 miles. Later the Springlawn area was used as a convict farm by Edwin Baker. Visitors can swim off the beach that bears his name but be wary of an undertow, and water skiing is allowed in designated stretches. Rangers operate in the west of the park leading guided walks in the summer. There are lots of picnic spots and some modern composting toilets.

📷 Photo spot

There are two really. One is at the entrance to Narawntapu when the wallabies are in the meadows. Use 100ASA film on a bright day, 200ASA on cloudy. Long lens advised (100–300mm). The other is along the beach, looking across the estuary to Port Sorell where terns dive for fish, skimming their beaks at tremendous speed along the water surface. Very hard shot to get as you really need a long lens moving at speed so using a high speed film (400–800ASA), but it is worth a go, especially if the light is good.

Getting to and around Narawntapu

By private vehicle or bicycle only. From Launceston, head north up the A7 Tamar Highway. If you want to take a 20km dirt-road, keep heading north through Beaconsfield and Beauty Point then take a left shortly before York Town. This will take you off road through a beautiful patch of forest. At a T-junction turn right for Narawntapu. If you would rather stay on the asphalt then at Exeter take the B71 left

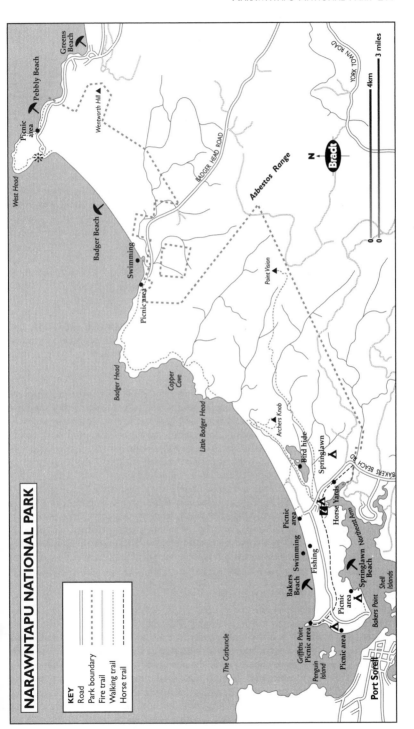

NARAWNTAPU NATIONAL PARK

KEY
Road
Park boundary
Fire trail
Walking trail
Horse trail

Greens Beach
Pebbly Beach
Picnic area
West Head
Wentworth Hill
BADGER HEAD ROAD
Badger Beach
Swimming
Picnic area
Asbestos Range
Point Vision
Badger Head
Copper Cove
Little Badger Head
Archers Knob
Bird hide
Springlawn
Horse Yards
Picnic area
Bakers Beach
Swimming
Fishing
Springlawn Northeast Arm
Beach
Shell Islands
Bakers Point
BAKERS BEACH ROAD
The Carbuncle
Griffiths Point Picnic area
Picnic area
Penguin Island
Port Sorell
YORK TOWN ROAD
N
Bradt
0   4km
0   3 miles

to Latrobe. The right turn for Narawntapu appears about 16km after West Frankford. Coming from Devonport, go through Latrobe and turn left onto the B71, then left again (signposted to Narawntapu) about three miles beyond Hartford.

When driving around the Dazzler Range forests just outside the park, keep watch for **yellow-tailed black cockatoos**. One showery afternoon on the C741 dirt-road passing through the forests between the park and York Town I saw three glide across the road, squawking and cackling, and sit on a branch muttering to themselves.

Where to stay and eat

Camping in the park is allowed at Springlawn, the Horse Yards, Bakers Point and Griffiths Point. The park authorities ask you to register at the Springlawn information hut. There are fireplaces, picnic tables and composting or pit toilets. Springlawn also has electric barbecues which are great when it is windy. Bring all food and water.

Greens Beach at the northern end of the C720 is a lovely spot to spend a lazy day. The beach itself is a magical sweep of sand, good for a long walk out to West Head. You can park or leave bikes at the general store at the end of the sealed road and head up the gravel track to join the beach. The store has good fish and chips but the seagulls here are ferocious. There is camping and a golf course.

The Seahorse Farm

Near Beauty Point on the Tamar River is **Seahorse World** (tel: 6383 4111; fax: 6383 4888; email: info@seahorseworld.com.au; web: www.seahorseworld.com.au), a seahorse farm which stocks 250,000 captive bred specimens and is currently sharing its ground-breaking technology with the Chinese, who use millions of wild seahorse each year for traditional medicine.

The founders of the project hope their new science will reduce the pressures on sea stocks and eventually convince consuming nations there is no further need for harvesting wild populations. If it works it will be a conservation breakthrough.

Professor Nigel Forteath, the founder of Seahorse Australia, started work on his dream almost a decade ago in the hope that it would reduce pressure on wild stocks which are fished for use also in the aquarium trade.

Tasmanian waters are home to the *Hippocampus abdominalis*, one of the world's biggest species. The work has been possible here as the young are big enough when born (20–25mm long) to be fed brine shrimps almost immediately.

Most recently, the seahorses have been branded with tiny marks to assist buyers to prove they are farmed and not wild. Bookings recommended. Adult $15; student and senior $12; pensioner $10; child (under 16) $8; child (under 4) free; family $35 (2 adults, unlimited children). Open daily 09.30–15.30. Closed Christmas Day.

Short walk in Narawntapu
Springlawn Nature Walk
Distance: 2km return. Time: 1 hour return. Difficulty: easy.
This circular walk starts at the visitor information hut by the main entrance and passes the relics of the farm. Information signs are clear. Look out for wallabies, pademelons and a wombat or two. Duckboarding runs through the wetlands to a bird hide. The track comes back behind high sand dunes with views out over the ocean and heaths.

As a longer option try Archers Knob Walk (an hour or two), the hike to Point Vision (three hours return), or an even longer (five hours one-way) stroll past

Badgers Head and along to West Head where there is a picnic spot (camping 2km on at Greens Beach).

Further information

More information on this region on the Tamar River from the travel and information centre in Main Road, Exeter (tel: 6394 4454: email: exeter@tasvisinfo.com.au).

INLAND TO THE GREAT WESTERN TIERS

This area has some interesting scenery and heritage towns as well as some terrific caves and a good national park. It is on the way to lots of other places for most visitors but definitely worth a day or two of your time.

Westbury

This was laid out in a very English pattern under the watchful eye of Lieutenant-Governor Arthur in 1828. He envisaged it becoming the chief town of the region through which goods and people would travel to and from the rest of the colony. You can see his point as it is centrally located, now only half-an-hour's drive from Launceston and 45 minutes from Devonport, but Arthur's dream for the town was not to be. It grew slowly and did flourish as a coaching stop and later when the Western Railway blew through around 1871. Most present residents are probably quite glad it stayed small because now it is a relaxing tourist spot with bed and breakfasts, teashops, and a good selection of colonial buildings. The A1 Bass Highway dissects it, but the street is so wide (following Australia's obsession with boulevards in the smallest of towns) that the traffic is only a minor nuisance.

The **village green** is a good place to get your bearings and a potted history of the place from the signboard. A must-see is the **White House** (tel: 6393 1171; fax: 6344 4033; email: nat_trust@vision.net.au), a handsome Georgian corner shop and house built in the early 1840s by Thomas White which stands near the village green. Adult $7.70; concession $5.50; child free; National Trust members (including overseas card holders) free with card. Open September–June, Tuesday–Sunday 10.00–16.00. Closed Christmas Day, Boxing Day, Good Friday. Lose yourself in the **Westbury Maze** (10 Old Bass Highway; tel: 6393 1840; fax: 6393 2356; email: dent_wma@vision.net.au) which is fun. Adult $5; child $4; family $18 (2 adults, 4 children). Open daily September–July from 10.00. The maze has a tearoom where they make excellent 'spiders', concoctions of ice-cream and fizzy pop.

📷 Photo spot

The maze is always good but rather than go for the postcard shot of the whole thing from a high vantage point, construct an abstract shot with a corner of the hedge and simple, cloudless blue sky beyond, or an empty stretch of maze with the hedge walls on either side and a child running away from you and just about to disappear out of shot around a corner. 100 or 200ASA and 50mm lens. If you have a bright day this is a good spot to use a black and white or sepia film too, and if your equipment bag stretches to an infrared film then the maze is perfect.

Where to stay and eat

For accommodation it is hard to beat the delightful **Gingerbread Cottage** (52 William Street, Westbury, TAS 7303; tel/fax: 6393 1140; mobile: 0409 931 143; email: cclarke@tpg.com.au; web: www.gingercottage.com), an award-winning self-contained place with picket fence and lovely garden (which is also up for an award as we go to press).

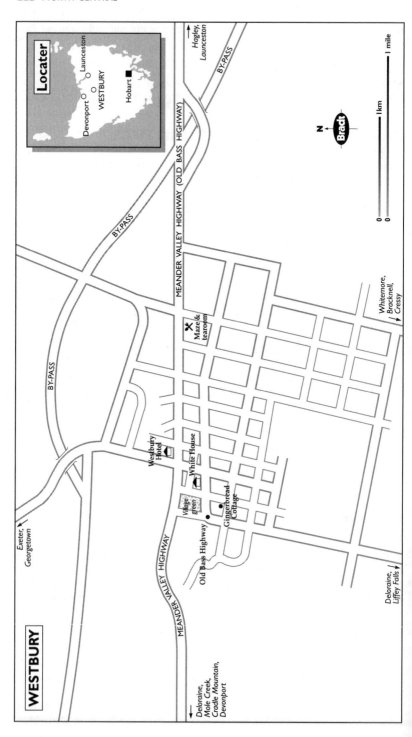

The owners leave fresh-roasted coffee beans, fruit and homemade biscuits as well as breakfast provisions in the kitchen for you. $125, single and double.
Egmont (429 Birralee Road, Westbury, TAS 7303; tel/fax: 6393 1164; email: egmont@vision.net.au; web: www.ontas.com.au/egmont) is a recommended self-contained cottage for rent for $88–99, single and double. It retains some of the original furniture first used when the place was built in 1838. You can fish and swim in the Meander River near by and there are short bushwalks.
The **Westbury Hotel** (107 Bass Highway, Westbury, TAS 7303; tel: 6393 1151) does good pub grub (main meals about $10–15) for lunch and supper.

Deloraine

This town is not as picturesque as its neighbour but is convenient for those heading for Cradle Mountain and Mole Creek Karst National Park. A good place to bed down is **Bowerbank Mill Cottages** (4455 Meander Valley Highway, Deloraine, TAS 7304; tel: 6362 2628; fax: 6362 3586; email: jmax@vision.net.au; web: www.view.com.au/bowerbank), built as a flour mill in 1853 near the foot of the spectacular Western Tiers. Now it is two self-contained romantic cottages and a suite. This is early colonial architecture, panelled and decorated, and furnished with antiques. There is a fine art gallery too. Your hosts will bring continental breakfast and can provide a candle-lit dinner. En-suite room $110/148, single/double.

Short walk from Deloraine
Liffey Falls
Distance: 2–5km return. Time: 1–3 hour return. Difficulty: moderate.
Drive south from Deloraine on the A5 and C513 to the Liffey State Reserve. There are two starting-points, one at each of two car-parks. Those in a car or on bicycle can reach the top car-park from where there is a shorter and better-defined track to the falls. Those in a campervan, bus or coach will access the lower car-park and walk a longer and not-so-clear track, but both are straightforward. If you are a fan of tree ferns then also drop by the Liffey Valley Fernery, which has a tearoom and good views looking up to Dry Bluff (1,297m).

Day walk from Deloraine
Meander Falls
Distance: 10km return. Time: 6 hour return. Difficulty: moderate.
This is an easy way of getting a taste of wilderness in a day from Deloraine. Drive south from Deloraine on the A5 and C167 to Meander, on the river of the same name, then follow signs to the Meander Forest Reserve. At the car-park there is a bush toilet and a shelter hut. From there, follow the signs for the walk to the first set of falls and then on to Meander Falls proper, at 183m the highest in Tasmania. There is some camping available up at the falls. This track takes you up to the edge of the Central Plateau Conservation Area, with Iron Stone Peak to the northwest marking the highest peak in the Great Western Tiers (1,443m). The track can become difficult or impassable in winter as it is hit with snow and ice.

Sheffield

Further west, **Sheffield** is a good spot if you are exploring the hills around Lake Barrington and south to the Mole Creek Karst National Park region. You can take a trip on the lake with **Lake Barrington Pleasure Tours** (Wilmot Boat Ramp, Lake Barrington, TAS 7306; tel: 6492 1150). Tours leave from the Wilmot boat ramp and take about three hours, visiting Forth Falls and the Lake Barrington

International Rowing Course. Platypus, waterbirds and black cockatoos all frequent the lake and its shoreline. Lunch provided. $60 per person fully catered; $45 per person with cheese platter and tea or coffee.

If your timing is good you will catch the **Claude Road Market** (Claude Road Hall, Sheffield), selling local crafts and produce and secondhand jewellery. Open every third Saturday of every third month 09.00 to 15.00.

It is worth seeking out two spots to stay. The **Silver Ridge Retreat** (Rysavy Road, off C136, Mount Roland, Sheffield, TAS 7306; tel: 6491 1727; fax: 6491 1925; email: info@silverridgeretreat.com.au; web: www.silverridgeretreat.com.au) sits on the slopes of Mount Roland on the edge of the wilderness. There is a track to the summit where wedge-tailed eagles fly. Accommodation is in modern timber cottages with wood heaters and an indoor heated pool. Horseback, 4WD motorbike, and an old 1870s silver mine with glow worms and stalactite formations. Mine tours available. Self-catering or there is a licensed restaurant. Apartment $95–180, single and double.

Loongana
The **Mountain Valley Wilderness Holidays Lodge** (1519 Loongana Road, Loongana, TAS 7315; tel: 6429 1394; fax: 6429 1229; email: mountainvalley@microtech.com.au; web: www.welcome.to/mountainvalley) is in a hidden valley just north of Cradle Mountain. Good bushwalks through fern glades and river gorges, trout fishing, and platypus-spotting trips all available. This 61-hectare property is registered with National Parks and Wildlife under the 'Land for Wildlife' scheme. Caving tours can be arranged, with all meals and equipment provided. Apartment $121–138, single/double.

Further information
More information from the Sheffield Visitor Centre (tel: 6491 1036; email: sheffield@tasvisinfo.com.au) in Pioneer Crescent behind the post office.

MOLE CREEK KARST NATIONAL PARK
This park (tel: 6363 5181) is quite new, having been created in 1996, and it is Tasmania's only one underground. It protects an area of deep limestone caverns that boast some spectacular stalactites, stalagmites and joined columns. There are more than 200 caves in the park's nine separate reserves all within 13km of Mole Creek. The main ones are Marakoopa Cave, King Solomon Cave, Crosesus Cave, Kubla Khan Cave, Sensation Gorge and Baldocks Cave reserves. South of Mole Creek are the Westmorland Falls and Wet Cave reserves, as well as a small parcel of crown land that had not been a reserve before the national park was created.

The caves formed about 450 million years ago when this region was under water. Layers of coral and bone sediment built up on the seabed over millennia, creating a limestone bedrock. About 165 million years ago significant volcanic activity squeezed molten dolerite up through cracks and fissures in the limestone. Over time the sedimentary limestone surrounding the more resistant dolerite eroded away, leaving this fluted rock which is similar to that found above ground in the Great Western Tiers. The caves began to 'grow' their decorative formations about 30 million years ago (which is an excellent reason not to touch anything in the caves in case you ruin such an ancient structure in a heartbeat).

King Solomon Cave was the first to be discovered by Europeans when dogs from a hunting party barked into it in 1906. Four years later the Byard brothers almost fell into Marakoopa Cave. Both were made reserves in 1939. Access to the caves is via Mole Creek. Take the B12 from Deloraine for 23km. Cave tour times and other information is here and should be checked before heading on to the park proper.

In Mole Creek, stay at the **Camping Ground** (2 Union Bridge Road, Mole Creek, TAS 7304; tel: 6363 1150) which has 20 tent sites costing $5–8/$10–12, single/double, or check into the **Mole Creek Guesthouse** (100 Pioneer Drive, Mole Creek, TAS 7304; tel: 6363 1399; fax: 6363 1420; email: sted.mcgh@tassie.net.au), a beautifully refurbished 19th-century guesthouse which offers comfortable accommodation with good home-cooked meals. En-suite rooms $70–90/$90–110, single/double; suite $100–110/$110–130, single/double. Try the **Mole Creek Tearooms** for snacks (open daily).

Activities

Cave tours regularly operate in Marakoopa and King Solomon and there are tougher trips in the other more technical caves. Debbie Hunter is your best contact. She runs Wild Cave Tours and is the conservation officer for the Mole Creek Caving Club and the first point of contact for the state's cave rescue operations. Her tours have a strong emphasis on environmental issues and she limits the groups to a maximum of eight but prefers two or three in the party (tel: 6367 8142, email: debhunter@tassie.net.au or debbie@wildcavetours.com; web: www.wildcavetours.com). Prices and schedules on enquiry. Or try the Australian Speliological Federation (web: www.cavesorg.au) who produce the *Australian Caver* newsletter.

For fabulous **views** head for Devil's Gullet at the end of a side-road off the C171.

📷 Photo spot

Caves are always difficult to photograph. Flash gives so much light it provides no atmosphere and yet it is far too dark without it. Therefore, once inside turn and face back out towards the mouth of the cave, set manual light meters for the reading of the outside forest and snap – you should get a green forest-scape framed by the silhouetted cave mouth. 100ASA and 50mm or wide-angle lens, whichever gives you the better-looking frame.

Honey

The R Stephen's Tasmanian honey plant is based at Mole Creek. The factory (tel: 6363 1170) is open year-round but is best from January to April when the honey is being extracted. Open weekdays 08.00–16.30. Admission free and there are tastings.

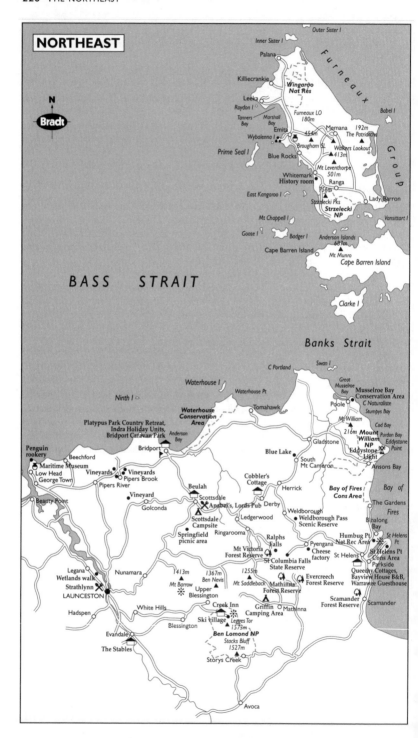

NORTHEAST

N

Bradt

Outer Sister I

Inner Sister I

Palana

Furneaux

Killiecrankie

Wingaroo Nat Rés

Leeka

Roydon I

Tanners Bay

Marshall Bay

Emita

Furneaux LO 180m

Memana

192m The Patriarchs

Wybalenna I

454m

Brougham SL

Walkers Lookout ▲413m

Prime Seal I

Blue Rocks

Mt Leventhorpe 501m

Whitemark
History room

Ranga

756m

East Kangaroo I

Strzelecki Pks

Strzelecki NP

Lady Barron

Vansittart I

Mt Chappell I

Goose I

Badger I

Anderson Islands
687m ▲

Cape Barren Island

Mt Munro ▲

Cape Barren Island

Clarke I

BASS   STRAIT

Banks   Strait

Swan I

C Portland

Great Musselroe Bay

Musselroe Bay Conservation Area

Waterhouse I

Waterhouse Pt

Poole

C Naturaliste

Stumpys Bay

Ninth I

Tomahawk

Waterhouse Conservation Area

Mt William ▲

216m **Mount William NP**

Cod Bay

Purdon Bay Eddystone Point

Platypus Park Country Retreat,
Indra Holiday Units,
Bridport Caravan Park

Anderson Bay

Gladstone

Eddystone Light

Penguin
rookery

Bridport

Blue Lake

South
Mt Cameron

Ansons Bay

Beechford

Maritime Museum

Low Head
George Town

Vineyards

Vineyards
Pipers Brook

Cobbler's
Cottage

Herrick

**Bay of Fires
Cons Area**

Bay of

Beauty Point

Pipers River

Vineyard

Beulah

Scottsdale

Derby

Fires

The Gardens

Golconda

Anabel's, Lords Pub

Ledgerwood

Weldborough

**Weldborough Pass
Scenic Reserve**

Binalong
Bay

Scottsdale
Campsite

Ringarooma

Pyengana

Humbug Pt
Nat Rec Area

St Helens
Pt

Springfield
picnic area

Ralphs
Falls

Cheese
factory

St Helens

**St Helens Pt
Cons Area**

Mt Victoria
Forest Reserve

St Columba Falls
State Reserve

Parkside
Queechy Cottages,
Bayview House B&B,
Warrawee Guesthouse

Legana

Nunamara

1413m

1367m

1255m

Mt Saddleback

**Evercreech
Forest Reserve**

Wetlands walk

Mt Barrow ▲

Ben Nevis ▲

**Mathinna
Forest Reserve**

Strathlynn
LAUNCESTON

Upper
Blessington

Scamander
Forest Reserve

Scamander

White Hills

Creek Inn
Camping Area

Griffin

Mathinna

Hadspen

Ski village

Legges Tor
1573m

Blessington

Evandale

Ben Lomond NP

The Stables

*Stacks Bluff
1527m*

Storys Creek

Avoca

12

The Northeast

This chapter looks at the corner of the state north of the A4 and east of the A1 and the Tamar River, including Launceston, two of Tasmania's least visited national parks (Mount William and Strzelecki), and the Furneaux Group of islands off the northeast coast. This area is tremendously diverse. The interior is almost all hilly, some parts mountainous, while the coast is gentle and sandy. There are not many places where you can ski in winter and sunbathe in summer at locations less than 80km apart but, at 1,573m, Legges Tor in Ben Lomond National Park is high enough to support a small winter sports base while down the road the magnificent Bay of Fires has arguably Tasmania's best beach.

The lower parts of this region are dry and comparatively warm and subsequently vineyards flourish, scattered around the rolling hills near the Tamar. The northeast is also known for its arts and crafts and there are numerous galleries and potteries in towns and out in the country, with Derby a notable centre.

The north coast from Bridport to Cape Portland and then down to Mount William is sparsely populated, and about one-third of it lies in protected areas, so if you really want to get away from it all but do not fancy roughing it in the southwest wilderness or the central highlands then this is the place.

The islands are the remnants of the land bridge that once linked Tasmania with the mainland and across which its first inhabitants walked. As islands they have a tragic history. It was here that some of the worst atrocities were committed against the Aborigines by Europeans and today they stand almost as memorials to a lost culture.

HISTORY

The northeast's first settlers were pastoralists who used the lush valleys for grazing sheep for mutton and wool. Tin, coal and gold were all struck in the hills in the late 1800s and fortunes made and lost as towns boomed and went broke. A freight railway was built through the foothills of the mountains between Launceston and Herrick to carry tin, grain, produce and supplies. It carried some passengers as well for a time. A goods train still runs on the section from Scottsdale to Launceston, but the rest of the line has been torn up.

In the far west of this region, George Town is the third-oldest European settlement in Australia after Sydney and Hobart. It was founded as Outer Cove in November 11 1804 after the Governor of New South Wales, Lieutenant-Colonel W Paterson became worried the French were about to invade and claim it as theirs. He rushed over a party of 181 people from the mainland, including soldiers, convicts, one free settler and a doctor, and named the place after King George III.

It later declined as Launceston grew into the major town in the region. Launceston was, and still is, the capital of the north and is famous as being the departure point for John Batman's expedition that founded Melbourne.

The Furneaux Islands were first spotted by Europeans in 1773 when Captain Tobias Furneaux briefly sailed up the east coast and around Cape Portland before heading east to New Zealand. Their history is important. Flinders Island was one of the first parts of the state to be settled as Aboriginal people travelled across the land bridge roughly 40,000 years ago. However, they abandoned the island and the rest in the Furneaux Group when the seas rose to their present level about 6,500 years ago.

They were to return later in 1832 as part of an experiment to 'Christianise' them. The man who brought them back, George Augustus Robinson, may have wanted the best for them (opinions differ) but the project was a disaster. He landed with a group of 135 Aborigines, including Truganini (see *Chapter 1*, page 10). They were first taken to Swan Island just off the north coast, then on to Vansittart Island, between Flinders and Cape Barren. Originally they were settled at The Lagoons, south of Whitemark, and then moved to Wybalenna, which means 'black men's houses'. Here a smattering of huts was erected to house the band.

But the indigenous people had been taken from different tribes as Robinson had toured the main island, and their juxtaposition was not always favourable. More to the point, the physical barrier of the stretch of water between them and the rest of their kin (one of the reasons the islands were abandoned in the first place) made them homesick. They could not adapt to the changes in diet and they were plagued by visits from whaling and sealing fleets of white sailors who brought western disease to which the Aboriginals had no resistance, and, more alarmingly, who bartered for, and in some cases stole, Aboriginal women.

The population withered, and almost 100 died, before the project collapsed and the remainder were relocated in October 1847 to Oyster Cove near Hobart.

There was another population on Cape Barren Island which had a school. They traded in mutton-birds, seal skins and sea elephant oil, and, as early as 1866 began asking for ownership of the land by virtue of their race. It was denied to them by the new European arrivals who instead deemed it necessary for them to adapt to Western ways and become farmers, a concept they could not understand and that was wholly unsuited to the poor soil of the island. The community imploded, and once the settlers started paying them with rations of alcohol there was no hope.

As a result of the loss of women and many deaths, the once 500-strong Northeast tribe on the islands and the mainland numbered only 72 men and six women by 1830.

Today, Cape Barren supports a small community of people descended from those few who never left the island, and some younger people who have moved there for its tranquillity. Other important Aboriginal sites are the nature reserves of Babel Island, Mount Chappell Island, Badger Island and Great Dog Island.

GETTING THERE AND AROUND
By air
Launceston airport is about a 20-minute drive south of the city near Evandale.

Qantas (tel: 13 13 13 in Australia; web: www.qantas.com.au) flies daily to Launceston from Sydney, Melbourne and Adelaide.

Kendell (tel: 13 13 00 in Australia; web: www.ansett.com.au or www.Kendell.com.au) flies regularly to Launceston from Melbourne.

Virgin Blue (tel: 13 67 89 in Australia; web: www.virgin.blue.com.au) flies daily to Launceston from Melbourne.

Island Airlines Tasmania (tel: 1800 645 875; email: bobpratt@bigpond.com.au; web: www.iat.com.au) flies between Melbourne and Launceston three times a week (Monday, Wedneday, Friday). Also between Launceston and Flinders Island two or three times a day, and Launceston–Strahan–Hobart return three times a week (Tuesday, Thursday, Sunday). And charter flights from Essendon to Strahan.

By road

From Hobart, take the A1 Midland Highway north to Launceston and then the A3 Tasman Highway east to Scottsdale; or the A1 to Conara, north of Campbell Town and the A4 Esk Highway east to Ben Lomond National Park and on to St Helens; or take the A3 up the east coast to St Helens. From the north coast and northwest, take the A1 Bass Highway through Devonport and to Launceston and on.

The following rental car companies operate in the region:

Autorent Hertz 58 Paterson St, Launceston, TAS 7250; tel: 6335 1111; fax: 6331 2788; email: mail@autorent.com.au. Branches also at airport.

Avis Tasmania Corner of Brisbane St and Wellington St, Launceston, TAS 7250; tel: 6334 7722; fax: 6334 6260; email: avishbt@netspace.net.au). Branch also at airport.

Budget Rent-A-Car Tel: 6391 8566; fax: 6391 8743; email: reservations@budgettas.com; web: www.budget.com.au. At airport only.

Economy Car Rentals 27 William St, Launceston, TAS 7250; tel: 6334 3299; mobile: 0419 132 599; fax: 6334 1500.

Delta Europcar 112 George St, Launceston, TAS 7250; tel: 6391 8000; fax: 6391 8008; email: restas@deltaeuropcar.com.au; wweb: www.deltaeuropcar.com.au). Branch also at airport.

Thrifty Car Rental Tel: 6391 8105; fax: 6391 8482; email: thrifty@tasvacations.com.au; web: www.tasvacations.com.au. At the airport.

Flinders Island Car Rentals Memana Rd, Whitemark, Flinders Island, TAS 7255; tel: 6359 2168; fax: 6359 2293).

Flinders Island Transport Services Patrick St, Whitemark, Flinders Island, TAS 7255; tel: 6359 2060; fax: 6359 2026.

By bus/coach

Tasmanian Redline Coaches (**TRC**) (tel: 1300 360 000 or 6336 1446) runs services from Hobart to St Helens and Launceston, and from Launceston to St Helens and Derby.

TWT's Tassielink Regional Coach Service (tel: 1300 300 520; web: www.tigerline.com.au) runs services between Hobart and Launceston via east coast and St Helens.

By bicycle

Rent bikes from Launceston (**Rent A Cycle**, 36 Thistle Street; tel/fax: 6344 9779) and St Helens (**East Lines**, 28 Cecilia Street; tel: 6376 1720). They also rent golf clubs, snorkel gear, tennis-rackets, scuba-dive gear and wet-suits.

By sea

In summer, the **Devil Cat** (tel: 13 20 10 in Australia; email: reservations@tt-line.com.au; web: www.tt-line.com.au) fast vehicle and passenger catamaran makes three six-hour crossings from Melbourne to George Town each week (daily over Christmas and New Year and holiday times).

The **Southern Shipping Company** (tel: 6356 1753; fax: 6356 1956) runs a mainly freight service from Bridport to Flinders Island once a week (schedules vary with the tides), and once a month it continues across Bass Strait to Port

Welshpool (three hours southeast of Melbourne), but you will have to rough it as there are no sleeping or dining facilities on board.

LAUNCESTON
Where to stay and eat
For the traveller keen on the outdoors and on seeing as much flora and fauna as possible, Launceston is somewhere you will want to breeze through. However, here are a few places for those staying a day or two:

Edenholme Grange Historic B&B (14 St Andrews Street, Launceston, TAS 7250; tel: 6334 6666; fax: 6334 3106; email: edenholme@microtech.com.au) is probably your best bet. It is a handsome 1880s house set in parkland with apartments for $168–176, single and double, and en-suite rooms for $112–176/$148–176, single/double. One has a four-poster.
Highfield House (23 Welman Street, Launceston, TAS 7250; tel: 6334 3485; fax: 6334 3492; email: highfieldhouse@bigpond.com.au; web: www.historichouses.
com.au) is pleasant too, with five en-suite rooms for $115/146, single/double.
The **Waratah on York** (12 York Street, Launceston, TAS 7250; tel: 6331 2081; fax: 6331 9200; email: info@waratahonyork.com.au; web: www.waratahonyork.
com.au) is a grand place and the winner of Tasmanian tourism awards both in 2000 and 2001. It is housed in a recently restored Victorian Italianate mansion, with views over the city and river. En-suite rooms $156–208, single and double.
A good cheaper option is **Kurrajong House** (18 High Street, Launceston, TAS 7250; tel: 6331 6655; fax: 6331 6455; email: info@kurrajonghouse.com.au; web: www.kurrajonghouse.com.au), opposite the croquet club, which has five en-suite rooms for $72–85/$90–126, single/double.
Another is **Fiona's Bed and Breakfast** (5/141a George Street, Launceston, TAS 7250; tel: 6334 5965; fax: 6331 1709), which is next door to the Roman Baths spa complex and has 12 en-suite rooms for $71/99, single/double.
The **Launceston Backpackers** (103 Canning Street, Launceston, TAS 7250; tel: 6334 2327; fax: 6394 7574, web: www.launcestonbackpackers.com.au) is not bad if you are on a budget. Dorms $15.50; twins $17.50; doubles $18.50.
Near the airport at Evandale is **The Stables** (5 Russell Street, Evandale, TAS 7212; tel: 6391 8048; fax: 6391 8047; email: thestables@vision.net.au; web: www.vision.net.au/~thestables), where there are three self-contained and award-winning cottages dating back to 1843 and National Trust and National Estate listed. $95/150, single/double.
The **Treasure Island Caravan Park** (94 Glen Dhu Street, South Launceston, Launceston, TAS 7249; tel: 6344 2600; fax: 6343 1764) is OK. Tent site $10–15, single and double; on-site van $38, single and double; cabin $63–70, single and double; serviced site $13–17, single and double.
Cucina Simpatica (corner of Frederick Street and Margaret Street; tel: 6334 3177) is a café with good modern Australian cuisine (mains $22–24) and great coffee.
Konditorei Café Manfred (106 George Street, Launceston; tel: 6334 2490) is good for light lunches, sandwiches, rolls and a yummy apple strudel.
For up-market dining, **Fee and Me** (corner of Charles Street and Frederick Street; tel: 6331 3195) is the most exciting place to eat. It offers multi-course *dégustation* menus that you can mix and match. The Tasmanian ocean trout and roasted crayfish are superb. $75–80 per head for all courses, wine and coffee. There is also a good selection of Chinese and Thai places.
For some up-market, out-of-town dining with a view, head for **Strathlynn** (95 Rosevears Drive, Rosevears; tel: 6330 2388), just north of Launceston on the A7, where executive chef Daniel Alps has established a restaurant, food and wine shop and wine-tasting centre. Open daily.

Above Red rocks at Eddystone Point at the northern end of Abbotsbury Beach, Mount William National Park (MB)

Left Vegetation around Blue Lake (MB)

Next page Sailing ship in harbour, Hobart (MB)

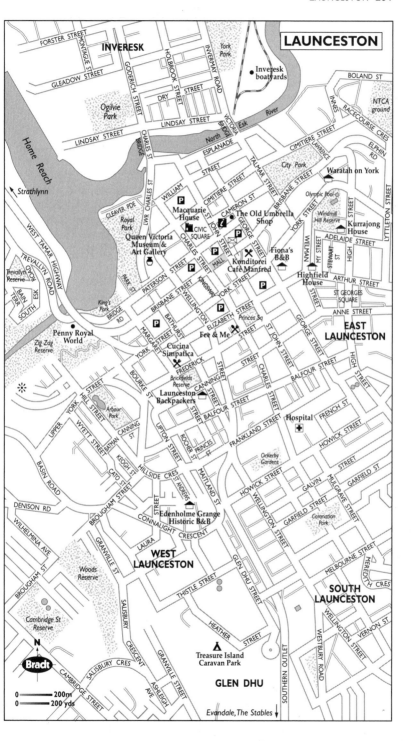

LAUNCESTON

INVERESK

FORSTER STREET
MONTAGUE STREET
GLEADOW STREET
GODERICH STREET
HOLBROOK STREET
DRY STREET
LINDSAY STREET
INVERMAY ROAD
VICTORIA BRIDGE
York Park
Inveresk boatyards
BOLAND ST
INNES
RACECOURSE CRES
NTCA ground

Ogilvie Park

Esk River
North Esk

Home Reach

Strathlynn

CLEAVER PDE
CHARLES ST
LWR CHARLES ST

ESPLANADE
North Esk
CIMITIERE STREET
WILLIAM STREET
CAMERON ST
TALBOT STREET
BRISBANE STREET
CIMITIERE STREET
LAWRENCE
ELPHIN RD

City Park
Waratah on York
Olympic Pool
Windmill Hill Reserve
Kurrajong House

WEST TAMAR HIGHWAY
TREVALLYN ROAD
ESK
BAIN TERR SOUTH
Trevallyn Reserve

Royal Park

Macquarie House
CIVIC SQUARE
Queen Victoria Museum & Art Gallery

JOHN STREET
CHARLES STREET
MALL
KINGSWAY
YORK STREET
GEORGE STREET

The Old Umbrella Shop
Konditorei Café Manfred
Fiona's B&B
Highfield House
ADELAIDE STREET
MY STREET
STEWART ST
HIGH STREET
WELMAN STREET
ST GEORGES SQUARE
YORK STREET
LYTTLETON STREET

King's Park
BRIDGE RD
PARK ST
PATERSON STREET
BRISBANE STREET
WELLINGTON STREET
BATHURST STREET
MARGARET STREET

Penny Royal World
Zig Zag Reserve

Princes Sq
Fee & Me
Elizabeth Street
ANNE STREET
EAST LAUNCESTON
ST JOHN STREET
GEORGE STREET
BALFOUR STREET
HIGH STREET

Cucina Simpatica
Brickfields Reserve
Launceston Backpackers
BOURKE ST
YORK STREET
FREDERICK STREET
CANNING STREET
BALFOUR STREET
CHARLES STREET
FRANKLAND STREET
Hospital
FRENCH ST
HOWICK STREET

Arbour Park
HILL STREET
WYETT STREET
UPPER YORK STREET
BATMAN STREET
CANNING ST
KEOGH ST
CATO ST
UPTON STREET
ROCHER ST
PRINCES ST
HILLSIDE CRES
MAITLAND STREET
ST ANDREWS STREET
Ockerby Gardens
HOWICK STREET
GALVIN STREET
MULGRAVE STREET
GARFIELD ST

BASIN ROAD
DENISON RD
BROUGHAM STREET
CONNAUGHT CRESCENT
LAURA STREET
Edenholme Grange Historic B&B
WEST LAUNCESTON
WELLINGTON STREET
GARFIELD STREET
Coronation Park

WILHELMINA AVE
BROUGHAM ST
Woods Reserve
GRANVILLE ST
THISTLE STREET
GLEN DHU STREET
SOUTH LAUNCESTON
MELBOURNE STREET
MEREDITH CRES

Cambridge St Reserve
SALISBURY CRESCENT
GRANVILLE AVE
HEATHER STREET
Treasure Island Caravan Park
GLEN DHU
SOUTHERN OUTLET
WESTBURY ROAD
WELLINGTON STREET
VERNON ST

N
Bradt
0 ———— 200m
0 ———— 200 yds
CAMBRIDGE STREET
SALISBURY CRES
ASHLEIGH
Evandale, The Stables

What to see and do

Launceston has a good variety of architecture and it is worth taking a walking tour of the town's **historical buildings**, either self-guided or through the visitor centre or a tour operator. One place not to miss is the **Old Umbrella Shop** (60 George Street, Launceston, TAS 7250; tel: 6331 9248; fax: 6344 4033; email: nat_trust@vision.net.au), a wonderfully eccentric place that looks like it belongs in a backstreet off Bond Street in London. It dates to the 1860s and is listed with the National Trust who also use it as an information centre. The interior design of rich Tasmanian blackwood and original Victorian fittings has been preserved so well that it calls itself the last genuine period shop in Tasmania. Adult $7.70; concession $5.50; family $15.40. Open Monday–Friday 09.00–17.00, Saturday 09.00–12.00. Closed Christmas Day, Good Friday.

It is also worth dropping by the **Queen Victoria Museum and Art Gallery** (Wellington Street, Launceston, TAS 7250; tel: 6323 3777; fax: 6323 3776; email: webmaster@qvmag.tased.edu.au), in particular to see the collection of colonial paintings and the Chinese joss-house temple, a reminder of the presence of Chinese tin miners here in the late 19th century. Open Monday–Saturday 10.00–17.00, Sunday 14.00–17.00. Closed Christmas Day, Good Friday.

Launceston Wilderness Walks (110 George Street, Launceston, TAS 7250; tel: 6334 3477; fax: 6334 3463; email: info@tas-ex.com) offer cycling, canoeing and walking tours in and around and departing from Launceston. Destinations include Freycinet, Cradle Mountain, Longford, Lake St Clair and Liffey Falls. All tours include meals, transport, accommodation and equipment. Rates on enquiry.

Take a trip up the river with **Tamar River Cruises** (Home Point, Launceston, TAS 7250; tel: 6334 9900; fax: 6334 9911) or do one of two moderate half-hour **cliff walks** on both sides of the impressive Cataract Gorge (steep in places). In summer try an after-dark walk to see the gorge lit up.

For a superb **wetland walk**, head north of Launceston about 11km on the A7 and turn off when you see signs for the **Tamar Island Wetlands Walk** (tel: 6327 3964; email: janine.keesing@dpiwe.tas.gov.au; web: www.dpiwe.tas.gov.au) and/or the Parks and Wildlife Centre. All boardwalks suitable for wheelchairs. Head out on a 40-minute walk over the marshes where the bird life is spectacular. Expect to see egrets, pelicans, wedge-tailed eagles and white-bellied sea eagles. There are two resident platypus, and copperhead and tiger snakes are present. There are guided walks run by volunteers during the summer. Donations: adult $2; child $1.

If you are in the northeast to check out the skills of arts and crafts designers then head for the **Tasmanian Wood Design Collection** (Macquarie House, Civic Square, Launceston, TAS 7250; tel: 6334 6558; fax: 6334 6559; email: info@twdc.org.au). Adult $2.20; child $1.10; family $5.50. Open Monday–Friday 10.00–13.00, from December 28 to Easter 10.00–16.00. Closed Christmas Day, Good Friday.

Further information

From the Gateway Tasmanian Travel and Information Centre (corner of St John and Paterson streets; tel: 6336 3122; fax: 6336 3118; email: info@gatewaytas.com.au). Open Monday–Friday 09.00–17.00, Saturday 09.00–15.00, Sunday and public holiday 09.00–12.00. Closed Christmas Day.

GEORGE TOWN AND THE COAST

This is a pretty seaside town blown clean daily by fresh winds from Bass Strait. It is bright and clean and well laid out and has retained many of its original buildings. There are newly painted weatherboard houses looking out over the water. It is a

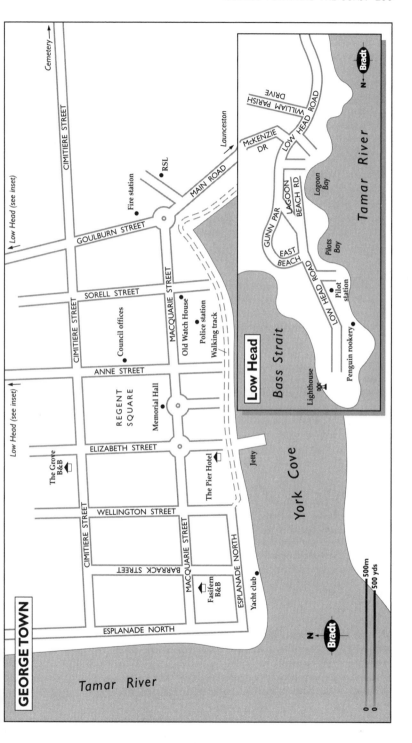

good place to stay for a couple of nights to get a good slice of early Australian history (only Sydney and Hobart pre-date George Town) and take some walks along the waterfront to see the penguins.

Along the coast is Bridport, a holiday town with several caravan and camping sites and B&Bs. This is a popular summer holiday spot for families as the weather is generally dry and sunny on this side of the island, the beaches here are good and the swimming is safe.

East of Bridport the coastal flats and thin eucalyptus forests are deserted. Roads run to Waterhouse Point, Tomahawk and Cape Portland via Gladstone, but most are gravel and some badly rutted.

Where to stay and eat

In George Town, try **Fasifern B&B** (13 Esplanade North, George Town, TAS 7253; tel: 6382 1424; fax: 6382 3290; email: georgetown@amcal.net.au), which was built in 1874 for an employee of the Extension Cable Company and from where one of the first primitive telephone calls was made to the Cable Station at Low Head. En-suite room $75/100, single/double.

Also **The Grove B&B** (25 Cimitiere Street, George Town, TAS 7253; tel: 6382 1336; fax: 6382 3352; email: thegrove@tas.quik.com.au), which was built in 1835 as a home for the port officer and magistrate, Matthew Friend, and has been restored. B&B in self-contained Nanna's Cottage, en-suite room $55–65/$65–85, single/double. The Grove also has an award-winning restaurant.

A motel to check out is **The Pier** (5 Elizabeth Street, George Town, TAS 7253; tel: 6382 1300; fax: 6382 2085; email: pierhotel@vision.net.au; web: www.pierhotel.com), which looks fairly ordinary but has won several awards and is well positioned on the waterfront opposite the Devil Cat terminal. There is a restaurant too. Apartment $130, single and double; en-suite room $110, single and double; standard room $55, single and double.

In Bridport, the **Platypus Park Country Retreat** (Ada Street, Bridport, TAS 7262; tel: 6356 1873; fax: 6356 0173; email: platypuspark@tassie.net.au) makes a nice stay. There are four cottages, set in lawns and gardens overlooking trout-stocked farm dams and a river valley. Platypus play in the dams and ponds in this river valley. Apartment $55–65/$70–136, single/double; en-suite room $60–80, single and double.

The **Indra Holiday Units** (53 Westwood Street, Bridport, TAS 7262; tel: 6356 1196; mobile: 0418 135 809; fax: 6356 1332; email: indra@vision.net.au) are functional, comfortable, only a couple of streets from the beach, and good for families. Apartment $60–70/$65–80, single/double.

The **Bridport Caravan Park** (Bentley Street, Bridport, TAS 7262; tel: 6356 1227) is right on the beach and has 43 serviced sites for $12–15 each.

There are several fast food places and fish and chip shops in Bridport.

Further east at **Waterhouse Point** and at Cape Portland there are campsites with no facilities but stunning locations, and in between at Tomahawk is the **Tomahawk Caravan Park** (Tomahawk, TAS 7262; tel: 6355 2268; fax: 6356 0560): tent sites $6/12, single/double; serviced sites $9, single and double; cabins $40, single and double. There is a boat ramp here too.

What to see and do

Take the excellent self-guided **heritage trails** of George Town and Low Head devised by the George Town and District Historical Society and George Town Council. Pick up a brochure from the visitor centre on the way into town on the A8. Both walks have maps and markers that will lead you on clear routes. The George Town one starts at the Old Watch House on the corner of Macquarie and Sorell streets (where the old gaol once stood) and passes a number of well-preserved former private homes and official buildings. The tour took me about an hour. The Low Head tour is longer at about 7km which takes about 3–4 hours and includes walking right out to the lighthouse. Walking is easy on both trails but wear sneakers (sand shoes) if you can.

📷 Photo spot

George Town has some wonderfully photogenic buildings. Try to find the ones painted in light colours and photograph with a darker sky behind. Ideal if a storm has blown through and you have sunlight behind you and the rumbling thunderheads blackening the sky behind the brightly painted weatherboards of the buildings. Gives a good sense of coastal-climate living. 64ASA and 50mm lens.

Also at Low Head is the **Pilot Station Maritime Museum** (tel: 6382 1143). Apparently this is Australia's oldest continuously running pilot station, having been established in 1805. Adult \$3; pensioner and student \$2. Open daily 08.00–20.00.

For **wildlife-watching** with emphasis on penguins, try **Nocturnal Tours** (mobile: 0418 361 860; fax: 6382 2310; rates on enquiry) that run nightly from July to April one hour before sunset. For seal-watching at Tenth Island, try **Seal and Sea Adventures** (mobile: 0419 357 028 or 0418 133 179, web: www.sealandssea.com; rates on enquiry).

In Bridport you are most likely to be spending time on the beach or fishing. Try the **Tasmanian Fly-Fishing School** (tel/fax: 6362 3441; email: tasflyfish@vision.net.au) to see which operators work this part of the island.

There is a good easy walk from Bridport through the 52-hectare (128-acre) Granite Point Coastal Reserve (tel: 6376 1550 for details and directions). Also near by is the 6,700-hectare **Waterhouse Conservation Area** with wonderful sand-dunes, rock-pools and tranquil beaches. There are some campsites too (tel: 6356 1173 for details and directions off the B82).

If you are following the **wine trail** around Tasmania you will not want to miss some of the jewels in its crown, the northern vineyards. They are situated on the gentle slopes halfway between George Town and Bridport. They are known throughout Australia, and increasingly Europe and North America, for their chardonnay, riesling and pinot noir and have won several awards. Wineries offer tours, tastings and cellar-door purchases. Try the **Pipers Brook Vineyard** (1216 Pipers Brook Road, Pipers Brook, TAS 7254; tel: 6382 7527; fax: 6382 7226; email: enquiries@pbv.com.au; web: www.pbv.com.au) whose chief winemaker, Andrew Pirie, is famous in Australia. Also the **Ninth Island Winery** (40 Baxters Road, Pipers River, TAS 7252; tel: 6382 7622; fax: 6382 7225) about 40 minutes in the car from Launceston. There is a restaurant at both open for lunches, coffee and cakes. Both wineries open October–April 10.00–17.00. Closed Christmas Day.

Otherwise one of the joys of this region is that you can wander for miles down side-roads, through eucalyptus woods, and along lonely beaches.

Further information

From the George Town Visitor Centre on Main Road (tel: 6382 1700; email: georgetown@tasvisinfo.com.au; web: www.georgetown.tas.gov.au).

📷 Photo spot

Vineyards are good because the lines of vines flow away in the viewfinder so gracefully. Try to take some heading uphill so they fill the frame (no sky or other background). 100ASA and 50mm lens (not wide angle as it can distort the lines).

MEET A TASMANIAN: MICHELE ROUND (RETAIL MANAGER FOR PIPERS BROOK WINERY)

A native Hobartian and die-hard Tasmanian patriot, Michele Round adores her homeland.

Tasmania is a total celebration of food and drink. We've got the fattest, lushest pastures anywhere. The pre-volcanic land across the north produces incredibly thick grass blades.

The ripening of our grapes is long and slow which is perfect for the most complex, elegant wines. The sparkling fruit is the first to come off the vine. Our 'Pirie' sparkling makes the top ten lists in Australia. We don't enter wines in competitions but it has had some marvellous reviews here and overseas. We have a big market in Japan and you can buy it by the glass in ten restaurants in New York City. We also sell to markets in Canada. That's not bad for a winery with only 180 hectares under vine.

I've been working here for more than 12 months, but I was an arts teacher for 20 years before that on the northwest coast and then set up a food and wine consultancy in Hobart. We have a cooking school, a promotional marketing division for food clients, and I'm also a wine writer.

I studied overseas for a while but probably always knew deep down I would come back to Tasmania. It's the most amazing place. I've lived here for a long time but I'm still blown away by the beauty of the sunlight on the vines at four o'clock on a wintry Saturday afternoon. How could I bear to leave this landscape? And we have this amazing variety of food: the honey, the cheeses from all across the north, the oysters that you can get all year round, the crayfish at Stanley, and the fantastic game meats like quail and venison. And then look at the aquaculture industry that is doing so well here, especially producing ocean trout; and the Huon is bursting with more fruit than they can deal with. Because of our geographical position and the variety of climate we seem to be able to grow virtually anything. The choice is incredibly wide for a small island – it's like living in nature's own kitchen.

CENTRAL UPLANDS

East from the A3 Launceston to Scottsdale road almost to the ocean is a series of small mountain ranges and hills. This region is virtually impenetrable unless you have a 4WD, apart from a few side-roads that can take 2WD, to Ringarooma and Mathinna for example.

The land is forested although little is protected and some is being logged. The peaks are quite high (up to 1,573m) and are snow-covered for the winter. Human presence in the wilds is minimal and the wildlife viewing is excellent, but there are marked trails through here like the Overland Track or the South Coast Track so you are much better going with a guide (see *What to see and do* section, page 237). If you are here in winter then you can ski up in Ben Lomond National Park.

By the time this book is published, work on a new $200m environment interpretation centre should be well under way. It was being planned and funded by Forestry Tasmania and the Dorset Regional Council.

Where to stay and eat

Scottsdale has a few high quality B&Bs and a pub with budget rooms.

Beulah (9 King Street, Scottsdale, TAS 7260; tel: 6352 3723; mobile: 0418 699 174; fax: 6352 3077) is charming and has a lovely garden. Rooms cost $80–110/$110–150, single/double.

Also **Anabel's** (46 King Street, Scottsdale, TAS 7260; tel: 6352 3277; fax: 6352 2144; email: anabels@vision.net.au), $88/99, single/double. The restaurant is well thought of and books up fast, so give plenty of notice.

For a budget night, try **Lords** pub (King Street, Scottsdale, TAS 7260; tel: 6352 2319) where the rooms are pretty basic and have shared facilities but the staff are friendly and it is fine for $22/35, single/double. The pub has a good bottle shop.

There is also a small **campsite** slightly out of town (tel: 6352 2017; fax: 6352 3309; email: dorset@dorset.tas.gov.au) for campervans, caravans and campers, with sites for about $10–15.

In Derby, try the fully self-contained **Cobbler's Cottage** (63 Main Road, Derby, TAS 7264; tel: 6354 2145; fax: 6354 2466) for $40/70, single/double. There is **camping** with facilities at **Branxholm** tent site for $6/12, single/double; serviced site $20, single and double; and at Weldborough at the **Weldborough Hotel** with tent sites for $5/10, single/double; serviced site $6/12, single/double. Also at Griffin near Mathinna, and Fingal. And at Ben Lomond try Tasmania's highest B&B, the **Creek Inn** (tel/fax: 6372 2444), which is open all year round. Rates on enquiry.

What to see and do

For an excellent tour, with plenty of wildlife and local history and humour, contact Craig Williams at **Pepper Bush Peaks Adventure Tours** (65 King Street, Scottsdale, TAS 7260; tel/fax: 6352 2263; mobile: 0419 570 887; email: pepper@microtech.com.au). The prices are higher than most but they are worth it. Even if you are not the sort of traveller who goes for organised tours (I am not, as a rule) you might make an exception here for this is quite tough terrain with little of it in national parks so there are not the information sheets, walking trails and wildlife species lists we are used to elsewhere in Tasmania. Craig, or 'Bushy' to his mates, was born in the country and knows the land well. He is friends with most of the local farmers who allow him on to their land, and over years of 'poking around' he has learned enough about the habits of the wildlife to be able to predict their movements. Kangaroos are common on the lower slopes, wallabies and pademelons higher up, along with a host of other native mammals. The freshwater crayfish living in the streams here are reputed to be the largest in the world.

His bush survival skills are fun too, like how to make a cup of reviving tea from the lemon myrtle tree, and how to disguise body odour after several days in the bush by rubbing yourself with leaves from the fragrant blackheart sassafras tree.

His main stomping ground is the Mackenzie Ranges south of Scottsdale which he reaches by 4WD. You can come on a full-guided tour or, if you have your own vehicle, do a tag-along with Craig leading the convoy. He is a former butcher and a wonderful bush chef so after a morning slogging it through the forests you can sit down on a hilltop looking out to the ocean and Cape Barren Island, and tuck into wallaby loin in crab-apple, port and native pepperberry sauce. Maybe it was the fresh air or the tang of the pepperberries, but this was one of the best meals I

MEET A TASMANIAN: CRAIG 'BUSHY' WILLIAMS (BUSH TOUR OPERATOR)

There is virtually nothing Craig Williams does not know about the bush; hence his nickname.

I was born in the bush, grew up here and I'll probably roll over and die here too. It's my home and I like it. It's almost not Australia, it's a very unique, Tasmanian landscape here, not like the mainland at all.

I've picked up all my knowledge from years of exploring and finding out things. My father, my grandfather and brother were all forest rangers so I used to spend time with them poking around in the bush and asking questions.

I learned about the bush compass, where you look at a tree trunk and the moss will always be growing on the southern side and branches, away from the sunlight, and the bigger branches of most trees tend towards the northeast to catch as much of the morning sun as they can.

I caught my first snake when I was five years old. I've been bitten a couple of times since and got pretty sick but I'm still here.

Within five hours I can show you scores of forest tree, animal and bird species, in four types of forest that are all very different from each other. On tours we also usually manage to find a freshwater crayfish. This is the largest species in the world here and its ancestors go back hundreds of years. I also usually let my guests in on some bush legends. They are all true of course.

Things have really changed in the past year or two. I was invited to America to talk to some travel people there about them pushing my tours, and also the business from England is going well. It's great to show so many people from so far away my own backyard.

When in need of inspiration Craig still relies on the most trusted of all Aussie bush techniques.

I was sitting on top of a nearby mountain one day in the Maczenzie Ranges trying to work out what to call my company. I had a sip of beer, looked down at this lovely plant next to me, and it came to me in a flash – Pepperbush Peak Tours.

have eaten in Australia. He also owns three bush cabins where guests can hide out fishing for their suppers.

If you are going to explore this area solo then first contact Forestry Tasmania (tel: 6374 2102 or 6352 2466) who operate the Forest Reserves, and the Parks and Wildlife department who run the State Reserves and Ben Lomond National Park (tel: 6390 6279).

Short walks in reserves
White Knights at Evercreech Forest Reserve
Distance: 1km return. Time: 30 minute return. Difficulty: easy.

Start at the reserve car-park which is at the end of the B43 from Fingal or the end of the C423 from Ringarooma. The loop walk takes you past some magnificent white gums, the tallest of which measures 91.3m and is almost 300 years old. Do not walk in stormy or very windy conditions.

Waterfall Walk at Mathinna Falls Forest Reserve
Distance: 1km return. Time: 30 minutes return. Difficulty: easy.
Start at the end of the dirt-road leading north from the C423 and B43. The track is even and leads to the base of the falls. Mathinna Falls is a four-tier waterfall which plummets over a total drop of 80m.

Ralphs Falls at Mount Victoria Forest Reserve
Distance: 2km return. Time: 1 hour return. Difficulty: easy.
Drive south of Ringarooma on the eastern spur of the C423, following signs to the falls and to Mount Victoria Forest Reserve. From the car-park, follow a clearly marked track to the falls (there are about 25 rough bush steps) and complete a circuit via Cash's Gorge Loop. Ralphs Falls drops over a fluted cliff.

Waterfall Walk at St Columba Falls State Reserve
Distance: 1km return. Time: 30 minutes return. Difficulty: easy.
This walk starts at the car-park at the end of the side-track leading from the C428 and follows an easy track with a gentle uphill gradient to the falls, one of the highest in Tasmania.

BEN LOMOND NATIONAL PARK
This park (tel: 6390 6279) covers 16,527 hectares and is about an hour's drive southeast of Launceston and three hours northeast of Hobart.

Ben Lomond, as its ancestral Scottish name suggests, is a high park, more than 1,300 metres above sea level. Ben Lomond itself stands 1,572m high and is only topped by Mount Ossa (1,617m).

The park sits on a plateau from where there are awesome views over the midland plains and to the east coast and even Flinders Island on a clear day.

Despite the vast high areas of southwest wilderness, Ben Lomond contains the biggest area of alpine vegetation. Mountain pepper, daisy bush and scoparia are among the alpine species. In spring the park is awash with colour from wildflowers, the most noted being the mountain rocket. On the lower slopes you will find eucalyptus and some rainforest trees. Here is where the majority of the

CHEESE AND BEER
Addicts of either, or both, should make for Pyengana where John Healey, a third-generation cheesemaker, creates Pyengana cloth-matured cheddar which is delicious. The cheese is only made on Tuesday, Thursday and Sunday, but visitors can drop in any day for tastings. Tel: 6373 6157. You can combine this with a drink at the **Pub in the Paddock** (St Columba Falls Road, Pyengana, TAS 7216; tel: 6373 6121; fax: 6373 6178; email: pubinthepaddock@bigpond.com) which has been licensed for more than a century. There are six standard rooms with good views for $35/45 single/double. It is in a beautiful setting with wildlife all around, including two 400kg beer-guzzling pigs, Slops and Priscilla, who finish off the dregs after a big night at the bar.

wildlife hides – wallabies, echidnas, pygmy-possums and Tasmanian devils are common. Also keep an eye to the skies for a wedge-tailed eagle.

The Plangummairreenner band of Aborigines spent time here, as did settlers in the 1930s when it became popular for skiing with the Northern Tasmanian Alpine Club. It was proclaimed a national park in 1946 but skiing was also encouraged. Visitors can ski from July to September for a separate fee. Summer is for bushwalkers but there is only one marked trail – to the summit of Legges Tor which takes about two hours return from the ski village. Experienced and well-equipped walkers only should attempt off-track walks across the rest of the park.

From Launceston, drive south to Evandale and take the C413 to Blessington. Then go left on the C420 (there should be a signpost here) and continue for about 12km to a crossroads just before Upper Blessington, and take a right and drive the 17km to the ski village in the park.

EAST COAST
From St Helens north to Cape Portland is a largely deserted and incredibly beautiful coastline. Few people make it this far to the northeast corner as it takes a good six or more hours to drive from Hobart and requires at least two nights' accommodation. The beaches are of the purest white sand, the waters translucent and seemingly free from any kind of pollution. In many hours of walking I saw not one piece of ship's debris, not one blob of oil. It was as if an army of cleaners had trawled their way along an hour or two ahead of me to cleanse the place. There is virtually no static accommodation or visitor services, yet this is one of the most enticing parts of the island state.

Where to stay and eat
St Helens has lots of places to stay, but most are standard B&Bs and holiday units which are reasonably priced and aimed at families so they book up quickly as the summer approaches.

Queechy Cottages (2 Tasman Highway, St Helens, TAS 7216; tel: 6376 1321; fax: 6376 1652; email: queechy@vision.net.au; web: www.queechycottages.com.au), on the south side of the Golden Fleece Bridge, is a good spot. The homestead is National Trust listed and there are 18 self-contained cottages. It is five minutes from the town centre and there is a restaurant on-site. Apartment $66–82, single and double.

Bayview House B&B (Binalong Bay Rd, St Helens, TAS 7216; tel/fax: 6376 2065; email: bayview.house@tassie.net.au) is pleasant and in a good location overlooking Georges Bay. The owners are planting bird-friendly trees to attract the many species that favour the gentle climate of this coast. Standard room $50–65/$70–85, single/double.

Also try **Warrawee Guesthouse** (Tasman Highway at Kirwan's Beach, St Helens, TAS 7216; tel: 6376 1987; fax: 6376 1012; email: warrawee@vision.net.au), which is up the hill a bit with good views and a paddock around it. En-suite rooms $100–150/$150–200, single/double.

The **Hillcrest Tourist Park** (Chimney Heights Rd, St Helens, TAS 7216; tel: 6376 3298; fax: 6376 3055) is good if you are mobile or camping. Tent sites $8/12, single/double; serviced site $10/15, single/double; cabins $55–71, single and double.

Bay of Fires Character Cottages (Main Rd, Binalong Bay, TAS 7216; tel: 6376 8262; fax: 6376 8261). Apartment $65/88, single/double.

If you want to stay in complete luxury, and money is no barrier, then contact the **Bay of Fires Walk and Lodge** (Tel: 6331 2006; fax: 6331 5255; email: cradle@tassie.net.au or info@cradlehuts.com.au; web: www.bayoffires.com). Set on a hilltop 40 metres above the beach and surrounded by Mount William National Park, the lodge is the only building on 20km of outstanding coastal wilderness. It is a dream beach house with long timber sun decks, open fires and huge windows framing the seascapes. Tasmanian hardwoods and plantation pines were lifted in by helicopter or carried by hand to the site to reduce habitat impact, and the lodge operates sustainably. Materials used were from sustainable sources, there is rain-water collection from the roof, grey-water treatment systems, composting toilets and solar power for lighting and hot showers. Guests can do a two-day beach walk starting north of Eddystone Point and staying the first night in the Forester Beach Camp, a de-mountable seasonal structure with twin-share rooms with timber floors, canvas roofs and full kitchen facilities. The company obtained special permission to operate this camp within the national park. Sea kayaking, snorkelling and wildlife-watching are all possible.

What to see and do
St Helens is charming. It is a popular seaside town with a lively buzz and beach-going families with buckets and spades. There is a good information centre and history room (61 Cecilia Street, St Helens, TAS 7216; tel: 6376 1744). Open Monday–Friday 09.00-17.00, Saturday 09.00–12.00, Sunday (January–April and long weekends only) 10.00–14.00. Adult $2; child $1. Apart from seaside fun, the main draw is Mount William National Park and the beaches.

MOUNT WILLIAM NATIONAL PARK
This park (tel: 6357 2108) on the northeast tip covers 13,899 hectares. The most dominant rock is 380 million-year-old granite which is best seen exposed on the coast. Granite has a high quartz content and breaks down into pure white sand, hence the tropical-looking beaches. The park is made up of gentle bays, low dunes and fairly flat coastal land. In the north is Musselroe Bay Conservation Area, a long spit goes the length of this bay. The parallel dunes behind Boulder Point were formed about 130,000 years ago when the earth was warmer and the sea-level higher. These dunes now rise to about 30m.

The vegetation is mainly coastal heath and woodland containing hundreds of plant species with many wildflowers which are best seen in spring and summer. Closer to the ocean there are salt-tolerant plants. The most common trees are black gum, banksia, she-oak and bull oak, and black peppermint. This is a favourite domain of the Forester kangaroo, but you might also see an echidna blindly sniffing along the ground; also wombats, devils and brush-tail possums. Almost 100 species of bird live here, from tiny superb blue wrens and flame robins to yellow-tailed black cockatoos and sea eagles. If you ask the Parks and Wildlife Service they will tell you the best location to spot the sacred ibis. Out to sea, whales and dolphins use this coast fairly regularly.

The park has great significance to descendants of Aboriginal people from the Northeast tribe who first lived here more than 30,000 years ago, living off seafood, kangaroo and wallaby. Some middens along this coast are so large that scientists believe they may have been the result of 1,000 years of habitation. As elsewhere in Tasmania, their days were numbered with the arrival of the Europeans. Sealers and whalers at first started trading with the indigenous groups but soon began ravaging communities and taking women by force. It is estimated that by 1830 the community here had been decimated from 400 or 500 to 72 men and only six women. The park was declared in 1973, primarily to protect the kangaroo.

Eddystone Point
As we go to press, members of the Aboriginal community are pressing the Tasmanian Government for the return of land at Eddystone Point in the park. Land at Oyster Cove, south of Hobart, has been successfully reclaimed and there is a similar campaign over parts of Rocky Cape National Park in the northwest.

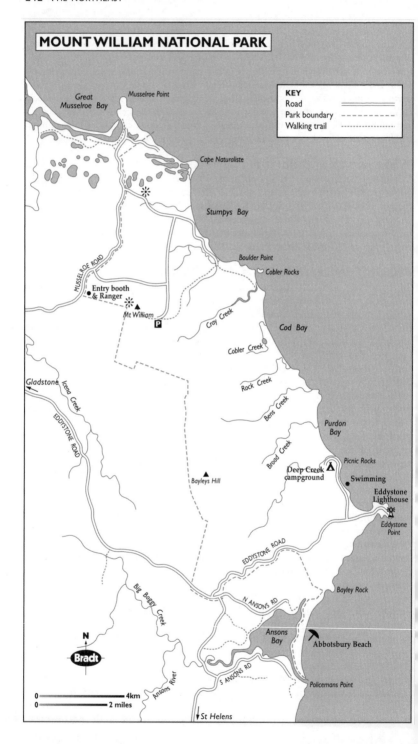

MOUNT WILLIAM NATIONAL PARK

KEY
Road
Park boundary
Walking trail

Great Musselroe Bay

Musselroe Point

Cape Naturaliste

Stumpys Bay

Boulder Point
Cobler Rocks

MUSSELROE ROAD

Entry booth & Ranger

Mt William

Cray Creek

Cod Bay

Cobler Creek

Rock Creek

Berrs Creek

Purdon Bay

Gladstone

Iceng Creek

EDDYSTONE ROAD

Brood Creek

Bayleys Hill

Deep Creek campground

Picnic Rocks

Swimming

Eddystone Lighthouse

Eddystone Point

EDDYSTONE ROAD

Big Boggy Creek

N ANSONS RD

Bayley Rock

N

Bradt

Ansons Bay

Abbotsbury Beach

S ANSONS RD

Ansons River

Policemans Point

0 ——— 4km
0 ——— 2 miles

↓ St Helens

📷 Photo spot

This entire coast is ravishingly beautiful. My favourite spot for pictures is the orange-algae-covered rocks at Eddystone Point. Shoot out to sea as the lighthouse clutters the shot. Orange-painted rocks in the foreground, brilliant blue ocean beyond, and sometimes a bright yellow fishing boat obliges by bobbing around the headland and giving you the icing on the cake. Use low-speed film (50 or 64ASA) to saturate the colour and a 50mm and wide-angle lens (take shots with both). Good for black and white as well, surprisingly, but really only if you have good equipment and a deep-red filter to make the contrasts strong.

Short walks in Mount William National Park
Stumpys to Cobler
Distance: 3–5km return. Time: 1–2 hours return. Difficulty: easy.
Drive the C845 to Stumpys Bay, where there is camping possible but no facilities. Head south to Cobler Rocks and back, or continue south to Cod Bay. There are usually lots of wallabies and wombats along this part of the coastline and you may even spot a quoll. Sea eagles are seen fairly regularly as well.

Mount William
Distance: 3km return. Time: 2 hours return. Difficulty: easy.
Drive the C845 and turn right to Mount William about 16km east of Gladstone. The walk starts at the car-park a little further on from the end of Forester Kangaroo Drive. The summit is only 216m but the flatness of the surrounding land means the views are good. You can see over to Cape Barren Island and some of its smaller islets.

Eddystone and Abbotsbury
Distance: 6km return. Time: 3 hours return. Difficulty: easy.
Leave your vehicle at the end of the C846 in the lighthouse and boat ramp car-park. Walk back up the road to the sign for Abbotsbury Beach and through the dunes to the beach. Wander south down the beach to the end of the spit and then north again, and on to Eddystone Point, where there are some good examples of granite rocks covered in red algae. Go past the lighthouse and a child's grave on the right surrounded by a picket fence. The track leads you back to the car-park.

Blue Lake
Just west of the park and off the B82 south of Gladstone is Blue Lake, a remarkable, cobalt-coloured lake which makes for some striking photographs. The cliff edges around the lake are crumbly and weak so do not get too close. The lake is so blue for two possible reasons: first because it has been coloured by a number of minerals that were turned up here during the time when tin mining was prevalent here (one of the biggest Chinese tin-mining communities in Australia lived here), and second because it has a light clay-and-sand bottom so reflects the sunlight as it filters through.

📷 Photo spot
Blue Lake is an amazing place and makes great photos but you need a sunny day and access to just the right spot is hard. The cliffs around the lake are soft and crumbly so take care. 50–100mm lens best to get closer without risking your life, and 64ASA.

FURNEAUX ISLANDS
The main island is Flinders, but Cape Barren and Clarke are also of a decent size. The rest are much smaller, the very tips of hills whose slopes once led down to the Bassian plain that linked Tasmania with the mainland.

The islands stand as a reminder of the rapid disintegration of the Aboriginal population at the hands of the Europeans, especially the lawless sealers and whalers. This brutal history is detailed in the *History* section of this chapter (see page 227) and the general *History* section in *Chapter 1*. For details on getting there and around, see page 229.

Protected islands include Outer and Inner Sister, Babel, Great and Little Dog, and Little Green, which are all mutton-bird reserves, and Cat, Storehouse, Big Green, Low Islets and the Mount Chappell Islands, which are all nature reserves. Wybalenna is a wildlife sanctuary, Chalky a bird sanctuary, and Goose Island a conservation area.

Flinders Island
Where to stay and eat
There are a surprising number of places to stay on Flinders considering it is somewhat off the main tourist trail. Here are three of the best for wildlife-watching:

Carnsdale Host Farm Cottage (Memana, Flinders Island, TAS 7255; tel/fax: 6359 9718; email: rd&jawilson@trump.net.au) is a self-contained property surrounded by a 950-hectare sheep and cattle farm in the middle of the island. There are wallabies, possums, wild pigs and turkeys, Cape Barren geese and pheasants. Apartment $88, single and double. The owners have a car they rent out.

Castle Cottage (41 Port Davies Road, Emita, Flinders Island, TAS 7255; tel/fax: 6359 8488) is self-contained and rents for $90–100 (sleeps four people). The owners live on the same property and can take guests on bush trips in their 4WD.

Partridge Farm (Badger Corner, Flinders Island, TAS 7255; tel/fax: 6359 3554; email: chris_rhodes@bigpond.com) is surrounded by bushland with honey-eaters, tree creepers and superb wrens by day and wallabies at dusk. Studio apartment $99; apartment $116; en-suite room $121, all single and double.

There are not many places to eat but much accommodation is self-catering and supplies are available from general stores in Whitemark and Lady Barron.

What to see and do
A good first stop is the **Furneaux Historical Research Association Museum** (Whitemark, Flinders Island; tel: 6359 2380; email: amdo@bigpond.com; web: www.flindersislandonline.com) in Emita. This three-room timber cottage was the first government school on the island. Relics from the numerous shipwrecks around the island are on display here and there are photographs and newspaper clippings depicting the life of the early settlers and mutton-birders. Adult $2; child (under 10 years) free. Open Saturday and Sunday 13.00–17.00, daily during summer school holidays and Easter.

Near by is the **Wybalenna Historic Site** (Flinders Island Aboriginal Incorporated; tel: 6359 3532; 126 hectares or 311 acres) where the disastrous, forced Aboriginal settlement was based between 1833 and 1847 (see *History* in this chapter and in *Chapter 1*). The National Trust owns the chapel and has restored it. There are some good swimming beaches near by and some boats for hire.

An excellent source of information on Flinders Island is the helpful and delightful Thelma Shaik, at the Gem Shop in Killiecrankie, who produces brochures with all the useful phone numbers and other contact details any tourist to the island could hope for. She can mail information too. She is registered as the Flinders Island Visitor Information Centre (tel: 6359 2160; email: flindersisinfo@bigpond.com).

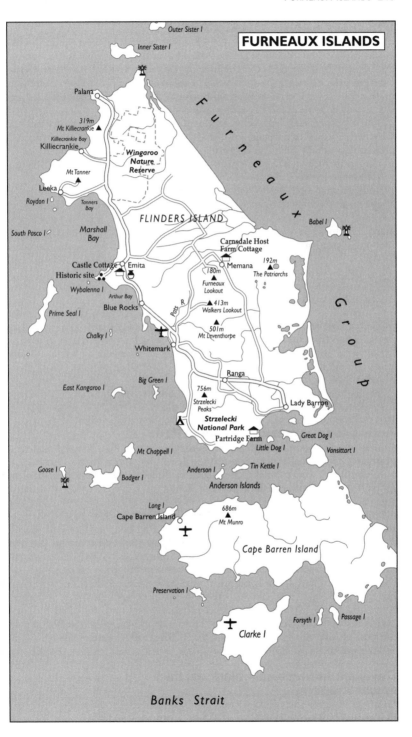

FURNEAUX ISLANDS

Outer Sister I

Inner Sister I

Palana

319m
Mt Killiecrankie ▲
Killiecrankie Bay
Killiecrankie

Mt Tanner ▲

Leeka

Roydon I

Tanners
Bay

South Pasco I

Marshall
Bay

*Wingaroo
Nature
Reserve*

FLINDERS ISLAND

F u r n e a u x

Babel I

**Carnsdale Host
Farm Cottage**

Castle Cottage
Historic site
Wybalenna I

Emita

Memana

192m ▲
The Patriarchs

180m ▲
*Furneaux
Lookout*

Arthur Bay

Blue Rocks

Prime Seal I

Chalky I

Pats R

▲ 413m
Walkers Lookout

501m
Mt Leventhorpe

Whitemark

Ranga

Big Green I

East Kangaroo I

756m
▲
*Strzelecki
Peaks*

Lady Barron

*Strzelecki
National Park*

Partridge Farm

Great Dog I

Little Dog I

Vansittart I

Mt Chappell I

Goose I

Badger I

Anderson I

Tin Kettle I

Anderson Islands

G r o u p

Long I
Cape Barren Island

686m
▲
Mt Munro

Cape Barren Island

Preservation I

Forsyth I

Passage I

Clarke I

Banks Strait

STRZELECKI NATIONAL PARK

This park (tel: 6359 2217) covers 4,215 hectares at the southwest tip of Flinders Island. Mount Strzelecki (765m) lies to the north of the park, while at the southern end you will find rugged granite mountains such as Mount Razorback, and some excellent seascapes at which to marvel. The splendidly named Trousers Point west of the park has some good examples of the park's floral emblem, the drooping she-oak, as well as some deserted beaches with good swimming.

The vegetation is varied, with sand-dunes and rocky shorelines, freshwater and saltwater marshes, sedge and heathlands, scrub, woodland and some isolated pockets of forest in gullies. A staggering 800 plant species have been recorded on Flinders, including bushy needlewood and southern blue gums. Spring wildflowers are spectacular.

You will not find devils here but to make up for it there are successful populations of echidnas, Bennett's wallabies, pademelons, wombats and brush-tail possums. Driving at dusk is a bad idea as there will be more wildlife on the road than cars. More secretive are the island's ring-tail and pygmy-possums, potoroos, marsupial mice, rats and bats, and if you are really lucky you will see an Australian fur seal sunning itself on rocks at the shore. All three species of snake are here, along with blotched blue-tongue lizards, skinks and little mountain dragons.

Birds are plentiful. About 150 species have been recorded and some are rare. This is also home to the forty-spotted pardalote.

The park is a major nesting site for mutton-birds, which return each September from their colossal migrations to burrows on the Furneaux Islands. The best place to see them is from the lookout at Port Davey at sunset between October and April.

Strzelecki was declared a national park in 1967, and named after a Polish count, Paul Edmund de Strzelecki, who climbed some of the highest peaks on Flinders Island in 1842.

To get here from Whitemark, drive south on the B85 and then C806. From Lady Barron, head northwest on the B85 and then the C806.

Activities in Strzelecki National Park

Conditions are good for **diving**, with calm, clear water, but the north and west coasts are best avoided as they are much rougher than the south and east. However, one lure of the west coast is the presence of three good wrecks off Settlement Point. Contact **Flinders Island Dive** in Emita (tel/fax: 6359 8429). **Fishing** is good from beaches and rocks but make sure you are not in a conservation area or national park. Contact **Corporate Fishing Charters** (tel: 9654 2022), or **Flinders Island Adventures** (tel: 6359 4507; fax: 6359 4533; email: jamesluddington@bigpond.com), who also do 4WD tours and group packages, or **Killiecrankie Enterprises** (tel: 6359 8560; fax: 6359 8575; email: mwheatley@trump.net.au), who also offer accommodation and car hire.

Visitors can also try their hand at diamond-hunting, not for real diamonds, but for slivers of topaz that splinter off from the decomposing rocks of Mount Killiecrankie in the far northwest, and can be found in streams and along the coast here. The locals call them Killiecrankie Diamonds and if you cannot find any on the beach then you will get one in the **Killiecrankie Enterprises** shop in Whitemark (tel: 6359 2130).

Day walk in Strzelecki National Park
Mount Strzelecki
Distance: 5–6km return. Time: 4–5 hours return. Difficulty: moderate.
Drive south of Whitemark along the C806 until you see signs for the track. It climbs

gradually to the 756m peak from where the views are great. If it is clear, you will be able to pick out most of the other 53 islands in the Furneaux Group. If it is really clear, you may even be able to see Wilsons Promontory on the mainland. There is no water on the track so bring your own and watch for snakes on the lower slopes. Although the path is fairly clear it is best to get hold of a large-scale map to find your way more easily and to identify accurately the landmarks around you.

Cape Barren Island

Cape Barren Island supports a small population of people, mainly descended from the former Aboriginal tribes. Until recently they had preserved the ancient tradition of making shell necklaces that was first seen by early French explorers and colonial artists who painted Tasmanian Aboriginal men and women wearing strings of tiny shells. It was about all that had survived and so was an important symbol for today's descendants, but the person who did the shell jewellery died in 2001 and it is not known if the tradition will continue.

However, an Aboriginal language, *Palawa Kani*, has been saved in the form of a retrieved word list. It is not a working language but the nine children at the tiny school on the island, run by principal Sandra Reid, are being taught it alongside their normal lessons in English.

Getting there
You will need to charter a plane from Peter Hay at the **Launceston Flying School** (tel: 6391 8477).

Where to stay
Sandra Reed (tel: 6359 3564) also rents out a cottage that sleeps three people. The building is the original schoolhouse dating from 1890 and has a laundry, microwave, hot water and open fires. All money earned from the cottage rents goes toward funding the present school.

You could also try a cottage rented out by the **Cape Barren Island Aboriginal Association** (tel: 6359 3533). Otherwise bring your tent.

Wildlife-spotting
This is the reason for coming to Cape Barren. Wildlife on the island is abundant, but there are no mutton-birds. Instead pelicans, sea eagles, seals, echidna, Forester kangaroos, Bennett's wallabies, and pademelons. Tiger and copperhead snakes are here too. You can join the school kids and watch pelicans landing right outside the schoolhouse.

The bushwalking is superb and the beaches pristine. However, the interior comes as a surprise. It is quite mountainous and much is inaccessible. Sandra Reid reckons it takes a week to walk fully around the island along the coast. There is a lot of private land and some crown land owned by the federal government. Bushwalkers must come prepared as there is little, if any, fresh water and no services, but, if it is isolation you are after and to be immersed in a wildlife paradise with only the wind for company, then Cape Barren is the place for you.

Chappell Islands

These islands to the southwest of Flinders are nature reserves and as such access is restricted. Apply to the Parks and Wildlife department for information (tel: 6233 6191; email: ParksEnquiries@dpiwe.tas.gov.au). They are renowned for one fantastic evolutionary process. The tiger snakes here are much bigger than elsewhere in Tasmania and the theory is that they had to increase their size rapidly once the land-based prey ran out and they were left with a choice of feeding off mutton-birds or going extinct. They chose the birds and now are of a rather alarming size. However, they are also said to be quite docile. When scientists were on the islands tagging and checking the snakes, they could place them back down at their feet and they slithered off nonchalantly into the bush. There are also reports that the group of tigers here are developing hypodermic fangs to be able to apply a much more deadly bite. If snakes are your thing, this would make a terrific day trip if Parks and Wildlife allow it. If snakes are your phobia, forget it.

Swan Island

This small island just off the northeast coast is privately owned and can be rented. There is a standard, fully self-contained guesthouse (the old lighthouse keeper's residence) with three double rooms and five single beds sleeping a maximum of 11 (tel: Nigel on 6357 2211). Guests have a laundry and kitchen.

The wildlife is good, with mutton-birds, a fairy penguin colony, pelicans and sea eagles. There are some tiger snakes, blue-tongued lizards, rabbits, and three elusive wallabies. Dolphins swim past fairly regularly, and seals and humpback and southern right whales are seen off the coast during migrations. A few years ago a pod of killer whales was seen but this is very rare. There is good diving in a small marine reserve but it is for the experienced and must be self-guided. Nigel charters flights with Peter Hay at the Launceston Flying School (tel: 6391 8477).

Tasmanian devils

The East Coast

13

This chapter covers a large section, from the Tasman Peninsula (including Port Arthur) right up the Sun Coast to St Marys.

The Tasman Peninsula is my favourite part of the island. Idyllic bays, a gentle and sunny climate, lots of chance to get out on the water and some dramatic history. I would recommend a good four days spent south of Dunalley if you have a vehicle, more if you are on bicycles. There are great short and long walks along the cliffs, an array of impressive geographical features to see (some quite rare), terrific seascapes with the biggest waves in Tasmania, and some excellent places to stay. And then there is Port Arthur, a must-see place cursed with tragedy and full of ghosts and reminders of past wrongs. A visit is always deeply moving.

Tasmania's Sun Coast stretches north from Triabunna to Bicheno. It is one of the most magnificent coastlines in Australia, if not the southern hemisphere. A rain shadow caused by the western and central highlands means this region receives little rain, roughly seven hours of sunshine a day and more than 300 sunny days a year. Subsequently it is Tasmania's seaside playground with plenty of accommodation. There are lots of short and long walks through the graceful eucalyptus forests of Freycinet, Maria Island and Douglas Apsley national parks and along the sweeping, oat-white sand of the Friendly Beaches and Bay of Fires. You can follow mysterious animal tracks as they scamper through the dunes. A sea eagle's mighty talons indent a similar span to a human hand; the eastern quoll's prints are tiny and delicate; and a trail of heavy round paws reveals the gait of a well fed Tasmanian devil.

In the north, beaches are separated by headlands of granite dusted with red algae. They offer unlimited photo opportunities against frequently clear skies, and natural playgrounds for children and adults alike. The adventurous can hop in a kayak to ride blue ocean rollers off the Freycinet Peninsula. Point your paddles south and there's nothing until Antarctica.

Beneath the water lie towering forests of giant kelp, swayed by the currents, and much marine life. Humpback and southern right whales cruise this coast during their migrations. In May and June they head north to warmer waters, returning south from September and November. A few cruise into Great Oyster Bay to frolic for a few days.

Bottlenose and spinner dolphins are also regular visitors all year, although they tend to be more active in summer. Australian fur seals congregate on rocky outcrops or 'haul-outs'. They are best watched from boats but strict limits are imposed on how close operators can get, so photographers might want to take a long lens and some fast film. Fairy penguins at Bicheno and Triabunna outnumber

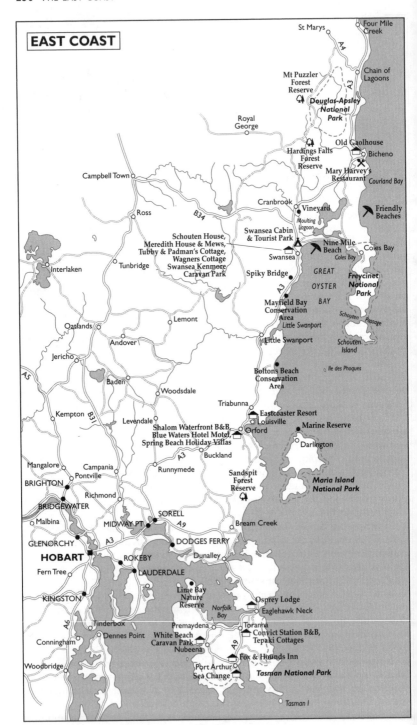

humans and can cause serious traffic congestion at penguin rush hours. August to Christmas is the best time.

Sea eagles nest on the precipitous cliffs of the Freycinet Peninsula, and mutton-birds winter here before their vast trans-Pacific migration. Shy albatross and Pacific gulls are also seen on the wing.

The coast produces some of the highest quality seafood in Australia. Sydney's most acclaimed chef, Tetsuya Wakuda, favours Tasmanian marine produce whenever possible. Oysters, abalone, crayfish, salmon and tuna are plentiful. And, to accompany them, this area boasts several vineyards.

The east coast is more sheltered than the wild west and was favoured for landing by convict boats and early settlers. As a result some of Tasmania's older buildings are found here. The principal holiday towns of Swansea and Bicheno, and the A3 that links them, all get busy during summer.

HISTORY

There are a few different versions of whose was the first European foot to set stand on Tasmanian soil but it is thought to have happened on the east coast. He was certainly Dutch and under the command of Captain Abel Janszoon Tasman, the first European to spot the island. Some accounts say it was Tasman himself. It is also unclear whether the landing party rowed or swam ashore for the seas were rough that day in 1642 (some say August, others November). They are believed to have landed somewhere in Blackman Bay on the Forestier Peninsula where they raised the Dutch flag.

They saw smoke coming from the hills, notches cut in trees and saw tiger-like prints (the thylacine we can assume) and realised they were not alone. They were not impressed and left for New Zealand.

About 200 years later this same region was picked as the site of a fortress prison. Port Arthur became the most famous penal site in Van Diemen's Land. If they slipped their chains and fled the prison itself they had to beat a line of vicious dogs and armed guards at Eaglehawk Neck and then survive in an unknown territory with an unpredictable climate. Transportation to Australia ceased in 1853 and the penal colony closed in 1877, its walls having heard the desperate laments of 12,000 prisoners.

Another major event happened at the Port Arthur Historical Site on April 28 1996, when lone gunman Martin Bryant shot dead 35 tourists and staff and injured many more. The incident prompted the newly elected Australian Prime Minister, John Howard, to hurry through tough new gun laws across the country.

Aborigines of the Oyster Bay tribe lived along the Sun Coast for generations in relative peace before the first visitors arrived. They prospered in the mild climate and on the bounty of food on land and offshore. Important ochre mines were dug on Maria Island and the rock used for wall and body painting.

Most early contact was at Maria Island. Tasman spotted this much smaller island from offshore during his 1642 voyage and diplomatically christened it after the wife of his patron, Anthony Van Diemen, the governor-general of the Dutch East India Company, but he did not land.

In 1789 John Henry Cox, on the brig *Mercury*, landed at Shoal Bay on the western side of the island. The passage of water that separates Maria Island and the mainland coast is named after his ship. He found supplies of wood and water on Maria Island and met Aboriginal people who he reported as peaceful, 'very merry, laughing and mimicking our actions'. In his diaries Cox describes Aboriginal boats made of hollowed trees, their bark huts and piles of shells.

In 1802 the French explorer Nicolas Baudin called at Maria Island with a group of naturalists who studied the island and its people. A doctor with that expedition, M F Peron, found the Aborigines cremated their dead, unlike their cousins on mainland Australia. With breathtaking ignorance, he was baffled why the Oyster Bay tribe were upset when he ransacked the remains of a cremation. He was lucky to escape with his life.

After the founding of Hobart in 1803, the new settlers spread out, finding land on the east coast suitable for farming crops, cattle and sheep. They found vast stands of eucalyptus and started a timber industry that still operates today. News went out that seals and whales were plentiful and, like sharks tasting blood, the capture ships raced south from Sydney and began a cull that took populations to the brink of extinction.

Seals and whales have since recovered and are now more common and protected.

The sealers also took Aboriginal women, either by bartering with tribes or by physical force. The decimation of the indigenous population was lightning fast and in less than 100 years they were wiped out here on the east coast and then across the whole island.

Timber and fishing kept the region alive until tourists first arrived, and now that is by far the biggest earner here.

GETTING THERE AND AROUND
By car
From Hobart, cross the Tasman Bridge and take the A3 to Sorrell. Take a right down the A9 to the Tasman Peninsula or straight on to Triabunna for the Sun Coast. From Launceston, drive the A3 through Scottsdale and Derby to St Helens and south, or head south along the A1 and turn left at Conara for the A4 to St Marys following the South Esk River. Alternatively, at Campbell Town take the B34 to Swansea past Lake Leake. Rent a vehicle in Hobart or Launceston.

By bus
Tasmanian Redline Coaches (tel: 1300 360 000 or 6336 1446) run services from Hobart and Launceston to the east coast towns of St Helens, Bicheno and Swansea. **TWT's Tassielink Regional Coach Service** (tel: 1300 300 520; web: tigerline.com.au) run services between Launceston and Bicheno via St Helens, and between Hobart and Swansea via Orford (for Maria Island ferry). They also run a service between Hobart, Nubeena and Port Arthur on Tasman Peninsula.

Bicheno Coach Service (tel: 6257 0293) runs services between Bicheno and Coles Bay. Check with companies for latest timetables and fares.

By bicycle
Getting to Triabunna from Hobart takes three leisurely days. The A3 Tasman Highway is fast and popular with logging trucks so back-roads are advisable. An easier option is to call the bus and coach companies (see *Getting Around* section of *Chapter 2*) and see if they will carry bikes. Or rent from the following places along the coast:

Eaglehawk Neck Backpackers Old Jetty Rd, Eaglehawk Neck; tel: 6250 3248
Triabunna Post Office Leonard St, Triabunna; tel: 8576 3849
Louisville Ferry Terminal Tel: 8262 3399
Swansea BP service station Terence St, Swansea; tel: 3736 9920
Coles Bay Post Office Eleanor St, Coles Bay; tel: 8556 0087
Bicheno Penguin and Adventure Tours A3 Tasman Highway, opposite triangle marker in town centre; tel: 6375 1333; fax: 6375 1533

Prices vary from $11 to $14 for a half day; around $20 for a full day; weekly rates available. Refundable deposits of around $60 per bicycle are usually required.

By sea
The Eastcoaster Express ferry (tel: 6257 1589) sails to Maria Island from Louisville, near Orford, three times a day at 10.30, 13.00 and 15.30. The trip takes about 25 minutes and the boat returns at 11.00, 13.30 and 16.00. Less frequent sailings in winter or bad weather. Call for current fares.

By air
You will have to charter your own plane as there are no scheduled flights to this coast. For a scenic flight, try Freycinet Air (109 Friendly Beaches Road, Friendly Beaches, TAS 7215; tel: 6375 1694) and see *Scenic flights* in *Specialist Tour Operators* section of *Chapter 2*.

TASMAN AND FORESTIER PENINSULAS
The main centres are Eaglehawk Neck, Nubeena and Port Arthur, all with good facilities. Both peninsulas are predominantly eucalyptus woodland with open spaces. The eastern coasts and coastal hinterlands are now protected in the Tasman National Park which features rare geological structures and handsome cliffs. The region is easily accessible and popular with tourists, with accommodation widespread.

Where to stay and eat
Convict Station Historic B&B (RMB 956 Arthur Highway, Taranna, TAS 7180; tel/fax: 6250 3487; email: evans@convictstation.com; web: www.convictstation.com) gets the top Bradt seal of approval for accommodation on the Tasman Peninsula and for the whole of Tasmania. It is run superbly by Dorothy and Michael Evans, two British botanists who have travelled the world. There is an 'almost organic' garden, Dorothy pots her own jams and marmalades and the place is licensed to sell beer and wines. The breakfasts are huge. The lounge has a log fire, all rooms are welcoming and some have glorious views over Little Norfolk Bay. Dorothy was also a museum interpreter and is responsible for the intricate and engaging exhibit at the Port Arthur Historical Site (see page 255). Michael is a guide at the site.

With the commencement of Port Arthur as a prison, supplies were needed, and, to save ships negotiating the wild seas off Cape Raoul south of the peninsula, it was decided to use the much calmer waters of Norfolk Bay. From here goods were hauled, by convicts of course, along a tramway to the prison. The house was built at the landing point as a commissariat clerk's residence and store, and after the closure of Port Arthur it became a post office attached. When renovating, Dorothy and Mike found a convict's navy blue jacket lying between the rafters in the ceiling. The jacket read PA798 and now hangs in the museum but they have kept a replica to show guests. PA798's fate is a mystery but he could have escaped by changing into a sailor's outfit here in the house and secretly joining the crew on a supply ship back to Hobart, and freedom. Rates on enquiry.

For a budget option in Taranna, try **Teraki Cottages** (RA19 Nubeena Road, Taranna, TAS 7172; tel: 6250 3436; fax: 6250 3736) which offers basic, self-contained cottages with log fires and provisions for cooked breakfast. $60, single and double. No credit cards.

At Port Arthur township there is a host of accommodation.

The **Fox and Hounds Inn** (Arthur Highway, Port Arthur, TAS 7182; tel: 6250 2217; fax: 6250 2590; email: info@foxtas.com; web: www.foxtas.com) has apartments for $111–155, single and double, and en-suite rooms for $95–137, single and double. Packages available, including entry to Historical Site or Ghost Tours.

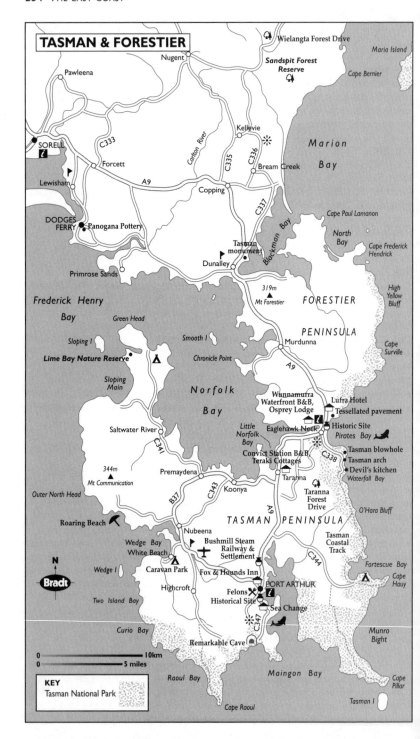

TASMAN & FORESTIER

Wielangta Forest Drive

Sandspit Forest Reserve

Maria Island

Cape Bernier

Nugent

Pawleena

Kellevie

Marion Bay

SORELL

C333

Forcett

C335

C336

Bream Creek

A9

Copping

C337

Cape Paul Lamanon

North Bay

Cape Frederick Hendrick

Lewisham

DODGES FERRY

Panogana Pottery

Blackman Bay

Tasman monument

Dunalley

Primrose Sands

319m ▲ Mt Forestier

FORESTIER

High Yellow Bluff

Frederick Henry Bay

Green Head

Sloping I

Lime Bay Nature Reserve

Smooth I

Chronicle Point

Murdunna

PENINSULA

Cape Surville

A9

Sloping Main

Norfolk Bay

Wunnamurra Waterfront B&B, Osprey Lodge

Lufra Hotel

Tessellated pavement

Saltwater River

Little Norfolk Bay

Eaglehawk Neck

Historic Site

Pirates Bay

● Tasman blowhole

Convict Station B&B, Teraki Cottages

C338

C341

344m ▲ Mt Communication

Premaydena

Taranna

● Tasman arch

● Devil's kitchen

Waterfall Bay

Outer North Head

B37

C343

Koonya

Taranna Forest Drive

O'Hara Bluff

Roaring Beach

TASMAN PENINSULA

A9

Tasman Coastal Track

Nubeena

Bushmill Steam Railway & Settlement

C344

Fortescue Bay

Wedge Bay White Beach

Caravan Park

Fox & Hounds Inn

PORT ARTHUR

Cape Hauy

Wedge I

Felons Historical Site

Highcroft

Sea Change

C347

Two Island Bay

Curio Bay

Munro Bight

Remarkable Cave

0 ——— 10km
0 ——— 5 miles

Raoul Bay

Maingon Bay

Cape Pillar

Tasman I

Cape Raoul

KEY
Tasman National Park

About 4km south of Port Arthur, try **Sea Change** (425 Safety Cove Road, Port Arthur, TAS 7182; tel: 6250 2719; mobile: 0438 502 719; fax: 6250 2115; email: bookings@safetycove.com; web: www.safetycove.com) for B&B and self-contained accommodation. Apartment $104–114/$128–140, single/double; standard room $84–100/$108–124, single/double.

At Nubeena, try the **Fairway Resort** (1583 Nubeena Road, Nubeena, TAS 7184; tel: 6250 2171; fax: 6250 2605; email: info@fariwayresort.com; web: www.fairwayresort.com) which has apartments for $132–140, single and double, studio apartments for $102, single and double, and en-suite rooms for $94, single and double.

The **White Beach Caravan Park** (White Beach Road, Nubeena, TAS 7184; tel: 6250 2142; fax: 6250 2575; email: wbcp@southcom.com.au; web: www.whitebeachcp.com.au) is in an idyllic spot on a sheltered bay. Tent site $14–16, single and double; serviced site $16–18, single and double; on-site van $35–65, single and double; cabin $70–110, single and double.

The best food in the Port Arthur region is probably at **Felons** at Port Arthur Historical Site (tel: 1800 659 101 or 6251 2314). The venison and stout pie ($22) is great and the seafood is fresh and reasonable (fish of the day $21). In season (spring) the crayfish is worth a try. Open daily 17.00–20.30. Closed Christmas Day.

At Eaglehawk Neck, try the spacious and stylish **Osprey Lodge B&B** (14 Osprey Road, Eaglehawk Neck, TAS 7179; tel: 6250 3629; fax: 6250 3031; email: osprey@southcom.com.au; web: www.view.com.au/osprey), which is a modern lodge with big windows and cedar panelling and tremendous views over Pirates Bay. $150–180 per couple. BBQ ingredients provided. Won a special guests' award in 2001 tourism awards.

On the same road is **Wunnamurra Waterfront B&B** (21 Osprey Road, Eaglehawk Neck, TAS 7179; tel/fax: 6250 3145; mobile: 0407 502 931; email: wunn.eaglehawk@blightanner.com.au), which is another delightful property. En-suite $80–110/$100–120, single/double.

The **Lufra Hotel** (Pirates Bay Drive, Eaglehawk Neck, TAS 7179; tel: 6250 3262; fax: 6250 3460; email: gwpcon@bigpond.com.au) is above the Tessellated Pavement and has good views over Pirates Bay. En-suite room $61/77, single/double.

What to see and do

The **Port Arthur Historical Site** (Port Arthur, TAS 7182; tel: 1800 659 101 or 6251 2310; fax: 6251 2311; email: bookings@portarthur.org.au; web: www.portarthur. org.au) is a must-see, mainly for the superb exhibition created by gallery interpreter Dorothy Evans. Your ticket gets you into the exhibition and around the spacious grounds to walk through the old stone cells of the main prison block and visit the other preserved buildings. As you enter you are given a playing card that relates to a real convict who was shipped to Port Arthur from Britain or Ireland, and for the next hour or two you become that character, learning of their crime (sometimes as petty as stealing vegetables from a garden), their ludicrous court trial, and their long and arduous journey to this distant and horrible place. There are leg irons to try on and lots of easily digested information. It is a splendid exhibit, worth every cent. Convicts were incarcerated here between 1830 and 1877, in wooden cells at first, and later in ones of stone which must have been even colder. You walk through the ruined prison block on wooden platforms and staircases getting a real feel for the sadness of the place. Prisoners worked long hours timber milling, shipbuilding, coal mining, and making bricks, nails, furniture and shoes. Adult $19.80; pensioners/senior citizens $15.80; student $15.80 (over 18 years); child (4 to 17 years) $9; family $43 (2 adults, up to 6 children). Open daily 08.30–17.00 restored buildings, 08.30–dusk historic site.

Tasmanian Seaplanes (tel: 6227 8808; fax: 6227 9721; email: scenic@tas-seaplane.com; web: www.tas-seaplane.com) have a base here and can fly you back to Hobart.

There is also a **ghost tour**. A guide leads the way with a lantern and tells chilling stories of apparitions and strange occurrences that have happened here. Adult $14.30; child (4 to 17 years) $8.80; child (4 and under) free; family $37.40 (2 adults and up to 6 children).

📸 Photo spot

Best angle is from over near the seaplane stand at the north end of the small bay, looking across the grass to the old prison building. In spring and autumn, come late in the day when the gloom is gathering to make it spooky and there are fewer tourists to spoil the shot. To brighten the scene, try shooting at lunchtime when the sun (in the north) warms up the sandstone of the buildings. Try to push the main prison block over to the right or left of your viewfinder rather than have it in the middle – it gives the picture a bit more interest and your picture will look less like a postcard. Wide-angle lens best here to get the wide scene in.

The **Bush Mill Steam Railway and Settlement** (Arthur Highway, Port Arthur, TAS 7182; tel: 6250 2221; fax: 6250 2344; email: info@bushmill.com.au; web: www.bushmill.com.au) is also fun for families. There is a working steam-powered sawmill, a working blacksmiths' shop, a convict saw pit, a bush camp, mill manager's cottage and a country store. Seven times a day the train leaves the station for a 4-kilometre steam-train ride on the 15-inch gauge track down the steep gully to the Fox and Hounds resort, then back up the incline. Adult $15; concession $12.50; child (2 to 16 years) $6.50; family $38. Includes train ride. Open daily 09.00–17.00 (July and August 10.00–16.00). Closed Saturday for maintenance in winter, Christmas Day.

Eaglehawk Neck Historic Site is the wafer-thin isthmus that joins Tasman Peninsula to Forestier Peninsula and the main island. There is a good information centre here at The Officer's Mess in Pirates Bay (tel: 6250 3635; fax: 6250 3637). You can walk through the original officers' quarters and walk the site of the Dog Line. If any convicts did manage to slip their leg irons and flee Port Arthur they had two choices: swim for it in icy waters patrolled by sharks or try to make it over the Neck. To make sure none made it by land, the authorities put a line of guard dogs tied by chains to barrels and allowed just enough movement to cover the width of the isthmus. Armed guards stood behind them. Apparently one bright spark who had escaped the prison killed and gutted a kangaroo, crawled inside its skin and proceeded to hop along the beach little knowing the guards used kangaroos as target practice. The whole exhibition at the Neck is free and there is a general store and restaurant, the Drunken Admiral (tel: 6234 1903). Open daily from 18.00.

On your way through Dodges Ferry have a quick look at **Panogana Pottery** (8 Payeena Street; tel: 6265 8481; fax: 6265 9310; email: panogana@yahoo.com; web: www.panogana.com), Tasmania's largest production workshop, producing distinctive, functional stoneware. Custom dinner services a speciality. Open Monday–Friday 09.00–17.00 (lunch 13.00–14.00), by appointment on weekends and public holidays. And in Dunalley check out **Potters Croft** (Arthur Highway; tel: 6253 5469; mobile: 0408 120 979; fax: 6253 5651; email: bholmes@southcom.com.au) for weaving, wood, silk and jewellery. There is also a teashop. Open Sunday–Friday 10.00–18.00. Closed Monday, Tuesday in July and August, Christmas Day.

Further information

From the Port Arthur and Tasman Region Marketing Limited (tel: 6251 2371) and from travel and information centres at Port Arthur (tel: 6251 2329; email:

portarth@tasvisinfo.com.au) and Eaglehawk Neck (tel: 6250 3722; email: eaglehawk@tasvisinfo.com.au).

TASMAN NATIONAL PARK

This park (tel: 6250 3497) covers 8,312 hectares and is the latest addition to Tasmania's wealth of protected areas, being declared a park in 1999. It includes the southwest tip of the Tasman Peninsula (Cape Raoul, Mount Brown, Remarkable Cave and Point Puer to Briggs Point) and the southeast tip (Cape Pillar, Tasman Island and the Abel Tasman Forest Reserve). The protected area also runs up the east coast almost to Eaglehawk Neck and continues north of the isthmus running up the coast almost to Cape Frederick Hendrick.

The area is noted for its dramatic organ-pipe formations rising from the waves. They are some of Australia's highest cliffs at 300m. The park includes unique coastal landforms created by millennia of erosions such as the Blowhole, Tasman Arch and the Devils Kitchen. All these can be seen from vantage points along the C338, but the car-parks get busy in summer and the cliffs here are wearing away so stay back from the edge. One other formation to mention which is just outside the park is a brilliant example of a tessellated pavement just north of Eaglehawk Neck. You can walk down a wooden ramp way and out over the pavement at low tide and there are signs that explain the complicated chemical and physical processes that have formed it and that are changing it daily.

Like South Bruny National Park, the vegetation of Tasman mainly consists of shoreline communities, heathlands, eucalyptus forest and rainforest in sheltered gullies. There are pademelons, potoroos, wallabies, wombats, brush-tail and ring-tail possums and Tasmanian devils. The coast is superb for watching southern right and humpback whales and dolphins.

Photo spot

The tessellated pavement is superb. It is best to walk along it at low tide to the southern end and shoot towards the northeast (out to sea) but this will have to be in the afternoon on a bright day when the sun has passed behind the trees and the low cliff (so the shot is not silhouetted). Make sure the pavement fills at least half the frame, its pools reflecting the clouds. 50mm lens best but 28mm wide-angle also good to get lots of the pavement in.

Activities in Tasman National Park

There are several short, day and long-distance walks in the park and around its borders. If you need a guide, contact Ruth Brozek (Tasman Nature Guiding, 70 Old Jetty Road, Eaglehawk Neck, TAS 7179; tel: 6250 3268; email: brozek@southcom.com.au) who comes highly recommended. Her tours are suitable for all ages and abilities (one has wheelchair access) and are leisurely. Groups of seven or less so book early. Or you can stride off under your own steam.

Sea kayaking

The kayaking is wonderful around the peninsula but it is best to go with a guide unless you are an experienced sea kayaker as the seas can be big here and tidal surges around the base of those giant cliffs can get novices into trouble. For operators, see *Specialist Tour Operators* in *Chapter 2*.

Diving

These waters offer some of the best temperate diving in Australia. There are several excellent wrecks to dive, mainly thanks to the reef around the Hippolyte Rocks that has claimed so many boats. A favourite is the *Nord* which went down with a boat-load of benzine on November 7 1915. The hull now lies upright on the sea bed about 35–40 metres down. It has held together remarkably well. Try **Eaglehawk Dive Centre** (178 Pirates Bay Drive, Eaglehawk Neck, TAS 7179; tel: 6250 3566; mobile: 0417 013 518; fax: 6265 2251; email: info@eaglehawkdive.com.au; web: www.eaglehawkdive.com.au) who dive the *Nord* as well as a host of other locations in the area. Sisters Rocks are rock columns at 40m with huge shoals of butterfly perch and long-finned pike, Waterfall Bay caves and canyons are spectacular underwater caverns, and the Hippolyte Rocks themselves support a small seal colony. If you are a beginner or a novice diver talk with the dive team first to see which dives are appropriate.

Short walks
Devils Kitchen to Waterfall Bay
Distance: 4km return. Time: 2 hours return. Difficulty: easy.
Take A9 Arthur Highway to Eaglehawk Neck then turn left and follow signs to Devils Kitchen car-park. Track starts here and heads south, with good views along the cliffs. You should see caves and a magnificent arch cut by the waves. Towards Waterfall Bay the cliffs rise and there are more views over to Clemes Peak. Retrace your steps to return.

To Canoe Bay
Distance: 4km return. Time: 2 hours return. Difficulty: easy.
Drive through the pretty town of Taranna on the shores of Little Norfolk Bay and about 5km beyond the junction with the B37 turn left on to the C344 and follow signs to Fortescue Bay (12km on). The beach here is beautiful and the walk begins with a stroll along it to the north end where you should see signs taking you up to the Tasman Trail (see *Long-distance walks*). Follow the trail for an hour to Canoe Bay as it drops and climbs through shady eucalyptus forest with kookaburras and song birds in the branches. Retrace your steps to Fortescue where there is an attractive campsite.

To Monument Lookout
Distance: 5km return. Time: 2–3 hours return. Difficulty: moderate.
Start from the boat ramp at Fortescue Bay and head east along the coast for about 1km, when the track turns inland and climbs through the forest (it is quite steep here). After about half an hour of steady walking there will be a sign pointing to Monument Lookout which you take. The cliff edge is just a few minutes away and what a cliff edge! Keep a close eye on children and keep back from the lip – there is a vertical drop of more than 200m. You will see The Lanterns rocks off the point and beyond them the Hippolyte Rocks which have claimed numerous ships in the past 200 years. The iron steamship *Tasman* sunk here on November 29 1883. Everyone was saved and washed up on Fortescue Bay.

Long-distance walk
Abel Tasman Trail
Distance: 70km. Time: 5 days. Difficulty: moderate (hard in places).
This relatively new trail covers most of the park's coastline from Eaglehawk Neck right down to Cape Pillar and then continuing further west. It is tougher than it looks and walkers need to take full gear with them. The best guide possible is *Peninsular Tracks* by Peter and Shirley Storey which is available from most good bookshops and from visitor centres on the peninsula itself. It also contains details of more than 30 shorter walks across this beautiful part of Tasmania.

MID-COAST AND MARIA ISLAND

Orford and Triabunna are fishing centres with great vistas over the ocean to the east and over lush farmland and eucalyptus forests looking west. Maria Island National Park is a wildlife haven with grassy meadows and cliffs inhabited by numerous sea birds. Its past is a reminder of the brutality and pain that sculpted Tasmania's modern history. Aborigines from the Oyster Bay tribe fled the island soon after the Europeans began arriving and a harsh penal colony was established here. The remains can be visited.

Where to stay and eat

Orford is the more picturesque place to stay and has easy access to Louisville for the ferry.

The **Shalom Waterfront B&B** (50 Tasman Highway, Orford, TAS 7190; tel: 6257 1175) is quite cosy for a night with three en-suites for $35–45/$60–95, single/double.
The **Blue Waters Hotel Motel** (Tasman Highway, Orford, TAS 7190; tel: 6257 1102; fax: 6257 1621) is fine too, with en-suites for $35–38/$45–50, single/double, and it does evening meals.
The **Eastcoaster Resort** (Louisville Point Road, Orford, TAS 7190; tel: 6257 1172; fax: 6257 1564; email: info@eastcoaster.com.au) at the Maria Island ferry terminal in Louisville is fine for a night if you are popping over to the island for a few days. Apartment $77–88/$87–110, single/double; en-suite room $77–88/$87–110, single/double. Evening meals, heated swimming pool.
Spring Beach Holiday Villas (Rheban Road, Orford, TAS 7190; tel/fax: 6257 1440; email: springbv@southcom.com.au) have two-bedroom villas which sleep up to six, with good sea views to Spring Bay and Maria Island. Apartment $100–130, single and double. There is a tennis court, children's playground and it is only 200 metres to the beach.
On Maria Island the **Penitentiary Units** (Darlington, Maria Island, TAS 7190; tel: 6257 1420; fax: 6257 1482) in the former penal colony at Darlington are much in demand. The accommodation is basic – just bunks and wood-fired heaters in cells – so bring your own bedding, torches/lanterns, camp cooker, food and water. They are run by Parks and Wildlife. There is one dorm for ten people and nine standard rooms that can sleep up to 54 in all. Adult $8 each; child $4.40 each; family/group $22 per room.
The only other accommodation on the island is **camping**. The **Maria Island Campground** (tel: 6257 1420; fax: 6257 1482) is also very popular so book ahead. Adult $4.40 each; children $2.20 each; family/group $11 (up to 6 people); school group $2 each. There are two more sites at Frenchs Farm and Encampment Cove which are a good 4-hour walk from Darlington and are free but have no facilities or water.

What to see and do

A detour from the A3 Tasman Highway south from Orford or north from Copping will take drivers to the **Wielangta Road Forest Drive**. A gravel road winds through one of Forestry Tasmania's oldest production forests. There are great ocean views framed by sentinel blue gums. From the Thumbs Lookout at the Orford end of the drive you can walk through the Sandspit Forest Reserve and picnic at designated spots.

The Wielangta Walk follows the path, a former tramway, to the deserted site of a long-dead timber town. Forestry Tasmania is still logging the Wielangta so watch for log trucks on the road. More information from Forestry Tasmania in Triabunna (tel: 6257 3243; web: www.forestrytas.com.au).

A miniature-golf course is situated at the Eastcoaster Resort by the ferry terminal at **Louisville**. The holes are not that inspiring but it must have the best view of any miniature-golf course in the world – the dazzling waters of the Mercury Passage with Maria Island looming dramatically behind. Watch for the rosellas in the trees by the course. More information from the **Triabunna Visitor Centre** (corner of Esplanade and Charles Street; tel: 6257 4090; fax: 6257 3675).

The **Tasmanian Seafarers Memorial** on Esplanade is dedicated to all Tasmanian seafarers and anyone who has perished in these seas. Plaques are fixed to the top of a low brick wall in the shape of the first Christian symbol, a fish, and the wall is surmounted by an anchor cross.

MARIA ISLAND NATIONAL PARK

The park (tel: 6257 1420) includes the whole island and covers 11,550 hectares. Parks and Wildlife Service took it over as a fauna reserve in 1965 and it was made a national park seven years later. It is beautiful and popular in the summer months. The park is really two islands joined by an isthmus. It is mostly low-altitude climbing to Bishop and Clerk peak at 630m and Mount Maria at 709m, both on the east side of the island. The coastline is made up of pristine beaches, limestone cliffs, rocky reefs and underwater caves. Vegetation is mainly light eucalyptus forest with some pockets of denser rainforest in gullies on higher ground. The fauna reserve must have worked because the island today has healthy populations of Forester kangaroos, Bennett's wallabies and pademelons, wombats, echidnas, pygmy, brush-tail and ring-tail possums, potoroos, eastern swamp and water rats. There are no shops on Maria Island so visitors must be completely self-sufficient. As ever in Tasmania, bring clothes for all four seasons. There is a ranger's office and public pay telephone at the Darlington settlement. Visitors can get maps and notes of the island and its walks from Land Information Bureau offices in Hobart and Launceston. National Park fees apply. No pets.

As well as the land being protected, 1,500 hectares of the waters immediately off the north coast are part of a **marine reserve**. Off Fossil Bay there are numerous rocky reefs, large underwater caverns and underwater forests of giant kelp with some strands growing to 20 metres. There are sandstone reefs at Howells Point and seagrass beds and fish nurseries in Mercury Passage. A detailed map of the perimeters of the marine reserve and a list of conservation care points are available from the Parks and Wildlife offices (see main park number above).

🐚 Photo spot
When diving on a sunny day, try a skyward shot from in among the kelp. Use flash to highlight the orange of the kelp fronds, and a wide-angle lens (28mm).

Activities in the park and reserve
A network of easy walking tracks takes you to Fossil Cliffs, Painted Cliffs and Bishop and Clerk Mountain. Longer hikes lead south to Chinamans Bay and beyond.

Diving
For information about diving the east coast, contact **Dive Tasmania** (mobile: 0417 013518 or web: www.divetasmania.com). Swim and snorkel only with extreme caution as rip tides and swell surges can be strong around the island. Fossil Bay is more protected and good for snorkelling. Check with the ranger if you have doubts. Collecting or harming any living or dead plants, animals or natural material in the marine reserve is prohibited. Fishing is not permitted between Return Point and Cape Boullanger but there are some excellent spots near by. White-painted rock cairns mark the northern boundary (northwest tip of Cape

Boullanger) and the southern extent (Return Point) of the 'no fishing' zone and it extends one kilometre out to sea.

Sea kayaking

Sea kayaking is available through **Freycinet Adventures** (PO Box 226, Coles Bay, TAS 7215; tel: 6257 0500; fax: 6257 0447; email: coastalkayak@vision.net.au; web: www.tasadventures.com). They run a four-day sea kayak tour around the island with side trips to the convict ruins and snorkelling in the marine reserve. Previous kayaking experience required. $890 for four-day tour; transport from Hobart, equipment, food, soft drinks included. Runs November to February. The office is at the corner of Esplanade and Freycinet Drive, Coles Bay.

Short walks
Fossil Cliffs

Distance: 4km. Time: 2 hours return. Difficulty: moderate but with high, open cliffs.
Bicycles allowed on the track. From Fossil Cliffs the view is north to Cape Boullanger and Ile du Nord and southeast to Mount Pedder.

Painted Cliffs

Distance: 4–6km. Time: 2–2½ hours return. Difficulty: moderate grade with no steep sections.
Bicycles allowed on wider road sections but not on beach or foot track. The path follows the island's west coast affording views over Mercury Passage. This can be walked en route to the campsite at Encampment Cove.

Bishop and Clerk

Distance: 8km return. Time: 4 hours return. Difficulty: difficult.
This challenging walk offers exhilarating cliff-top views over the ocean, but it is a struggle for those who are not fit. The path climbs and descends steeply over large boulders to the summit of Bishop and Clerk Mountain (named after two early European explorers). There are also some big cliffs so it is not ideal for children unless they are budding Everest challengers.

The more ambitious can attempt **Mount Maria**, the highest point on the island at 709 metres but it can take 7 hours to get up and back in good weather. On all walks you can see kangaroos, wallabies, pademelons and Cape Barren geese, but also be on the lookout for whales, dolphins, albatross and sea eagles. Aboriginal sites are marked on maps of the island and should be viewed with care. There are some good middens near Hopground and Four Mile Beach.

Beach stops to Swansea

Along the road from Triabunna to Swansea, stop off at the two conservation areas, Boltons Beach and Mayfield Bay. Boltons is down a side-road off the A3 and has a picnic area, while Mayfield is near the main road and has a campsite as well as picnic spot. These are good spots to take a day and do nothing. If you have the time, pitch the tent and just read or bird spot or go for short beach walks.

If you wish to stay the night along this road, **Little Swanport** has **Gumleaves** (Swanston Road, Little Swanport, TAS 7190; tel: 6244 8147; fax: 6244 7560; email: ldjackson@h130.aone.net.au) with self-contained cabins for $100 per double, and cottages and a hostel for $20 each. **Kabuki by the Sea** (Tasman Highway, Swansea, TAS 7190; tel/fax: 6257 8588; email: rockyhills@vision.net.au; web:

www.kabukibythesea.com.au) is an exclusive Japanese hotel and restaurant clinging to the cliff. Its Zen ambience makes it a superbly peaceful spot. Apartment $95/120, single/double. Packages including dinner at the excellent restaurant.

FREYCINET TO ST MARYS

Brilliant white beaches, towering cliffs inhabited by sea eagles, and bays of the purest blue water. In terms of pure natural beauty this is hard to beat. Fortunately visitors can also get to the green heart of the area, bushwalking, camping or staying in luxury lodges with hopping guests peering in at the windows. Freycinet is Tasmania's shop window for nature tourism. This is not a place to be rushed. Four to five days are recommended including a couple of bushwalks, a spot of sea kayaking and some reflective moments beachcombing. While in Bicheno, spare a thought for two Tasmanian heroines. Mary Harvey saved her policeman husband from being beaten to death on a lonely dark road one night by bashing his assailant on the head. She also single-handedly arrested two absconding ne'er-do-wells from a whaling ship. A good restaurant in the town is named after her. Waubedebar, a local Aboriginal woman taken as a slave by sealers, showed immense courage and forgiveness by rescuing two of their sealing fellows from a shipwreck. A grave in the town commemorates her heroism.

Where to stay and eat
Swansea

Most accommodation in Swansea is in the higher price range and books up well in advance before holidays and summer weekends.

The luxurious **Schouten House** (1 Waterloo Road, Swansea, TAS 7190; tel: 6257 8564; fax: 6257 8767; email: schoutenhouse@bigpond.com; web: www.classicallytasmania.com.au) has four en-suite rooms for $120/130, single/double. There are four-poster beds and the owners leave goodies to make a continental breakfast. Their restaurant, Schouten House, is worth trying but popular, so book ahead.

National Trust listed **Meredith House and Mews** (15 Noyes Street, Swansea, TAS 7190; tel: 6257 8119; fax: 6257 8123; email: olbery@vision.net.au; web: www.meredith-house.com) has ten en-suite rooms $110–170/$146–180, single/double. There are evening meals by arrangement in advance, and the house is licensed.

Tubby and Padman's Cottage (20 Franklin Street, Swansea, TAS 7190; tel: 6257 8901; mobile: 0409 624 855; fax: 6257 8902; email: tubby&padman@tassie.net.au) has two suites for $100/$140–155, single/double, and two apartments for $100/$120–135, single/double.

Self-contained **Wagners Cottage** (Tasman Highway, Swansea, TAS 7190; tel: 6257 8494; fax: 6257 8267; email: wagners.cottages@tassie.net.au; web: www.wagnerscottages.com.au) is peaceful and relaxing and has three apartments $112–178, single and double.

Camping and caravaning is good at the **Swansea Cabin and Tourist Park** (north of town on Shaw Street, Swansea, TAS 7190; tel: 6257 8177; fax: 6257 8511; email: enquiries@swansea-holiday.com.au; web: www.swansea-holiday.com.au) with tent sites $8–11/$11–14, single/double and cabins $33–44/$33–55, single/double.

Also the **Swansea-Kenmore Caravan Park** (2 Bridge Street, Swansea, TAS 7190; tel: 6257 8148; fax: 6257 8554; email: kenmore@vision.net.au), with on-site van $38, single and double; cabin $57–68, single and double; serviced site $16–18, single and double.

Freycinet Peninsula

On the Freycinet Peninsula there is the **Freycinet Lodge** (Freycinet National Park, Coles Bay, TAS 7215; tel: 6257 0101; fax: 6257 0278; email: info@freycinetlodge.com.au; web: www.freycinetlodge.com.au) which has won awards for its design and should have received others for the view over Great Oyster Bay. The lodge is inside Freycinet National Park, a bone of contention for some conservationists, but much effort has gone into minimising the effect on the landscape. There are 39 en-suite rooms for $185–248, single and double, and 21 apartments for $232, single and double. There is a restaurant, playground and convention facilities.

North of Coles Bay by 4km, and outside the park, is the stylish **Edge of the Bay** (2308 Main Road, Coles Bay, TAS 7215; tel: 6257 0102; fax: 6257 0437; web: www.edgeofthebay.com.au). The 11 spacious family cottages ($135–137, single and double) sleep up to six and have their own barbecue facilities, sun decks and log fires. The six waterfront suites ($126-166, single and double) have all the modern panache of a big city hotel but with the wild Southern Ocean lapping just feet away from the private deck. The resort is a haven for local wildlife. **The Edge** restaurant is also popular for modern Australian cuisine. All activities are free, including bicycle hire (there is a range from tiny tots' bikes with stabilisers to full-size adult models).

The **Freycinet Experience** (Friendly Beaches, Friendly Beaches, TAS 7215; tel: 6223 7565; fax: 6224 1315; email: walk@freycinet.com.au; web: www.freycinet.com.au) is a four-day wildlife extravaganza which includes a couple of nights in a luxury bush camp and staying at the wonderful Friendly Beaches Lodge. It is expensive (upwards of $1,000 per person) but a marvellous experience. The guides are fun and knowledgeable, the food good and the location unbeatable. Every effort has gone into making sure the impact on the environment is minimised, including staff carrying all waste (including human) out of the park. The lodge has been built back beyond the tree line so it is invisible from the beach. A real treat. See *What to see and do*, page 265, for full details.

A few others to try are **Churinga Farm Cottage** (1474 Coles Bay Road, Coles Bay, TAS 7215; tel: 6257 0190; fax: 6257 0397; email: churinga@tassie.net.au; web: www.view.com.au/churinga), 12km north of Coles Bay with seven self-contained cottages surrounded by bush land for $75–130, single and double; in Coles Bay itself, **Gum Nut Cottage** (50 Freycinet Drive, Coles Bay, TAS 7215; tel/fax: 6257 0320) which has one apartment for $70–95, single and double (the owners also rent out two more places); and **Jessie's Cottage** (7 Esplanade East, Coles Bay, TAS 7215; tel: 6257 0143; email: janelazaroff@hotmail.com), which has two apartments for $90–100/$90–120, single/double.

Bicheno

At Bicheno, try **Mary Harvey's Restaurant** for great oysters, salmon and local Tasmanian game (disabled access and toilet). A two-course meal is about $36 with wine. The owners also keep the excellent B&B next door, the **Old Gaolhouse** (corner of Burgess Street and James Street, Bicheno, TAS 7215; tel: 6375 1430; mobile: 0418 340 766; fax: 6375 1866; email: head.n.home@tassie.net.au; web: www.bichenogaolcottages.com), which is the best in Bicheno and well worth a couple of nights. Hosts Wayne and Gill Homan have taken great care with the fine detail. The provisions left for breakfast are good and plentiful, the rooms well appointed, and there is lots of firewood for chilly nights. The place was built in 1845 and is National Trust listed. Guests can stay in the gaol itself (sleeps a party of four in one double and one twin, in rooms which used to be the magistrate's office and the interview room). The toilet and shower rooms occupy the former cells, the original heavy oak doors and bolts are still there. The gaol and the nearby **Old Schoolhouse** (which is good for a family stay as it has bunks) are both self-contained, as is the **Stables**, a smaller and more intimate detached cottage which would suit a couple. Old Gaolhouse $130, single and double, $180 for four; Old Schoolhouse $130 for two adults, $180 for four, and $160 for a family with two children under 16; Stables $115. The Old Schoolhouse has a wheelchair ramp and some disabled facilities in the bathroom (shower and toilet). All breakfast ingredients are provided in cottages, along with complimentary port.

What to see and do
Swansea
Little Swanport boasts some tremendous beaches which are still relatively undiscovered. You might miss **Spiky Bridge** whizzing along the A3. Heading north, keep an eye out on your left. The bridge dates back to 1843 and was an important piece of early Tasmanian engineering. Convicts spent two months slaving to erect the structure and placing jagged sandstone and granite chunks on end for decoration.

Swansea was the former centre of the Oyster Bay tribe and later became Australia's oldest rural municipality, registered in 1828. It is a popular seaside town with plenty of fishing, surfing and boating. A leisurely morning can be spent on a walking tour of the town, its historical buildings and nearby mutton-bird breeding colony.

There are vineyards with cellar-door tasting at the **Swansea Wine and Wool Centre** at Bark Mill on the Tasman Highway north of town and at **Freycinet Vineyard**, a 30-minute drive north of town.

From Swansea to Freycinet by sea is even more fun than by land (and a lot quicker if you are on a bicycle). A former fishing boat chops across Great Oyster Bay between the months of October and April (tel: 6257 0239). It costs $12 each plus a bike and any baggage. It goes from the tip of Dolphin Sands across the Swan River, and from the other side it is 6km to Coles Bay.

Short walk
Around Swansea
Distance: 5km return. Time: 1 hour return. Difficulty: easy.

Begin at the Great Short Walks 'W' sign in the centre of town and follow the path along the coast past stunning scenery and through a mutton-bird breeding area. Birds can be seen at dusk in the summer months when they return to their burrows after feeding at sea during the day. In order to protect breeding mutton-birds, dogs are not permitted between dusk and dawn between September 15 and April 15. Keep dogs on leashes at all times. Then relax on Jubilee, Waterloo and Schouten House beaches for the rest of the day.

FREYCINET PENINSULA
This magical area could occupy the mind and body for at least a week. Most roads in Freycinet National Park are unsealed but mainly fine for two-wheel drives. Bush and beach walking, fishing, snorkelling, sea kayaking and rock climbing are favourite pastimes.

FREYCINET NATIONAL PARK
The park (tel: 6257 0107) covers 11,930 hectares and includes Schouten Island. Its spotless white beaches are its trademark, washed by brilliant blue water and overlooked by granite mountains, the highest being Mount Freycinet at 620 metres. Vegetation includes wetlands, heaths, coastal dunes and dry eucalyptus forest. The peninsula has many wild orchids that bloom throughout the year. Humpback, southern right and pilot whales can all be seen between May and August. Watch out for seals at Ile Des Phoques (small rocks off the peninsula), and also look out for dolphins, penguins and sea eagles.

The Oyster Bay tribe occupied this area, numbering about 700 in the 19th century. The local band was the Toorernomairremener and they left numerous shell middens along this coastline. Abel Tasman named Schouten on his famous 1642 expedition in which he was the first European to see Tasmania. This coast ran red with blood at the height of the whaling and sealing boom in the 1800s.

In 1905 the peninsula and Schouten Island were declared game reserves and 11 years later the former became Freycinet National Park. Schouten was added in 1977, and the coast including the Friendly Beaches not until 1992.

Activities in Freycinet National Park
Scenic drives
Take the 6.4km road to Cape Tourville from the main road just after the Freycinet Lodge. The road is unsealed and rough in places but there are sweeping views along the coast from the lookout at the road's end. Reach the Friendly Beaches by taking the turn-off on the Coles Bay Road. There are gravel roads leading to car-parks overlooking the beaches. Basic camping is allowed at Isaacs Point and Ridge Camp but there is no fresh water.

On the water
Sea kayak tours explore the coastline of the peninsula and Schouten Island.

Freycinet Adventures (tel: 6257 0500, mobile: 0419 321 896; fax: 6257 0447; email: coastalkayak@vision.net.au; web: www.tasadventures.com) run one-, three- and five-day kayak tours around Freycinet coast and Schouten Island, observing Aboriginal middens, walking to Wineglass Bay and spending nights at wilderness camps. Rates on enquiry. This same company also organises rock climbing and abseiling tours in the park.

Aardvark Adventures (tel/fax: 6249 4098; mobile: 0408 127714; email: aardvark@tasadventures.com) also offers a full complement of adventure trips and tours in Freycinet.

The best spots for **snorkelling and diving** are the more sheltered bays on the western side of the peninsula where the swell is lower. Sleepy Bay is a great place for those with a bit of experience, while Honeymoon Bay is safer for beginners and children. There are spectacular rock pools at both spots and at Ranger Creek. For the more experienced, the eastern coasts offer kelp forests. Whales and dolphins are common in winter and wetsuits required all year. Tidal surge can be big so seek advice from experts at **Dive Tasmania** (mobile: 0417 013518; web: www.divetasmania.com).

Fishing is by charter. Try Rob and Ann Stevenson at **Roban Coastal Charter** (tel: 6376 3631; mobile: 0407 134031). Boat can carry four passengers and two crew, and costs from $66 per hour, including equipment, and morning and afternoon tea. Crew will clean and pack catch for guests.

Other
The Freycinet Experience (Friendly Beaches, TAS 7215; tel: 6223 7565; fax: 6224 1315; email: walk@freycinet.com.au; web: www.freycinet.com.au)is the ultimate in luxury adventure on the peninsula.

Day one Guests are bussed from Hobart to Coles Bay and taken by boat to the southernmost tip of the peninsula and around Schouten Island. There are sometimes whales and dolphins in the bay (especially in winter) and sea eagles nest on the cliffs. After lunch, and a short, easy walk, there is a spot of fishing to catch supper. Camp that night is an hour's hike from the boat.

Day two 12km coastal stroll or tougher trek over Mount Graham, arriving at an eco-camp in Bluestone Bay for the night. The camp is only there for six months of the year and is fully removed from the park (including all human waste) every autumn.

Day three 9km cliff-top walk from Bluestone Bay to the beautiful Friendly Beaches and a night at self-contained Friendly Beaches Lodge, the first tourism venture in Tasmania to win a national architectural award.

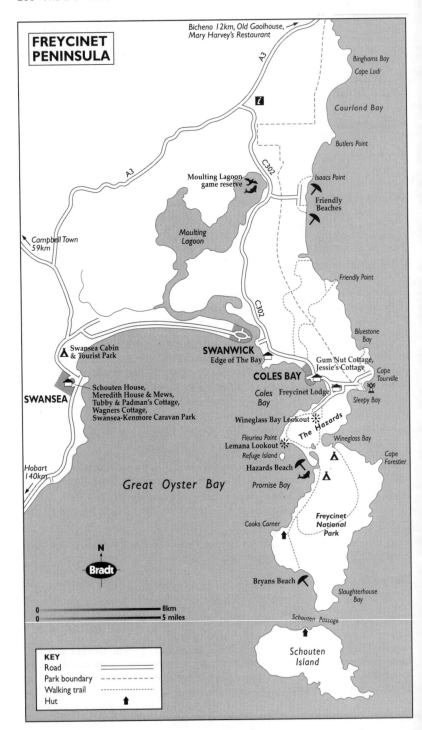

**FREYCINET
PENINSULA**

Bicheno 12km, Old Gaolhouse,
Mary Harvey's Restaurant

A3

Binghams Bay

Cape Lodi

Courland Bay

Butlers Point

C302

Moulting Lagoon
game reserve

Isaacs Point

Friendly
Beaches

*Moulting
Lagoon*

Campbell Town
59km

Friendly Point

C302

*Bluestone
Bay*

Swansea Cabin
& Tourist Park

SWANWICK
Edge of The Bay

Gum Nut Cottage,
Jessie's Cottage

*Cape
Tourville*

COLES BAY

Schouten House,
Meredith House & Mews,
Tubby & Padman's Cottage,
Wagners Cottage,
Swansea-Kenmore Caravan Park

*Coles
Bay*

Freycinet Lodge

Sleepy Bay

SWANSEA

Wineglass Bay Lookout

The Hazards

Hobart
140km

Fleurieu Point
Lemana Lookout
Refuge Island

Hazards Beach

Wineglass Bay

*Cape
Forestier*

Great Oyster Bay

Promise Bay

*Freycinet
National
Park*

Cooks Corner

N

Bradt

Bryans Beach

*Slaughterhouse
Bay*

0   8km
0   5 miles

Schouten Passage

*Schouten
Island*

KEY
Road
Park boundary
Walking trail
Hut

Day four Beach or bush walks for bird spotting and wildlife tracking, transfers to Hobart. Guests must adhere to strict environmental guidelines, even brushing their teeth into a bucket that is later carried out of the park and disposed of soundly.

All Aboriginal sites are carefully preserved and taking rocks and shells from such areas forbidden. Two experienced and knowledgeable guides are with the group for safety, environmental awareness and to point out rare flora and fauna.

Tasmanian Expeditions (110 George Street, Launceston, TAS 7250; tel: 6334 3477 or 6334 0427; fax: 6334 3463; email: info@tas-ex.com; web: www.tas-ex.com) also run a **Freycinet Walking Tour** exploring the national park and the Douglas Apsley National Park near by. It includes scaling Mount Amos and visiting Wineglass Bay and Hazards Beach. At Douglas Apsley, guests will walk through groves of Oyster Bay pines, past sheer cliffs and a rock pool fed by waterfalls. The walking is easy and suitable for bush novices. $495 per person (includes experienced guides, two nights' cabin accommodation, group equipment, wet-weather gear, meals, park fees, transfers from Launceston).

Short walks
Wineglass Bay
Distance: 6km return. Time: 3 hours return. Difficulty: moderate.
From the A3, take the C302 to Wineglass Bay car-park in Freycinet National Park (toilets and picnic facilities). First section steep and difficult in places with rough bush steps. At the pass, turn left for the Lookout and one of Tasmania's most stunning and famous vistas, looking down on Wineglass Bay. The reason for its name becomes instantly obvious. Then head on via a moderate-grade path to the bay for lunch and a swim in pure turquoise waters. Safe swimming but watch children. Take water and food.

Shorter option Just do the lookout then head back to the main car-park (takes a leisurely 1½ hours).

Longer option From Wineglass Bay, continue across the isthmus to Hazards Beach (give yourself a total of 3½ hours return for the whole walk. Return the same way. Beaches are not patrolled so swim with caution.

Friendly Beaches
Take a ½-hour stroll or a 6-hour hike along one of Australia's most pristine beaches. From the A3, take the C302 and turn off to Friendly Beaches. There are bush toilets near the car-park. The walking is easy but the beach is not patrolled. Tempting as it may be, it is advised that people do not swim. The water is perishing for much of the year and there are rips.

Sleepy Bay
Distance: 1km return. Time: 40 minutes return. Difficulty: easy
Drive to the signposted turn-off to the left, just past Freycinet Lodge. Stop at Sleepy Bay car-park. Gently graded steps lead to the rocky shoreline of Sleepy Bay, which can be rough. Then go on up the track leading to the right. This provides beautiful coastal views before a steep descent to this delightful cove. While the track is easy to follow, it is rough underfoot in places and passes close to some high cliff tops.

Long-distance walks
The favourite walk is the Hazards Beach/Cooks Beach/Wineglass Bay circuit which takes a leisurely three or four days, depending on whether you can drag

yourself away from the beaches. Campsites are situated at Wineglass Bay, Hazards, Cooks and Bryans beaches. Water is normally available in water tanks at Cooks Beach and in Jimmys Creek between Mount Graham and Cooks Beach. Less reliable sources can also be found in Laguna Creek at Hazards Beach and where the track crosses the top of Grahams Creek. There is no water at Wineglass Bay or Bryans Beach. Please check with the ranger regarding water availability before commencing overnight trips. Full details and maps for this long-distance walk are available from the park authorities (number above).

📷 Photo spot
Wineglass Bay must be the most photographed beach on the east coast so you are probably better off buying a postcard. However, a good shot is with a 28mm wide-angle lens from the Wineglass Bay Lookout. You will get in a fabulous vista with the beach in the bottom quarter, Great Oyster Bay beyond and the eucalyptus slopes to your right. If there is a boat moored in the bay, try a long lens (100–300mm) to foreshorten everything else and keep the boat centre-frame.

Bicheno
This lovely little town is seen as Freycinet's poor relation but in fact it is remarkably scenic and there is lots to do. It is the best place on the east coast to see fairy penguins. **Bicheno Penguin and Adventure Tours** (Tasman Highway, Bicheno, TAS 7215; tel: 6375 1333; fax: 6375 1533) can get you to the thick of the action on their nightly tours that leave from the information centre or your accommodation. Adult $15; child (4–14 years) $7; child (1–4 years) $3. The company also organises day tours to Freycinet, glass-bottom boat trips to Governor Island Marine Reserve, fishing trips, short flights and a nocturnal wildlife discovery tour. Rates on enquiry.

Divers can explore up to 30 dive sites in the Bicheno area, mainly in the 60-hectare Governor Island Marine Reserve just beyond The Gulch. There are unusual rock faces and vast caverns housing invertebrates such as seawhips, seafans and yellow zooanthids. Other areas sport huge granite boulders 23 metres down on the sea floor which lean against each other to create swim-throughs, undercuts and drop-offs. There are giant kelp forests here too. In winter, whales and dolphins are common. **Dive Tasmania** (mobile: 0417 013518; web: www.divetasmania.com) has full details on diving packages and rates.

In Bicheno check out the **Crohill Gallery** (60 Burgess Street; tel: 6375 1535; fax: 6375 1070; email: dstronac@tassie.net.au) which is one of the largest galleries in Tasmania and features exhibitions by leading local artists and craftspeople. Open daily. Closed Christmas Day, Good Friday.

DOUGLAS APSLEY NATIONAL PARK
The park (tel: 6257 0107) covers 16,080 hectares and is one of least visited in Tasmania. It combines rugged river gorges, waterfalls and tranquil pools with large stands of dry eucalyptus forest. In fact this park has the last large undisturbed area of dry sclerophyll forest in the state. There are large stands of Oyster Bay pine, Barbers gum, the very rare South Esk pine and a newly described heath – *Epacris apsleyonis*.

You are unlikely to see the rare Tasmanian grayling, a silvery fish that only lives here, but there are some about. More likely will be sightings of Bennett's wallabies, pademelons, long-nosed potoroos, Tasmanian devils, bandicoots, bettongs, eastern quolls and possums. There are an estimated 65 species of bird here and the park is good for bats too. All three species of snake exist too so watch your step.

There is a no-frills campground at the Apsley Waterhole (follow signs from A3 north of Bicheno). On hot summer days the waterhole is perfect for a swim. There is a short walk to a lookout (wheelchair access) and another longer return trek up the Apsley Gorge. Roads into the Douglas Apsley National Park are gravel and can get badly corrugated after rare spells of wet weather. Two-wheel drives are fine but care is advised.

In the north of the park there is a day return walk to Heritage Falls where a campsite is located. Long-distance walking is via the Leeaberra Track (three days) which takes hikers north to south through the park. For details on Leeaberra Track and other long-distance walks, contact the park direct. Douglas Apsley was designated a park in 1989.

For a tour including this park, see Tasmanian Expeditions' Freycinet Walking Tour (see page 267).

📷 Photo spot

The swimming pools in Douglas Apsley make lovely family shots if you have children playing in the water or even picnicking by it. 50mm lens fine.

Thylacine

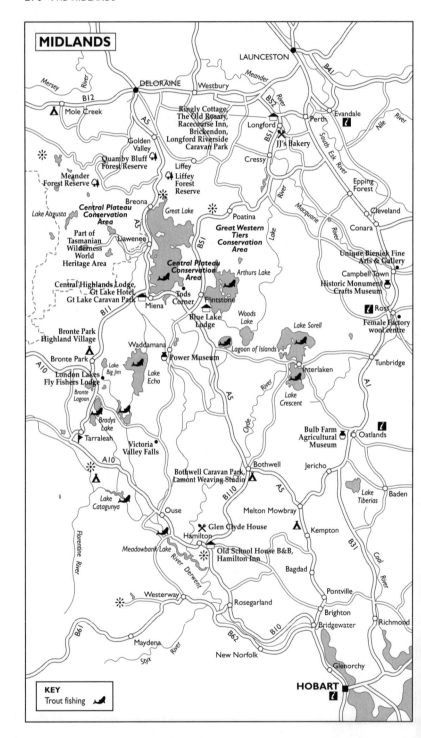

MIDLANDS

LAUNCESTON

DELORAINE
Westbury

Mersey River
B12
Mole Creek

Meander River
BA1
B52
Perth
Evandale
Longford
Nile River

Golden Valley

Ringly Cottage,
The Old Rosary,
Racecourse Inn,
Brickendon,
Longford Riverside
Caravan Park

JJ's Bakery

South Esk River

Quamby Bluff
Forest Reserve
Liffey
Cressy

Meander
Forest Reserve
Liffey
Forest
Reserve

Epping
Forest

Breona
Great Lake
Poatina
Cleveland

Lake Augusta

Central Plateau
Conservation
Area

Great Western
Tiers
Conservation
Area

Macquarie River
Conara

Part of
Tasmanian
Wilderness
World
Heritage Area

Liawenee

Lake River

Unique Bieniek Fine
Arts & Gallery

Campbell Town

Central Plateau
Conservation
Area

Arthurs Lake

Historic Monument
Crafts Museum

Central Highlands Lodge,
Gt Lake Hotel
Gt Lake Caravan Park

Tods
Corner

Flintstone

Woods
Lake

Ross

Female Factory
wool centre

Miena

Blue Lake
Lodge

Lake Sorell

Bronte Park
Highland Village

Waddamana

Power Museum

Lagoon of Islands

Tunbridge

Bronte Park

London Lakes
Fly Fishers Lodge

Lake
Big Jim

Lake
Echo

Interlaken

A1

Bronte
Lagoon

A10

Bradys
Lake

Tarraleah

Victoria
Valley Falls

Lake
Crescent

Clyde River

Bulb Farm
Agricultural
Museum

Oatlands

Lake
Catagunya

Ouse

Bothwell Caravan Park,
Lamont Weaving Studio

B110

Bothwell

A5

Jericho

Baden

Lake
Tiberias

Melton Mowbray

Florentine River

Glen Clyde House
Hamilton

Kempton

B31

Coal River

Meadowbank Lake

Old School House B&B,
Hamilton Inn

Bagdad

River Derwent

Westerway

Rosegarland

Pontville

Brighton

Richmond

B61

B62

Maydena

River Styx

New Norfolk

B10

Bridgewater

Glenorchy

HOBART

KEY
Trout fishing

14

The Midlands

Tasmania's central region lies between the A10 and the Walls of Jerusalem National Park in the south and west, the A1 in the east and the Great Western Tiers in the north. The land consists of a high plateau in the west and rolling open bushland further east. This region is not renowned for as great a variety of wildlife as elsewhere and it receives a smaller entry in our guide. However, it is one of the most important heritage areas of the state and contains some fantastic fishing opportunities.

GETTING THERE AND AROUND
Many places in the Midlands region are not well served by public transport so having your own vehicle here will make things a lot easier (check bus companies in *Chapter 2, Getting Around*). Also, as the land is flatter, it is good bicycle country.

WHERE TO STAY AND EAT
There are some excellent fishing lodges in the lakes area of the Central Plateau, all in beautiful wild settings and with good food. The towns along the A1 Midland Highway offer plenty of National Trust heritage homes to spend the night.

Lodges
Three of the best are:

London Lakes Fly Fishers Lodge (c/o PO Bronte Park, Bronte Park, TAS 7140; tel: 6289 1159; fax: 6289 1122; email: garrett@londonlakes.com.au; web: www.londonlakes.com.au) takes ten guests at a time in five twin-bedded en-suite rooms and offers fly-fishing only on a 5,000-acre private estate. The food is excellent and there are lessons available. It is run by Jason and Barbara Garrett. Jason has represented Australia in six fly-fishing world championships. The lodge offers a number of packages, from guided stays, including all tackle, to fishing and hunting trips. Rates on enquiry.

Blue Lake Lodge (Arthurs Lake Rd, Arthurs Lake, TAS 7030; tel: 6259 8030; fax: 6259 8031; email: highland.fly@tassie.net.au) is on the shores of Arthurs Lake, a reliable fly-fishing lake and one of Tasmania's most prolific wild trout fisheries. It offers modern, relaxed and comfortable lakeside living. Blue Lake Lodge is situated on 100 acres of native bush land with wallabies, wombats, echidnas, fallow deer, possums and devils, and numerous bird species. Accommodation and guided fishing packages available. Rates on enquiry.

Central Highlands Lodge (Haddens Bay, Miena, TAS 7030; tel: 6259 8179; mobile: 0411 800 607; fax: 6259 8351; email: chl@tassie.net.au) is on the shores of the Great Lake and is close to the famous fisheries of the Western Lakes, Arthurs Lake, Penstock Lagoon and Little Pine Lagoon, all of which contain an abundance of wild brown trout. It is open during the fishing season from August 1 to the end of April. All equipment and professional guides can be hired. The lodge has its own 81-hectare private lake, full of wild brown trout. Rates on enquiry.

You could also try the **Great Lake Hotel** (Swan Bay, Miena, TAS 7030; tel: 6259 8163; fax: 6259 8147) for a more reasonably priced stay. It is on the shores of Great Lake and has en-suite rooms and self-catering units. The hotel has information about trout-fishing tours, guides and the mayfly waters. $77–110, double.

There are campsites at caravan parks at Miena (**Great Lake Caravan Park**, Swan Bay Miena, TAS 7030; tel: 6259 8163; fax: 6259 8147; rates on enquiry), Bronte Park (**Bronte Park Highland Village**, 378 Marlborough Highway, Bronte Park, TAS 7140; tel: 6289 1126; mobile: 0419 105 443; fax: 6289 1109; email: bronte@netspace.net.au; with campsites $12, serviced site $14, and standard rooms in cabins $20–25, all single and double) and Bothwell (**Bothwell Caravan Park**, Market Place, Bothwell, TAS 7030; tel: 6259 5503; fax: 6259 5722), and camping only with facilities at Interlaken between Lake Sorell and Lake Crescent.

Heritage stays
Longford

In **Longford**, south of Launceston, try the **Racecourse Inn** (114 Marlborough Street, Longford, TAS 7301; tel: 6391 2352; fax: 6391 2430; email: innbaker@vision.net.au; web: www.racecourseinn.com), a brick building with climbing roses built by convicts in 1840. This racecourse is the oldest continuously operating track in Australia. The inn is classified by the National Trust and on the register of the National Estate, is only 20 minutes from Launceston airport and has 5 en-suite rooms for $105–165/$132–165, single/double.

Ringley Cottage (16–18 Union Street, Longford, TAS 7301; tel: 6391 2305; mobile: 0419 503 702; fax: 6391 1608) is a charming self-contained cottage with a four-poster bed and some generous accessories such as perfumes and oils. $100–110/$110–120, single/double.

The Old Rosary (Longford Hall-Malcombe Street, Longford, TAS 7301; tel: 6391 1662; fax: 6391 1077) is a two-storey self-contained cottage tucked away in the gardens of the stately home, Longford Hall. This was originally the stables. You can play tennis on the court in the garden or ask your hosts to arrange a fishing guide. $143, single and double.

📷 Photo spot

The Old Rosary is a lovely house to photograph from deep in the middle of a flowering bush in the garden. Do not try to get the whole house in, just give a sense that you have just stumbled upon this idyllic little spot in the middle of a lush flowerbed and you are admiring from a distance. Full sunlight, 50mm lens, 100ASA film.

Brickendon (Woolmers Lane (C520), Longford, TAS 7301; tel: 6391 1251; mobile: 0418 127 767; fax: 6391 2073; email: brickendon@eudoramail.com; web: www.brickendon.com.au) is one of Tasmania's oldest farming properties, settled in 1824 by William Archer. Amazingly, his 7th-generation descendants still run it. It is a historic farming village and guests can stay in restored, self-contained farm cottages for $110–21/$143–154, single/double.

Also try the **Longford Riverside Caravan Park** (Archer Street, Longford, TAS 7301; tel: 6391 1470) which has tent sites $10/12, single/double; serviced sites $14, single and double; cabins $14–40/18–40, single/double; on-site vans $28–55, single and double.

For great cakes, breads, sourdoughs and pastries, try the award-winning **JJ's Bakery** (52 Wellington Street near the Uniting Church; tel: 6391 2364), which has been awarded a gold medal in the Aussie Pie Competition and in 2001 won the best cake and pastry award in a statewide contest. There is also a wood-fired pizza oven (pizzas about $14). Open from 07.00 but not for supper unless pre-booked for a function.

Ross

The **Ross Bakery Inn** (Church Street, Ross, TAS 7209; tel: 6381 5246; mobile: 0419 879 347; fax: 6381 5360; email: rossbakery@vision.net.au; web: www.rossbakery.com.au) is a cosy sandstone former coaching inn with en-suite rooms for $69/110, single/double.

📷 Photo spot

This picture has been taken many times but it is a good one. The Ross Bakery looks good at dusk on a summer evening. Take from the front but not square on, maybe just to the right so it is at a slight angle. Make sure the outside lights are on and you are catching the last of the light (about one hour before the sun sets). 200ASA film or 400ASA if you want the stone to have a more grainy feel. 50mm lens, or a wide-angle lens if you want to stand closer.

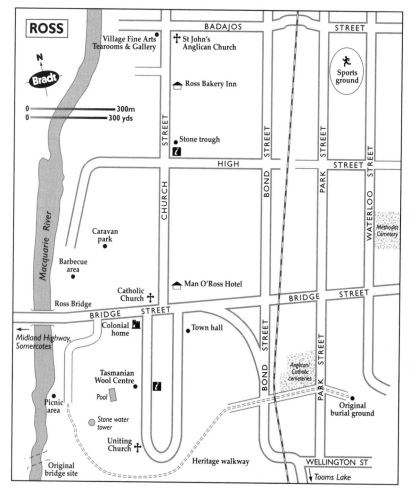

At **Somercotes** (Midlands Hwy, Ross, TAS 7209; tel: 6381 5231; fax: 6381 5356; email: somercotes@bigpond.com.au) guests stay in cottages built for the workers on one of the island's big country estates. The cottages have been restored and furnished to retain their original historic feel. $120/150, single/double.

The **Man O'Ross Hotel** (Church St, Ross, TAS 7209; tel: 6381 5240; fax: 6381 5423) has 8 standard rooms $35–40/$55, single/double. It also does good pub food.

For snacks, try the **Ross Bakery Inn** (details above) which has its own 19th-century wood-fired oven, and the **Village Fine Arts Tea Room** (6 Church St, TAS 7209; tel: 6381 5251), opposite St John's Anglican church, for Devonshire teas. Open Thursday–Sunday 10.00–16.00.

Oatlands

Try the **Oatlands Lodge Colonial B&B** (92 High Street, Oatlands, TAS 7120; tel/fax: 6254 1444; mobile: 0408 176 362; email: oatlandslodge@excite.com), a convict-built sandstone house. It has a real feel of history to it especially when you notice some of the hand-made bricks in the interior walls bear the thumbprints of the convict workmen. There are 3 en-suite rooms costing $75–85/$95–110, single/double.

There is also the National Trust listed **Thimble Cottage** (101 High Street, Oatlands, TAS 7120; mobile: 0409 481910), a self-contained, stone-built cottage which sleeps 6 in 2 attic bedrooms and 1 ground-floor double bedroom. Rates on enquiry.

Waverley Cottage Collection of Colonial Accommodation (Waverley Cottages, Oatlands, TAS 7120; tel: 6254 1264; mobile: 0408 125049; fax: 6254 1527) has a selection of 12 lovely properties to choose from. Rates and details on enquiry.

Blossom's restaurant (116 High Street, opposite Oatlands Mill, tel: 6254 1516) does light lunches (around $7.50) and delicious Devonshire teas ($4.50).

The **Midlands Hotel** (91 High Street, Oatlands, TAS 7120; tel: 6254 1103; mobile: 0418 135 759; fax: 6254 1450) does pub food and has a few basic rooms $35/45, single/double.

Hamilton

The award-winning **Old School House B&B** (Lyell Highway, Hamilton, TAS 7140; tel: 6286 3292; mobile: 0408 863 290; fax: 6286 3369; email: jcrook@southcom.com.au; web: www.schoolhouse.southcom.com.au) makes an excellent stay. It is a sandstone country house built in 1856 as a school and headmaster's residence. There are three en-suite rooms $99/$132–140, single/double. A stone self-contained cottage is also available which sleeps six (rates on enquiry).

The **Hamilton Inn** (Tarleton Street, Hamilton, TAS 7140; tel: 6286 3204; fax: 6286 3281) does big lunches and suppers and has log fires. The white sandstone inn was built in the late 1820s by William Roadknight as his house and boasts cedar doors and panels. He was a bit of everything – farmer, constable, convict and postmaster. The inn also does rooms for $30–45/$45–80, single/double.

The **Glen Clyde House** (Lyell Highway, Hamilton, TAS 7140; tel: 6286 3276; fax: 6286 3295; email: glenclyde@southcom.com.au; web: www.glenclyde. southcom.com.au) serves good lunches.

WHAT TO SEE AND DO
Fishing

If you have never fished then this area of Tasmania is one of the best in the world to learn. They hold world championships here and respected anglers from all over the world write rave reviews about the quality of the water, the accommodation, the food and the fish. The lodges mentioned above offer beginner courses which are probably among the best in the world. If you are an experienced angler you may be familiar with this region's reputation already. Another place for information is

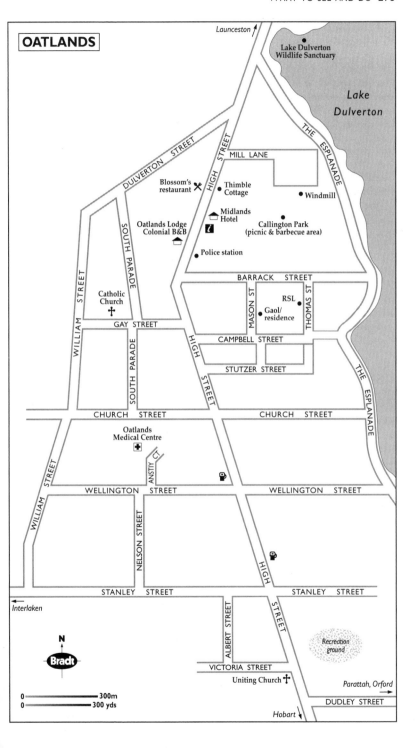

OATLANDS

Launceston

Lake Dulverton Wildlife Sanctuary

Lake Dulverton

DULVERTON STREET

HIGH STREET

THE ESPLANADE

MILL LANE

Blossom's restaurant

Thimble Cottage

Windmill

SOUTH PARADE

Midlands Hotel

Oatlands Lodge Colonial B&B

Callington Park (picnic & barbecue area)

Police station

WILLIAM STREET

BARRACK STREET

Catholic Church

MASON ST

RSL

THOMAS ST

Gaol/ residence

GAY STREET

SOUTH PARADE

HIGH STREET

CAMPBELL STREET

STUTZER STREET

CHURCH STREET

CHURCH STREET

THE ESPLANADE

Oatlands Medical Centre

ANSTIY CT

WELLINGTON STREET

WELLINGTON STREET

NELSON STREET

WILLIAM STREET

HIGH STREET

STANLEY STREET

STANLEY STREET

Interlaken

N

Bradt

ALBERT STREET

HIGH STREET

Recreation ground

0 — 300m
0 — 300 yds

VICTORIA STREET

Uniting Church

Parattah, Orford

DUDLEY STREET

Hobart

the **Tasmanian Fly-Fishing School** (tel/fax: 6362 3441; email: tasflyfish@vision.net.au) which organises beginner schools and trout guiding trips.

📷 Photo spot

Even if you or your companion are shockingly bad anglers you can make yourselves look professional by taking a shot of yourselves knee-deep in the lake with the rod in the water or just as you cast. Position the angler to the far right or left of the shot but get them close enough so you can recognise them. Bright sunlight is best and use a polarising filter to make the foreground water transparent. If you can work it so the bait hook (or float) is in the near foreground under the water so much the better (best if the bait is bright red to stand out). Use 28mm wide-angle lens and 100ASA film. Also check your background to make sure you have not got your 4WD in the shot.

Scenic highland drives

The central highlands have some good scenic drives but these are best taken in the summer months as fog can block out the view in winter. Try the Great Lake loop by starting in Bothwell and heading north on the A5 to Great Lake, maybe having booked lunch at one of the lodges, then heading south along the B11 to Bronte Park where there is a caravan park and some good short walks near the lake. Head southeast on the A10 having a quick look at Tarraleah, a ghost town that once serviced the hydro-electric plant and is soon to be revived into a highland resort, and ending with a night in Hamilton. If you have a 4WD then any of the dirt-roads inside this loop, like the ones to Victoria Valley Falls or Dee Lagoon, are worth trying but winter weather can be severe.

CENTRAL PLATEAU CONSERVATION AREA

This area (tel: 6259 8148) covers 93,000 hectares (229,808 acres) in the middle of the state and much of it is within the World Heritage Area. West is the Walls of Jerusalem National Park and then Cradle Mountain-Lake St Clair. South and east lie the central lakes and plains leading to the east coast. This 'land of a thousand lakes' contains some of the best trout-fishing in the world and some lovely scenery. The weather, however, can be ghastly so come prepared.

Heritage Trail

The A1 Midland Highway acts as a kind of heritage spine down the centre of the state linking the important towns of Campbell Town, Ross and Oatlands with Launceston and Hobart. This was the old coaching road pioneered by one Lieutenant Thomas Laycock of the 102nd New South Wales Corps and his small party who, with just the aid of a compass and the southern stars, navigated from the north coast to Hobart, arriving on February 11 1807.

As you might imagine with so many convicts present, as the road developed there was no shortage of highwaymen to hold up and rob wealthy land owners and businessmen making their journeys north and south.

Tasmanian Expeditions (110 George Street, Launceston, TAS 7250; tel: 1800 030 230 or 6334 3477; fax: 6334 3463; email: info@tas-ex.com; web: www.tas-ex.com) organise a Heritage Cycling Tour through the north of this region from Launceston to the east coast, stopping each night at a National Trust property. The tour passes through Longford and Campbell Town. Winner of state's Adventure Tourism award in 2001.

Longford was originally called Latour and was established by free settlers rather than convicts. You may hear Australians talk about 'catching a brumby' when they mean a wild horse. That word was named after James Brumby, who came to Van Diemen's Land with the first settlers and is buried at Christ Church in Longford.

Campbell Town has a tremendously wide main street with small buildings and houses down each side. There is a good general store and some other smaller shops. The town is famous for a couple of reasons. The first recorded telephone conversation in the southern hemisphere was made here by Alfred Barrett Briggs, and it is the birthplace of Harold Gatty, the aviation pioneer who completed the first round-the-world flight in 1931. There is a memorial to him on the northern edge of town.

In Campbell Town, visit the **Unique Bieniek Fine Arts and Gallery** (at 120 High Street, Campbell Town, TAS 7210; tel: 6381 1438; email: uniquebieniek@telstra.easymail.com.au) to see works by the noted Tasmanian artist, Sonja Bieniek, as well as other Tasmanian artists' contributions in wood, glass and ceramics. Lots of good wilderness oil paintings. Open daily 10.00–18.00. Closed Christmas Day, Good Friday.

Ross was a lawless place for many years and its four main town buildings gained nicknames: temptation (the hotel), recreation (town hall), salvation (church) and damnation (the gaol). Such was the level of unrest here that an illegal militia was established to protect the town's citizens from marauding bushrangers who came to plunder. These militiamen later went on to become the first Light Horse Brigade.

There is a quite good **Walking Tour of Ross** (Church Street, Ross, TAS 7209; tel: 6381 5354; fax: 6331 1895; email: mjohnson@southerncom.com.au), with a knowledgeable guide, which visits the local church, Ross Bridge and several buildings in the tree-lined streets. Rates on enquiry.

The **Village Fine Arts Gallery** (6 Church Street, opposite St John's Anglican Church; tel: 6381 5251) is the only one in Tasmania stocking paintings by the New South Wales outback artist, Pro Hart. Ross is also home to the **Tasmanian Wool Centre** (Church Street, Ross, TAS 7209; tel: 6381 5466; fax: 6381 5407; email: taswoolcentre@tassie.net.au) where visitors can follow the evolution of the sheep and wool industry in the state, and see samples of superfine wool cloth. See a depiction of the 180-year history of Ross with its many convict buildings and famous bridge completed by convict builders in 1836, replete with 186 carvings by highwayman Daniel Herbert. Admission to museum by donation (rates apply for tour groups). Open daily 09.00–18.00 (09.00–17.00 in winter). Closed Christmas Day, Good Friday.

Oatlands was first settled in 1821, after which it became a key coaching stop on the main north–south run. It has arguably the largest collection of well-preserved Georgian buildings in Australia, including the country's oldest Supreme Courthouse and the world's southernmost wind-powered mill (Callington Mill, which dates back to 1837). The visitor centre has an excellent **information booklet** with details of all the historic buildings and a map to find them with. The **Ghost Tour** (7 Gay Street, Oatlands, TAS 7120; tel: 6254 1135) is fun as it creeps through the streets by candlelight, visiting an old gaol building, historic homes and other notable sights. Tours depart from address above at 21.00 summer and 20.00 winter. Adult $8; child (5–12 years) $4.

Further west on the A10 Lyell Highway, **Hamilton** was founded shortly after New Norfolk (1807) by mainly Scottish settlers. It is thought the first settlement was known as Macquarie Town in the Sorell Plains district, and later as Lower Clyde. By 1828 the first few weatherboard houses were up and occupied on the banks of the River Clyde, a tributary of the Derwent. Alcohol soon played a key role according to the Hamilton Historical Society, who say in their helpful brochure to the town, *Historic Hamilton*, that one visitor noted there were some 30 'sly grog shops' which must have meant virtually every house was a speakeasy.

The **Glen Clyde House** (Lyell Highway, Hamilton, TAS 7140; tel: 6286 3276; fax: 6286 3295; email: glenclyde@southcom.com.au; web: www.glenclyde. southcom.com.au) is a restored 1840s convict-built coaching inn with a craft gallery, licensed tearooms and open garden. The garden, craft centre and restaurant have all either won tourism awards or been recommended. Open daily 09.30–17.00. Closed Christmas Day.

The **Lamont Weaving Studio** (10 Patrick Street, Bothwell; tel/fax: 6259 5698; email: lamontweaving@hotmail.com) is also worth a look for hand-dyed yarns and hand-woven garments. There are three looms operating at all times and the place is the home of the Tasmanian Tartan. Open daily 09.00–16.30. Closed Christmas Day, Good Friday, every second Friday.

Further information
From the visitor centres in Oatlands (tel: 6254 1212; email: centas@trump.net.au) and Ross (tel: 6381 5466; email: taswoolcentre@tassie.net.au).

Where Next?

15

The community of Antarctic scientists, engineers and logistics experts in Hobart is the biggest and most varied in the world outside the frozen continent itself. Many travel to Antarctica regularly, some for long tours of duty.

In Hobart there are several reminders of the long history the city, and Tasmania generally, has of providing logistical support to Antarctic expeditions. Just south of town in Kingston is the big Australian Antarctic Division headquarters; there are ice-breakers in the harbour during winter, and, from the post office on the corner of Macquarie and Elizabeth streets, Roald Amundsen sent the telegram that told the world he had made it to the South Pole.

Up to this point Antarctica has been a place for scientists, explorers and wildlife cameramen but we are now in an age where just about any kind of travel is possible (people are already planning trips to space) and this harsh continent is becoming more and more accessible to all.

The most popular departure point is still Ushuaia in southern Argentina, which offers the shortest sea crossing, but Hobart is becoming a contender. Already several Southern Ocean tours leave from here, taking between 300 and 400 people each summer.

Two Antarctic operators use Hobart as their base for tourism and scientific voyages of exploration to Antarctica and the Southern Ocean:

Quark Expeditions (in US: 980 Post Road, Darien, CT 06820; tel: 1 203 656 0499; fax: 1 203 655 6623; tollfree: 1 800 356 5699; in UK: 19a Crendon Street, High Wycombe, Bucks HP13 6LJ; tel: 01494 464080; fax: 01494 449739; web: www.quarkexpeditions.com) is advertising (as we go to press) a 23-night voyage called 'The Great Explorers' which sets sail from Lyttleton Harbour in Christchurch, New Zealand, in February 2003 on the polar ice-breaker *Kapitan Khlebnikov*. It will include visits to Macquarie Island (technically part of Tasmania, although a good 1,500km southeast of the main island) and New Zealand's sub-Antarctic islands. The destination is the Ross Sea, reaching the most southerly point at McMurdo Sound before heading north again and ending the journey in Hobart. The ship has on-board helicopters and a fleet of Zodiac landing craft. Rates and full details on enquiry.

Ocean Frontiers (tel: 02 9979 3155; email: elaine@oceanfrontiers.com.au; web: www.oceanfrontiers.com.au) is an Australian company set up by adventurers Don and Margie McIntyre, with their 37-metre Finnish-built ice-breaker *Sir Hubert Wilkins*. The ship is available for charter and will carry paying passengers.

The McIntyres spent 1995 living alone and isolated in a tiny prefabricated hut at Cape Denison, an achievement which won them the Australian Geographical Society's Adventurer of the Year award in 1996. They established the company partly as an educational endeavour to host exploration and discovery programmes, scientific research, filming and environmental monitoring.

The *Sir Hubert Wilkins* will be available to support projects by scientists from universities, government agencies and elsewhere, and may be fitted out to meet the needs of specific projects. Ocean Frontiers say their project provides the opportunity, through sponsorship, for companies to support and be identified with important environmental and marine research. It will carry a helicopter on some voyages and longer term a small submarine is planned. The McIntyres are also looking for **volunteer crews to Antarctica** and elsewhere, and for people to fill positions of ship's doctor, electricians, cooks and helicopter pilots. Contact by email above.

Qantas operates over-flights on 747s from Sydney and Adelaide that last about 12 hours and have scientists on board to explain the view. Seat rotation ensures everyone gets a view. The flights are organised by Croydon Travel (in Australia, tel: 1800 633 449).

MACQUARIE ISLAND

Wild, remote and with a history of bloodshed, this small island 1,500km southeast of Hobart (yet still part of Tasmania) lies in the sub-Antarctic region of the Southern Ocean, and is accessible by tourists.

From 1810 to 1830 gangs of sealers raided the black sand beaches, slaughtering hundreds of thousands of elephant seals and penguins until they virtually wiped out their populations. The remnants of this hideous industry still exist today in the form of rusting vats which were used to cook the animals and extract their lucrative oil. There was opposition to the practices but this was the last outpost of an already remote colony of Van Diemen's Land and laws were almost non-existent here (apart from the whalers, only the occasional explorer came through en route to Antarctica) and it would be almost another 100 years before the island was protected. It was declared a reserve in 1933 and scientific monitoring began in the late 1940s. That work continues today with Australian teams monitoring the populations of albatross, penguins and seals. The island is an important nesting site for four species of albatross (sooty, wandering, grey-headed and black-browed). There is much concern over the numbers being accidentally caught on longlines by fleets fishing the Southern Ocean for tuna and Patagonian toothfish. Macquarie Island was listed as a new World Heritage Area in 1997, the second for Tasmania.

The only way on to Macquarie is by boat and the crossing can take between five and seven days from Hobart, depending on the weather. As we go to press it is unclear who will be running future trips to Macquarie so the best advice is to contact the Australian Antarctic Division (tel: 6232 3209) which manages the island.

MAATSUYKER ISLAND LIGHTHOUSE

If you have plenty of books to read and a high boredom threshold contact Parks and Wildlife in Tasmania for details on how to apply to spend a stint producing weather reports from the lighthouse on the remote rock stack of Maatsuyker Island off the south coast. A good level of meteorological competence is required. Contact Parks and Wildlife (tel: 6233 6191; email: ParksEnquiries@dpiwe.tas.gov.au).

ENVIRONMENTAL DILEMMA

The future for passenger travel from Hobart could be even more exciting. The city's airport is capable of supporting direct flights between Australia and Antarctica and in October 2001 the Australian government's department of Antarctic Affairs had put out to tender the operation of a new airstrip at Casey

Station (one of the Australian bases). It is expressly for scientific and logistic flights but there is always the possibility in the future that regulations could be changed to allow paying passengers.

However, the number of visitors to Antarctica has doubled since 1993 and will do so again in another five years according to a report in 2001 by the international body of Antarctic tour operators, IAATO. The report said 6,700 people visited Antarctica in 1993 for a holiday. More than 12,000 came in 2000 and by 2006 at least 25,000 will visit annually. Tourism will soon overtake fishing as the biggest industry, but Antarctica is more at risk than almost anywhere else on earth. Environmentalists fear degradation, but tour operators argue tourism is strictly monitored. Its environment is extremely fragile and precious to science, and, because most of it is not subject to normal planning laws, there are concerns tourism could increase rapidly without the usual checks and balances to regulate it. The tourists are not just coming to watch the penguins. The British Antarctic Survey reports that some 'fly into a blue ice airfield and climb mountains or ski to the South Pole. More recently there have been sky-diving attempts and scuba-diving holidays will be available next year.'

There are also plans to set up bases for kayaking, snowboarding, camping and even marathon running. IAATO says some of these have already been established.

The international watchdog, the Antarctic and Southern Ocean Coalition (ASOC), fears an unchecked rise in tourism could spell disaster for Antarctica. 'It will herald the use of larger ships, intercontinental aircraft, and even accommodation facilities on land,' said the director of ASOC's Antarctic Project, Beth Clark.

> The usual control methods for tourism found elsewhere do not operate in Antarctica. In 1998 the World Tourism Organisation reported cruise holidays are the fastest growing component of world tourism. Some in the industry are already anticipating that very large numbers (100,000 or more) will be travelling to Antarctica in the near future.

Greenpeace are also worried. The campaign group's Antarctic campaigner, Denise Boyd, said:

> We didn't save Antarctica to see it ruined by thousands of tourists. We have to take a strongly precautionary approach to Antarctica because we don't want to love it to death.

> It's not like anywhere else; you can't just go marching in *en masse* because humans are an introduced species in that environment.

All that tour operators require at the moment to get access is an Environmental Impact Assessment (EIA) which ASOC argues is too weak and it wants tougher regulations.

It is not yet known if flora and fauna will be affected irreversibly by tourist activity over a longer period of time.

Dr Julia Green from the University of Tasmania, who has been to the Antarctica as an observer, explained that tourism could bring with it

> water pollution from oil spills, [motorised dinghy] operations and sewage disposal; the introduction of bird and plant diseases; littering; the collection of souvenirs especially very valuable meteorites; the introduction of exotic flora via ballast water; pollution from incineration on board ships; and potential disturbance to natural habitat and natural behaviour of wildlife.

In 1990 countries with a stake in Antarctica signed the Madrid Protocol, agreeing to long-term conservation and designating it 'a natural reserve, devoted to peace and science'.

ASOC wants to see a cap on all tourism for 20 years to limit visitor numbers, a ban on all intercontinental tourist flights, land-based accommodation, fuel dumps and permanent runways. It also wants to ensure countries that signed the Madrid Protocol do not allow their sectors to be used for tourism by operators from countries who have not signed up and are therefore not subject to the same rules.

And ASOC would like to see independent observers on tourist trips to check operators are sticking to environmental rules.

IAATO's senior representative, Denise Landau, said Antarctic tourism is already of the highest standard. She said,

> The IAATO member companies are excellent and have worked together
> to develop strict operating guidelines over the years and have significantly
> raised the standard of Antarctic operations. To guarantee that all of
> tourism in Antarctica will be monitored strictly is a near legal and political
> impossibility. We have always taken observers, we take several per year
> [and have] been carrying them for over ten years. Legally no-one can put
> a cap on tourism at the moment. Antarctic tourism is a legitimate activity
> and there is freedom of access to Antarctica. By denying access to
> Antarctica you're taking away freedom of travel.

IAATO describes visitors to Antarctica as 'ambassadors' and says their experience will encourage them to spread the word about the beauty and wonder of the continent, thereby assisting its future protection.

The decision is yours.

Appendix 1

NOMENCLATURE

Tasmania is blessed with some great place names. After lengthy research, Tourism Tasmania has compiled some answers and suggestions as to who named them and why.

Bagdad, Jericho, Jerusalem, Lake Tiberius and the Jordan Range All in southern Tasmania and can be credited to the explorer-soldier Hugh Germaine who was a private in the Royal Marines and landed in Van Diemen's Land in 1804. He had two books with him – the Bible and *Arabian Nights*. Jerusalem is now Colebrook.

Bay of Fires Lady Jane Franklin, the wife of Governor Sir John Franklin, gasped as she sailed past what is now Eddystone Point en route to Hobart and saw the shoreline alight with Aboriginal fires.

Beauty Point A Ms Garrett named this spot after her favourite bullock, called Beauty, when he died in the 1890s.

Bruny Island After Rear-Admiral Bruni D'Entrecasteaux who explored this part of Tasmania.

Doctors Rocks After the property of Dr Thomas Wilson, who for many years was the only GP west of Ulverstone.

Eggs and Bacon Bay Probably after the plant 'eggs and bacon' and named by Sir John Franklin.

Hobart After Lord Hobart, Secretary of State for the Colonies at the time the town was founded.

Ile de Phoques French for 'seal'.

Marakoopa Aboriginal for 'handsome'.

Mother Cummings This is the name of a local school mistress who was bet by some of her pupils that she could not make it to the top of this peak. When she proved them wrong, the peak was named after her.

Nowhere Else Settler Charles Ivory stopped people on his land saying, 'This is far enough, the track leads nowhere else.'

Nubeena Aboriginal for 'crayfish'.

Porky, Porky Sandblow and **Porky Creek** After echidna that were thought to be porcupines.

Salamanca After battle of Salamanca in Spain in 1812.

Smokers Bank Possibly after a beloved bullock or where passengers waiting for the stage coach would have a cigarette.

Squeaking Point In 1834 Captain James Friend of the ship *Rebecca* was preparing to land when a pig escaped and had to be recaptured in the bush.

Strahan After Major Sir George Cumine Strahan (governor 1881–1886).

Tinderbox This is a high fire danger area.

Trousers Point A box of moleskin trousers was washed ashore here in 1875 from the wreck of the *Cambridgeshire*.

Pronunciations

Bicheno	_bish_-en-no
Bruny	_broo_-nee
Freycinet	_fre_-ji-nay
Geeveston	_jeeves_-tun
Huon	_hew_-on
Launceston	_lon_-ses-tun
Maatsuyker	mats-_eye_-ker
Maria Island	mar-_eye_-ah
Marrawah	_mar_-ra-war
Melaleuca	mel-al-_oo_-ka
Narawntapu	nar-_ran_-ta-poo
Schouten	_shoo_-ten
Strahan	_strorn_
Strzelecki	strez-_lec_-ki
Waratah	_war_-ra-tar
Wynyard	_win_-yud
Zeehan	_zee_-yan

Appendix

FURTHER INFORMATION
Further reading
Tasmania

Nash, M *The Historic Shipwreck Brahmin 1842–1854* Bulletin of the Australian Institute for Maritime Archaeology 13(1):15-18, 1989

Lemon, A and Morgan, M *Poor Souls They Perished – The Cataraqui, Australia's Worst Shipwreck* Hargreen Publishing, 1986

Storey, Shirley and Peter *Tasman Tracks* and *Peninsular Tracks* contact Parks and Wildlife for details

Fenton, James *Bushlife in Tasmania* Regal, 1989

Simpson, Lindsay and Miller, Bruce *The Australian Geographic Book of Tasmania* Australian Geographic, 1997

Kneale, Matthew *English Passengers* Penguin, 2000

Tasmanian Trail Association *Tasmanian Trail Guide Book* from PO Box 99, Sandy Bay, Hobart, TAS 7005; email: tastrail@dpiwe.tas.gov.au

General Australia

Coppell, Bill *Australia in Facts and Figures* Penguin, 1999

Reed, A W *Aboriginal Myths, Legends & Fables* Reed New Holland, 1999

Lord, Mary (ed) *Best Australian Short Stories* Penguin, 2000

Chambers, John *Australia: A Traveller's History* Windrush Press, 1999

Hughes, Robert *The Fatal Shore* Harvill, 1996

Other information sources

Parks and Wildlife Service Hobart HQ 134 Macquarie Street, Hobart, TAS 7000; tel: 6233 6191; email: ParksEnquiries@dpiwe.tas.gov.au

Parks and Wildlife Service Launceston HQ Prospect Offices, Bass Highway, South Launceston, TAS 7249; tel: 6336 5312

Cradle Mountain parks office Cradle Mountain, PO Box 20, Sheffield, TAS 7306; tel: 6492 1133; fax: 6492 1120

Lake St Clair parks office Field Centres, Lake St Clair, Derwent Bridge, TAS 7140; tel: 6289 1172; fax: 6289 1227

Department of Primary Industry, Water and Environment (Tasmania) Tel: 6267 4649

Tourism Tasmania Tel: 6230 8175; web: www.discovertasmania.com

Qantas Tel: 13 13 13; web: www.qantas.com.au

Ansett Mark II Tel: 13 13 00; web: www.ansett.com.au

BRADT WILDLIFE GUIDES

Full colour, quality guides focusing on regions specially rich in natural history, written by experts.

Madagascar Wildlife
A Visitor's Guide
Nick Garbutt, Hilary Bradt and Derek Schuurman

This companion guide to Bradt's *Madagascar* is a celebration in full colour of Madagascar's wildlife. It includes the most important parks and reserves, plus features on evolution, camouflage, conservation, wildlife watching and photography.

Galápagos Wildlife
A Visitor's Guide
David Horwell and Peter Oxford

Excellent colour photographs and lively text make this the guide for wildlife enthusiasts. Includes detailed maps and descriptions of all the visitor sites, island habitats, conservation and ecology.

Antarctica
A Guide to the Wildlife
Tony Soper and Dan Powell

A superbly illustrated and attractive traveller's companion to the wildlife of the Antarctic wilderness by TV naturalist Tony Soper. Full species identification is aided by specially commissioned paintings by Dafila Scott.

The Arctic
A Guide to Coastal Wildlife
Tony Soper and Dan Powell

An introduction for visitors to the birds, animals and marine life of the Arctic Ocean and its polar fringes, and a fascinating and informative armchair read. Tony Soper's expert knowledge is richly supplemented with full-colour illustrations by award-winning wildlife artist Dan Powell.

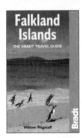   

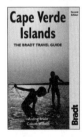 

MEASUREMENTS AND CONVERSIONS

To convert	Multiply by
Inches to centimetres	2.54
Centimetres to inches	0.3937
Feet to metres	0.3048
Metres to feet	3.281
Yards to metres	0.9144
Metres to yards	1.094
Miles to kilometres	1.609
Kilometres to miles	0.6214
Acres to hectares	0.4047
Hectares to acres	2.471
Imperial gallons to litres	4.546
Litres to imperial gallons	0.22
US gallons to litres	3.785
Litres to US gallons	0.264
Ounces to grams	28.35
Grams to ounces	0.03527
Pounds to grams	453.6
Grams to pounds	0.002205
Pounds to kilograms	0.4536
Kilograms to pounds	2.205
British tons to kilograms	1016.0
Kilograms to British tons	0.0009812
US tons to kilograms	907.0
Kilograms to US tons	0.000907

5 imperial gallons are equal to 6 US gallons
A British ton is 2,240 lbs. A US ton is 2,000 lbs.

Temperature conversion table

The bold figures in the central columns can be read as either centigrade or fahrenheit.

°C		°F	°C		°F
−18	**0**	32	10	**50**	122
−15	**5**	41	13	**55**	131
−12	**10**	50	16	**60**	140
−9	**15**	59	18	**65**	149
−7	**20**	68	21	**70**	158
−4	**25**	77	24	**75**	167
−1	**30**	86	27	**80**	176
2	**35**	95	32	**90**	194
4	**40**	104	38	**100**	212
7	**45**	113	40	**104**	219

Index

Page numbers in bold indicate major entries, those in italics indicate maps.